PULLMAN PORTERS AND THE

RISE OF **PROTEST POLITICS** IN

BLACK AMERICA, 1925–1945

THE JOHN HOPE FRANKLIN SERIES IN
AFRICAN AMERICAN HISTORY AND CULTURE

WALDO E. MARTIN JR. AND PATRICIA SULLIVAN,
EDITORS

PULLMAN PORTERS AND THE
RISE OF **PROTEST POLITICS** IN
BLACK AMERICA, 1925–1945

BETH TOMPKINS BATES

THE UNIVERSITY OF NORTH CAROLINA PRESS | CHAPEL HILL AND LONDON

Designed by April Leidig-Higgins
Set in Minion by Keystone Typesetting, Inc.
Manufactured in the United States of America

The paper in this book meets the guidelines for permanence and
durability of the Committee on Production Guidelines for Book
Longevity of the Council on Library Resources.

Library of Congress Cataloging-in-Publication Data
Bates, Beth Tompkins. Pullman porters and the rise of protest politics
in Black America, 1925–1945 / by Beth Tompkins Bates.
p. cm.—(The John Hope Franklin series in African American history
and culture) Includes bibliographical references and index.
ISBN 0-8078-2614-6 (cloth: alk. paper)
ISBN 0-8078-4929-4 (pbk.: alk. paper)
1. Pullman porters—Labor unions—United States—History.
2. Afro-American labor union members—Political activity—History.
3. Discrimination in employment—United States—History.
4. Race discrimination—United States—History. I. Title. II. Series.
HD8039.R362 U63 2001   331.88'1138522'097309041—dc21   00-047974

Portions of this work have been published previously, in somewhat
different form, as "A New Crowd Challenges the Agenda of the Old
Guard in the NAACP, 1933–1941," *American Historical Review* 102:2
(April 1997): 340–77, and are reprinted here with permission.

05 04 03 02 01   5 4 3 2 1

FOR MY PARENTS

Marion Duncan Tompkins and

Harold Willers Tompkins

AND TO THE MEMORY OF

Lillian Green Duncan

CONTENTS

A section of illustrations follows page 106.

ACKNOWLEDGMENTS

The list of those who helped me with this book is much longer than these acknowledgments suggest. A few of the many include Robert V. Daniels, Peter Seybolt, Mark Stoler, and the late Milton Nadworny, who planted seeds that led to graduate school while I was a farmer attending the University of Vermont. I left rural Vermont for graduate study at Columbia University where I had the good fortune to work with Eric Foner, my dissertation adviser. When the project was in the formative stage—with many questions and very little focus— he patiently encouraged me. Every day in the archives, his example as a scholar inspired me to dig deeper. At important junctures, he knew how to pose the critical question to push me to consider the implications of my argument, go back to the archives, and dig deeper still. For all this, the manuscript is much stronger. I also value the integrity and humanity that infuse all of his endeavors, an example that has influenced my approach not just to history but to life. While at Columbia, I was also fortunate to be able to work with Elizabeth Blackmar. From the moment I walked into Professor Blackmar's intellectually scintillating graduate seminar on social history, I began to find my voice. She closely read numerous drafts of this manuscript, pushing me to clarify my often ambiguous positions, and providing encouragement at every step of the process. The book is more nuanced and stronger thanks to the hours of discussion we have had. I shall be forever in debt to her for invaluable "brainstorming" sessions and for a fuller comprehension of the nature of power relations. Daryl Michael Scott critiqued the manuscript and helped me to understand the larger implications of my research. Joshua Freeman, Robert Lieberman, and Anthony Marx read and critiqued various stages of the manuscript, strengthening the final text. Barbara Jeanne Field's seminar on the postbellum South was enormously helpful for understanding the terrain that shaped many of the actors in my narrative before they migrated to Chicago, and her own work influenced my approach to the present topic. Hampton Carey provided intellectual sustenance throughout the long process and helped me better understand the context for nineteenth-century political struggles. Tami Friedman and Mai Ngai offered valuable critiques that sharpened the focus.

While in Chicago conducting research I was especially lucky to meet several

Chicago historians who provided necessary information for exploring the politics of black Chicago past and present. Charles R. Branham, James R. Grossman, Archie Motley, and Rima L. Schultz provided entree to resources, both in archives and within the black community on Chicago's South Side, that made this study possible. Rima L. Schultz's knowledge on the history of Chicago women proved invaluable. Not only did she selflessly share her knowledge of Chicago's social history with me, but she also helped me sort out the web of connections within local networks. At the Chicago Historical Society, Archie Motley eased the complicated task of piecing together the history of black Chicago through his inspiration, which fuels attention to archival details. He is to the researcher what the muse is to the writer. Rosemary K. Adams and Lesley A. Martin generously took time to help me locate pictures for this book, some of which appeared in an earlier article I wrote for *Chicago History*. I would also like to thank Greg LeRoy for letting me review his important interviews with Chicago Pullman porters and Timmuel Black, Margaret Burroughs, Ishmael Flory, Michael Flug, Linda Evans, Charles Hayes, and Les Orear for taking time to talk with me about Chicago history.

Several archivists and librarians outside the Chicago history network helped with materials. In Washington, D.C., Randy Boehm offered guidance during my initial search in the Brotherhood of Sleeping Car papers. Fred Bouman helped me find my way in the Manuscript Room at the Library of Congress. Pablo Calvan came to my rescue on several occasions, locating materials in the Library of Congress that the computer never heard of. Some of my research at the Library of Congress focused on the National Association for the Advancement of Colored People (NAACP). Parts of an article about the NAACP, which originally appeared in the *American Historical Review*, are in chapter 5 and chapter 6. Thanks also go to Esme Bahn at Howard University's Moorland-Spingarn Research Center and the staff of the Reuther Library of Wayne State University, especially Louis Jones, Tom Featherstone, and William Lefever.

Colleagues and friends in the greater Detroit metropolitan area have helped me keep up the momentum to complete this project. Earl Lewis found time in his packed schedule to read part of the manuscript, helping me think through the politics of the twenties. Grace Lee Boggs talked with me about her participation in the March on Washington Movement. General Gordon Baker encouraged me with his comments on a chapter of the manuscript. Linda Housch-Collins enthusiastically discussed the project with me, offering valuable suggestions and lots of encouragement. I am especially grateful to the faculty in the Department of Africana Studies at Wayne State University for steadfast support of my project. In particular, Melba Boyd's work on Frances

E. W. Harper influenced me greatly and sharpened the focus of the discussion on Ida B. Wells-Barnett. On countless occasions, Debbie Hardy Simpson and Michelle Hardy helped me stay on track with both their technical expertise and good humor. I am also grateful for the financial support of the College of Urban, Labor, and Metropolitan Affairs at Wayne State University.

I have discussed this project in various settings, receiving suggestions and testing ideas that sharpened the focus of the manuscript. For comments on papers at professional meetings and in reviews, I want to thank Ernie Allen, John Beck, Carolyn A. Brown, Ardis Cameron, Colin Davis, Elizabeth Faue, Nancy Gabin, Kevin Gaines, Susan Hirsch, Robin D. G. Kelley, Robert Korstad, Peter Rachleff, Randi Storch, and Paul Young. I also benefited from discussions with participants who attended the Black History Workshop, sponsored by the African American Studies Program and Department of History at the University of Houston during the spring of 1998. Thanks to Richard Blackett and Linda Reed for making that possible. Richard Pierce contributed important suggestions for the book that have been the basis for our ongoing discussions of black political history. Timothy Tyson read part of the manuscript and never failed to brighten my spirits with his candor.

Working with the editors and staff of the University of North Carolina Press has been a pleasure. In particular, I want to thank Lewis Bateman for launching the project and David Perry for carrying it forward, as well as Alison Waldenberg, Ron Maner, Elizabeth Gray, and Brian R. MacDonald for their attention to countless details both large and small. Eric Arnesen, a reader for the University of North Carolina Press, reviewed the manuscript with meticulous care and offered suggestions for revision that greatly improved the finished product. A special thanks to Professor Arnesen. I am also grateful to an anonymous reader for reviews and an extremely constructive critique.

A community of scholars and friends guaranteed that this project would finally be finished. Sharon Anderson, Jerry Anderson, David Arsen, Sue Gronewold, Mark Higbee, Martha Kehm, Larry Koblenz, Dr. Lilian Lai, Maggie Levenstein, Margo and Ethan Lowenstein, Bob and Jean McCrosky, Robyn Spencer, and Peter Winn all did their part to make sure I crossed the finish line.

Finally, this book is imbued with support and inspiration from my family. Through his example, my father taught me a love for learning, an inheritance worth more than gold. My mother gave me the grit to keep moving forward. Both never stopped believing in me, even when the needle on my compass pointed in several directions. Brother Barry's quest to build a twenty-five-foot wooden sailboat from scratch, including the one and a half ton keel, was a model for my project. His tenacity and ability to work independently and creatively with the resources at hand inspired me on numerous occasions. Stephanie Nietzel kept the faith despite the fact that it was taking a long time to finish.

Throughout this process, Tim Bates's contribution was crucial. Not just because he read, reread, and read yet again every word on every page. Nor because he kept the home fires burning even when there was no fuel. Nor even just because he cheered me on through every phase. He did all that, for which I am grateful. But most important has been his unfailing belief in the project since its inception. What is more, he is also a constant source of joy and the light of my life.

ABBREVIATIONS

The following abbreviations are used in the text. For abbreviations used in the notes, see page 189.

AFL	American Federation of Labor
AME	African Methodist Episcopal
ANLC	American Negro Labor Congress
ANP	Associated Negro Press
ARU	American Railway Union
ASC	Alpha Suffrage Club
BSCP	Brotherhood of Sleeping Car Porters
CCNO	Chicago Council of Negro Organizations
CIO	Congress of Industrial Organizations
CNLU	Colored National Labor Union
CORE	Congress on Racial Equality
CP	Communist Party
CWA	Civil Works Administration
ERP	Employee Representation Plan
FEPC	Fair Employment Practice Committee
ILD	International Labor Defense
ILGWU	International Ladies Garment Workers' Union
JCNR	Joint Committee on National Recovery
MIA	Montgomery Improvement Association
MOWM	March on Washington Movement
NAACP	National Association for the Advancement of Colored People
NAACP LDF	National Association for the Advancement of Colored People Legal Defense Fund
NACW	National Association of Colored Women
NAWSA	National American Woman Suffrage Association
NNC	National Negro Congress
NUL	National Urban League
OPM	Office of Production Management
PPBAA	Pullman Porters Benefit Association of America

PPMPA	Pullman Porters and Maids Protective Association
PWA	Public Works Administration
PWOC	Packinghouse Workers Organizing Committee
SLC	Stockyards Labor Council
SNCC	Student Nonviolent Coordinating Committee
SWOC	Steel Workers Organizing Committee
TUUL	Trade Union Unity League
UAW	United Auto Workers
UAW-CIO	United Auto Workers, Congress of Industrial Organizations
UNIA	Universal Negro Improvement Association
WLB	War Labor Board
WTUL	Women's Trade Union League
YMCA	Young Men's Christian Association
YWCA	Young Women's Christian Association

PULLMAN PORTERS AND THE RISE OF **PROTEST POLITICS IN** BLACK AMERICA, 1925–1945

No more powerful a statement of the cause of freedom has ever been stated than in one of the sorrow songs of the race, which eloquently challenges arrogant tyranny, in the immortal phrase: "Before I'll be a slave I'll be buried in my grave and go home to my lord and be saved." We, who have come after these noble souls, who suffered and sacrificed and wept and prayed and died that their children might be delivered from the cruel oppression of the Slave Power of the South, are bound in duty, in reverence and devotion, to re-dedicate our hearts and minds to the unfinished task of emancipation, so that Denmark Vesey, Nat Turner, Sojourner Truth, Harriet Tubman and that vast throng of unknown and unsung heroes whose hearts beat true to the hymn of liberty, of that matchless champion of human justice, Frederick Douglass, shall not have died in vain.

Yes, my brethren, let us stand firm, undismayed, with our heads erect and souls undaunted, ever vigilant and devoted to the Brotherhood whose chart and compass are truth and justice. . . . More hinges on the successful consummation of our job than the welfare of the Pullman porters, the destiny of the entire race is involved.

A. PHILIP RANDOLPH, *Messenger*, April 1926

> We are creatures of history, for every historical epoch has its roots in
> a preceding epoch. The black militants of today are standing upon the
> shoulders of the New Negro radicals of my day, the twenties, thirties,
> and forties. We stood upon the shoulders of the civil rights fighters of
> the Reconstruction era, and they stood upon the shoulders of the
> black abolitionists. These are the interconnections of history, and
> they play their role in the course of development.
>
> A. PHILIP RANDOLPH

When Asa Philip Randolph migrated to Harlem on the eve of World War I, he was in search of a place where he could be whole and human. Turn-of-the-century Jacksonville, Florida, where A. Philip Randolph had been raised, offered few opportunities for a well-educated, self-assured, ambitious young African American. During his youth in that Florida community, Randolph had learned valuable lessons about his rights and responsibilities as a citizen, but he realized he must leave the South in order to begin to realize full membership in American society.

In 1927 Richard Wright, like Randolph before him, left the South for the promise of freedom that lay in the mythic land to the north of the Ohio River. As he recounted in *Black Boy*, "my deepest instinct had always made me reject the 'place' to which the white South had assigned me. It had never occurred to me that I was in any way an inferior being." Moreover, the white South said it not only knew Wright's "place" but also who he was. Wright noted, with some irony, that not only did the white South not know who he was, neither did he. In order to find himself, he had to leave.[1]

Wright's autobiography painstakingly depicts the multiple ways that Jim Crow tried to silence his humanity.[2] He felt he must go north to free himself from the suffocation of the southern caste system. Randolph went further and thought all African Americans needed to create as much distance as possible between themselves and the social relations of slavery—those customs, beliefs, and practices, recorded by Wright, that, when acted upon and repeated daily in white America, create and recreate racism even as they spawn a "rationaliza-

tion" for relegating a group of people to an inferior status.³ Neither Wright nor
Randolph found the equality he sought up north: relations between black and
white Americans, albeit different from those in the South, were polluted by the
refuse from slavery that had floated to northern shores. While Wright used his
artistic talents to "hurl words into this darkness," narrating the "hunger for
life . . . to keep alive . . . the inexpressibly human" yearnings of black Americans,
Randolph dedicated a good part of his life to helping African Americans challenge the legacy of slavery.⁴ Both men were engaged in what Vincent Harding
called the struggle to develop one's "whole being."⁵

When Randolph arrived in Harlem in 1911, the lack of self-reliance and
independence from white control among African Americans frustrated him.
He criticized black leaders who were part of what he called the Old Crowd,
"subsidized by the Old Crowd of white Americans—a group which viciously
opposes every demand made by organized labor for an opportunity to live a
better life." As an editor of the *Messenger* beginning in 1917, Randolph placed
the need for new tactics and new leaders high on his agenda for claiming an
equal place in society. Black politicians "owe their places, not to the votes of the
people, but to the white bosses who appointed them," warned Randolph.
"Power over a man's subsistence is the power over his will."⁶ Randolph thought
the tactics of the Old Crowd of black leaders perpetuated servile relations
between black and white Americans. Although slavery as an institution, legal-
ized by the state, had ended in 1865, he believed that certain perspectives and
practices engendered under slavery continued to hold the rights of African
Americans in thrall well into the twentieth century; black Americans would not
be free until they directly challenged servile social relations.

This concern with the legacy of slavery defined the position of "New Negroes," who, like Randolph, believed that actual emancipation could no longer
be denied.⁷ Legal equality achieved in 1865 did not erase the image of black
people as moral inferiors which had been stamped on the consciousness of
white America through years of slavery. For example, at the end of the nineteenth century, economic competition with black workers was translated by
white trade unionists into a "high-stakes moral contest" involving race: white
workers felt accepting black workers on an equal basis would be degrading,
which provided a rationale for maintaining racial barriers in unions.⁸ Reluctance to recognize the moral equality of black Americans complicated the task
of claiming equal economic opportunity for black workers decades after the
end of slavery. Randolph felt that moral inequality and economic discrimination in the workplace were inextricably linked to what Eric Foner reminds us is
the "unresolved legacy of emancipation," the struggle for equality in social

relations, which is still "part of our world, more than a century after the demise of slavery."[9]

This book is about a group of African American Pullman car porters, under the leadership of Randolph, who pressed the claim that they had the right, as Americans, to live and work on an equal basis with white Americans. The memory of slavery that was carried forward in the home, the church, and community organizations provided the subtext of the battle by the Brotherhood of Sleeping Car Porters (BSCP) to claim economic rights of citizenship.

Pullman Company porters were ever mindful of servile relations engendered in the antebellum South, for the work culture for porters, nurtured by the Pullman Company, was inherited from slavery. George Pullman, founder and president of the Pullman Company, consciously perpetuated the link between African Americans and slaves when he chose black men to be porters on his Pullman sleeping cars in the early 1870s. From the beginning, the porter's job was a black man's job, and by the end of the century the term "porter" raised an image of a black person while the term "conductor" raised the image of a white person. The BSCP organized to rewrite the master-servant narrative which had been fostered for so long by the Pullman Company. The Brotherhood's organizational campaign drew upon the memories of slavery and emancipation to connect the union's challenge to the Pullman Company to the larger quest for first-class citizenship in the broader political arena.[10]

That quest was given new life during the First World War as thousands of black Americans journeyed north for jobs in industry. Their passage etched new coordinates on the racial map of America, changing the geography of the color line, as African Americans discovered the urban North also had constructed narrowly defined "places" for black Americans to work and live. Many African Americans seized economic opportunities opened up during the war, bidding farwell to the torturous, confining life in the rural South, to change their status and place within the larger political entity. Despite discriminatory policies of labor unions and employers, which kept black workers in so-called "Negro jobs," often those that were hot, dirty, and dangerous, they made significant inroads in manufacturing industries, such as meat-packing in Chicago. In the process, however, tensions with organized labor increased. In Chicago, during organizing campaigns in the stockyards just after World War I, the majority of the 12,000 black packinghouse workers, drawing from their experiences with racist unions in the past, kept their distance from the "white man's union." At the same time, over 90 percent of the white workers favored the union effort. Tension between black workers and white unionists was rooted in the exclusion practiced by the predominately white labor movement.

Twenty-four national labor unions, ten of them affiliates of the American Federation of Labor, barred blacks completely.[11]

Barriers also restricted where blacks in the Promised Land could live, walk, and play. Racially restrictive covenants limited the space "allocated" for black residents even as the urban black population mushroomed. When one black youth in Chicago innocently crossed over an invisible "color" line, marking the area restricted by custom to black bathers, on a hot July day, a race riot erupted. It was only one among many racial disorders during the summer of 1919, but it raised again the perennial question, asked by W. E. B. Du Bois, "Where do we come in?"[12]

In addition, the crusade to make the world safe for democracy unleashed the hope that World War I would mark a significant turning point in the black freedom struggle. Black soldiers who returned from fighting met massive resistance from white Americans, determined that black Americans would not assume an equal place with white citizens. In addition to the race riots, more than seventy lynchings—ten of black soldiers in uniform—and the resurrection of the Ku Klux Klan demonstrated during the first year of "peace" that America was not safe for black citizens. Historian Carter Woodson had predicted as much when he observed that with northward migration "maltreatment" of African Americans would be "nationalized" when both sections "strike at this race long stigmatized by servitude but now demanding economic opportunity." African Americans demonstrated their willingness to fight back in their own defense during the postwar racial strife, reflecting the impatience they felt toward a second-class place.[13]

In the aftermath of the war, the quest for full citizenship rights was carried forward through a variety of movements. One was the black nationalist Garvey Movement, based on race pride. In another, African Americans, defining themselves as "New Negroes," formed a social movement to put an end to their subordinate place in American democracy. The New Negro Movement, whose leaders included Randolph, Chandler Owen, Cyril Briggs, Hubert Harrison, and many others, showed that they, like Marcus Garvey, had little fear of white men and women and proclaimed that "the time for cringing is over."[14]

In the wake of the devastation wrought by the summer of 1919 and the economic recession that followed in 1921, leadership of the traditional black betterment organizations, such as the National Association for the Advancement of Colored People (NAACP) and the National Urban League (NUL), spoke in moderate voices. While James Weldon Johnson, the first black secretary of the NAACP, often used militant rhetoric to rebuke "spineless men who are relying on 'good white friends' to give them citizenship rights," the black leadership of the NAACP followed an approach that favored moderation over militancy and issuing appeals to white benefactors rather than demanding rights.[15] Not until the late 1930s did the NAACP change course and hew its policies to the interests of the black working class and the politics of a new crowd committed to direct, mass action. By the early 1940s many within the old guard were supporting the protest politics of a new crowd of black activists.

The question is how did the protest politics espoused by the New Negro Movement—what I call new-crowd protest politics—take root in the black community between the wars? To approach such a large question, this study uses the struggle by the Brotherhood of Sleeping Car Porters to form a union of black workers in Chicago as a vehicle for analyzing the process. In August 1925 a group of disgruntled Pullman porters in New York City asked Randolph to head an effort to form an independent union of porters and maids. Although the effort was successful in New York, the BSCP needed to win support in Chicago, headquarters of the giant Pullman corporation and the city where the largest number of porters and maids lived. The organizing effort stalled when the BSCP headed west to Chicago in October. A major problem was resistance from the majority of the middle-class leaders who, believing porters should not rattle the notoriously antiunion Pullman Company, spoke against the BSCP. At that time black leaders placed little faith in the power of labor unions to advance the interests of black Americans. The BSCP needed the support of the middle-class black community and its institutions because they controlled the press, the pulpit, and public opinion.

This inquiry traces how the BSCP won allegiance in black neighborhoods and used a union movement to counter resistance by addressing the community's growing concern over citizenship. The story begins by examining political change from the point of view of participants in networks formed under the tutelage of the BSCP, then charts the path that linked the politics of local networks to the national agenda of the NAACP. Thus, the larger concern is how tactics of local protest networks contributed to reconfiguring the range and direction of national protest politics. The argument is that initiatives for changing the approach to gain a more equal place in American society flowed from grass-roots networks to the boardrooms of national black organizations and then back again, somewhat like a double-arrowed chemical reaction in a nonlinear, interactive process.

"Hindsight," as David Potter noted in reference to writing about the decade preceding the Civil War, is the historian's "chief asset and his main liability."[16] Potter's comment reminds us of the risk involved in studying groups that have been hailed as "social visionaries," as though the outcome of the organization of the Brotherhood of Sleeping Car Porters were preordained.[17] In fact, it was the problem of hindsight that led me to the question that important studies on the Brotherhood of Sleeping Car Porters raised but never answered. While the struggle of the BSCP against the Pullman Company has been documented with scholarly care, previous histories did not examine fully the relationship between the BSCP and the larger black community.[18] We know that the black press, ministers, and politicians resisted the Brotherhood's efforts to organize in 1925 but not how long the Brotherhood faced resistance from the larger community, as well as how it was able to proceed without the support of the middle class and the institutions it controlled. Yet, by the time the Brotherhood won its contract from the Pullman Company in 1937, the porters could do little wrong in the eyes of the community and its leaders. The shift was historic: the efforts of the BSCP contributed significantly to changing the antiunion perspective embraced by a large portion of the black leadership class. This study was undertaken with the hope that, by examining the organizational process of the BSCP as it intersected with the black community, I might understand why that community came to support the BSCP, and, further, why the Brotherhood's initial efforts created such turmoil in middle-class circles.

When the Brotherhood first tried to mobilize support within the community, some members of the black elite claimed that the BSCP threatened to "bite the hand that feeds you" with its challenge to the Pullman Company, considered a friend of black labor in many circles. Yet, by the early thirties, black, old-guard leaders—once committed to using individual appeals to white patrons when negotiating racial inequities—began to view labor unions, collective solidarity, and grass-roots mobilization as important tools in the ongoing fight for first-class citizenship. The reasons for the shift from a one-on-one approach to a protest strategy grounded in making demands backed by collective action is a key theme of this book.

A major target of the Brotherhood of Sleeping Car Porters was the Employee Representation Plan (ERP), a company union. The Brotherhood's labor rhetoric emphasized the handicap of working under a company union because there were "too many Uncle Toms in the service with their slave psychology" who "bow and kowtow" to the company officials.[19] In the battle against the paternalism of the Pullman Company, the BSCP employed the legacy of slavery to depict the Pullman Company as "callous and heartless as Nero," treating the Pullman porter "like a slave." To make its point, BSCP used the idiom of manhood rights to describe the servile relations that prevailed. "The porter has no manhood in the eyes of the company," according to BSCP. He could be addressed as "George" by some sixteen-year-old "Whipper snapper messenger boy" even though the porter might be four times the boy's age. "And if . . . he should assert his rights as a man, immediately he is branded as a rattled brain radical, and hounded and harassed out of the service."[20]

But the idiom of manhood and manhood rights conveyed more than taking a stand against Pullman paternalism. Organizers drew upon the concept of manhood as it had developed in nineteenth-century conflicts over the meaning of suffrage and citizenship in African American history and built upon understandings of manhood carried forward through sacred as well as secular texts, such as W. E. B. Du Bois's *The Souls of Black Folk*. Du Bois recalled resistance in the nineteenth century when people "strove singly and together as men . . . not as slaves." Referring to Frederick Douglass, one of the heroes cited often in Brotherhood organizing literature, Du Bois noted that "Douglass, in his old age, still bravely stood for the ideals of his early manhood—ultimate assimilation *through* self-assertion and on no other terms."[21]

Manhood rights appealed to a broad audience. Many black Chicago clubwomen were drawn to the Brotherhood, for example, because they, too, employed the concept manhood rights, which they defined in universal, humanistic terms. Ida B. Wells-Barnett, internationally renowned antilynching activist, was among them. Wells-Barnett initiated her antilynching crusade after a thorough investigation led her to conclude that the increase in lynching in the late nineteenth century was a deliberate response to black economic gains and political potential. When black men were accused of rape against white women, the charge was often a subterfuge, suggesting that lynching was punishment for the crime of black progress, viewed as a move toward social equality.[22] It was within the context of Wells-Barnett's antilynching campaign that she, and several other women, organized the first civic club among black women in Chicago, the Ida B. Wells Club, fusing race and gender issues.[23] While many clubwomen inextricably linked the interests of black womanhood and race progress—and believed, as Deborah Gray White argues, that solutions to the race problem "began and ended with black women"—there was a price to pay in terms of black feminism.[24] Black clubwomen were instrumental in advancing citizenship interests of African Americans through their alliance with the Brotherhood, but there were indications that female assertiveness sometimes created tensions between male organizers and the clubwomen network.[25] Nevertheless, the concept of manhood rights connected the Brotherhood and clubwomen who defined their gender interests mainly in racial terms as they worked with black men to improve the place of black Americans.[26] During the 1920s and 1930s, the larger problem—claiming rights of first-class citizenship—usually overshadowed other issues.

The Brotherhood pitched its campaign as a struggle not just over bread-and-butter issues, but for larger claims to status as first-class Americans. This was, they insisted, "the unfinished task of emancipation."[27] The narrative that follows chronicles the BSCP's attempt to use a labor-based movement as a tool for shaping a protest strategy that sought civil and economic rights. To explore the intersection of the BSCP's union movement and the culture of protest politics, the study probes the evolving relationship between the BSCP and the black community in order to understand influences each had on the other. Efforts undertaken by the BSCP in its Citizens' Committee and through its labor conferences to educate the community and win the hearts and minds of a critical mass of the black middle class move the narrative forward through the first several chapters. The BSCP developed these entities to connect its movement for workplace rights with the interests of African Americans in general and to counter the troubled history between unions and black workers as well as the thousands of dollars the Pullman Company poured into black neighborhoods to influence the press, ministers, and politicians. Because studies of the BSCP have been institutional in design and national in scope, these networks have received little attention from scholars. Yet the networks are the connective tissue between the porters' union and the politics of the black community. As members of the BSCP protest networks mobilized black Chicagoans around the "unfinished task of emancipation," they broke down resistance to organized labor even as they expanded the boundaries of citizenship to include equal economic opportunity. Between 1936 and 1940, the BSCP protest network gained a platform at the national level when it fused Brotherhood activities with those of the National Negro Congress organizing around a labor-oriented approach to civil rights.

While not an institutional study, this book emphasizes the influence that the tactics and agenda of the NAACP, led by Walter White, and the National Negro Congress (NNC), headed by John Davis and A. Philip Randolph, had over the direction of protest politics. Activities of key players in protest networks in Chicago are traced to these national organizations in order to connect micro- and macrolevel politics. Before the 1920s, the majority of mainstream black leaders—but certainly not all—deferred to etiquette prescribed by the dominant culture when they made petitions or requests to renegotiate established boundaries of citizenship. By 1941, when White, executive secretary of the NAACP, and Randolph won the first executive order issued by a president to address discrimination in the workplace against black citizens, black Americans negotiated from a position of greater strength than they had in the 1920s. In negotiating Executive Order 8802, which outlawed discrimination against black workers in defense industries, black Americans challenged the civic paternalism that determined rules for petitioning the president when they backed their demands with the threat of mass protest.

A shift also occurred, between the First and the Second World Wars, in the role labor organizing and trade unionism played in calculations for overcoming racial inequities. After fighting and supporting a war to make the world safe for democracy during World War I, African Americans turned their attention to challenging the racial status quo on the home front. At that time, black leaders did not view unions as a tool for gaining democratic rights.[28] Nevertheless, by World War II when Walter White stood outside the gates of the River Rouge Plant near Detroit to show his support of the United Auto Workers (UAW) effort to unionize black and white workers at the Ford Motor Company, a labor-oriented approach to civil rights had gained acceptance.

Although new-crowd activists during the interwar period did not eschew tools of conventional politics, traditional politics was viewed merely as one route among many for gaining a more equal place in society. The key factor in protest politics for the Brotherhood was the added measure of power that could be derived from using aggressive tactics to make demands on society. The BSCP's strategy for gaining power was shaped by concerns Randolph had expressed in the *Messenger*: black politicians had no practical influence and would continue to be powerless until black Americans gained a measure of economic security and power. Neither government, political parties, nor even paternalistic gestures by the Carnegies, Rockefellers, or Rosenwalds would take the responsibility for redressing racial inequities. Nor should they, Randolph decided. For power, as Randolph often reminded his audiences, was the "product and flower of organization—organization of the masses, the masses in the mills and mines, on the farms, in the factories."[29]

Though the BSCP focused on claiming rights of citizenship, it was the tactics and strategies—transgressions against civic proprieties—advanced by the Brotherhood that distinguished its politics. The goal was to move out of the shadow of second-class status and assume a position of first-class citizenship. I have tried to recover the processes that brought protest politics to the fore in Chicago in the late 1920s and early 1930s. In doing so, I have found that new-crowd activists shared a desire to overcome what I call a "politics of civility," which defined relations between black and white Americans. The concept is drawn from William Chafe's perceptive analysis of the dialectic of social control and social change over the issue of race relations in Greensboro, North Carolina, from the 1940s to the 1960s. There he found a "culture of white progressivism" that dominated North Carolina's political and economic life. The culture, driven by a strong sense of obligation to take responsibility for those who are less fortunate, was replete with assumptions regarding correct behavior in the patron-client relationship it encouraged between white benefactors and black petitioners. Chafe argues that the negotiation process between patron and client was driven by an "etiquette of civility," which set the limits for good behavior between citizens and determined what tactics would be condoned for expressing grievances or making requests. Because the goal was to maintain social and political consensus, no room was left for conflict, which could only destroy harmonious relations. Black North Carolinians understood "the chilling power of consensus to crush efforts to raise issues of racial justice" and that civility also meant assuming "deferential poses . . . in order to keep jobs." Finally, he reasons, the etiquette of civility "offered almost no room for collective self-assertion and independence. White people dictated the ground rules, and the benefits went only to those who played the game."[30]

A similar culture set the tone in the North, imposing boundaries upon the degrees of freedom black citizens enjoyed and structuring relations between white and black old-guard leaders. The politics that the Brotherhood introduced in Chicago was designed to break the pattern of petitioning the dominant culture for rights that already belonged to black Americans. In the process of using tactics that challenged civic decorum, the Brotherhood helped shape the rise of protest politics by connecting its manhood rights campaign to African American struggles from the past. That connection pushed protest politics in the direction of an attack on what the new crowd considered the uncivil nature of relations between black and white Americans: that to be black in America was to be less than whole, only half a "man." When new-crowd politics directly challenged the politics of civility, it was trying to mop up flotsam from the social relations of slavery.

"Community," for black urban dwellers, is an entity characterized not by static unity but the active participation of individuals negotiating with other dwellers over the best means to achieve goals thought to advance the interests of the entire group.[31] The term "black community" assumes, on the one hand, that black Americans in a particular locality share a general goal for overcoming racial inequities and gaining greater freedom within the larger white community. On the other hand, black communities were divided along lines of religion, gender, and economic status, among other differences, and its habitants shaped by different experiences, what Earl Lewis refers to as the "multipositional" self that defines a black American. Building on this outlook, I consider various aspirations that drove participants in the community formation process. Black Chicagoans in the 1920s were driven by several impulses, defined by overlapping community interests, which included the aspirations of recent migrants and the desire to attain an equal place with white Americans in society.[32] This book looks at the negotiation process as it was played out within the protest networks developed by the Brotherhood. Protest networks were the enclaves where the BSCP sought to tie overlapping community interests together in order to strengthen the power of black Americans, to win over those opposed to labor and new-crowd style activism and to push back boundaries and barriers to greater freedom.

The Communist Party plays a relatively small but supporting role in the following narrative of the rise of protest politics. I have tried to convey what I learned from both primary documents as well as interviews with black activists from the 1930s by keeping the larger interests of the party in the background, which is where they generally resided in the minds of those who collaborated with Communists in the thirties. Not too many years ago, organizations that captured the attention of large numbers of black Americans, the National Negro Congress among them, were often dismissed if they were thought to be under the influence of the Communist Party. The result was that several otherwise fine studies failed to penetrate the mood of black protest politics.[33] Yet the impact that local councils of the NNC had on community affairs emerges as an important part of this book.[34] My sources indicated that African Americans did not view the Communist Party through the same lens used by white Americans.[35] Although my interest is not whether certain activists were or were not Communists, Communist participation in the politics of the black community during the 1930s is hard to miss, and the activities of the local council of the NNC in Chicago form a significant part of this study. I approach Communist participation hoping to understand what it meant to black activists in the 1930s, not through the perspective of the Cold War era. If I seem to pay little attention to Communists working in close alliance with Christian clubwomen, ministers, and Republican politicians within BSCP protest networks, it is because the players themselves did not dwell on whether an organizer was or was not a Communist. This was a perception shared by black middle-class and working-class activists alike, particularly during the 1930s.

A word of caution is in order about my usage of terms related to first-class citizenship. From the perspective of African Americans in the 1920s, second-class status referred to their inability to access what were considered entitlements and rights of freedom and citizenship guaranteed in the Thirteenth and Fourteenth Amendments. For example, during Reconstruction, the right to compete as an equal in the marketplace with white workers was viewed as a right of citizenship.[36] Freedmen and freedwomen came to understand emancipation in terms of enjoying a share of the political and economic power once in the hands of the planter class.[37] The Brotherhood carried this perspective forward by emphasizing economic rights, competing equally with white workers, and exercising the right to join a union and write economic contracts. When the Brotherhood campaigned for equal economic opportunity, it was to lay claim to economic rights of citizenship. Too often concepts like citizenship are interpreted *for* African Americans. My concern was to discover how black Americans between the wars understood the term. None of this is to imply, however, that all white Americans enjoyed first-class citizenship or equality of economic opportunity commensurate with the ideal harbored by black Americans coming of age in the urban, industrial North. Many white workers did not possess the right to write their own contracts during the 1920s, a decade noted for employers' staunch antiunionism, surveillance of workers, and profusion of company unions.

The Brotherhood viewed politics broadly.[38] It first set its sights on exposing the politics of civility that structured relations between the Pullman Company and the black community on Chicago's South Side. To understand the relationship between Pullman porters and the larger community, chapter 1 begins by focusing on the work culture of Pullman porters, which was embedded within that of slavery. The chapter builds on observations made by W. E. B. Du Bois in 1920 in *Darkwater: Voices from Within the Veil*, about "The Servant in the House," where he argued that until white America stopped attaching the servant stereotype to black people, black Americans would not approach freedom. Chapter 2 analyzes the political context that shaped the efforts of the BSCP to form a labor union in Chicago, laying out the web of connections African Americans had with the Pullman Company and the Republican Party political machine.

Chapter 3 traces the formation and development of the alliance between the BSCP organizers, Chicago clubwomen, and ministers between 1925 and 1927, a phase that was critical for anchoring the Brotherhood's movement within the community. The clubwomen, together with a couple of sympathetic ministers, formed a citizens' committee to promote the Brotherhood, offering the fledgling union a harbor from the storm of protest by the black press and most of the clergy. For more than two years, while the *Chicago Defender* opposed the BSCP, this core of citizens broadcast the message of the Brotherhood's movement and advanced its agenda, particularly among the reformed-minded middle class.

In January 1928 the newly formed Citizens' Committee of the BSCP sponsored its first labor conference in Chicago and introduced the idea of using a labor organization as a vehicle to claim rights of first-class citizenship to a broad audience of black Americans. From this beginning, a network emerged over the next several months as the BSCP sought to gain the support of middle-class citizens and to turn its labor-organizing process into a tool to expand citizenship rights for all. Chapter 4 reconstructs the Brotherhood's strategy to win the hearts and minds of black Chicago, which included weaving black political history into its challenge to Pullman paternalism as a way to connect its agenda with larger concerns about rights of black citizenship. The chapter focuses on following the transformation of community opinion toward the BSCP and unions that was underway by the end of the 1920s.

Chapter 5 follows the development of new-crowd networks between 1930 and 1935, a period when the Brotherhood helped forge alliances with other networks around issues such as unionization of black and white workers and the plight of Angelo Herndon, a black Communist sentenced to eighteen years in prison on the charge of inciting insurrection. In the process, the BSCP network branched out deeper into the community.

In 1936 when the National Negro Congress elected A. Philip Randolph as its president, the Brotherhood gained a national platform for mobilizing African Americans, modeling its approach, in part, on the labor conferences of the Chicago Division of the BSCP. Between 1936 and 1940, the BSCP network, in alliance with the NNC local network, participated in many of the challenges that led the old guard to reorder its priorities, which resulted in a realignment of power relations within black Chicago, a process explored in chapter 6.

In 1941 the BSCP used the threat of the power of collective organization to protest discrimination in the defense industry. That effort, the subject of chapter 7, led to the first major effort by the federal government to remedy distinct abuses suffered by African Americans since Reconstruction with the enactment of Executive Order 8802 and the formation of the Fair Employment Practice Committee (FEPC). When the executive order was issued, Randolph canceled the threatened protest march on Washington. But the BSCP, in the interest of perpetuating the momentum generated for the threatened march, formed a March on Washington Movement (MOWM). Strategically, the most provocative aspect of the MOWM was limiting membership to black Americans. Its primary goal was to have African Americans run and control this movement to secure full citizenship rights.

Chapter 8, by way of conclusion, evaluates the evolution of protest politics by looking at ways black workers utilized protest politics on the shop floor in the trade-union movement of the Congress of Industrial Organizations (CIO). Not only had protest politics come of age, but so had many thousands of black Americans who explored various avenues for asserting rights. When management, government, and union officials dragged their feet over issues involving discrimination in hiring, black workers initiated wildcat strikes, taking matters into their own hands by applying the lessons of new-crowd protest politics in the workplace.

Protest politics may have come of age, but the legacy of slavery endures to this day. The struggle carried forward by African Americans that is described in the pages that follow covers only a part of the still largely unmapped terrain of grass-roots activities during the twenties and thirties. But even this perspective reveals the wisdom of Randolph's refrain, drawn from Frederick Douglass, that "power concedes nothing without a demand."[39]

No More Servants in the House

Pullman Porters Strive for Full-Fledged Citizenship

> So long, then, as humble black folk, voluble with thanks, receive
> barrels of old clothes from lordly and generous whites, there is much
> mental peace and moral satisfaction. But when the black man begins
> to dispute the white man's title to certain alleged bequests of the
> Fathers in wage and position, authority and training; and when his
> attitude toward charity is sullen anger rather than humble jollity;
> when he insists on his human right to swagger and swear and waste,—
> then the spell is suddenly broken and the philanthropist is ready
> to believe that Negroes are impudent, that the South is right.
>
> W. E. B. DU BOIS, *Darkwater: Voices from Within the Veil* (1920)

> The nearest thing to a slave observable in this country is the Pullman
> porter. He has the same color, to begin with, and to conclude, he
> toils under conditions that are not remarkably dissimilar.
>
> From *America: A Catholic Review of the Week* (1927)

Shortly after the Civil War, when George Mortimer Pullman revolutionized intercity travel with his Pullman sleeping cars, he consciously recruited recently freed slaves for the position of porter. He did so, as his official biographer noted, because they had been "trained as a race by years of personal service in various capacities, and by nature adapted faithfully to perform their duties under circumstances which necessitate unfailing good nature, solicitude, and faithfulness."[1] The Pullman porter was a servant whose job was to attend to all the needs of passengers as they traveled across the country on Pullman's luxurious hotels on wheels. When George Pullman created the Pullman porter to serve his passengers, some predicted that this new niche would improve the occupational status of African Americans within American society.[2]

Although the question of Pullman porter status remains open, no one disputes the fact that the porter helped make the Pullman Company an industrial giant in corporate America. By the 1920s, over 35 million passengers annually slept on Pullman sleeping cars, served by approximately 12,000 porters, making Pullman the single largest private employer of African Americans in the United States. A key factor in the company's success was the style of service delivered by porters. For the price of a ticket on a sleeping car, a white person could be pampered and waited on in the manner once reserved for privileged gentry in the antebellum South.[3] Porters were, according to one of the company's executives, "Pullman's greatest assets," and the company featured a smiling, submissive-looking black servant in its advertisements for Pullman sleepers.[4]

By the twentieth century, the Pullman porter was a national figure, perhaps the most easily recognized African American in white America. As early as 1913, Hollywood had such demand for Pullman porters in films that one actor made a good living—much better than actual porters—cast as a porter for nearly three decades.[5] In the 1927 silent movie, *The Girl on the Pullman*, a porter was portrayed as bowing and grinning, while receiving a handsome tip from his customer.[6]

To the white public patronizing Pullman sleeping cars, porters often were not fully formed, three-dimensional characters; they were just "George"—after the founder of the Pullman Company. The implication was that porters were the property of George Pullman.[7] Although slavery images were not necessarily on the minds of white clients when they called for "George," the person who responded to that call was, as Murray Kempton observed, "at once omnipresent and nonexistent" to the customer.

> The Pullman porter rode his car, silent with all the chaff round him, always most agreeable when he was of the old school, accepting the generic designation of "George" as though it were a balm instead of an affront, a domestic apparently unaltered by the passage of time or the Emancipation Proclamation. . . . Any white man who spoke to him spoke consciously to a Negro, which is a terrible barrier even for the best of men . . . life was a process of enforcing recognition of his personality from a world which treated him as possessed of color without feature. It was always mixing him up with the porter in the car ahead and asking him in simple bewilderment if he was its porter, because he was, after all, only a piece of furniture set out for the convenience of persons who saw no need to be connoisseurs of this sort of furniture."[8]

Within the black community, the porter was a model citizen and enjoyed a measure of prestige since he had fairly steady employment.[9] On the road, Pullman porters connected rural African Americans with news from urban areas. Black youth, in particular, looked up to them as agents of exotic ideas from faraway places, like New York, Chicago, and Los Angeles. They distributed copies of the *Chicago Defender* at stops throughout the country, which boosted circulation, and helped make it the largest selling black newspaper in the United States with a circulation exceeding 200,000 by 1925.[10] Managing editor Lucious C. Harper credited the paper's wide circulation—two-thirds of which was outside of Chicago—in part to its practice of giving Pullman porters copies to distribute en route.[11] Not only did porters make extra money distributing news of the wider world and its possibilities, they became spokesmen for African Americans and influenced the historical and cultural formation of black America.[12] Edgar Daniel Nixon, an ex-porter and civil rights activist, conveys the role porters played.

> Everybody listened because they knowd the porter been everywhere and they never been anywhere themselves. In cafes where they ate or hotels where they stayed, they'd bring in the papers they picked up, white papers, Negro papers. He'd put 'em in his locker and distribute 'em to black communities all over the country. Along the road, where a whole lot of people couldn't get to town, we used to roll up the papers and tie a string around 'em. We'd throw these papers off to these people. We were able to let people know what was happening.[13]

On the job, Pullman porters sustained a cloak of invisibility, smiling as though they were content with the racial status quo. It was a protective mechanism that shielded them from the charge of stepping out of place—the place assigned by the white world—or "being uppity." The porter's role, as one historian observed, resembled that of the black minstrel who wears a mask on stage to protect not just his self-esteem, but also to shield the actor from revealing his true feelings toward the audience.[14] Benjamin McLaurin, a Pullman porter in Chicago during the 1920s, made a similar observation: porters wore two faces in order to survive.[15] As Thomas Holt might explain the process, porters had been "marked" or stereotyped by the culture of Pullman labor relations as "natural" servants. The status was recreated in the Pullman car on every trip by the traveling public, whose "seemingly trivial" and innocent expectations reinforced the myth that porters were content and happy; after all, they were always smiling.[16]

The issue of achieving status and recognition as fully formed human beings ultimately united the larger black community and Pullman porters against the Pullman Company. Within the black community, issues of human dignity were often referred to as manhood rights, drawing from the ongoing African American quest for participation as equal human beings in American society. The Great Migration and World War I unleashed yearnings for all of the rights that black Americans—as both citizens and workers—had long been denied, desires that shaped the Harlem Renaissance and the New Negro Movement in the twenties.

When a group of porters set out to form an independent union in 1925, they anchored their challenge to the Pullman Company in a call for "manhood rights," connecting the union effort to a larger impulse in black America against the pariah status to which African Americans had been relegated. In this chapter, we explore the place of Pullman porters as labor aristocrats within the social matrix of black America and as workers without full citizenship in their native land.

The Pullman Palace Sleeping Car Company
Creates "George" for the Traveling Public

When discussing their work, Pullman porters sometimes noted that "Lincoln freed the slaves, and the Pullman Company hired 'em."[17] There is a measure of truth in this assessment. At the end of the Civil War, George Mortimer Pullman built a sleeping car like no other that existed at the time. Called the "Pioneer," the car transformed the industry in terms of comfort and elegance. The Pullman sleeping car, as Eric Arnesen points out, "addressed not merely passengers' need for rest but their psychological preference for luxury as well."[18] Before the Pioneer, "sleepers" were hard, uncomfortable, and crowded; each car cost no more than $5,000 to build. The Pioneer—fully equipped and ready for service—cost over $20,000. "Never had the wildest flights of fancy imagined such magnificence," according to Pullman's biographer.[19] The interior featured "brocaded fabrics . . . door frames and window sashes . . . of hand worked and polished woods . . . a plush red carpet, and several gilt-edged mirrors [that] reflected the light of silver-trimmed coal-oil lamps."[20]

Before George Pullman could realize a return on his investment, he needed to sell his concept of a palace on wheels to both railroad companies and the traveling public, for he had constructed this impressive car—longer, wider, higher, and heavier than any other railroad car—without a contract for its use. The car, located in Chicago, was so large that before it could run, bridges, trestles, and station platform dimensions needed alteration. Had President Lincoln not been assassinated, Pullman might have gone broke before he could persuade railroad companies to change the space allotted for passage of rail cars. It was Pullman's good fortune that when the body of Abraham Lincoln reached Chicago, state officials, who wanted the very best conveyance to carry Lincoln to his final destination in Springfield, Illinois, chose the Pioneer. All along the way, the new sleeping car was hailed as a conveyance of beauty. He soon received contracts from several rail lines willing to make the necessary alterations, and in 1867 had organized the Pullman Palace Car Company.[21]

To win the hearts of the public, George Pullman added distinctive service by creating the position of Pullman sleeping car porter to serve his patrons in a princely manner. Porters were at the beck and call of customers to prepare berths, clean the cars, and render whatever small services customers desired to make them comfortable while traveling. In order to maintain a smooth-running operation, Pullman carefully divided the work of his employees between conductors who sold and collected tickets and porters who waited upon clients.[22] That Pullman hired only white men to be conductors and only black men to be porters may have seemed fitting to him in 1867. Indeed, he once claimed, according to historian William Harris, that black Americans were chosen out of concern for their welfare in the aftermath of the Civil War, a time when black workers were anxious to leave agriculture and enter new occupations. Nevertheless, black Americans could not be conductors on his sleeping cars, and very few black workers found employment in maintenance shops in Pullman yards until World War I.[23] Although until the late sixties African American males were never hired as conductors, who received considerably higher base (monthly) salaries—in 1915, $70 for conductors and $27.50 for porters—they often did the work of conductors as "porters-in-charge," saving the company a fortune in wages. Finally, the white conductor had supervisory authority over the behavior, actions, and work requirements of the porters.[24]

Pullman sleeping car porters were exclusively African Americans except for a brief period in the late twenties when the Pullman Company, in an effort to break the back of the fledgling Brotherhood of Sleeping Car Porters (BSCP), hired Filipino porters. When the BSCP threat persisted, Pullman management abandoned that tactic, returning the position of Pullman sleeping car porter to the preserve of black Americans. At that point, Filipinos were placed in separate job categories as attendants, cooks, and busboys.[25]

In testimony delivered in 1915 before the U.S. Senate's Commission on Industrial Relations, Pullman officials explained the company's preference for African Americans. L. S. Hungerford, general manager, told the hearing that while they found no shortage of applicants in St. Louis and Chicago, they were not always able to hire the "right caliber" of men from northern areas. Management had found that "the old southern colored man makes the best porter on the car." Not only was the stereotypic older black servant more "pleasant" and "adapted to waiting on passengers," but he represented an image that was "more pleasing" to white clients than the "younger colored man that is found around in the slums of Chicago."[26]

White clients found it easier to have an African American wait on them in the limited and intimate space of a sleeping car, for the social distance that societal caste distinctions had created made the servile black porter seem less intrusive than a white worker. Pullman intended that the smiling, polite porter would increase the comfort level of his clients and that comfort was linked to *seeing* porters—black men—as servants. Veteran porters talked about white women who thought nothing of undressing in front of them, as if they were invisible. The *visibility* accorded white service workers makes it hard to imagine a white woman undressing in front of a white hotel bellboy.[27]

Finally, a porter's ability to make a living wage was linked to tips he received for services rendered, perpetuating the role of the porter as servant to the traveling public.[28] As one Pullman porter put it, "this tipping question is the nub of the whole situation."[29] The porters learned to utilize their "invisibility" in order to attract tips. Although pretending not to understand or be privy to conversations, for example, porters took mental notes of the likes and dislikes, interests, and habits of clients as a way of anticipating the patrons' needs. One ex-porter in Chicago told his interviewer, "Pullman made hustlers out of us. They had us constantly on our knees." Two other ex-porters, writing for *Coronet* magazine in 1948, revealed that the "porter caters first to your *mental* comfort. He massages your ego, flatters your vanity, helps you enjoy your trip. . . . Most porters would be out of work if they didn't add applied psychology to their job of running errands."[30]

The tipping system influenced the porter's sense of self-esteem as well as images of porters within larger society. As early as 1904, the tipping system was cited as the most demeaning aspect of the job in *Freemen Yet Slaves*, a book discussing Pullman porter grievances written by a porter.[31] The art of solicitation for "alms" entailed degrading gestures sometimes referred to as kowtowing, hustling, or "Uncle Tomming," creating a stereotype of the porter as a clown, scuffling for a handout. Nevertheless, some porters recall the tipping tradition favorably. One, interviewed by the Commission on Industrial Relations, said he did not feel "disgraced or humiliated" by working for tips. "The degradation would be if we did not get them." This porter, who acknowledged he was working "indirectly" for the Pullman Company while giving testimony, was an exception.[32] The majority of those interviewed over the years remembered working for tips as a humiliating experience. Retired porters interviewed by Jack Santino in the early 1980s were acutely sensitive to the fact that selling themselves for tips resembled slavery.[33] Officials of the Pullman Company admitted in 1915 to the Commission on Industrial Relations that porters were underpaid, that the standard salary of the porters—$27.50 per month— "obliged" porters to secure tips from the public in order to live.[34] Moreover, Robert Todd Lincoln, son of Abraham Lincoln, ex-president of the Pullman Company and chairman of the board of directors of the Pullman Company, admitted that the porter's low monthly salary bothered him greatly, but emphasized that there was no plan to increase the base pay and abolish tipping. Lincoln thought porters would get tips no matter what their wages were.[35] The commissioners noted that if wages were doubled and tipping abolished, the Pullman Company's annual surplus would be reduced by about $2.3 million, suggesting that stockholders of the Pullman Company—not the porters—were "the real tip takers."[36]

Lincoln did not think tipping robbed porters of their self-respect.[37] Frank P. Walsh, chairman of the committee, who probed the issue of parallels between the Pullman work relations and slavery, must have noted the irony of having the son of the Great Emancipator testify about the status of porters. The Pullman Company saw no problem with a system that Walsh described as compelling men, "struggling up from slavery . . . to depend on receiving gratuities from another race for their livelihood. "[38] Lincoln justified the company's position by pointing out that the "colored race, as we know, were subject to great limitations in the past to obtain employment in this country." But "outside of what you might call the learned professions . . . the one large element which has done more to uplift them is the service in the Pullman Co."[39]

Labor Aristocrats in the Neighborhood

By the World War I era, the approximately 12,000 porters who worked for the Pullman Company included many of the best-educated black men in the country. Historian William H. Harris makes this point by citing the case of a porter, killed in a train wreck, whose body was identified by his Phi Beta Kappa key from the class of 1922, Dartmouth College.[40] Although the job of porter offered no possibility for advancement, many black professionals were Pullman porters and several used employment with the Pullman Company as a source of income for furthering their education. Benjamin E. Mays, president emeritus of Morehouse College, financed his education by working for Pullman, but felt no loyalty to the company after he was fired for writing a letter objecting to being held on call without pay.[41] Others like Perry Howard, Republican national committeeman from Mississippi, Jesse Binga, head of Binga State Bank in

Chicago, Melvin Chisum, member of the National Negro Press Association, and J. Finley Wilson, grand exalted ruler of the Elks, were grateful to the Pullman Company for hiring them when most employers excluded African Americans.[42]

Before the Great Migration of the World War I era, most porters lived in northern cities. The Pullman Company recruited porters primarily in the South, but then transferred them north to regions with the greatest demand, particularly Chicago and New York. New recruits usually moved north alone and then sent for their families later.[43] Initially, porters' letters to former neighbors in the South served as a pipeline for information about life in the urban North. Because porters were always, while at work, on the move, they were a conduit between new centers of population and rural areas.[44] While Pullman officials advertised its service to white patrons by selling the image of porters as "old southern colored men," black Americans associated porters with urbanity and sophistication. Many rural residents were introduced to the values of urban society by porters, who also helped shape ideas—from politics to music—as they crisscrossed the country.[45] Lawrence Levine credits Pullman porters with introducing rural districts to hit blues records, keeping black music alive and connected between the North and the South.[46]

For the majority of porters, the job was the best they could do in a world structured by barriers that severely restricted occupational mobility for all black workers.[47] In 1910 more than 45 percent of employed black men in Chicago, the city with the largest number of porters, worked as porters, servants, waiters, and janitors; and over 60 percent of employed black women were laundresses or domestic servants. The percentage of black, male workers in the professions was 2.9 percent; for females it was 3.2 percent. The Pullman porter job exemplified a pattern that had persisted for decades: black men were driven to jobs white men considered beneath them. Generally, these were low-paying service jobs, held little chance for advancement, and were considered servile.[48] In this context, the job of Pullman porter was sought after.

In Chicago, before World War I, the Pullman porter was not only considered a member of the black middle class but was thought of as among its "leading men."[49] Unlike the white community, African Americans assigned middle-class status as much on the basis of a refined, sober life-style as sources of income. Positions that provided a relatively steady income, were clean, and did not involve manual labor, such as Pullman porters, waiters, and postal clerks, qualified.[50] Pullman porters had the trappings of middle-class respectability, particularly as homeowners. In Chicago, home ownership among union porters was high. In 1927, 57 percent of porters owned their homes and 42 percent listed themselves as renters. By comparison only 33 percent of a matching sample of black residents in the same neighborhoods owned their own homes and 66 percent rented from someone else.[51]

In Chicago, the status of porters declined as World War I and migration led to rising expectations. Porters did not lose their middle-class status so much as slip within the class hierarchy. St. Clair Drake and Horace Cayton, scholars of Chicago's black neighborhoods, suggest that the change reflected a growing population of younger men who would rather labor in a factory job than work as a servant. As possibilities outside of the personal-service sector opened up, other occupations gained prestige at the expense of the Pullman porter. Jobs in industry opened opportunities long denied black workers, giving industrial workers a measure of prestige. Policemen and firemen ranked high in terms of prestige—almost as high as teachers and social workers—because as symbols of authority they provided proof that black workers in the North were closer to white citizens in terms of the job categories they could enter. Moreover, these new occupations carried hope for advancement, something that was lacking for porters. Young male migrants in the 1920s did not come north to work as Pullman porters; they came north hoping to enter new fields and improve their place within the American political economy.[52] In Chicago, 119 manufacturing establishments employed 19,070 African Americans in 1920 compared with 5,947 in 1915.[53] By 1920 the proportion of black men doing servant work had fallen to 25 percent, while the proportion in industry rose from 40 to 55 percent.[54]

Writing in the twenties, Claude Barnett, founder of the Associated Negro Press, a national news service headquartered in Chicago, noted that:

> A few years ago the Pullman porter was one of the most gainful occupations colored men could aspire to. The Pullman Company as the first large employer of colored labor has meant untold good in an economic way to the Negro race. In early days the Pullman porter was a big man. With the growth, however, in business and professional life among colored people, the increased cost of living, coupled with the fact that many skilled workmen make much more money than the porters, plus the important angle that the daily press and racial press, and public opinion, have tended to ridicule the job; the position that the Pullman man and his family have occupied in the community has steadily declined.[55]

Migration north and openings in fields previously closed to African Americans helped shatter the mystique of the Pullman porter's job.

When World War I closed off European immigration, the Chicago stockyards hired increasing numbers of black workers. By 1917 there were approximately 12,000 black workers in meat-packing, which included 1,490 semiskilled operatives, in Chicago.[56] During the twenties, the most important source of jobs for workers from Chicago's black neighborhoods and one of the better routes for economic advancement was the meat-packing industry. Close to half of the 4,500 African American packinghouse workers in 1930 were classified as semiskilled butchers. According to the son of a longtime Swift employee, "To be a top man at Swift's or Armour's meant that you could pay your bills, feed your family, have your kids in clothes and shoes, and have more than a little bit of respect from your neighbors."[57] In 1920 even unskilled black packinghouse workers earned $22 a week for approximately 60 hours a week, or 240 hours a month. Porters earned $60 a month, plus tips, for an average 400 hours a month. Work in the stockyards may have been dirty, smelly, and dangerous, but porters usually worked for fifteen years before they received a token 5 percent increase in pay, and there was no advancement. Black meat-packers could hope to advance up the ladder to butcher or skilled meat-packer. In the twenties, over 500 black slaughterhouse workers were promoted to butcher, a position previously dominated by whites that paid between $35 and $48 a week in 1920.[58]

Vitally important for thousands of new residents in Chicago was independence from direct white control. Almost every aspect of life in the rural South was supervised and monitored by whites. In factories and stockyards, supervision was limited to working hours and was impersonal. Not only did recent migrants gravitate toward industrial work, but they often did so even if it meant earning less money. Between 1918 and 1920, service employers had difficulty finding domestic help even when they offered higher wages than competing factories. Increasingly, black Chicagoans would rather work for less if they felt like more of a human being at the end of the day.[59] Joe Trotter reminds us that the process of making a black industrial working class took place within a context reflecting the experiences of workers shaped by the subjugation and exploitation of sharecropping and the servility demanded by domestic and personal-service jobs.[60] Recent migrants viewed work through a different lens than laborers from other experiences.

No More Servants in the House

Barnett's proposed solution to the problem of low self-esteem among porters by 1920 was to produce a magazine devoted to the accomplishments of porters.[61] W. E. B. Du Bois had another solution to the problem represented by the Pullman porter's job.

In 1920 Du Bois connected the problem of partial freedom to the persistence of social relations that had originated in slavery and lingered into the twentieth century. It was, he argued, the assumption that "Negroes are servants; servants are Negroes" and "upon such spiritual myths" that the "anachronism of American slavery [was] built." The result "was the degradation that once made menial servants the aristocrats among colored folk."[62] The house servant, able to secure better food, clothing, and shelter, imagined that the special relationship with the master might mean a chance to gain freedom. But that was not to be. In the United States, "as every Negro soon knew and knows," the way to climb "out of slavery into citizenship" lay "in escape from menial serfdom."[63] In fact, Du Bois measured the rise of black Americans in terms of the percentage of servants and serfs among workers. In 1860, 98 percent of black Americans "were servants and serfs. In 1880, 30 per cent were servants and 65 per cent were serfs." He warned that "until this hateful badge of slavery and mediaevalism has been reduced to less than 10 per cent," black people "will not approach freedom."[64]

In Chicago, on the eve of the Depression, over 25 out of every 100 employed black men and 56 out of every 100 black women were doing some kind of servant work.[65] Du Bois counted among what he called the "million menial workers" and "upper servants" positions like "hotel waiters, Pullman porters, janitors, and cooks, who, had they been white, could have called on the great labor movement to lift their work out of slavery, to standardize their hours, to define their duties and to substitute a living, regular wage for personal largess in the shape of tips, old clothes, and cold leavings of food." The problem, observed Du Bois, was the "labor movement turned their backs on those black men when the white world dinned in their ears" that African Americans belong in the servant caste. Until that perception is erased, black workers will never receive equal consideration and pay with white workers.[66]

Du Bois noted that the rules of labor unions were designed "not simply to raise wages, but to guard against any likeness between artisan and servant." In his mind, there was "no essential difference in ability and training between a subway guard and a Pullman porter, but between their union cards lies a whole world."[67] Pullman porters' jobs exemplified "the last and worst refuse of industrial caste." Menial service was "an anachronism, —the refuse of medieval barbarism."[68] Menial service work was directly related to what Du Bois called the "'manure' theory of social organization," a belief that "at the bottom of organized human life there are necessary duties and services which no real human being ought to be compelled to do. We push below this mudsill the derelicts and half-men, whom we hate and despise, and seek to build above it— Democracy!" Because the majority "consciously and unconsciously" still subscribe to this theory, Du Bois advocated getting the servants out of the house to restore "half-men" to their full manhood—that is, full humanity.[69] Until black Americans were above Du Bois's mudsill, freedom and democracy would remain a chimera.

Manhood Rights and the Quest for Democracy at Home

Historians often cite 1919 as the year black Americans fought back when attacked by white citizens in northern urban areas. Black citizens fought back many times before 1919, but the year is useful, nonetheless, to mark a change in the geography of the color line. By then, World War I had come to a close and President Woodrow Wilson had enunciated his Fourteen Points at the Paris Peace Conference, suggesting an expansion of rights for racial groups. By then, African Americans, aspiring to first-class citizenship, demanded the elimination of traditional and imaginary dividing lines, which sorted humanity according to color. No matter where black people had stood on the debate over Du Bois's appeal to "close ranks" behind President Wilson's war effort, black Americans expected they would be rewarded with democracy at home once the war was over. Indeed, Senator James K. Vardaman of Mississippi, fearing black soldiers would earn a stake in democracy for all black Americans, argued against conscription of black men for just this reason.[70]

Senator Vardaman's fears were partially realized. The war, as Du Bois told a packed audience at Chicago's Wendell Phillips High School in 1919, changed forever the consciousness of soldiers. They would "never be the same again," Du Bois told the crowd. "You need not ask them to go back to what they were before. They cannot, for they are not the same men any more."[71] But the war's influence extended beyond soldiers. Throughout the war, the *Chicago Defender* brought the war to the home front by tracking the battles and heroism of black soldiers, especially the Eighth Illinois Regiment, which was awarded twenty-one Distinguished Service Crosses by the United States and sixty-eight *Croix de Guerre* pins by the French. Black Chicago was reminded that black men fighting for democracy, "will provide a fuller measure of equality for you and for them when it is over—that the democracy for which they are fighting will include the American Negro when peace is signed in Berlin."[72] Writing for the *Crisis*, the monthly magazine of the National Association for the Advancement of Colored People (NAACP), Du Bois added, "make way for Democracy! We saved it in France, and by the Great Jehovah, we will save it in the United States of America, or know the reasons why."[73]

The mostly younger black southerners who migrated north to Chicago carried aspirations for economic and political integration into American society. Pulled by the booming economy and the desire for increased opportunity, black southerners, in the process of traveling north, invested in the promise of democracy. Those who traveled the rails during the first phase of the Great Migration broke from a caste system and reached for the better life they expected lay at the end of the road. The hope was to take their place as equal participants in American civic and economic life.[74]

African Americans spoke of the post–World War I era as a new era, a "grand and awful time" where the "yesterdays are gone forever."[75] The call went out for New Negroes, those willing to make demands and fight for rights of American citizenship. The Old Negro, described as "bent and twisted" from "bowing" and "kow-towing" to the wishes of white America, and "his methods must go," for "his abject crawling and pleading have availed the Cause nothing."[76] The *Chicago Whip* noted that "we have witnessed the decadence of Negro rights, manhood rights. We have witnessed the deterioration of brotherly love (commenting on black soldiers drafted into a Jim Crow army to come home and face lynching and bombs)." The solution offered by the *Whip* was to "Take a man's stand." Old Negroes, those who were "spineless, cringing, would-be leaders," were a "species" that could not "be placed in the genus of man; men have backbone and invertebrates belong to the class reptila, example rattlesnake."[77]

Black Americans fought back in twenty-six cities during the summer of 1919 when attacked by white mobs. Concerned citizens studied the uprisings at great length in an attempt to understand why African Americans were "suddenly" dissatisfied, why they were exhibiting a "dangerous tendency" toward violence.[78] Illinois Governor Frank Lowden formed the Chicago Commission on Race Relations, a panel of six white and six African American civic leaders, businessmen, and politicians to study the Chicago race riot that began on July 27, 1919, and ended two days later. A 700-page report, published three years later, had little impact on public policy, minimized evidence of white racism, and faulted black Chicagoans for "thinking and talking too much in terms of . . . race" pride. The commission advised the black press, criticized for inciting a growing race consciousness that interfered with "racial adjustment" and assimilation, to educate its readers about the "means and opportunities of adjusting themselves and their fellows into more harmonious relations with their white neighbors and fellow-citizens."[79] In other words, black Chicagoans should learn to be more civil and acquiesce to conventions of correct behavior prescribed by the status quo.

The African American press, in contrast, saw the racial status quo as the root of the problem. The Richmond *Planet* said the "primary cause . . . is the inborn hatred that is in the hearts of those who resent the human aspirations of colored people."[80] The *Chicago Whip* pointed to the fear from "white friends" that the "Negro is breaking his shell and beginning to bask in the sunlight of real manhood."[81] A new spirit in black America, a new assertiveness was observed. Militant voices across the country hailed the New Negro, who "unlike the old time Negro 'does not fear the face of day,'" as a role model.[82] The *Crusader* suggested that there was more "respect for the Negro following the race riots" because black America fought back against the racial status quo.[83] Claude McKay's poem "If We Must Die," written in and of the summer of 1919, and published in black journals, magazines, and newspapers across the country, captured the essence of the spirit of the New Negro. "If we must die, let it not be like hogs . . . (but) like men we'll face the murderous cowardly pack, pressed to the wall, dying, but fighting back!"[84]

Restoring George's Manhood Rights

During the summer of 1925 five Pullman porters, operating out of New York City, wanted shorter working hours and higher pay. But—like Du Bois—they also wanted to destroy the myth connecting black people with the status of servants, for they believed that the historical circumstances that created "George" continued to define social relations restricting freedom of opportunity for black Americans as workers. They proposed that porters form a labor union.

The problem was not representation. Since 1920, the Employee Representation Plan had been representing the porters. During World War I the federal government assumed control and operation of railroads and decreed that Pullman employees had the right to organize and select their own representatives for collective bargaining, a historical moment for the Pullman Company. The conductors seized the window of opportunity and organized the Order of Sleeping Car Conductors in February 1918. But Pullman porters' organizational efforts soon splintered into several small, regional unions. One of the strongest, at least initially, was the Brotherhood of Sleeping Car Porters Protective Union, which operated out of New York and Chicago. In July 1919 some 5,000 people gathered in Harlem to hear how the Protective Union planned to "lay a better foundation for future Colored Americans." One porter claimed the grievance among porters was not work, but the kind of labor. "We are willing to work and at the same time be courteous, but we are going to insist that we are men and as such entitled to a living wage. . . . We are men and added to this WE ARE UNION MEN."[85] When that effort was co-opted by porters sympathetic to management, the Pullman Company used the shell provided by Protective Union as a foundation for the Plan—the Employee Representation Plan—which was presented to porters for their approval. Not all porters accepted the ERP as their representative. Among those who refused was Ashley L. Totten who led the New York Central District.[86]

Nevertheless, Totten remained both militant and active in the ERP. In 1924 he was elected by a vote of 9,131 out of a total national count of 9,780 to be a porter delegate at a wage conference organized by the Pullman Company. His popularity suggests that porters wanted representatives willing to stand up to Pullman Company officials.[87] During negotiations at this conference, Totten decided the time was ripe to try to organize a national union. The delegates had hoped to win a concession, at the least, reducing their 400-hour month closer to 240 hours per month, which was the minimum negotiated by the Order of Sleeping Car Conductors. Conductors also made over twice as much per month while working many fewer hours and enjoying a six-hour-a-night sleep allowance. Not only did management not budge on the issue of hours, it offered a paltry $7.50 pay increase, which raised their monthly wages to $67.50 compared to a $150 base for conductors.[88] Company officials had made it a point, according to Totten, to bury important proposals in intricate details that were hard for the porter delegates to grasp.[89] But issues of pay and hours of work were related to larger issues of dignity and manhood rights. Totten called the company's efforts to buy the allegiance of porter delegates a "soothing salve," which it administered in the form good wine, cigars, nightly feasts with entertainment from the Pullman Porter Band, and a $5.00 per diem in addition to normal wages. It was an attempt to keep the porters passive and subservient.[90]

Because both the work and community life of Pullman porters were closely scrutinized by Pullman Company officials, assisted by a cadre of black men, usually ex-porters, employed as Pullman welfare workers or what Totten characterized as "stool pigeons," secrecy was a key consideration for the five porters who laid plans between June and August 1925 for the Brotherhood of Sleeping Car Porters (BSCP).[91] Fear of reprisal from the Pullman Company—widely known for its antiunion policies—led Totten and his colleagues to look for a leader who was beyond the direct reach of the Pullman Company, capable of standing up to the company and its officials. Totten thought he found all the necessary traits in A. Philip Randolph, editor of the *Messenger*, a monthly magazine published in Harlem, which had heralded the arrival of the New Negro during World War I. The magazine could serve as the voice of the new union; Randolph was considered one of the best public speakers the streets of Harlem had produced, and he was fiercely committed to the organization of black workers. Finally, Randolph was also known as a tireless fighter for rights of black Americans within the larger society.[92]

The five porters asked Randolph if he would consider being chief organizer for the Pullman porters. Randolph accepted, and the BSCP was launched. Its first public meeting on August 25 was so secret that the New York organizers did not invite leading porters from other districts to lessen the risk of sabotage from Pullman porter spies.[93]

Randolph immediately used the *Messenger* as a means for educating the porters, other black workers, and the larger African American community about the BSCP's effort to restore George's manhood rights. Although Randolph and other organizers initially referred to the BSCP as a labor union, from the first they revealed the contours of a larger vision, for they regarded their union effort as a vehicle for social and economic change for African Americans. "The Brotherhood was born," Randolph wrote, to pursue the "quest for the holy grail of economic freedom." But in order to reach that goal, "we must destroy the engines of industrial slavery ere we breathe the air of free men."[94] Industrial slavery and the paternalistic relations embedded in company unions embodied most of the servile relations that Randolph thought held porters and most black Americans in second-class status.

The union movement concentrated its educational efforts around claiming manhood rights for porters and maids, viewed as a first step in the struggle for economic freedom. It ran articles in the *Messenger* on other specific issues, such as the ERP or previous struggles of the porters to organize, but the larger theme underlying the BSCP's propaganda was manhood rights, which was, in the minds of BSCP organizers, inextricably linked with economic freedom.[95] Asserting one's "manhood rights" was, therefore, part of the process of regaining one's self-esteem and claiming a place as an equal to white citizens.[96]

For Asa Philip Randolph, actively involved in Harlem's radical politics and fighting for manhood rights since before World War I, the BSCP provided a means to carry forward the spirit of the New Negro. Randolph helped shape the concept of the "New Negro" in the pages of the *Messenger*, which began publication in Harlem in 1917.[97] The New Negro, unlike the Old Negro, "cannot be lulled into a false sense of security with political spoils and patronage" from white America. The New Negro demanded the right to "select his representatives." As a worker, the New Negro "advocates that the Negro join the labor unions. Wherever white unions discriminate against the Negro worker, then the only sensible thing to do is to form independent unions." Socially, the New Negro stood for absolute and unequivocal "social equality," a "decidedly different" goal from the Old Negro.[98]

Although his writings helped shape the New Negro and fused the concept with the quest for black humanity, few knew better than Randolph that the New Negro sat on the shoulders of past struggles in African American history for manhood rights. The contours of this tradition can be traced through Randolph's family history. Randolph was born on April 15, 1889, in Cresent City, Florida, located near Jacksonville. His father, the Reverend James Randolph, an African Methodist Episcopal (AME) minister for several small churches scattered in the vicinity of Jacksonville, formed his political outlook during Reconstruction within the context of the militancy of those times when he and many others often armed themselves to defend their rights.[99] Reverend Randolph taught his two sons, Asa and James, that they were the equal of all other people in the United States in terms of both abilities and rights. "Now I got that from my father before the fireplace," Randolph recalled years later. "He drilled into us the idea that there was nothing beyond you if you studied to equip yourself for it." Randolph credited his parents and early family life for his strong positive self-image and confidence in his capacity to overcome obstacles.[100] Asa's father also exposed them to black politics through the *Voice of the Negro*, a monthly journal, and taught them about great figures in black history. One of those figures, a colleague of the elder Randolph, was the Reverend Henry McNeal Turner, bishop in charge of the Georgia and Florida districts of the AME Church.[101]

During Reconstruction, Turner was a leading black Republican and was elected to the state House of Representatives in Georgia in 1868.[102] When the Georgia legislature expelled him, Turner protested with a speech that influenced both Randolph and his son.

> I hold that I am a member of this body. . . . I shall neither fawn nor cringe before any party nor stoop to beg them for my rights. . . . I am here to demand my rights, and to hurl thunderbolts at the men who would dare to cross the threshold of my manhood. . . . The black man cannot protect a country if the country doesn't protect him; and if, tomorrow, a war should arise, I would not raise a musket to defend a country where my manhood is denied.[103]

Turner may not have been directly responsible for Randolph's opposition to black participation in World War I, but the passage suggests that the spirit of Turner's legacy was carried forward when Randolph condemned "Old Crowd Negroes" for counseling men "first your country, then your rights."[104]

Reverend Randolph also taught his sons about other great men in black history including Crispus Attucks, Nat Turner, Denmark Vesey, Toussaint

L'Ouverture, Richard Allen, and Frederick Douglass. Role models from black history reinforced his father's stern warning to stand up for your rights. Thus Randolph gained self-confidence from the firm belief that he was as capable as any white person and was not "supposed to bow and take a back seat for any-body."[105] Randolph remembered his father as a "highly racially conscious" person who wanted "us to be that way." His father told him "there isn't a single Negro in Jacksonville who has any immunity from persecution by whites . . . and therein lies the major problem of our life." At the same time, the elder Randolph's race consciousness did not preclude working with whites who "be-lieve in social justice." He recalled that Jacksonville had a good number of black people "who had courage and determination and were deeply racially oriented, and who believed in their rights and were willing to fight for them."[106]

W. E. B. Du Bois's *The Souls of Black Folk*, published in 1903, provided some of the intellectual foundation for Randolph's migration northward. The book captured the essence of Du Bois's argument against the racial accommodation espoused by Booker T. Washington, who represented, wrote Du Bois, "in Negro thought the old attitude of adjustment and submission." Moreover, "Mr. Wash-ington withdraws many of the high demands of Negroes as men and American citizens." To counter this tendency, Du Bois called for "the assertion of the manhood rights of the Negro by himself."[107] The great debate between Du Bois and Washington, which began in 1895, continued throughout the entire first decade of the twentieth century and shaped Randolph's racial radicalism. *Souls of Black Folk*, which he later recalled as "the most influential book" he ever read, further developed his belief in the importance of fighting "for social equality," rather than accommodating to the racial status quo.[108]

Du Bois also strengthened Randolph's belief that he was potentially a mem-ber of the Talented Tenth. From his early childhood, he had been taught that one's purpose in life was to help other black Americans attain greater economic security and civil rights. As a young man in Florida, he daydreamed about "carrying on some program for the abolition of racial discrimination."[109] Al-though Randolph was class valedictorian when he graduated from the Cook-man Institute in 1907 and earned what was then considered a prestigious job as an insurance agent, he did not see much hope for advancing the race, or himself, by remaining in the South.[110] Du Bois critiqued Washington for insist-ing on "thrift and self-respect" while at the same time counseling a "silent submission to civic inferiority such as is bound to sap the manhood of any race in the long run."[111] Randolph, who wanted to escape from a region that de-manded submission to civic inferiority, may have read Du Bois's assessment of

Washington as a personal warning. Armed with ideas that imbued Du Bois's protest politics, Randolph migrated to New York City in 1911.

He spent several years studying economics, sociology, and history at City College of New York, while pursuing an "independent colloquium" in the "theory and history of socialism and working-class politics" and "their application to the racial problem in America" through the offerings of the New York Public Library.[112] Randolph first read socialist literature in a course at City College and devoured Marx in his spare time. Forums held at the Rand School, an institute of the Socialist Party commonly known as New York City worker's university, where he heard lectures by Elizabeth Gurley Flynn, Morris Hillquit, and Eugene Debs, broadened his critique of the nation's economic life. He began to think that the struggle for racial freedom must be coupled with a movement for social and economic change.[113]

Perhaps most important in Randolph's political development was the thought of Hubert Henry Harrison, whom Winston James calls the "intellectual father of A. Philip Randolph and the radical socialism of the *Messenger* magazine."[114] Harrison, known as the black Socrates, was a pioneer in shaping early-twentieth-century black radical thought and one of the most gifted intellectuals and street-corner orators to appear in Harlem.[115] When Randolph and other economic radicals or New Negroes associated with the *Messenger* adopted socialism, their model was more likely Harrison, not Eugene Debs.[116] James argues that Harrison "remained a socialist from the time he discovered Marx to the end of this life," never wavering from the belief that the capitalist system could never serve the interests of black people. He did not long remain a member of the Socialist Party of America, however, because it did not put race issues high on its agenda, and he was humiliated by the paternalistic attitudes of some socialists. Harrison, according to James, was pushed, "reluctantly," by racial reality in America, into black nationalism. He was "waiting for a better day that he feared would never come, working in the meantime as a black nationalist."[117]

Randolph joined the Socialist Party about the time Harrison left to become a free-lance agent for black socialism. It is hard to imagine that Randolph did not seriously consider Harrison's critique of the party—his announcement that he would not put the party above his race—while he continued to espouse economic socialism as the foundation for a "race first" politics. In "New Politics for the New Negro," in 1917, Harrison wrote that "any man today who aspires to lead the Negro race must set squarely before his face the idea of 'Race First' . . . Striving to be men."[118] Harrison was highly critical of "good white people" who did not seem to understand that black people were not children, which no doubt appealed to Randolph.[119] Years later, Randolph said that he and Chandler Owen had told Harrison he was their mentor: "We want to extend your work, what you're doing."[120] When Harrison died in December 1927, the New York *Amsterdam News* emphasized that Harrison "bowed to nobody, and that was his strength." He stood alone and was not willing to stoop "to the powers that want a Negro leader to go so far and no further."[121] From Randolph's perspective, this characteristic was perhaps the most important trait not just for black leaders but for the entire African American population.

Although one of the lesser known of the black radicals that emerged during the twenties, Harrison may have been the quintessential New Negro. But the sentiment associated with the New Negro manifested itself in many ways. The question was, How would the impulse be directed? In the early twenties that question remained open. The movement that initially carried forward Harrison's ideas, and was unquestionably received as putting race first, was the Garvey movement. During the summer of 1919, black citizens, soldiers, and workers flocked to the Universal Negro Improvement Association (UNIA), which Marcus Garvey had founded in Jamaica in 1914. Garvey's appeal can be traced to themes emphasized by the New Negro radicals' race first, race pride, and black self-determination.[122]

Although Randolph and the *Messenger* crowd were later to play a significant role in dismissing Garvey, Randolph worked with him up until 1921. They formed a group called the International League of Darker Peoples toward the end of World War I to issue a list of demands in behalf of colonized peoples, which they hoped would be presented at the peace conference in Versailles. The UNIA selected Randolph, antilynching activist Ida B. Wells-Barnett, and Garvey as delegates to attend the Versailles Peace Conference.[123] The *Messenger* applauded Garvey for "having put into many Negroes a backbone where for years they have had a wishbone" and for "having stimulated race pride" and interest in black history, literature, and art.[124]

Unlike Garvey, Randolph was willing to work with white people. He applauded Garvey when he denounced white paternalism and white patronage, but he did not advocate retreating into a separatist society. The *Messenger* benefited from the financial support it received from unions and other sources committed to the Socialist Party.[125] Randolph's aim was integration into white society but on black terms, through assertion of black self-determination. His goal created tension with implementation. It was a conundrum he never quite resolved.[126]

Garvey and Randolph also differed sharply over economic philosophy. Garvey praised black capitalism and advised black workers to be willing to work for less than white workers as a way to maintain the "goodwill of the white employer." His call for expanded black business ownership appealed to middle-class black shopkeepers, professionals, and schoolteachers. Randolph's variety of black socialism had less appeal to the petite bourgeoisie supporters of UNIA. Garvey accepted the unequal power relations that drive capitalism and thought the system was necessary to the progress of the world. Those who "unreasonably and wantonly oppose or fight against it are enemies of human advancement," he said.[127] Randolph disagreed; instead, he attempted to direct the New Negro sentiment toward unionization.

By the middle of the twenties, Randolph still espoused black socialism but withdrew from activism in the Socialist Party, which, as he told his biographer, "had no effective policy toward Negroes, and didn't spend enough time organizing them." Eugene Debs had summarized the problem for the party when he said, "We have nothing special to offer the Negro."[128] Socialism did not appear to be the vehicle for launching a movement for the advancement of black America. Socialist financial support for the *Messenger* declined predictably. But the Socialist Party was not the only group that needed monitoring when it came to race issues. Communism received some attention from the Harlem radicals in the early twenties. It, too, was tainted by the perception that white radicals did not put black issues at the top of their agenda. In addition, reports about white comrades treating black members "like children" and as though "whites had all the answers" must have reached Randolph and the *Messenger* crowd through his radical connections.[129]

When the *Messenger* shifted gears from emphasizing economics and politics to increasing the space devoted to music, art, and black culture, its agenda reflected the defeat of political forces in the aftermath of World War I. The political militancy of the New Negro unleashed by the war and harnessed, in part, by Garvey was largely transformed by 1925 into a cultural awakening among the educated elite. Alain Locke, who best exemplified this spirit with his promotion of the arts, in his text, *The New Negro*, thought a cultural flowering would promote the race through its artistic genius. Locke said that "for generations in the mind of America, the Negro has been more of a formula than a human being—a something to be argued about, condemned or defended, to be 'kept down,' or 'in his place,' or 'helped up,' . . . harassed or patronized." Shifting from the "status of a beneficiary and ward . . . [to] that of a collaborator and participant in American civilization" should lead to a reevaluation of old stereotypes of black people.[130] David Levering Lewis, in *When Harlem Was in Vogue*, questioned Locke's approach, suggesting it seemed "irresponsibly delusional." "Harlem was turning its back on Garveyism and socialism to gawk in perplexed admiration at Phi Beta Kappa poets, university-trained painters, concertizing musicians, and novel-writing civil rights officials."[131]

The *Messenger* in the mid-1920s also reflected the more moderate approach Randolph was adopting to issues involving black workers. Whereas he once blasted the American Federation of Labor (AFL) in the *Messenger*, he had come to believe that black workers should seek membership in the AFL. He did not think black workers should cease their efforts to break down color bars in the AFL. But the larger economic and social backdrop of the 1920s, reinforced by the state's hostile stance toward labor, persuaded Randolph that black workers needed to operate from a base of strength within the House of Labor.[132] The question was how do black workers gain entrée to the house, via the front door, and claim an equal seat at the bargaining table? It was a question that Randolph would spend a lifetime trying to resolve.

Although Randolph had worked with Communists in the early twenties, he increasingly adopted an anti-Communist posture. Randolph's opposition to the Communists may be related to the desire of Randolph and the *Messenger* staff that black Americans become "full-fledged citizens of the United States," a position best served by keeping some distance from a group known to have a problem with white chauvinism during the twenties. The Communists identification with Moscow may also have caused concern in the aftermath of the era of the Red Scare and Palmer raids.[133] He once had said that the Communists sought to destroy the existing trade-union movement. By the mid-twenties, Randolph thought the AFL might be the only weapon labor had to work with; he did not advocate alliance with the Communists. When the Communists inaugurated an alternative, the American Negro Labor Congress (ANLC), Randolph was trying to form a labor union in another arena and was courting the American Federation of Labor.[134] In addition, as Mark Solomon notes, the ANLC effort, against the advice of Otto Huiswoud, Richard B. Moore, and other black Communists, placed white Communists in the forefront of organizational work and "ignored the social and cultural roots of the ANLC's proposed constitutency."[135] Randolph worked with the Communists later on, particularly during the United Front period in the 1930s, but his rejection in the 1920s of the Communist approach was a product of both tactical expediency and race consciousness.

Randolph's primary interests in the mid-1920s were twofold. First, he wanted to have an impact on the liberation of black Americans from their inferior status, and, second, he remained convinced that without economic power, black Americans could not attain and secure full citizenship rights. Randolph was thirty-six in 1925 and groping for organizational direction. His principles and beliefs were about to find a vehicle for expression in a movement that would ultimately capture the attention of black America. His new direction emerged when Randolph accepted the offer of five disgruntled Pullman porters to help them organize a union independent of the Pullman Company. Years later, Randolph remembered the Pullman sleeping car porters as a group like no other in America, "who constituted the key to unlocking the door of a nation-wide struggle for Negro rights."[136]

CHAPTER TWO

The Politics of Paternalism and Patronage in Black Chicago

I believe a rich plunderer like Pullman is a greater felon than a
poor thief, and it has become no small part of the duty of this
organization [American Railway Union] to strip the mask of
hypocrisy from the pretended philanthropist and show him to the
world as an oppressor of labor. . . . The paternalism of Pullman is
the same as the interest of a slave holder in his human chattels.
You are striking to avert slavery and degradation.
EUGENE DEBS, May 16, 1894

Shortly after the Brotherhood of Sleeping Car Porters began its organizing
campaign in New York City during August 1925, Randolph made plans to take
the BSCP west to Chicago, the city with the largest population of Pullman
porters. If the Brotherhood wanted to represent Pullman porters and maids, it
had to win support in Chicago. But the shadow of the giant Pullman Company
hovered over that city's black community. In one direction a couple of miles
north of the area where the majority of African Americans lived, Pullman
Company headquarters loomed large on the horizon. In the other direction, a
few miles south of the black community, was the town of Pullman, founded in
the late nineteenth century as a model community for white workers of the
Pullman Company. Pullman town, though no longer owned and operated by
the Pullman Company, cast a shadow over the black community, for the town
stood as a reminder of George Pullman's dedication to industrial paternalism
and his resolve to fight unions. The Pullman strike of 1894 began in the town of
Pullman when George Pullman refused to respond to grievances brought by its
workers and residents against Pullman's paternalistic living and working ar-
rangements, which, the residents said, resembled feudalism. When the workers
decided their only recourse was to join the American Railway Union, the attorney general ordered federal troops to put down the unrest—14,000 armed

agents guarded Chicago at the height of the offensive—in one of the bloodiest labor struggles in all U.S. history.[1] Memory of that strike was still fresh.

The Brotherhood's campaign came to a halt when it reached Chicago and discovered that launching a union movement there would be very difficult. Recent migrants getting off at Chicago's Illinois Central Railroad Station discovered a new world when they disembarked. Although Richard Wright buffered his journey from rural Mississippi to Chicago by spending two years in urban Memphis, he recalled that "My first glimpse of the flat black stretches of Chicago depressed and dismayed me." It was "strange to pause before a crowded newsstand and buy a newspaper without having to wait until a white man was served . . .," he remembered, yet "I began to grow tense again. . . . I knew that this machine-city was governed by strange laws and I wondered if I would ever learn them."[2]

It is customary to associate the paternalism of George Pullman with the model town he built in the 1880s for white workmen and their families employed by the Pullman Palace Car Company. Yet, starting in the 1890s, Pullman, his family, and their successors at the Pullman Company attempted to engrave Pullman benevolence on the social and political system of black Chicago by making large financial contributions to such key institutions as churches, the Urban League, and the Young Men's Christian Association (YMCA). By the time the BSCP set out to organize porters and maids in Chicago in 1925, the community was steeped in a mystique identifying the Pullman Company, along with the Swift and Armour meat-packing companies, as a friend and supporter of black Chicagoans.[3] Union porters found their first order of business had to be gaining support and respect from a community that felt the Pullman Company had done more for black Chicago than any labor union. A. Philip Randolph, head of the BSCP, and Milton P. Webster, head of the Chicago Division of the BSCP, felt Pullman could not "stand up against the Brotherhood and the community, too."[4]

The Pullman Company Befriends Black Chicago

When the Pullman Palace Car Company was formed in 1867, George Mortimer Pullman became president and general manager of what became a model modern American corporation. The company manufactured luxury cars for railroads, but it was the operation and leasing of Pullman sleeping cars that generated most of the company's profits. Leasing a Pullman car was a package deal; the Pullman Company received all proceeds from the sale of tickets for its accommodations on Pullman sleeping cars above the regular train fare, and required the railroads to use sleeping car porters supplied by the Pullman Company. George Pullman's strength when negotiating with railroads rested on public demand for the superior Pullman sleeper. If a train did not have a Pullman sleeper, customers would travel on a train that did.[5] In 1893, the corporation earned $11.4 million, of which $9.2 million was revenue from operation of palace cars and the remainder was largely income from the manufacture of cars. The Pullman Company was considered one of the financially strongest institutions in the United States. Organized in a hierarchical chain of command, both the operating and manufacturing divisions were under the control of George Pullman. The board of directors merely rubber-stamped his recommendations and annually went through the formality of reelecting Pullman president of the company.[6]

The same control George Pullman exerted over the administration and operation of the corporate body of the Pullman Company was applied to managing his employees. He believed that capital and labor must cooperate for their mutual benefit, that the task of the employer was to improve employee morale by alleviating the squalor of city life and introducing workers to the advantages of reading rooms, libraries, and concert halls. Behind his devotion to improving his workers' lives was both concern for maximum profits and minimum labor problems as well as an obsession with order and control, concerns that also contributed to his passionate antiunion position. Perhaps most important was making his employees feel they were members of one large, happy family, without strife or conflict.[7] To this end, George Pullman utilized industrial paternalism to manage and control his workers. When he constructed a separate town—complete with library, churches, schools, and even a hotel—for his white car manufacturers, it was a "strictly business proposition," intended to apply the " 'Pullman system,' which had succeeded in railroad travel . . . to the problems of labor and housing." His motives were not philanthropic, he insisted; they made good business sense. Workers who benefited from the foresight of Pullman would return the investment with loyalty and reduced absenteeism and drinking.[8]

A similar labor policy shaped the paternalism that George Pullman applied to the black community on Chicago's South Side, home to more than one-third, or approximately 4,000, Pullman porters and 100 maids during the twenties, the highest concentration living in any one city. The presence of Pullman philanthropy in black neighborhoods helped the company extend its influence over both the porters and maids as well as the larger black community. The goal was to gain allegiance of porters and maids to the Pullman family. When

George Pullman decided to invest in the welfare of his black workers in the early 1890s, he did not choose to integrate the planned community of Pullman, Illinois. Instead, Pullman, his daughter Florence, and Pullman's successors poured money into black institutions on Chicago's South Side and financially backed prominent black citizens, linking the name of Pullman with assistance and philanthropy and creating what many South Siders thought of as a Pullman company town.[9] Pullman's presence was reinforced by the considerable influence other industrialists had over civic, social, and political affairs.[10]

Without the financial backing of George Pullman and his daughter Florence, it is questionable whether Provident Hospital, the first large-scale civic project of the black community, begun in 1891, would have succeeded.[11] The hospital, unlike any other in the country at the time, received black citizens on an equal basis and provided opportunities for black doctors and nurses who were discriminated against at most "white" hospitals. Black and white citizens and medical professionals served as members of the advisory board and on the medical staff.[12] When Provident Hospital was established, it marked an important departure in the black community, giving black neighbors an unprecedented sense of control over health care. The hospital also became a symbol of the advancement of black professionals. How, after all, could black doctors and nurses serve if hospitals would not allow them on the staff?[13] In 1893 Ida B. Wells-Barnett and Frederick Douglass, both lecturing at the Chicago World's Fair, took part in the ceremony to open the country's first and only interracial hospital while every black citizen in Chicago, according to one account, stood on the sidewalks to watch.[14]

During the depression that began in 1893, Florence Pullman's liberal contributions helped save the hospital from foreclosure. Another difficulty was finding properly trained nurses to serve on the staff of Provident Hospital. That problem was addressed when, in 1896, George Pullman and Marshall Field purchased additional land, across the street from the Provident, for a nursing school, which was training an average of twenty-five black nurses a year by World War I.[15] A close relationship between Provident Hospital and the Pullman Company continued well into the 1920s. Shortly after the first organizational meeting for the Brotherhood of Sleeping Car Porters in Chicago in 1925, the president of Pullman Company reminded porters about the company's most recent and substantial contribution to Provident Hospital, praising its work and its training school for nurses.[16]

The Pullman Company also gave large sums to the Wabash Avenue YMCA and the Chicago Urban League.[17] Both were important in shaping work habits of black Chicagoans and placing them in jobs, particularly during and after World

War I as large numbers of southern migrants headed north to Chicago. The South Side branch of the YMCA on Wabash Avenue, known as the Wabash Avenue YMCA, was established in 1911 as a Jim Crow twin after black Americans were barred from the downtown YMCA in 1910. Ida B. Wells-Barnett was among those who protested the exclusion of black citizens from the beds, reading rooms, and gymnasiums of the YMCA,[18] and black leaders rallied the community for funds to construct a YMCA for the black citizens in South Side neighborhoods. But widespread support from the black community, usually individual dollar donations, did not amount to enough to pay for the project, which depended on larger contributions from white capitalists representing the Pullman Company, meat-packing plants, and Sears Roebuck.[19]

The Wabash Avenue YMCA was one of the most important institutions for newly arrived male migrants aspiring to land industrial jobs. Industrialists took an active part in setting the agenda and encouraging YMCA programs that taught the newcomers the virtue of maintaining good relations with employers. George Arthur, executive secretary of the Wabash Avenue branch, portrayed the South Side "Y" as a "common ground" where thousands of black men working at Pullman Car Company shops, in steel mills, and meat-packing plants gathered "with their fellow workmen, foremen, superintendents, general managers and presidents" to discuss "plans relating to the welfare of both employer and employee."[20] After one year of service at Armour, black workers were entitled to a free membership in the YMCA. Other meat-packers invited YMCA staff to sign up black workers inside their plants.[21] Not only did the Pullman Company encourage porters to become members, the company used the facilities of the Wabash Avenue Y for meetings of its fraternal and benevolent association and had George Arthur address porters about the value of being "loyal to yourself and in being so, loyal to the Association."[22] Membership carried many privileges: access to room and board, glee clubs, reading rooms, swimming pools, picnics, concerts, and leagues and tournaments for various sports, including the popular YMCA Industrial Baseball League.[23]

Major employers of black workers, including five packinghouses, International Harvester, and Pullman, sponsored "efficiency clubs" through the Wabash YMCA. Arthur claimed the work of the efficiency clubs had "brought about a sense of responsibility on the part of the industrial worker and sympathetic understanding and good will on the part of company officials." Recent migrants were led to believe that promotions could result from participation in efficiency club meetings.[24] Efficiency clubs taught black men that the way to stay in the good favor of employers was to stay out of unions.[25]

The Chicago Urban League received substantial contributions from Pullman, both during its first financial campaign and for several years following its founding in 1915, and close ties between certain league members and the company existed well into the 1930s.[26] League officers often met migrants at the Illinois Central Station, suggesting places for them to work and live, shepherding migrants through various stages of settlement in the industrial North. The league helped place migrants in jobs, finding over 20,000 jobs for black workers between spring 1917 and summer 1919.[27]

The company also bestowed favors on certain individuals, such as Julius Nelthrop Avendorph, society editor of the *Chicago Defender*. In 1897 the Pullman Company placed Avendorph on its staff as what has been variously described as a "messenger" or "assistant" to the president of Pullman. Avendorph, known as "Chicago's undisputed social leader," was reputed to act as the eyes and ears in the black community for Pullman executives.[28]

In addition, positive relations were forged between the Pullman Company and the emerging black elite through membership in the Appomattox Club, an organization for politicians and professionals founded in 1900 by Edward H. Wright, a lawyer, politician, and Chicago's first black ward committeeman. The 40 charter members fashioned the club into one of the most important gathering places in black Chicago by the 1920s when its membership had grown to 450. By then, as the *Broad Ax* observed, the Appomattox Club "quietly but constantly exerted its influence for the welfare of the community," whose interests, as defined by club members, were linked with the Pullman Company. The bond was graphically reflected in the life-size portrait of George M. Pullman that hung in the front parlor of the Appomattox Club.[29]

But perhaps the most important factor involved in cultivating deep roots in the black community was the company's long-lasting relationship with the congregation and the minister of the city's largest African Methodist Episcopal (AME) church, Quinn Chapel. When the Reverend Archibald James Carey took over Quinn Chapel in 1898, the church faced foreclosure. Within a few years, however, Carey reversed its financial problems and attracted new parishioners, capturing the attention of Pullman executives and other industrialists who were impressed by his skill as a money manager and wise administrator. Carey rose to prominence early in the twentieth century as a major player in the politics of the Chicago Republican Party machine. As he quickly made his mark on both ecclesiastical and political affairs, his ascent was aided by financial help from his chief benefactors, including executives of the Pullman Company. He invited local and national reformers and political figures to speak from the pulpit of his church and established his reputation as a leader and activist in a church noted especially for its role as a meeting place for black abolitionists, decades before, and as a station on the Underground Railroad. In 1912 Carey took a position against the Republican political machine when he supported Edward Wright's unsuccessful attempt to become the first black alderman in Chicago. By the 1920s he was bishop of the AME Church, making him one of the most powerful black leaders in Chicago.[30]

First at Quinn Chapel, and then from 1909 at Institutional Church, Reverend Carey acted on the belief that a church should be a combination community center, town hall, spiritual sanctuary, and recreational area. Support for Carey by the Pullman Company meant more than blessing the religious affairs of the community. Pullman's contributions translated into support of the nursery and kindergarten and care for the children of working mothers. Civic and community affairs occupied a major place in the weekly activities at Institutional with speakers addressing issues such as human welfare, housing, and racial affairs. During these meetings, the church functioned as a town hall for the larger community, filling a void and providing a vital center for organizing urban life. It was a role that became increasingly important with the influx of newcomers pouring into the South Side neighborhoods with the Great Migration. Between 1880 and 1910, Chicago's black population increased from 6,480 to 44,103, and between 1910 and 1920, the black population increased from 44,103 to 109,458.[31]

Reverend Carey's employment service expanded the secular role of the church further than most clergy and created a strong bond between the Pullman Company and his congregation. When Pullman hired an additional 500 to 600 porters during the summer, Carey would announce from the pulpit that employment was available. In addition, some black workers got the few coveted jobs in Pullman repair shops and yards through referrals from Carey. While the position often was only as a car cleaner, it held out the promise of advancement to a skilled job in the Calumet shops where by 1925 there were over 300 black workers.[32] When Reverend Carey announced these positions—particularly during the period between 1910 and 1915—Pullman was seen as a friend of black workers.[33]

Reverend Carey's employment service also obtained jobs for black Chicagoans in domestic and personal service work in the homes of the white elite, reinforcing Carey's relationships with wealthy families such as the Swifts, the Armours, and the Pullmans. This relationship may explain his lifelong aversion toward organized labor. But it is also true that when Carey put down roots in Chicago, the city's trade unions had not extended a helping hand to black workers. Black participation had been shunned since early in the 1890s when black Americans, following in the path of Lithuanians and Poles, broke into basic industries as strikebreakers. When Eugene Debs tried to get the American

Railway Union (ARU) to abolish its color bar limiting membership to "railway employees born of white parents" in 1894, he was defeated by the white rank and file. Black workers responded by forming the Anti-Strikers' Railroad Union, which later that year joined with Polish immigrants to help break the Chicago stockyards strike. Years later, Debs thought the exclusion of black workers by ARU was one of several reasons for the union's defeat by Pullman in 1894. Tension between black and white workers over unions' racial discrimination persisted despite several significant exceptions, causing many black Chicagoans to conclude that unions were largely white institutions.[34]

In few industries, however, was the exclusion of black labor from unions more complete than in railroads. Although black workers were represented in almost every branch of railroading, they remained unorganized in the midst of a highly unionized industry. By the end of the nineteenth century, trade unions representing white railroad workers had clauses codifying the exclusion of black workers from positions as conductors, locomotive engineers, firemen, and brakemen. The big four brotherhoods all maintained constitutional bars against black workers as members. In the North, railroad brotherhoods won contracts with companies barring employment of blacks. A different situation prevailed in the South because the brotherhoods were weaker and labor markets were different. There, unions often were not able to win contractual or informal exclusion, at least not until the period around the Great Migration, because black southerners were well entrenched in these jobs, unlike in the antebellum and postbellum North; thus, black workers made up the majority of firemen and brakemen in many locations. While not barred from their craft, they were excluded from the brotherhoods. The big four railway brotherhoods not only worked against recruitment of black workers, they worked toward eliminating them from all operating crafts within the industry.[35]

During the white car cleaners strike against the Pullman Company in 1916, Pullman demonstrated its understanding of the reciprocal nature of the paternalistic bargain. The company not only hired male and female black workers to replace the strikers, but protected its newly hired car cleaners from retaliation by feeding them in Pullman dining cars and offering them beds in Pullman sleeping cars. Finally, Pullman kept most the replacements on as permanent car cleaners after the strike. The *Pullman Porters' Review*, a Pullman Company publication, observed that Pullman's benevolence during the strike toward its black replacement workers "again shows the attitude and loyalty of the company to the colored race."[36] Reports indicate that workers were grateful to Pullman for the place the company cultivated for black workers in this hostile industry.[37]

In the aftermath of the First World War, Reverend Carey continued to re-inforce the Pullman Company message and reiterate his antipathy for orga-nized labor. His outlook was similar to that of Booker T. Washington, who also favored appeals for aid from prosperous white and northern philanthropists over direct protest. Washington believed labor unions were responsible for destroying the strong position black craftsmen once had in the skilled trades, and white employers held the keys to opening doors to economic oppor-tunity.[38] Carey felt so strongly that economic opportunity would come from cooperation with industrial magnates rather than solidarity between black and white workers that during the 1920s he "forbade the congregations in his bish-opric in Chicago to allow A. Philip Randolph to speak before them."[39] His reasoning grew out of his positive experiences with wealthy benefactors who recognized black Americans and opened up jobs for them—often the very jobs that labor unions excluded black workers from with their color clauses. "The interest of my people lies with the wealth of the nation and with the class of white people who control it," Carey argued in 1924. "Labor and capital cannot adjust themselves by rival organizations; they must work together."[40] Carey's close working relationship with the Pullman Company opened up networks within the community where the company could boost its antiunion approach to labor relations, while cultivating its image as friend of the black belt.[41]

Pullman's Other Family

With porters and maids the company wanted to develop more than a friend-ship. Edward F. Carry, president of Pullman Company in the 1920s, hoped all Pullman employees would think they were part of a happy, prosperous family.[42] Pullman promoted the idea that the company gave black workers opportunities they could get nowhere else, raising their status in the black community, much as a parent raises a child. John Ford, a porter from New York, once told a Dartmouth College audience that the Pullman Company took "the best of my race" and gave them a chance to advance by acquiring education with money made during summer employment. Well-known leaders reinforced the mys-tique linking work as a Pullman porter with increased opportunity. Perry Howard, Republican national committeeman from Mississippi, and J. Finley Wilson, grand exalted ruler of the Elks, were successful ex-porters. In the *Pullman Porters' Review*, familial terms were employed by correspondents and writers to refer to relations between the company and its employees.[43] Labor relations were often thought of as "problems that are confronting the family." Porters and maids loyal to the company talked about porters in the BSCP as "brothers" who had "wandered away from the family circle." Years after George Pullman died in 1898, he remained the titular head of the family, and some employees regarded the Pullman Company "as the living embodiment of its founder."[44]

For the large number of porters who "had little early opportunity," as the company phrased it, to receive education, the company provided a chance to build certain skills. Pullman provided music lessons and organized porters into bands, orchestras, and choruses. Pullman president Carry hired Major N. Clark Smith, director of music at Tuskegee Institute, to give the porters a "thorough training in fundamentals of music," along with free lessons on instruments such as the trombone and saxophone. At least one porter was trained to direct a sixty-piece band as a pupil of Major Smith.[45] Hundreds of Pullman porters took advantage of this opportunity to develop their musical talents. Carry did not, however, extend the opportunity to Pullman conductors, perhaps because he thought white conductors were not blessed with African Americans' "gift of music." As a Pullman company official explained, the music program was good because black porters "are of a singing race and music adds to their cheerfulness and contentment."[46]

The musical program had a dual purpose. While it was designed to provide recreation and education for porters, President Carry also hoped the quartets and choruses would "be in a position to sing a song or two for the edification of the patrons."[47] The bands and choruses also performed at Pullman porters' picnics and special quartets sang throughout the country. One was known as the Hungerford Quartette, named after a company manager. Another, and one of the most celebrated, was the Pullman Porters Quartet of Chicago, whose four harmonizers, personally selected by President Carry, were known as the "president's own." This group traveled extensively, appearing in concerts before "leading men in every branch of commerce, industry and the professions."[48]

Other activities, such as baseball games, field days, and picnics, at which officials of the company were always present, encouraged what President Carry called an *"esprit de corps,"* which had a remarkably beneficial effect, management thought, on employees.[49] But the esprit also effectively segregated black and white workers. The *Pullman News*, a publication for all Pullman Company employees, had a special section, "News of the Big Pullman Family." The place reserved for news about porters always followed that of "storekeepers," and "yard" employees, throwing disorder to an otherwise alphabetized list and suggesting their second-class status within the larger family.[50]

What Pullman executives did for porters in the field of education, however, revealed the racial and sexual divide within the Pullman Family. The role for the model woman was to enhance the esprit of the company family by supporting her family and her husband. Short of recognition through the ladies auxiliary of the Pullman Porters Benefit Association of America, a company fraternal organization, women received few of the benefits Pullman Company reserved for its family. There was no evidence of softball teams for Pullman maids, which may simply reflect the small number of maids employed by the Pullman Company. In the *Pullman Porters' Review*, a company publication, mention is made of visits, parties, and illness involving women of the Pullman family, but a reader might never guess Pullman sleeping cars also had maids.[51] Brother porters were reminded of the importance of smiling; but sister maids were never mentioned.[52]

As early as 1914, Pullman inaugurated a pension plan making retirement, with pension, available to porters and maids who had worked for the company for twenty years. The plan made retirement compulsory at sixty-five for Pullman maids and seventy for Pullman porters. Pension allowances, paid monthly, were calculated to equal 1 percent of the average monthly pay during the last ten years of service multiplied by the total number of years in service, with no pension to be less than $15.00 a month. The company was not bound by contract to pay and could terminate payment for any reason. A death benefit plan also existed for dependents of employees who died after a year in service. The equivalent of one year's salary was paid entirely by the company. Another benefit for Pullman porters and maids was the yearly physical examination at company expense. Loyal porters reminded the community that many porters "had tuberculosis and did not know it." When Pullman discovered such a disease, the porters "were given treatment and cured without cost or obligation."[53] It was not mentioned that public knowledge of tuberculosis among Pullman porters and maids would have been very bad for business. Moreover, as Roy Lancaster, secretary-treasurer of the BSCP during the early years, thought, the medical examinations required by the company were "most humiliating to the men."[54] Beginning in December 1925, the company began an employee stock ownership plan, opened equally to all its employees, who could purchase shares for $140 in installments of $3.00 a month. However, because employees could purchase only one share for every $500.00 earned in salary per year, porters and maids could not purchase more than two shares a year. The plan was not popular with porters.[55]

Despite the extent of Pullman influence over the institutional life of black Chicago, not all porters were convinced that the company's benevolence was designed to serve their best interests. Disgruntled porters emerged between 1900 and 1920 to challenge the company's paternalistic policies. The earliest agitation by porters occurred around 1900, when the obsequiousness and dependency built into the tipping system were challenged by the Pullman Car Porters' Brotherhood, an organization founded by porter Charles Frederick Anderson. Porters claimed that they were receiving between $25 to $35 per month while other railroad men such as "colored train porters" working for other railroad companies were earning between $50 to $80 a month. Because they did not receive a "living wage," Pullman forced porters to rely on "tips" to earn enough to live on. That effort was short-lived.[56] At least three other attempts at organization surfaced. Two—one in 1909, and another in 1910—enjoyed a brief existence, and then died because of lack of interest or scattered memberships.[57] In 1915, a Pullman conductor, R. W. Bell, lost his job while trying to organize Pullman porters into a union, utilizing the support of Ida B. Wells-Barnett's Negro Fellowship League in Chicago.[58] After the railroads came under federal control during World War I, the Railway Men's International Benevolent Industrial Association, a federation of black railroad workers organized by Robert L. Mays, enlisted over 1,000 porters into its ranks. Most porters abandoned the organization as soon as they won an increase in pay.[59] The War Labor Conference Board, in March 1918, declared that Pullman employees had the right to organize and select their own representatives for collective bargaining, a right not to be "denied or abridged or interfered with in any manner whatsoever."[60]

Taking advantage of federal policies, several Pullman porters and maids formed independent unions. One, the Pullman Porters and Maids Protective Association (PPMPA),[61] inspired Pullman Company executives to form the Employee Representation Plan (ERP) in 1920. According to William Harris, rather than opposing independent unions, Pullman simply presented its own company union while allowing the PPMPA to remain as well. When the poorly organized PPMPA failed, the Pullman Porters Benefit Association of America (PPBAA), a fraternal and insurance arm of the ERP, took its place. The PPBAA, basically an organization to extend company influence, posed as much a threat to the organization of the Pullman porters as the ERP.[62]

Although Randolph strongly opposed the PPBAA and the Employee Representation Plan as "two wings of the same bird," porters and maids viewed the two organizations differently. The ERP was designed to silence dissidents among the rank and file and served as a vehicle for settling grievances between porters and maids and the company. Employees and management were equally represented on the various joint committees set up to address labor relations. Although Pullman's Board of Industrial Relations was at the center of the entire system and was, in terms of grievances, the court of last resort for disputes, the company did not actually convene the board to hear porters' grievances until after the BSCP began organizing.[63] In the minds of porters and maids loyal to the company, ERP was not a company union but, as one stated, "simply a co-operative Plan to bring the two groups together in a true co-operative spirit for the mutual benefit of all concerned."[64] President Edward F. Carry pictured his role as protector of porters and maids from the cutthroat negotiations employed by white unionists.[65] Nevertheless, the ERP's general ineffectiveness in dealing with issues of major importance to the porters and maids—such as wage revision, shortening the 400-hour or 11,000-mile monthly working standard, and inadequate overtime pay—raised questions among many porters and maids long before BSCP began organizing.[66]

The feeling of being part of one big family found its deepest and most meaningful expression for men in the PPBAA, a voluntary organization open to all black male workers at Pullman Company, not just porters. Approximately 8,000 of the 12,000 Pullman Company porters belonged to the PPBAA in the late 1920s. In return for dues of $28.00 a year for those under forty-five and $32.00 for those over forty-five, men could receive disability benefits of $10.00 per week after the first five days on the sick list, and relatives were eligible for up to $1,000 in death benefits. Although porters bore the expense of financing the insurance aspect by monthly payments, Pullman Company paid for all the administrative expenses of the organization as well as the lavish yearly conventions. PPBAA's appeal extended beyond insurance benefits to its role as a fraternal and social network.

Jobs were more secure for members in good standing, which is exemplified by the role Perry Parker, "grand chairman," played promoting interests of loyal porters to Pullman officials. Parker was known to argue cases of dismissed porters to Pullman officials, a method that, though often successful, placed a worker's job security at the whim of an individual. Parker was one of the people the Pullman Company contacted for the names of prospective mechanics for the coveted repair shop jobs. Porters valued the sense that PPBAA members looked after one another because it was one of the few safety nets available.[67] Parker, formerly a parlor car porter from Cincinnati, was promoted by Pullman executives to his position as head of PPBAA as a reward for his years of loyal service to the company. After the formation of the BSCP, Parker was responsible for several "Loyal Pullman Porters' Clubs" that assembled to "condemn all actions regarding said Randolph Union and . . . to pledge our sincere support and work for the support of The Pullman Company." Perry's motives may have been explained in a letter he and several PPBAA board members wrote to Pullman Company management. His concern with the BSCP lay, in part, with the way the labor organization had "besmirched the reputation of the Negro Race for loyalty and fidelity by conspiring with outside agitators to incite trouble."[68]

In life as well as in death, ceremony and ritual were important components of the PPBAA. Funerals were elaborate for members and always included eulogies from officials of the company. Annual conventions were large, grand affairs held in Chicago with fraternizing among members as well as all executive officers of Pullman and socially prominent members of black Chicago. The 1927 convention, which cost over $10,000, was entertained at the Wabash Avenue YMCA by a jazz orchestra and big-band music. Other convention events, many taking place at Pullman Company headquarters in downtown Chicago, were prominently featured as great social occasions in the local newspapers.[69]

The 9,000-member national association commanded respect from black businesses who noticed the multiplier effect within the community when the organization paid out close to $25,000 in sickness, accident and death benefits to Chicago porters alone during 1927. In addition, Chicago PPBAA was known to have a deposit of over $10,000 in Jesse Binga's bank.[70] At the 1927 annual meeting in Chicago, Binga, an honorary member of the PPBAA, spoke of his rise from Pullman porter to banker, emphasizing that it was "service that makes a man in demand." Binga pledged to help PPBAA members get mortgages and loans from his Binga State Bank, highlighting one of the many benefits to membership in the Pullman family. The Pullman Company, Binga announced as though taking the audience into his confidence, kept a special vault for loans to porters in his bank, overseen by a nonunion porter.[71] But he also reminded the audience that it was George Pullman who first placed his trust in porters and showed that "it pays to hire a black man" in the wake of Emancipation, comparing Pullman with Abraham Lincoln. Porters therefore owed "a debt of gratitude" to the Pullman Company for paving their way into the "industrial life of the world." Finally, he suggested that black Chicago appreciated the large, positive role Pullman had played supporting the infrastructure of the black community.[72]

Because the PPBAA was popular with many porters, the BSCP limited its attack on the PPBAA to questions of who controlled the organization. PPBAA was in the hands of seven directors, consisting of "instructors" or "welfare" workers, company-selected porters receiving twice the salary of the average porter.[73] Although the BSCP wanted to sever the porters' paternalistic relationship with Pullman, it did not want to destroy the benefits porters received from PPBAA. Many Chicago porters held membership in the BSCP and the PPBAA simultaneously, particularly between 1925 and 1929, which led Brotherhood officials to conclude that they had to formulate an insurance program.[74] In the interim, the PPBAA conventions continued to attract many porters, and the PPBAA meetings remained important as a site where the company could inculcate its employees with Pullman values.[75] Nevertheless, evidence suggests that many porters perceived the company's elaborate PPBAA conventions as a subterfuge designed to treat the men like children while doing nothing concrete to restore their sense of dignity.[76]

Pullman's culture of paternalism took root in Chicago decades before the BSCP began organizing in 1925. At a time when the larger white community condoned Jim Crow's color line in the job market and restricted black participation in the economic system, Pullman represented opportunity for black workers, giving the company a decided edge in maintaining the loyalty of both porters and maids as well as the larger community. In return for Pullman support, Chicago's black leaders reinforced all appearances of harmony and allegiance with Pullman over the upstart union of porters and maids. Bishop Archibald Carey not only banned the BSCP from all AME churches in the Chicago area but reminded AME ministers it was their responsibility to warn members against the evil influence of labor unions. In 1925 he expanded his opposition beyond Chicago, giving his position against BSCP more clout, when he successfully shepherded an antiunion resolution through an AME conference in Missouri.[77]

The black press greeted the formation of BSCP in 1925 with skepticism and outright hostility. With the alleged exception of the *Chicago Bee*,[78] most black newspapers, including the *Chicago Whip* and *Chicago Defender*, ignored the activities of the BSCP for more than two years, many even longer. Claude Barnett, founder of the Associated Negro Press (ANP) in Chicago in 1919, spoke for many black journalists when he claimed that it would be "difficult to overestimate the economic value to the entire colored group what the business of 'pullman portering' has been" as the backbone of the community.[79] The *Chicago Defender* agreed that Pullman was a friend of black labor, while the *Pittsburgh Courier* was a major exception in befriending the BSCP during its first two years of organizing.[80]

As head of the ANP, Barnett sent press releases to most black weeklies throughout the country that either ignored the Brotherhood entirely, praised the Pullman Company for all it had done for black America, or criticized the black union's efforts to organize porters and maids.[81] Barnett never tired of reminding his readers that the "Pullman Company ranks as the employer of the largest number of colored men in the country" and encouraged a "cooperative" spirit between employer and employee. The harmonious working

relationship was illustrated by stories about Pullman's musical education project under the tutelage of Major N. Clark Smith.[82] In addition, Barnett, as a
member of the Chicago Urban League, probably influenced the league's policies
in support of Pullman. Finally, Barnett published the *Heebie Jeebies*, a magazine
supported by financial contributions from the Pullman Company, which gave
Pullman management another outlet to spread its anti-BSCP propaganda. It was
through the *Heebie Jeebies*, advertised as a porters' organ sponsored in cooperation with the PPBAA, that A. Philip Randolph was called "Philip the Fooler," and
Philip the "Great Pretender."[83]

Patronage Politics

Patronage politics, another factor structuring life in black Chicago, influenced
the community's approach to group advancement. Even as Richard Wright,
along with thousands of other black southerners, learned the strange rules that
governed the Chicago machine, he often felt anxiety during his "fevered search
for honorable adjustment to the American scene."[84] Wright portrayed the Chicago machine as an exchange system that entailed trading black votes for jobs,
and, he added, "our boys consent, for here is the promise of a job behind a desk,
the kind of job that the white population does not want us to have." Although
the "law says that we are *all* free," Wright observed, "we are caught in a tangle of
conflicting ideals; we must either swap our votes for bread or starve."[85]

Yet because politicians, like the Reverend Archibald Carey and others who
were part of the established, pre–World War I black community, had played by
the rules of the Chicago machine, political possibilities that migrants found
when they arrived in Chicago were greater than in most urban areas. Reverend
Carey used the relationship he established with the machine while advancing
the career of William Hale Thompson from second ward alderman in 1900 to
mayor of Chicago in 1915 to jockey for a greater role for black citizens in shaping
public policy. This exchange of votes for favors led Ralph Bunche to describe
Chicago in the 1920s as a political mecca for black Americans, a "seventh
heaven." Indeed, black Chicagoans exercised more political power than black
citizens in any other place in North America. Chicago had a black alderman by
1915, twenty-six years before New York, and sent that alderman, Oscar DePriest,
to Congress in 1928, the first black congressman from the North.[86]

One factor accounting for a measure of political success was the concentration of large numbers of black migrants in a couple of wards on the South Side,
a population that increased by 65,491, or 148.5 percent, between 1910 and 1920,
an increase that took on special significance after black women gained the vote

for municipal and presidential elections in 1913. A second factor was the dependence of the Republican machine on black votes to remain in power.[87] In return for delivering the second ward, which contained the largest proportion of black voters, in 1900, Thompson enacted an ordinance for establishing the first children's playground in the city, funded with $1,200 tax dollars, and built it across the street from Quinn Chapel, Reverend Carey's church.[88] Thompson appointed Reverend Carey, over Booker T. Washington, as one of four speakers to commemorate the Centennial of Admiral Perry's victory at Put-in-Bay on Lake Erie in 1913, giving several prominent federal government officials, including ex-president Taft, a chance to hear Carey plead that the "most effective forces" of American life be turned upon "injustice and unrighteousness as exhibited in every form of discrimination, disenfranchisement, segregation . . . and jim crowism." When Thompson ran for mayor in the Republican primary in 1915, he won largely through the efforts of black voters in Carey's second ward. Thompson was mayor from 1915 to 1923, then again from 1927 to 1931, and it was Archibald Carey who was most responsible for the favorable image of "Big Bill" in black neighborhoods. In a mass meeting to celebrate the fiftieth anniversary of the passage of the Thirteenth Amendment, Carey said there were "three names which will stand high in American history—Abraham Lincoln, William McKinley and William Hale Thompson," who is the "best mayor Chicago ever had."[89]

Reverend Carey did not make this claim lightly. Thompson was popular with black Chicagoans because at least he understood "the question," which as A. L. Jackson, executive secretary of the Wabash Avenue YMCA, once noted, was the key to winning black votes. Thompson was right on "the question" when he called the film, *The Birth of a Nation*, an abomination and an insult to millions of Americans, appointed African Americans to patronage jobs in City Hall, and justified his actions by noting that "as American citizens they are entitled to their quota of representation in governmental affairs."[90] On another occasion, Carey referred to Thompson as the second Abraham Lincoln; "Whatever Mayor Thompson has done, whatever he will do, he will not do out of sympathy for the descendants of a race once enslaved, but for American citizens who have earned their position." Carey then informed 22,000 cheering black Chicagoans gathered at the Coliseum that Mayor Thompson appointed black citizens to jobs in City Hall because he recognized "the worth of a people." The audience went mad applauding Carey's speech, the *Defender* reported.[91]

So many black Chicagoans were appointed by Mayor Thompson that his opponents contemptuously referred to City Hall as "Uncle Tom's Cabin!"[92] Rather than hide his black appointees in a back room, the mayor gave them regular places to which their positions entitled them. One of those places was given to Carey in 1915 as librarian in the office of the corporation counsel, where he supervised seven employees and drew an annual salary of $2,000. When Mayor Thompson made Carey a member of the Civil Service Commission, a cabinet appointment, in 1928, Carey held the highest office ever given to a black citizen in a northern municipal government. The job carried a yearly salary of $6,000 as a member of a board of three that supervised recruiting more than 30,000 city employees, including the members of the police and fire departments.[93]

Thompson acknowledged that he had been criticized for appointing "Negro citizens to positions of honor, trust and dignity," that his enemies and political opponents tried to "arouse race prejudice against me" because he had given "undue recognition to the Colored people of Chicago." He replied that he made such appointments because the person was qualified for the position and "because in the name of humanity it is my duty to do what I can to elevate rather than degrade any class of American citizens."[94] On several occasions, Mayor Thompson took actions against the prejudices of white politicians who did not like to mix socially with black politicians,[95] giving black Chicagoans the kind of recognition that made them feel that they had entered the playing field as equal contenders, first-class citizens.

But when Carey presented petitions to City Hall for the welfare and rights of black residents, he went as an ambassador from the South Side, a broker dealing with the administration on an individual basis. Dependence on the preexisting political culture of the machine limited collective approaches to reform, for political advancement and control over patronage jobs resulted from cultivating an individual relationship with a white mentor in the machine. Rather than acting in concert—utilizing group power to make demands—black politicians acted individually within the narrow channels that linked the South Side neighborhoods to City Hall. Group advancement would come by working within the established political organization: the best way to contest racial exclusion was through political inclusion.[96]

Black leaders approached white benefactors individually, offering services to the machine in exchange for benefits for themselves and their political base. But the individual approach to jobs and political advancement, noted by all scholars of South Side Chicago, could undermine racial solidarity. The power that brokers placed on the negotiating table did not match that of the dominant culture, and at the ward and precinct level aspiring black political leaders often competed with each other to deliver the vote, further diluting the power of individuals.[97] Still, racial solidarity—the belief that black citizens "must learn to stick together" through "mutual self-help and racial co-operation"—was highly valued and touted repeatedly through the black press.[98] The fact that political channels blocked its expression when political mentors cultivated individual relationships would ultimately be a factor in the BSCP's organizing strategy that appealed to certain members of the black middle class.[99]

World War I: Fighting for Democracy at Home

Expectations raised during World War I created a new community of interests on the South Side and strained the compact with the political machine. In addition, the migration of over half a million men and women to the urban North and the entry of thousands into the ranks of industrial labor helped lay the foundation for renegotiating the social and economic boundaries constructed by leaders such as Reverend Carey. But hopes were dashed during the summer of 1919 as black and white Chicago clashed over housing and jobs.

As black migrants jockeyed to maintain their place within the economy in the first months after Armistice, bitterness set in when the doors of economic opportunity began closing, first on black women, then on black men. By early May 1919, black unemployment was at 10,000, a figure representing 20 percent of the city's unskilled unemployment. Returning soldiers, heading for Chicago and other northern cities for the first time because they did not want to return to former homes in the South, added to the already large numbers of black southerners who had entered the labor market during the last months of World War I.[100] While the black population increased by 65,491 between 1910 and 1920 in Chicago, 50,000 of the new residents arrived during a period of eighteen months in 1917–18.[101]

Despite some signs of progress toward interracial cooperation in the stockyards during the summer of 1919, most newcomers had little experience with unions in the industrial North. The prospect for union drives, such as the meatpacking organizing campaign during 1919, was ambiguous.[102] Although most black leaders lobbied against alliance with organized labor, Dr. George Cleveland Hall, a prominent physician on the staff of Provident Hospital and a member of the Chicago Urban League's board of directors, advocated union membership, as did the Reverend Lacy Kirk Williams of the Olivet Baptist Church and John F. Thomas of Ebenezer Baptist.[103] The hesitancy of black southerners toward unions contributed to increased tensions between black and white workers during July 1919 when 250,000 workers were either on strike, threatening to strike, or locked out.[104] Interracial violence over union issues erupted several times in the weeks before Chicago's July race riot; whereas 90 percent of white stockyard workers were unionized, 75 percent of black stockyard workers remained outside unions.[105] Yet, to conclude that working-class racism was a significant factor in causing the riot misses the restraining influence on white packinghouse workers played by the Stockyards Labor Council (SLC), the Polish press, settlement house workers, and at least one parish priest. As Rick Halpern argues the SLC was pivotal in sustaining ties between black and white packinghouse workers by holding mass interracial meetings and organizing relief for black families during the riot.[106]

Although African Americans in Chicago had access to the ballot, their limited political influence did not translate into an unqualified access to other resources in the city. Housing covenants restricted where blacks could live in Chicago, and other racial codes limited their physical mobility. The huge increase in the black population was confined to the "black belt," which had an acute shortage of housing. [107] Pressure to push outward the boundaries of the black belt heightened racial tensions. When black residents tried to expand their area of settlement on the South Side, they faced bombs, bullets, and collective efforts designed to keep them in a space narrowly circumscribed by the wishes of associations of white property owners. The Kenwood and Hyde Park Property Owners' Association draped a large banner proclaiming, "They shall not pass," across Grand Boulevard at Forty-third Street in 1918. The object, as Kenwood and Hyde Park property owners stated, was simply to "make Hyde Park white." Public space restricted black mobility. Residential districts adjacent to black neighborhoods were areas that black citizens learned to avoid lest they be physically attacked by white gangs. Contested public areas even included several streets that black workers had to pass through on their way to the stockyards and other industries. Literature published by white residents attempting to restrict the ability of black wage earners to purchase property in "white" neighborhoods emphasized keeping "the Negro in his place" or declared that "the place for a Negro aristocrat is in a Negro neighborhood."[108] The Kenwood and Hyde Park Property Owners' Association wrote Mayor Thompson complaining about a movement by the vicious element among black people "haranguing about constitutional rights" and encouraged by a black press laying claims to social equality. Black Chicagoans had stepped beyond their boundaries, they asserted, when they placed "legal rights of Negroes . . . above his moral obligation to the white people."[109]

In the eyes of white Chicago, black citizens' most egregious error was stepping out of the place white Chicago had designated for them. The presence of 50,000 additional black people increased the tension in the conflict over private space—and increasingly structured the relationship between black and white

Chicagoans whenever they met in public places. Despite the fact that over 90 percent of the migrants settled on the South Side in the very areas that had long had black residents, when a few black families dared move into de facto white neighborhoods, a stereotype was born in the minds of many whites of an uppity black person demanding an equal place in social and civil society. When black citizens protested about their constitutional rights, white citizens were correct in thinking that black residents meant to claim a measure of social power and control over their lives.[110]

As early as the summer of 1918, the *Defender* carried headlines declaring that the beaches belong to "all citizens of Chicago."[111] It was not until Sunday, July 27, 1919, that issues of space, race, and work erupted into the Chicago race riot. That day was one of several during July that averaged close to thirteen degrees Fahrenheit above normal. Both black and white citizens had taken to the streets and beaches for relief. When a raft of young black boys floated across an imaginary line dividing the Twenty-ninth Street Lake Michigan beach into "white" and "black" sections, Eugene Williams, one of the boys, was pelted by a white man, fell unconscious into the water, and drowned, sparking the riot.[112] By the time the disaster was over, the toll—38 dead, 537 wounded—inspired Walter Lippmann to note that the riot was an "event infinitely more disgraceful than . . . [the] Red Terror about which we are all so virtuously indignant."[113]

In the aftermath of the riot, black Chicagoans learned to loathe invisible Jim Crow boundaries; white Chicago learned that the city's black citizens were, as Du Bois had observed, a different people than before World War I. Not only did white rioters kill twenty-three black people, but black people fought back, killing fifteen white citizens, no doubt reinforcing the worst suspicions harbored by those white people against equality for black neighbors.[114] Nevertheless, the two sides were far from equal in the contest over public space. Despite the doubling of black representation on the police force between 1915 and 1919, thanks to efforts of black officeholders and Mayor Thompson, black Chicago had insufficient protection.[115] It was in the political arena that black people had a measure of power. Although it was a frail lifeline, when the riot was over, patronage politics seemed to be the one refuge that remained for making some advances.

The Chicago riot also gave birth to multiple black belts. A physical boundary emerged marking the physical space decreed for black residents of the city.[116] But the black belt was also a statement about how "color hate," as Richard Wright called it, defined "the place of black life as below that of white life."[117] Both boundaries, physical and mental, fueled the process that eventually united various factions within the black community around a profound suspicion of white people and increased the value of racial solidarity. Racial solidarity, which had strengthened during the age of Booker T. Washington in response to barriers thrown up against the economic and political development of black citizens, would be transformed from a moderate response to an aggressive tactic for demanding rights through collective action. Historically, the term was coupled with moral uplift and self-help and reflected expectations and an outlook that were reinforced through black institutional development. The hope had been that black Americans who followed the prescriptions of the white, middle class—by linking racial solidarity with economic development and moral virtue—would ultimately be rewarded with full citizenship. Black workers were to follow the path carved by the black middle class and elite or, alternatively be uplifted by them.[118] But the multiple boundaries, which confined black Americans as citizens to an inferior place within the social order, reduced the chance that any black American would attain first-class status. And that, in turn, raised the possibility of uniting across lines of class around the issue of black citizenship.

During the first weeks after the riot, the *Chicago Defender* circulated 30,000 handbills throughout black neighborhoods urging black citizens to cease fighting, stating that "this is no time to solve the Race Question."[119] That action anticipated much of the public sentiment in the aftermath of the riot. In the first years of the twenties, a conciliatory demeanor seemed to characterize relations between black leaders and the white community. "Some of us forget that the white man has given us freedom, the right to vote, to live on terms of equality with him, to be paid well for our work and to receive many other benefits," as one leader expressed it in the *Chicago Tribune*.[120] But this sentiment and demeanor may have been for the consumption of the white public. The Chicago Commission on Race Relations, established to study the causes of the 1919 riot, placed partial blame on the black press for not promoting harmonious relations between the races.[121] While newspapers, such as the *Defender*, toned down the rhetoric, the dream of citizenship rights did not die in the streets during the riot. Others such as Alderman Oscar De Priest and T. Arnold Hill of the Chicago Urban League issued a statement declaring that, "the Negro is demanding an equal share in the democracy he fought for."[122] For the time being, however, such talk was not backed by action.

Life in Chicago's black belt during the 1920s resonated with possibilities, as black newspapers, social clubs, churches, stores, and politicians flourished within the community. The *Chicago Defender*, other newspapers, and some politicians promoted the goal of reaching, as politician Edward Wright wrote, "the status of absolute equality as an American citizen."[123] But given the serious downturn in the economy between 1921 and 1924, black Chicagoans sustained a cautious approach to claiming those rights while community-based constraints deflected attacks on patronage and paternalism—often lumped together and referred to as "biting the hand that feeds you."[124] The 1919 riot marked a period when many black people of Chicago renewed their commitment to claiming their place as American citizens while understanding the necessity for restricting expression of that goal to the black belt. Although the riot fortified economic, social, and political barriers, the dream remained, deterred, but by no means forgotten.

Biting the Hand That Feeds Us

The BSCP Battles Pullman Paternalism, 1925–1927

> Of the many inhuman outrages of this present year, the only case
> where the proposed lynching did *not* occur, was where the men armed
> themselves. . . . The lesson this teaches and which every Afro-American
> should ponder well, is that a Winchester rifle should have a place of
> honor in every black home, and it should be used for that protection
> which the law refuses to give. When the white man who is always
> the aggressor knows he runs as great risk of biting the dust every
> time his Afro-American victim does, he will have greater respect
> for Afro-American life. The more the Afro-American yields and
> cringes and begs, the more he has to do so, the more he is insulted,
> outraged and lynched.
>
> IDA B. WELLS-BARNETT, June 1892

When A. Philip Randolph and several Pullman porters set out to organize the
Brotherhood of Sleeping Car Porters in Chicago in October 1925, they faced two
related tasks. They had to gain recognition from the Pullman Company and its
executives who allegedly vowed never to "sit down at the same table with a
'bunch of black porters.' "[1] But before they could gain recognition from Pullman, they needed to win the support of a larger black community accustomed
to Pullman paternalism. The immediate target of the BSCP was the Pullman
Company's union, the Employee Representation Plan. For the BSCP to make
sense to the porters and maids, union organizers had to expose what they
thought was wrong with a company that had been a "friend of black labor." In
short, union organizers had to answer the question Jesse Binga, head of Binga
State Bank, posed to porters at a Pullman Company benefit association meeting: why would the porters and maids want to go against the wishes of the
Pullman Company, which placed black workers in positions of trust and
showed the world that it pays to hire black people?[2]

While not everyone's faith in the goodwill of Pullman was as strong as that of Jesse Binga, the roster of defenders of the Pullman Company in its campaign against the upstart union read like a who's who within the black community. It included most ministers, including Bishop Archibald J. Carey (see chapter 2) and the Reverend Lacey Kirk Williams of Olivet Baptist Church, the largest Baptist church in a community where more than half the population was Baptist, members of the editorial staff of the *Chicago Whip*, and Robert S. Abbott, editor of the *Chicago Defender*. As BSCP organizers soon discovered, they had to gain recognition and support from community leaders, a group that considered cooperation with employers, not challenges against corporations, the practical approach for gaining a foothold in industry. But the Brotherhood also had to gain support from leaders like the Reverend L. K. Williams, who had previously supported unionization of black workers when the risks had not appeared so great. Reverend Williams's opposition to the BSCP reflected the power of the Pullman Company over the community. Initially, many, perhaps most, simply did not take the Brotherhood's challenge seriously, in view of the Pullman Company's success in defeating unions in the past.[3] Yet, opposition from leaders of black Chicago mattered because they used the press and the pulpit to influence public opinion, framing the way the community approached the question of black advancement. In order to reach porters and maids, the BSCP needed support from a large cross section of Chicago's black community.

Despite what seemed like overwhelming odds against the BSCP's effort to gain support, opportunities to gain allies did exist. There was much discussion, and less agreement, during the 1920s on what strategies would advance the large and varied interests of the increasingly complex black community.[4] Generally, political leaders valued organizing black voters for the larger interests of the Republican machine, which rewarded black citizens with patronage jobs and services, while civic leaders in the women's clubs and a few fraternal organizations advanced reform agendas espousing assertive solutions based on collective action.

How did the Brotherhood begin to make inroads into black Chicago? The prime movers during the first two years were a group of clubwomen and several ministers who formed an alliance with the organizers of the BSCP.[5] Clubwomen in Chicago came to the fore politically in 1913 after Illinois granted women suffrage in municipal and presidential elections. Within a year, one group of clubwomen, the Alpha Suffrage Club, asserted its political weight and gained prominence by challenging the dependency embedded in the relationship between black politicians and the white political machine. The fact that clubwomen had led the way in biting one of the hands that fed black Chicago may explain why they were more open than most black men to the Brotherhood's battle against the paternalism of Pullman in 1925.[6]

Chicago Clubwomen and the Politics of Manhood Rights

Milton P. Webster, general organizer of the Chicago division of the Brotherhood, summed up the situation in Chicago during the fall of 1925 by observing that "Everything Negro was against us."[7] Webster had approached some forty-five or fifty prominent black citizens before the first meeting for the BSCP. These were people he held "in the highest esteem." "There was going to be a movement started to organize Pullman porters and I wanted them to come out and give us a word of encouragement," he recalled. "Lo and behold, only five agreed to come and speak, and when the time came only one showed up."[8] That one was Dr. William D. Cook, minister of the Metropolitan Community Church where the meeting was held on October 17, 1925. For the next two weeks BSCP meetings were held every night, but the men in Chicago, as Randolph told Jervis Anderson, were "nowhere near as eager to sign up as the New York men had been."[9] Porters in Chicago, unlike those in New York City, lived in the shadow of the giant Pullman Company.

Pullman's benevolent treatment of the South Side black community paid off in terms of keeping what Webster referred to as "big Negroes" from lending their prestige to the Brotherhood's efforts. The *Chicago Defender, Chicago Whip*, and the Associated Negro Press were important organs for anti-Brotherhood propaganda. In addition, the company relied on the stealth of stool pigeons, loyal company porters who informed upon union members. Brotherhood organizers equated them with the "Uncle Tom, hat-in-hand, me-too-boss" type of person who "in slavery times . . . worshipped his master and his family." A stool pigeon was like the master's favorite slave, who "whenever he saw one of his fellow-slaves do anything . . . ran to the master, for which he would be rewarded with a ham knuckle, or a suit of old clothes."[10] Benjamin McLaurin, an organizer in Chicago in the 1920s, recalled that the stool-pigeon or "Pullman slave" was "better than the CIA. They were so good that if a porter bought furniture for his family the superintendent knew about it and that porter would be called in and told if you want to pay for that furniture you'd better be a good porter."[11]

In this hostile climate, the BSCP formed an alliance with several Chicago clubwomen whose civic interests converged with the larger agenda of the Brotherhood. The key issue uniting them was that of fuller citizenship rights for all African Americans, for which the BSCP employed the idiom of manhood rights. Black women, active in the fight for suffrage in Illinois and later for the Nineteenth Amendment, viewed the struggle for manhood rights as part of broader efforts to claim full citizenship for all African Americans. Arguably, Ida B. Wells-Barnett was the most important figure assisting the union. Webster told Wells-Barnett the Brotherhood was "very grateful to you, and other women in Chicago, who rendered us such noble assistance when we were passing through our most critical period." Wells-Barnett's club members were important to the larger goal of getting the Brotherhood's message on "economic subjects of vital importance to Negro workers" out to the community, despite all attempts of the press to silence the BSCP.[12] The political career of Ida B. Wells-Barnett since the 1890s helps illustrate the foundation for the alliance between Wells-Barnett, the clubwomen, and the BSCP.

On March 9, 1892, three successful black businessmen were lynched in Memphis, where Wells-Barnett lived at the time, for the crime of stepping out of place. Wells-Barnett remembered the lynching, which she exposed in her newspaper, the *Free Speech*, as the event that "changed the whole course of my life."[13] She argued that the three businessmen, prominent leaders of black Memphis who thought they could solve the problem of black disenfranchisement by "eschewing politics and putting money in the purse," broke a southern code through the success of their "flourishing grocery business." The People's Grocery Company was located in a "thickly populated suburb of Memphis" on a busy corner opposite a white grocery store, which had once "had a monopoly on the trade" of the area.[14] Because the People's Grocery successfully cut into the business of the white store owner, he charged his black competitors with conspiring against whites, secured warrants for their arrest, and told the black entrepreneurs that his friends planned to clean out the People's Grocery Company. When deputy sheriffs, dressed in civilian clothing, broke into People's Grocery store at night to deliver arrest warrants, they looked like a white mob and were fired upon.[15] No one was killed and the wounded sheriffs were out of danger two days later. Nevertheless, the three black businessmen were lynched for the crime of what Wells-Barnett called "getting too independent." The black community had to be taught the "lesson of subordination," the price for asserting one's manhood rights to "defend the cause of right and fight wrong wherever . . . [they] saw it."[16]

Wells-Barnett drew from American history to link the striving for black manhood—humanity—to the barbaric response it elicited from the white people who condoned lynching. Noting that there was little difference between the "Ante-bellum South and the New South," she said, ". . . white citizens are wedded to any method however revolting . . . for the subjugation of the young manhood of the race. They have cheated him out of his ballot, deprived him of civil rights or redress therefor [*sic*] in the civil courts, robbed him of the fruits of his labor, and are still murdering, burning and lynching him. The result is a growing disregard of human life."[17]

In the post-Reconstruction South, black and white people understood well that full manhood rights reached beyond the ballot and political citizenship. The Ku Klux Klan and lawless mobs "redeemed" the South by lynching black Americans when they dared defend their rights as human beings. She explained that "the Negro clung to his right of franchise with a heroism which would have wrung admiration from the hearts of savages. He believed that in the small white ballot there was a subtle something which *stood for* manhood as well as citizenship, and thousands of brave black men went to their graves, exemplifying the one by dying for the other" (emphasis added).[18]

With disenfranchisement in the South, lynchings increased, revealing that more was at issue, more had to be "redeemed" than just voting rights. It was at this point, Wells-Barnett noted, that the white South manufactured the excuse "that Negroes had to be killed to avenge their assaults upon women."[19] Yet, Wells's research revealed that much more than the "honor of white women" was at stake when white mobs lynched black Americans. Black women and children, not just black men, were among the lynched. In addition, the "reasons" recorded in the white press more often included "suspected robbery," "arson," "race prejudice," "wife beating," "alleged barn burning," "poisoning wells," "insulting whites," than "rape."[20] Finally, as a white newspaper in Memphis declared, "aside from violation of white women" the "chief cause of trouble between the races in the South" was "the Negro's lack of manners. In the state of slavery he learned politeness from association with white people." After emancipation the "tie of mutual interest and regard between master and servant was broken," and black Americans stepped out of the place that white southerners had deemed appropriate for black citizens.[21]

Wells-Barnett noted that "the whole matter [of the race issue in lynch law] is explained by the well-known opposition growing out of slavery to the progress of the race," something captured in the slogan, "this is a white man's country and the white man must rule."[22] The Memphis incident opened her eyes to what lynching really was: "An excuse to get rid of Negroes who were acquiring wealth and property and thus keep the race terrorized and 'keep the nigger down.'"[23] Through her writings, Wells-Barnett framed her argument in terms of the ongoing search for black manhood in America. "Nothing, absolutely nothing, is to be gained by a further sacrifice of manhood and self-respect." She advised black citizens to fight back and "ponder well, . . . that a Winchester rifle should have a place of honor in every black home."[24]

She also denounced lynching by drawing from the discourse on civilization dominant in mainstream culture in the 1890s. White Americans of northern European heritage raised the issue of civilization to justify colonial adventures carried out globally during the last decades of the nineteenth century under the guise of the "White Man's Burden." As they saw it, white America had a duty to raise "backward" people out of their barbarity into a more civilized state. White southerners used this ideology to rationalize lynching as an act to protect white women, who represented the purity of the "superior" white civilization, from the "barbarous" black man.[25] Wells-Barnett turned this rationale on its head, first, by exposing the myth of rape as the cause for lynching. She then portrayed the true barbarians as those who lynched and cast aside the laws of civilization, democracy, and human decency. "No torture of helpless victims by heathen savages or cruel red Indians ever exceeded the cold-blooded savagery of white devils under lynch law." Finally, she declared, "the more I studied the situation, the more I was convinced that the Southerner had never gotten over his resentment that the Negro was no longer his plaything, his servant, and his source of income."[26]

After her own life was threatened and her newspaper office destroyed, Wells-Barnett took her antilynching campaign first to New York City and Chicago, then to England in 1893. Her experiences abroad provided the foundation for her interest in starting a women's club in Chicago. Just as her British speaking tour had inspired audiences to organize clubs called the "Society for the Recognition of the Brotherhood of Man," so she hoped black women would become "more active in the affairs of their community, city, and nation" and use civic clubs as the means to become more politically responsive.[27] Wells-Barnett was instrumental in organizing the first black women's club in Chicago in 1893, the Wells Club.[28] In 1895 she settled permanently in Chicago and married attorney Ferdinard L. Barnett.[29]

After the turn of the century, Wells-Barnett's activism took place largely, though not entirely, through her Wells Clubs and other organizations in Chicago. Her antilynching perspective of the late nineteenth century imbued all her efforts for equal rights for black Americans, which she continued until her death in 1931. In 1910 she organized the Negro Fellowship League and used the league and its social center for men and boys to hold discussions about the unionization of Pullman porters in 1915.[30] Also in 1910 Wells-Barnett published

"How Enfranchisement Stops Lynching," linking arguments for black suffrage with those for manhood and full citizenship, which received national attention. Back in Chicago, she organized the Women's Second Ward Republican Club to help "men in getting better laws and having representation in everything which tends to the uplift of the city and its government."[31]

In the early teens, women were disenfranchised politically; black men in the North could vote, but they were disenfranchised economically and socially. In this milieu, Wells-Barnett continued to struggle *against* the disenfranchisement of all African Americans as she fought *for* enfranchisement of African American women. We can see how the two themes were woven together in the suffrage battle for all Illinois women.

In 1913 Wells-Barnett and Belle Squire, a white colleague in the Illinois suffrage movement, formed the Alpha Suffrage Club (ASC), the first suffrage organization for black women in Illinois, placing the interests of African American women on the state agenda for suffrage. Wells-Barnett was its first president, all elected officers were black women, and ASC remained under black control.[32] As a representative of the ASC and the state of Illinois, Wells-Barnett went to Washington, D.C., in March 1913 to take part in a parade sponsored by the National American Woman Suffrage Association (NAWSA). At the last minute, the NAWSA told Wells-Barnett she could not march with the white Illinois state delegates because the national association did not want southern white suffragists to think African American suffrage and female suffrage were connected. She was, however, welcome to take up the rear of the march with other black delegates. That she refused to do. One white women said, "If I were a colored woman, I should be willing to march with the other women of my race." Wells-Barnett replied, "there is a difference, . . . which you probably do not see. . . . I shall not march with the colored women. Either I go with you or not at all. I am not taking this stand because I personally wish for recognition. I am doing it for the future benefit of my whole race."[33] Wells-Barnett did march in the parade with white suffragettes under the Illinois banner.

In June 1913 the Illinois legislature gave women the vote, the first state east of the Mississippi to do so. The Illinois enfranchise meant African American females could vote in presidential and municipal elections. Wells-Barnett mobilized women in the ASC to "vote for the advantage of ourselves and our race."[34] The ASC women conducted a house-to-house canvas of the second, fourteenth, thirtieth, and sixth wards, "urging the colored women to register and explaining the importance of making a showing."[35] Initially, some women were "jeered at" and told "they ought to be at home taking care of the babies."

But the women persisted, encouraged by Wells-Barnett who kept the women focused on the larger goal—registering female voters, "so that they could help put a colored man in the city council."[36]

The Alpha Suffrage Club concentrated its efforts on registering women and canvassing votes. Its goal during a 1914 primary election was to elect William R. Cowan, an African American businessman, seeking the Republican nomination despite the fact that he was not the "choice" of the Republican machine for alderman from the second ward. The ASC was attempting to take advantage of a new direct primary law, which allowed voters in the primary, not political bosses, to determine who would be the party's candidate.[37] Under Wells-Barnett's direction, the Alpha Suffrage women lobbied throughout the community; they even canvassed female inmates in the Bridewell prison.[38] All black Chicago women did not heed the ASC's advice to stick together as a "race." Some favored following the traditional approach for selecting the party's candidates and threw their support behind the "nominee" selected by the white Republican machine, Hugh Norris, a white candidate.[39] These women, as historian Wanda Hendricks reminds us, were, like the Alpha Suffrage women, acting for what they believed was best for black Chicago. Because of the Republican Party machine, black Chicago had received a considerable measure of influence. Those supporting the Republican candidate may have equated backing a black candidate with a reduction in patronage handed out to the second ward.[40] The election left a "trail of hot blood" within the black community, for the contest exposed, as the *Broad Ax* suggested, the "dangerous business" of questioning the racial status quo and of "setting the Whites and the Blacks against each other in their effort to establish the 'color line'" in Chicago.[41] Norris won, but Cowan was only about 265 votes shy of the nomination.[42]

The number of female registered voters, and the collective action of the ASC, took the men by surprise. "Not one of them," said Wells-Barnett, "not even our ministers, had said one word to influence women to take advantage of the suffrage opportunity Illinois had given to her daughters."[43] Black and white men in Chicago began to listen when black women discussed politics.[44] Representatives from the ward organization of the Republican machine paid a visit to the Alpha Suffrage Club the night after the near upset by Cowen, urging the clubwomen not to back independent candidates for alderman in the future, lest the Democratic candidate win, and promising to nominate a black man for alderman next time.[45] When the next opening for city council occurred in 1915, three black men, for the first time, campaigned for alderman. All three presented themselves and their platforms for questioning by the ASC, seeking its endorsement. The concentration of black voters in the second ward caught the attention of any sensitive politician, but it was the way the women of the Alpha Suffrage Club managed to focus this power bloc that increased their value within black Chicago.[46]

The Alpha Suffrage Club, which numbered over 200 members by 1915, threw its weight behind Oscar Stanton DePriest, an African American and the choice of the Republican machine. The ASC also passed a motion stating any member of the club who supported a white candidate would be expelled.[47] In reporting its decision to endorse DePriest, the *Alpha Suffrage Record* said: "We pledge ourselves to leave no stone unturned to secure their election on April 6; we realize that in no other way can we safeguard our own rights than by holding up the hands of those who fight our battles."[48] DePriest won the primary and the general election to become the first black alderman of Chicago.

DePriest understood as well as any man that the women's unity around one candidate, focusing their efforts on registering voters with that specific goal in mind, was a decisive factor in the outcome. He wrote glowingly about the virtues of extending the vote to women in the *Crisis*, inspiring discussion of black Chicago politics at the national level. The significance of the newly enfranchised Chicago women could be seen as far South as Alabama, as Rosalyn Terborg-Penn shows, where a periodical published pictures of black Chicago women campaigning for African American candidates.[49] The *New York News*, in an editorial reprinted in the Alpha Suffrage Club's newsletter, applauded Chicago for pointing "the way to the political salvation of the race," noting that black Americans had gained "political recognition" because they had demanded it.[50]

The white Republican machine yielded ground to the demands of the newly assertive political bloc in the second ward. Whereas black men had focused largely on relations between the black and white communities, as brokers negotiating for greater access to scarce resources, the ASC women entered the political arena defying the power of the political machine, not beholden to it. Earlier in the decade, before women had the vote, some black politicians had tried unsuccessfully to defy the white machine.[51] But it took the organizational focus of the ASC clubwomen to help awaken the community to the power the black women's vote could command. The ASC boldly challenged the social relations embedded in the racial status quo, placing these clubwomen in the vanguard of a new approach to politics.[52]

Passage of the Nineteenth Amendment did not eclipse the political activism of black, middle-class clubwomen. Those who had been involved in the movement for suffrage continued to focus on issues that plagued both black men and black women, a pattern that distinguished their agenda from that of their white

sisters, whose major focus always was gender.[53] Racism in the suffrage movement at the national level was similar to what Wells-Barnett experienced in
Illinois in 1913. The situation in the 1920s had not changed terribly since the
nineteenth century when, as Melba Joyce Boyd shows, Frances E. W. Watkins
Harper found that for white women the struggle for human rights was based on
gender, not race.[54]

Wells-Barnett's network joined forces, on several occasions, with the People's
Movement, a group formed in 1917 by DePriest to promote his candidacy as an
independent politician. The two groups worked together to publicize the mas-
sacre of black workers in Elaine, Arkansas.[55] Wells-Barnett remained active and
influential politically precisely because she could back her protestations with
activism from members of her club network, a fact the black Republican leadership documented in minutes taken during a political strategy meeting in 1928.
The report disclosed that the men were told to back off from their position on a
particular issue because, as the leader explained to others present, "You know
how Mrs. Barnett would act. she [sic] and her cohorts held a meeting of protest
last night."[56]

The same spirit of independence, which had characterized the activities of
clubwomen affiliated with Wells-Barnett, led several Chicago clubwomen in
December 1925 to ignore public opinion against the Brotherhood and invite
A. Philip Randolph, head of the BSCP, to hear what he had to say. Randolph
spoke at the Chicago and Northern District Federation of Women's Clubs in
early December 1925.[57] Two weeks later, another group, the Woman's Forum,
heard Randolph speak in home of Ida B. Wells-Barnett.[58]

Wells-Barnett told Randolph, when they met in her home for the Sunday
Woman's Forum, that her group wanted to hear his side of the story because
they had not been able "to find anything in our press favorable to this movement" and had heard so much propaganda against it. Wells-Barnett's home was
not her first choice for a meeting place. She had tried unsuccessfully to get the
Appomattox Club for the meeting. The Appomattox Club officials told Wells-
Barnett they could not "afford to have Mr. Randolph speak" on its premises
because so many of "the men who are opposing him are members here and it
would embarrass them with the Pullman Company." To the twenty-five business and professional women gathered at her home she said, "I can hardly
conceive of Negro leaders taking such a narrow and selfish view of such vital
problems affecting the race." After Randolph's remarks about the aims and purposes of the BSCP, the Woman's Forum endorsed the new porters' union and
volunteered to help the BSCP, which the women called a "great movement."[59]

The BSCP readily accepted the offer. Milton P. Webster drew upon Wells-

Barnett's network of clubwomen, especially the Wells Club membership list, to contact the women directly.[60] He also asked Wells-Barnett to encourage the women to attend BSCP meetings in the hope that they would become a conduit within the black community to enlighten others about the Brotherhood's cause and serve as a counterweight to the "hostility of our local newspapers against this movement." Wells Club women were ultimately instrumental, Webster believed, in helping the BSCP gain a voice in black Chicago.[61]

Clubwomen activists who educated the community about the Brotherhood appreciated the fact that the BSCP aspired to be not just a labor organization but a social movement. Webster discussed the goals of the BSCP with Wells-Barnett. "The Race has a staunch, progressive, militant movement" in the new union, he assured Wells-Barnett. The BSCP "will ever be on the alert to wield its power whenever the interest of the Race demands." Although the Brotherhood addressed bread-and-butter issues in some of its appeals to porters and maids, organizers harbored a vision that reached beyond Pullman workers to all black Americans. One announcement discussed a Brotherhood that would lead black Americans into a "new day," one where "Black folks shall take their place in the sun of democracy, of citizenship, and economic welfare."[62]

Throwing their support behind the Brotherhood, clubwomen from Wells-Barnett's networks were carrying forward the spirit of previous activities for social, political, and economic enfranchisement of all black Americans started decades earlier in Chicago. Thus, although within the union movement, to be a "man" meant to become self-reliant, stand tall, and move out from under the control of paternalism, the concept applied to porters and maids alike. Clubwomen, part of a long line of black, female activists, did not think of breaking their work into categories of gender or class. As Deborah Gray White argues, "the general problem was, of course, the race problem . . . [but for] black women, race, class, and gender issues were so inseparable that one could not work on one front without working on all three."[63] Wells-Barnett, as Linda McMurry observes, recognized that for African Americans race was the primary lens through which their lives were experienced. Although she cared deeply about many issues, "nothing was more important than her color."[64] Concepts like manhood and manhood rights carry gendered understandings. But when black Chicago clubwomen mobilized their community around these concepts, they were connected to the larger battle against the racial status quo, which diminished black humanity. It is the social and historical context within which terms like manhood rights are utilized that gives social meaning to the politics of manhood rights in practice. In the context of the BSCP's movement, manhood and manhood rights referred to the larger ongoing struggle for acceptance as full human beings. Manhood cannot be understood as a concept cut loose from its historic mooring, loaded with understandings gathered from shores washed by another time.[65]

Voices of Opposition

The Brotherhood portrayed community leaders who backed the Pullman Company as part of the old guard, whereas union porters and their supporters were New Negroes, who, the *Messenger* reminded its readers, had the backbone to demand full civil rights.[66] But Brotherhood organizers were not the only ones waving the New Negro banner. The college-educated editors of the *Chicago Whip*, a local weekly newspaper, espoused a more moderate version of economic radicalism than the BSCP but had, according to Allan Spear, supported labor unions in 1919. They declared it was to the black workers' "decided advantage to join the A.F. of L." at the time of the organizing efforts in the stockyards and steel mills.[67] They also dissented from the self-help philosophy of Booker T. Washington to distinguish their position from that of Republican leaders in Chicago's second ward who, they charged, were "big-fake politicians who for a 'mess of pottage' have preached submissiveness to the black masses." Joseph Bibb and Arthur Clement MacNeal (known in the newspaper as A. C. MacNeal) identified themselves as New Negroes, taking black patronage politicians to task for ties to the political underworld. Is "vice immunity" the only plum that Negro Aldermen can secure in the way of patronage? they asked. Oscar DePriest openly rendered financial support to the *Whip* during its first year, perhaps to mask his connection to that very graft and vice he was often associated with.[68]

As far as we can tell, the *Whip's* interpretation of "New Crowd" did not include challenging the Pullman Company, provider of thousands of jobs for black Chicago.[69] In 1923, the *Whip*, according to the *Messenger*, called for the organization of Pullman porters.[70] When porters actually began organizing, however, the *Whip* first supported the union, then suddenly withdrew that support, warning the porters to support the company union instead. Its reasoning sounded similar to that of the Reverend Archibald Carey: "Black people at large," wrote the *Whip*, "align themselves as far as possible with the wealthier classes in America."[71] After noting that the *Whip* carried an ad for the Pullman Company, which bought large stacks of the *Whip* for distribution to the porters, Randolph claimed Pullman paid the *Whip* for stories against the Brotherhood.[72] Chandler Owen, Randolph's colleague and coeditor of the *Messenger* in the teens and early twenties, charged that *Whip* editors attempted to silence

Randolph by offering money to Owen who was, in turn, supposed to persuade Randolph to stop writing favorable articles about the BSCP. Owen claimed the money that Joseph Bibb offered him was supplied by Pullman Company officials.[73]

After Daniel J. Schuyler, an attorney for the Pullman Company, gained controlling interest in the *Whip*, the newspapers' policy toward the Brotherhood shifted 180 degrees, according to Owen, and it began printing scorching stories against the porters' union. In January 1926 Owen wrote a series of articles in the *Messenger* accusing Bibb and MacNeal of shady deals, including selling an interest in the paper to Schuyler.[74] Owen claimed that Oscar DePriest "swears that he was an eye-witness to the passing of 55 percent of the Whip stock to Mr. Daniel J. Schuyler."[75] This charge was never denied by the *Whip* or by DePriest. The *Messenger* reported that the *Whip* responded by suing Randolph and Owen, with the assistance of Pullman lawyers, for libel. They won indictments against Randolph and Owen, but a judge dismissed the suit without sending it to jury when the *Whip* could not substantiate its libel charges.[76] According to scholar Greg LeRoy, the case was reassigned after Milton Webster exercised his clout as a Republican ward heeler to have it heard by a sympathetic judge. "This other judge threw the case out, and that is why Randolph did not go to jail," Webster recalled several years later.[77] That New Negroes associated with the *Whip* moderated their militancy once Daniel J. Schuyler gained controlling interest in the newspaper suggests the extent of Pullman influence in the black community. [78]

The *Chicago Defender*, the major black newspaper in America, spoke out against the BSCP when it mentioned the Brotherhood at all.[79] Since early in the BSCP campaign the *Messenger* referred to the *Defender* as the Chicago "Surrender" and the "World's Greatest Weakly" and allocated much space to attacks against the *Defender* and other black periodicals.[80] The *Defender* continued its opposition until late fall of 1927. Of the national publications, the *Pittsburgh Courier* was the only newspaper to support the BSCP during its first two years.

Opposition to the BSCP was so widespread that a representative from New York told Congress that this attempt "by porters to organize has met with an avalanche of Pullman funds to thwart their efforts. Negro publications have been subsidized; Negro pulpits have been bought."[81] Nevertheless, at least one pulpit was not for sale, and the clubwomen were not the only members of the black middle class that by the 1920s had decided that pragmatic accommodation to the racial status quo was no longer acceptable.[82] Dr. William D. Cook, minister of the People's Church and Metropolitan Community Center, donated his facilities to the Brotherhood from the beginning of its organizational campaign and worked with the clubwomen who promoted the union. Randolph spoke about "The Negro and Industrial Emancipation" at the end of December 1925 at Cook's church.[83] From a base supported largely by the clubwomen's network, a proto–citizens' committee to publicize the vision of the porters' union began to emerge.[84] Dr. Cook, independent of Pullman control, was known, as Webster once observed, as a "kind of an outlaw preacher."[85] He had a history of social and political leanings "not in harmony" with the majority of the ecclesiastical community that stretched back to years before World War I when he was head of one of the largest and most prominent churches, Bethel AME. After the Reverend Archibald J. Carey became AME bishop for the Chicago area in 1920 and removed Cook from Bethel forever, Cook's "outlaw" tendencies increased. Out of that turmoil, the People's Community Church of Christ and Metropolitan Community Center, dedicated to the service of humanity and the welfare of the community, was formed. Ida B. Wells-Barnett and her family were among Metropolitan's first members. Activities sponsored under Cook's tutelage included educational programs, seminars on industrial relations, and the Sunday Forum, which Wells-Barnett directed. The first meeting of the American Negro Labor Congress, organized by the Communist Party, was held at the People's Church just before Cook threw his support behind the Brotherhood. Cook found and rented office space for the porters and maids during the first crucial two years and addressed many of the Brotherhood's meetings until his death in 1930.[86]

Another early ministerial supporter of the Brotherhood was Dr. Junius C. Austin, who opened up the Pilgrim Baptist Church for mass meetings of the Brotherhood soon after he came to Chicago from Pittsburgh in 1926. Known nationally as a "dynamic personality" and business leader as well as a minister, Austin, an outsider to Chicago politics, was not entangled in local patronage or paternalistic relations. In Pittsburgh, Austin was the most prominent minister supporting the UNIA, allowing Garvey supporters to speak from his pulpit.[87] He arrived in Chicago hoping to make strides toward uplifting the race and building a progressive church. Offering protection and advice to workers was just one of the church-sponsored services that Austin initiated. Pilgrim's mission statement said its purpose was to reach the unreached, upon the "highway and in the hedges." To execute this charge, it utilized a "Gospel Bus." Austin's approach to Christian ministry filled a need, for by 1930 the church had over 9,000 members and was counted among the largest and most prosperous of the hundreds of churches on the South Side.[88]

Despite Webster's attempt to win their support, the majority of Chicago's black clergy either ignored the Brotherhood or actively opposed it. Webster called a meeting during the spring of 1927 to talk with several directly about the BSCP but found the ministers did not feel "very friendly toward this movement." He also tried, with little success, to win the cooperation of the president of the Ministers' Alliance, an African American organization with an antiunion history going back to the Chicago Federation of Labor's biracial organizing efforts in 1919–21. Bishop Archibald Carey continued to ban the Brotherhood from AME churches, and the Reverend Lacy Kirk Williams of Olivet Baptist Church and president of the National Baptist Conference also actively opposed the Brotherhood.[89]

Yet in 1919 Williams had granted both packinghouse and steel organizers permission to discuss labor issues at Olivet. It is possible that Williams made a distinction between opposition to the Pullman Company and opposition to steel companies and packinghouse plants, convinced that Pullman had done more for black Chicago and its community institutions than any other single company.[90] More than opposition to labor unions, Williams's opposition may also have been rooted in a rivalry with Reverend Austin of Pilgrim Church. Olivet and Pilgrim were the two largest Baptist churches in Chicago during the twenties. Olivet was the established church, Pilgrim the newcomer, having started as a prayer meeting in the home of recent migrants in 1915 at a time when Olivet already had 4,000 members. Olivet benefited greatly from the migration and was the largest black Baptist church in the world. But Pilgrim grew in the 1920s and seemed a threat to Williams who envisioned making Olivet the community center of Chicago, complete with a labor bureau and a welfare department, along with athletic facilities and day care.[91] Williams may have not wanted to risk losing members over the Brotherhood issue. Whatever the reason, Williams's opposition was significant because he carried weight both in South Side neighborhoods and within the larger national community of Baptists.

Clergy who opposed the Brotherhood could have been responding to what they thought were the sentiments of their constituents. The years between 1924 and 1929 were, according to Horace Cayton and St. Clair Drake, "no doubt the most prosperous ones the Negro community in Chicago had ever experienced." Such an assessment can be misleading, for there was also a great deal of unemployment among black workers during this period. The "fat years," as Cayton and Drake phrased it, enriched the earnings of the professional and business class who enjoyed the fruits of a captive market restricted to living, spending, and consuming in segregated black neighborhoods.[92] Many within the black middle class thought, despite the many daily reminders of second-class status, that South Side Chicago had come a long way. There were black policemen, firemen, mail carriers, sales clerks, aldermen, precinct captains, state representatives, doctors, lawyers, and teachers. Although every public position and inch of space allotted black citizens and workers represented tough negotiations over the boundaries imposed by the dominant society, concessions gained through patronage and politics bolstered the argument against rocking the boat or biting the hand that feeds. Chicago had scored notable gains via electoral politics. But for the great majority of African Americans during this period, Chicago's opportunities amounted to an unfulfilled dream. Finally, the subtext during the "fat years" was that those who utilized their talents to gain access gradually would gain full participation in American society.[93]

Although prominent black leaders, the press, and clergy resisted the Brotherhood's ideas, voices of opposition often carried mixed messages about the route black Chicago should follow. While broadcasting uplifting sermons on the value of moderation as an approach to full participation in the Promised Land, they simultaneously promoted American democratic values such as self-determination, freedom, and equality.[94] Bishop Carey, for example, was known to endorse gratitude toward industrialists while applauding some of the same rights of citizenship—life, liberty, the pursuit of happiness—curtailed by discriminating practices of industrialists.[95] Oscar DePriest understood the tangled web of beliefs that were projected in the black community from the press, pulpit, and politicians better than most: he used his Peoples' Movement between 1917 and 1928 to promote his image as a defender of political and civil rights for black Chicago while maintaining allegiance and support for the Republican machine run by William Hale Thompson, his mentor.[96] Projecting an image of independence from white control may have tapped into the wishes of many within the black community, but it was left to the Brotherhood to confront the Pullman Company, the greatest symbol of white control over black workers on the South Side of Chicago.[97]

Publicizing the Brotherhood's Message

The Brotherhood began the work of gaining the support and allegiance of the larger community through the clubwomen's networks. With no access to newspapers, Webster leaned on the canvassing ability of Wells Club women to publicize the BSCP's message. The women distributed Brotherhood propaganda and helped organize mass meetings for the BSCP.[98] The first test of the BSCP with the clubwomen and Reverend Cook came in October 1926. By that time, Irene Goins, a pioneer clubwoman in Illinois, actively worked for the BSCP. She was president of the Chicago and Northern District Federation of Colored

Women's Clubs, the Illinois State Federation of Colored Women's Clubs, and the Douglass League of Women Voters.[99] The Illinois State Federation was known for its citizenship department, and the Douglass League helped develop "citizenship schools" in the 1920s.[100] Goins was also the first African American woman in the Midwest to take an active part in the labor movement, where she was an ally with Agnes Nestor, president of the Chicago branch of the Women's Trade Union League and the International Glove Workers Union, in 1913 on the campaign for an eight-hour day. During and after World War I she organized black women workers at the Chicago stockyards. She was also a member of the executive council of Chicago's Women's Trade Union League (WTUL) from 1917 to 1922.[101] Because of her work with the black working class, Goins was able to take the Brotherhood's labor message beyond middle-class club circles.

Mary McDowell, first president of the Chicago branch of the Women's Trade Union League (WTUL) and University of Chicago settlement house worker, also joined the cadre of citizens backing the Brotherhood by fall 1926. During the BSCP's formative years, she was the only white Chicagoan contesting the politics of Pullman paternalism alongside BSCP organizers. McDowell had a history of agitating for the rights of less skilled workers with little power in the workplace, which explains her interest in black workers. After the Lawrence Strike in 1912, she advocated the use of organizers who spoke the language of foreign-born workers.[102] Through the years, McDowell was one of the most loyal supporters and was known never to miss a Brotherhood mass meeting in Chicago.[103]

The newly formed alliance between the BSCP, black female activists, including Wells-Barnett and Wells Club members, and McDowell planned the mass meeting of October 3, 1926. How best to broadcast the BSCP message to the larger community and canvass the neighborhoods were critical concerns of the alliance. They spent time on the quality of paper, the images projected to the black community, and the actual words in the publicity messages. The alliance was determined to "mobilize all of the forces in Chicago, religious, social, fraternal and otherwise," to make the meeting, held in Reverend Austin's Pilgrim Baptist Church, a success.[104] It was, according to Webster, the "talk of the town." He doubted if the Brotherhood could have "bought the same publicity in Chicago with the expenditure of a thousand dollars."[105]

McDowell spoke at the meeting about a workers' right to make and sign contracts. "You must have the right to sign your own contracts," she informed her audience. "Until we have that we are not men and women." You must use "your power to organize for your own interests." She concluded by contrasting union porters and other Pullman porters. When the union first began in 1925, the porter assigned to her Pullman sleeping car was reluctant to talk to her directly about his union status. In 1926, however, she again asked a porter if he belonged to the BSCP. "He didn't stop a minute, he said, 'Yes, indeed, I do.' " She praised union porters for their self-confidence and the strength to "be unafraid of a lady." It was a self-confidence born in the process of throwing away deferential posturing that is a by-product of second-class status. She received special applause at this juncture of her speech.[106]

Although Pullman would not publicly recognize the union for porters and maids, privately the company expended huge resources gathering information on BSCP meetings and the influence of the union on the larger community. Company detectives noted the heavy advertising that preceded another Brotherhood meeting on October 26, 1927.[107] A large crowd gathered at Dr. Cook's Metropolitan Community Center to hear Randolph blast the *Chicago Defender*, charging that it had surrendered to "gold and power."[108] That strategy, in conjunction with a boycott campaign carried out by friends and members of the Brotherhood, struck a chord, for beginning with the November 19, 1927, issue, the *Chicago Defender* began supporting the Brotherhood.[109] Roi Ottley, biographer of *Defender* editor Robert Abbott, claimed that Abbott changed his policy toward the union in response to both decreased circulation and charges made by the BSCP that black editors supporting Pullman "were traitors to their race."[110] Over 2,000 people attended the BSCP's October 26 mass meeting.[111]

Whether the *Chicago Defender* was in the pocket of Pullman is debatable. Brailsford R. Brazeal, author of the first scholarly study of the Brotherhood of Sleeping Car Porters, argued that Abbott started endorsing the Brotherhood because the boycott of the *Defender* by porters, maids, and supporters of the BSCP hit "the paper's most vulnerable spot." Circulation and maintaining a favorable image within the black community was more important than ad revenues from Pullman Company.[112] William Harris, a more recent scholar of the BSCP, believes that while union leaders never proved direct financial dealings between Abbott and Pullman management, "some incidents do cast suspicion on the paper's early position."[113] But from the perspective of the black community, it may not have mattered so much if the *Chicago Defender* was in the pay of Pullman as the fact that the black community *thought* that was the case. To educate black Chicago, the *Messenger* exposed the $10,000 deposit in an account for the Pullman Porters Benefit Association (PPBA), controlled by Pullman, in Binga State Bank, while Abbott was a bank director. Randolph suggested that Abbott needed to be in the good graces of Pullman in order to maintain this account.[114] Even before the boycott, Abbott may have realized he risked losing subscribers by continuing to oppose the Brotherhood.[115] Randolph told Abbott's biographer many years later that at the time, when BSCP and the *Defender* staff buried the hatchet, a *Defender* staff member informed Webster and Randolph the paper had received "generous payments [presumably advertising] from the Pullman Company for material carried against the Brotherhood." Randolph also claimed that Nathan Magill, general manager of the *Defender*, even showed him the figures in the paper's accounting books of the *Defender*. The exact amount, however, was not revealed.[116]

Gaining the support of the *Chicago Defender* was an important victory for the Brotherhood. The *Defender*, with a circulation of well over 200,000 per week by 1925, two-thirds of that outside of Chicago, was the largest-selling black newspaper in the United States. Some 23,000 copies went to New York City.[117] Its circulation within Chicago was more than double either the *Chicago Bee* or *Chicago Whip*, its closest rivals. In addition, the *Defender* was a forum on public opinion. In its pages, black Americans discussed local, national, and international issues affecting people of African descent.[118] As a public forum, the *Defender* offered a means for gauging the views of African Americans. Measuring public opinion is far from a science in the best of circumstances, yet *Defender* circulation was one measure in Chicago's black neighborhoods. During the early fall of 1927, *Defender* circulation dropped, suggesting that public opinion toward the Brotherhood had begun to favor its cause. A group of black and white citizens delivered "a bushel basket of mail" to the *Defender*, demanding to know why the newspaper did not support the BSCP.[119] The BSCP exposed the contradiction inherent in advocating black freedom through paternalistic relations. Abbott, who wanted desperately to be considered a good "race man" within the African American community, came to understand that supporting Pullman was no longer in the interest of Abbott and the *Defender*.[120] Perhaps to make amends, the *Defender* ran a story in December that announced a "remarkable change of attitude on the part of the Negro community toward trade unions" had occurred because Pullman refused to "recognize the right of its porters to join an organization of their own choosing and be represented by agents of their own choice in wage negotiations with the company."[121]

Chicago Citizens' Committee for the Brotherhood

Webster built upon the alliances' success in 1927 by officially organizing a Chicago Citizens' Committee for the BSCP.[122] Irene McCoy Gaines, a prominent clubwoman and industrial secretary of the Young Women's Christian Association (YWCA) in the early 1920s, asked to be included as "one of the original committee."[123] Gaines proved to be a significant addition for her ability to reach a broad cross section of the black population. She came in contact with women workers through her YWCA position, yet she was also a member of the educated elite. Both she and her husband, Harris Barrett Gaines, who served in the Illinois State Legislature and was assistant state's attorney for Cook County in 1925, were graduates of Fisk University and had entrée to the social and political world of leading black Chicagoans. From 1924 to 1935 Irene Gaines was president of the Illinois Federation of Republican Colored Women's Clubs, a group that she helped to organize.[124] In January 1928 she was appointed secretary of the BSCP Citizens' Committee.[125]

Maude Smith, president of the Chicago and Northern District of the Federation of Women's Clubs, also supported the Brotherhood but more as a member-at-large. She spoke at labor conferences but did not appear on the official masthead listing Citizens' Committee membership until 1929.[126] Dr. J. B. Redmond, pastor of the St. Mark's AME Church, was an active member of the Citizens' Committee, lending his name and status to the Brotherhood's movement and using his influence to educate the community around its causes. His support pleased Webster, who thought Dr. Redmond "wields quite an influence here in Chicago."[127]

The BSCP gained additional access to the YWCA network when Lula E. Lawson, executive secretary of the South Parkway YWCA, joined the Citizens' Committee. The YWCA emphasized collective action and the importance of participation in "group work," which it believed was the means to give the individual a connection to social change.[128] Lula Lawson brought this perspective and experience to the BSCP.

The activities of the Chicago Colored Women's Economic Council, an auxiliary of the BSCP formed in 1926 for wives and relatives of the porters, were significant in keeping union porter families informed, strong, and united. The council was organized to cultivate support and resources from within the union family for the benefit of the BSCP. Its efforts were especially important to union porters and maids suffering from reprisals and firings by Pullman Company officials.[129] As Melinda Chateauvert has shown, the Women's Economic Council raised money to finance union activities, collected dues from members, visited families of porters to educate them about the meaning of the union, informed family members about important meetings, and delivered messages for union porters away from the suspecting eyes of Pullman spies. In short, their efforts helped secure the "strength of the Brotherhood" so it could function as a union.[130]

At the community level, resistance to the BSCP gradually was breaking down thanks to the efforts of Dr. Cook, Dr. Austin, Ida B. Wells-Barnett, Lula Lawson, Mary McDowell, and others. Meetings about the Brotherhood's movement were held several nights a week with as many as fifty to sixty porters and maids attending. Larger "mass" meetings, aimed at educating the broader community, were held monthly, commanding good publicity because BSCP organizers would literally blanket key parts of the community using connections opened up through Citizens' Committee networks.[131]

With the addition of George Cleveland Hall to the Citizens' Committee by early 1928, the Brotherhood gained access to circles frequented by Chicago businessmen. Dr. Hall, considered one of the most prominent leaders of the local professional and business class, appeared to exemplify much that Booker T. Washington stood for. He and his wife were personal friends of Washington. Hall, a surgeon and board member of Provident Hospital, promoted black business in Chicago and became, in 1912, the president of the Chicago branch of Washington's National Negro Business League. Yet, at the same time, he was one of two active black members of the executive staff of the Chicago branch of the National Association for the Advancement of Colored People. The Alpha Suffrage Club included Hall in its forums in 1914.[132] In addition, Hall helped found the Chicago Urban League.[133] His leadership in organizations that stood for two different approaches to group advancement—the Washington-sponsored National Negro Business League, which favored a gradual approach based on making progress through economic growth, and Du Bois's NAACP, which promoted active protest for civil and political rights—represented a cluster of beliefs drawn from several sources.[134] While he may have supported Washington out of personal loyalty or even because he subscribed to certain aspects of self-help, that relationship did not preclude his believing that black Americans had to fight white prejudice and discrimination directly. Hall was a leader in economic and civic life in Chicago from 1900 until his death in 1930 and represented business and professional men whose outlook was shaped in the process of defining a place for black businesses and institutions while barriers to an integrated society were being raised. As Allan Spear noted, Hall and his colleagues built the "institutional ghetto only after whites had created the physical ghetto."[135] Although Hall's perspective on racial solidarity was forged as a defensive reaction to racial barriers and white hostility, he was eventually drawn to the BSCP's interpretation of the concept.

Where was racial solidarity, the Brotherhood asked, when black politicians put organizational accommodation before the larger interest of group advancement?[136] The BSCP appealed to Hall when it argued that group solidarity and collective action were diluted by the demands of machine politics. Hall also approved of self-assertiveness as a tactic. When the Stockyards Labor Council attempted to bring black meat-packers into unions in 1918, Hall encouraged the council's organizational drive because it provided a good opportunity, "for Negroes to show that they are not natural-born strikebreakers."[137] The Brotherhood interpreted racial solidarity as a tool for asserting a group's right to challenge the political framework of machine politics, which controlled the allocation of government resources to Chicago's citizens. Racial solidarity meant protesting the inferior status assigned to black Chicago. It did not mean retreating within the community and settling for the measure of goods and services the white city fathers deemed sufficient for black Chicago. As a member of the Chicago Commission on Race Relations, which studied causes of the 1919 Chicago race riot, Hall was aware that racial solidarity had elicited explosive reactions within the white community and on the commission, which claimed that racial solidarity contributed to social unrest.[138] It seems likely that Hall was attracted to the Brotherhood because it dared to advocate group solidarity as a tool to challenge the racial status quo.

Finally, Hall's support of the BSCP was proof that even within the Chicago Urban League—often considered a bastion of proemployer sentiment, supported financially by the Pullman Company—differences were emerging on the issue of unionism. While Claude Barnett, an active member of the league's board, strongly opposed the BSCP,[139] Hall became a member of the Citizens' Committee of the BSCP. Hall threw his weight behind the Brotherhood's efforts during a particularly delicate moment when the Pullman Company withheld its annual contribution following the endorsement of the BSCP by Eugene Kinckle Jones, national executive secretary of the National Urban League.[140]

Most black business leaders were not as comfortable as Hall with the BSCP's fusion of racial solidarity and independence from white control.[141] Jesse Binga and others closed ranks behind the Pullman Company. Binga regarded the community as a self-sufficient, economically viable "black metropolis." The Brotherhood's challenge put the community's stability at risk, as Binga never tired of reminding the porters. Unlike many other members of the business and professional class, Binga never did support the Brotherhood.

Dr. Charles Wesley Burton, a black professional, not only became chairman of the Citizens' Committee in December 1927 but remained one of Brotherhood's staunchest supporters as it branched out nationally as a civil rights organization.[142] Webster chose Burton to chair its Citizens' Committee because he thought Burton had a "world of experience in the various social problems that concern the Negro." He had a law degree from Yale University and until 1926 was minister of the Lincoln Memorial Congregational Church, where he started a strong community outreach program on social issues.[143] Burton was one of only three ministers who responded to the Chicago Federation of Labor's invitation, in 1920, to mobilize the community in support of the organization of packinghouse workers.[144] His legal skills helped the fledgling union on several occasions, and he was aided in his position as chairman by fellow lawyer C. Francis Stratford, president of the National Bar Association, an association of African American lawyers, who joined the Citizens' Committee in 1928. Burton probably encouraged David W. Johnson, president of the Lincoln Community Men's Club of the Lincoln Memorial Congregational Church, to join the Citizens' Committee. Key members of the Lincoln Community Men's Club influenced the gradual breakdown of opposition, during the next couple of years, among middle-class, professional black men not normally familiar with the merits of labor organizing. Johnson helped the Brotherhood by writing letters to friends and acquaintances in the community about the BSCP and encouraging other members of the Men's Club to do the same.[145]

The Citizens' Committee network broadcast the Brotherhood's message and advanced its agenda during a time when the BSCP had few alternative sources for publicity. By activating the ever present impulse in black Chicago against white control and for full citizenship rights, the Citizens' Committee helped mobilize support for the Brotherhood and educated the community about the costs of Pullman paternalism. The breadth of the BSCP appeal was influenced as much by the alliance formed with the clubwomen, several ministers, and black professionals as by the BSCP's original vision for a labor union. Had the culture of Pullman paternalism not restricted Brotherhood activities in Chicago, the clubwomen's role in promoting the BSCP's approach to first-class status may not have been as crucial. Because it was necessary to utilize the clubwomen's network to gain an audience and have a platform for BSCP propaganda, clubwomen reinforced the human rights component of the BSCP's labor agenda. The ground clubwomen had plowed in earlier antilynching and suffrage campaigns provided rich soil to plant the seeds of the Brotherhood's battle for manhood rights. From the start of the Chicago phase of the Brotherhood's campaign against the Pullman Company, the BSCP had to speak a language that transcended bread-and-butter unionism. Had it not, it may not have appealed to the black community.

The BSCP's success notwithstanding, the Brotherhood still faced an uphill battle. It won allegiance from some leaders of black Chicago along with the endorsement of the *Chicago Defender*, but the culture of paternalism, though blemished, was not banished. Most ministers, including the Reverend L. K. Williams and the Reverend Archibald Carey, opposed the porters' efforts to unionize; the influential Appomattox Club had not changed its position; and the *Chicago Whip* did not begin to write favorably about the BSCP until 1930. Many potential recruits did not have faith in the Brotherhood's approach.

Those individuals who supported the Brotherhood by 1927 came from diverse backgrounds. Clubwomen identified with the issue of manhood rights because they had been wrestling in an organized fashion against a caste system that condoned lynching and robbed black men and women of their humanity since the nineteenth century. George Cleveland Hall viewed the Brotherhood's movement as a way to uplift the station of black workers as well as to attack discrimination directly. Dr. Cook and Dr. Redmond had reputations as independent thinkers who believed the church had a part to play in changing the racial status quo. Dr. Austin carried his support for the Garvey movement and principles of self-determination to Chicago from Pittsburgh. Generally, those for the Brotherhood did not have much faith in the goodwill of the Pullman Company and other white patrons. Many of those against the Brotherhood, like Jesse Binga, were openly in the pay of Pullman, while others may have shared resentment toward the status quo, desired independence from white control, but felt, nevertheless, that the Brotherhood's approach carried too many risks.

At this stage of the Brotherhood's struggle, the challenge to the racial status quo revealed the complexity involved in negotiating a new approach for overcoming second-class status. The Citizens' Committee recognized that the BSCP needed broader exposure to increase support. Beginning in January 1928, the Citizens' Committee gave the agenda of the Brotherhood's labor movement greater exposure through a "Negro Labor Conference," the first of several it sponsored over the next five years. In the process, as labor conferences connected labor issues with concerns over second-class citizenship, the union raised questions about the nature of the political culture that had, ostensibly, served black Chicago so well. Those questions, challenging patronage politics, broke down resistance within the community even as they expanded the civil rights component of the Brotherhood's agenda.

Launching a Social Movement, 1928–1930

And at its best the river of our struggle has moved consistently toward
the ocean of humankind's most courageous hopes for freedom and
integrity, forever seeking what black people in South Carolina said
they sought in 1865: "the right to develop our whole *being*."

VINCENT HARDING

Pullman porters and maids have a fundamental right to such
organization as they themselves see fit to choose. . . .
This right is just as sacred as those guaranteed under the 14th and 15th
amendments in the federal Constitution. Their selection of the
brotherhood as their representative is an exercise of that right and
they cannot and will not forfeit that right on the insidious threat of
wholesale loss of jobs and incidental starvation.

MILTON P. WEBSTER

The first Negro Labor Conference held in Chicago during January 1928 raised,
as Milton Webster observed, "the vital questions involved in this fight" for a
union in hopes of soliciting community support.[1] At that conference, the
Brotherhood declared that a worker's right to organize was an American right,
an entitlement embedded in American citizenship, laying the foundation for
connecting a labor movement with a civil rights agenda. As labor conferences
brought together people interested in the Brotherhood's message, a network of
activists began to expand. The network-building process illuminates the way
the Brotherhood used its challenge to Pullman paternalism as a vehicle for
reshaping how black Chicago approached and thought about the politics of
patronage. The politics the Brotherhood attempted to introduce in Chicago
relied on tactics that challenged the prevailing ground rules and prescribed new
patterns for conducting negotiations between the black and white communities. The BSCP sought to break the pattern of petitioning the dominant culture for rights that already belonged to black Americans.

Between 1925 and 1928, the *Messenger* articulated the historical underpin-nings of the BSCP's manhood rights campaign by connecting the Brotherhood with larger, ongoing struggles for humane and just treatment as American citizens. From the black press we see that many understandings of citizenship held by freedmen and women during the time of Emancipation and Recon-struction still resonated in the 1920s. The *Messenger* anchored much of the discussion of manhood rights and citizenship to what Patricia Sullivan calls "traditions of freedom and citizenship, born in the crucible of Reconstruction," which were carried forward through communities of resistance.[2]

The Brotherhood's efforts to link its unionization campaign with the larger black freedom struggle were challenged by setbacks along the way. A strike planned for early June 1928 against the Pullman Company was overwhelmingly endorsed by porters and maids. When Randolph canceled that strike, BSCP membership dropped significantly, leading several contemporary sources to declare that the union for porters and maids was dead. While this was a low point for the BSCP as a labor union, the canceled strike breathed new life into the Brotherhood as a social movement and broadened its horizons. The broader approach not only set the BSCP apart from conventional labor unions but offered a challenge to the culture of black machine politics with its em-phasis on individual advancement and organizational accommodation.[3] BSCP labor conferences in Chicago provide a window on the prolabor turn within the black community that emerged by the end of the 1920s.

The Legacy of African American History

The Brotherhood expanded on a traditional theme, independence from white control—a marker in the black freedom struggle and a stage on the way to gain full "manhood rights"—drawing from the legacy of black freedom fighters of the nineteenth century. Despite the failure of Reconstruction to secure the rights of black Americans as citizens and free laborers, the quest for manhood rights was kept alive through story, song, and history.[4] Frances Watkins Harper, Ida B. Wells-Barnett, Frederick Douglass, and others pointed the way through relentless agitation around the unfinished agenda of Reconstruction. On the twenty-fourth anniversary of Emancipation, Douglass reminded his fellow cit-izens that the work of the Republican Party in enfranchising and emancipating black Americans was "sadly incomplete. We are yet, as a people, only half free. The promise of liberty remains unfulfilled."[5] In order to claim the rightful place for black people, Douglass advised that "manly self-assertion and eter-nal vigilance are essential to Negro liberty," while "shrinking cowardice wins nothing."[6] For Douglass, as Waldo E. Martin argues, "slavery more than black skin color caused white prejudice against Negroes"; even after the Civil War, Douglass stated that although black Americans had "ceased to be the slave of an individual," they had become in some sense the slave of a society that coupled color with servility, ignorance, dependence, and human inferiority. "The lingering shadow of slavery," Martin suggests, "poisoned" the moral climate of the nation in Douglass's eyes.[7]

The BSCP echoed Douglass on the link between power and humanity. "The exercise of absolute and irresponsible power of man over man," Douglass said, "develops manliness neither in the oppressed or the oppressor. It breeds a haughty spirit and hot temper, in the one, and cowardly servility, in the other." Thus Douglass, says Martin, concluded that the irresponsible power by one over another "diminished the humanity of both parties." But Douglass saw power as a complicated phenomenon: there was an interdependency between power and powerlessness that made it both elusive and attainable. Through struggle the powerless could engage the powerful and reshape the relationship. Douglass said "power concedes nothing without a struggle. It never did, and it never will." Randolph and the BSCP used that quotation often in their rhetorical battle against the Pullman Company.[8] BSCP flyers, handbills, and literature revived the usage, articulated by Douglass, equating manhood with full humanity, first-class citizenship. A popular "bulletin," published by the Brotherhood, harked back to nineteenth-century manhood rhetoric with a sketch of Douglass and a caption that said: "Douglass fought for the abolition of chattel slavery, and today we fight for economic freedom. The time has passed when a grown-up black man should beg a grown-up white man for anything," a reference to the tipping system that porters and maids had to rely upon to make a "living" wage.[9]

BSCP organizers asked audiences in black neighborhoods to "re-dedicate our hearts and minds" to other figures from African American history: the spirit of Denmark Vesey, Nat Turner, Sojourner Truth, and Harriet Tubman, so they "shall not have died in vain." The Brotherhood proclaimed that "we, who have come after these noble souls who suffered and sacrificed" in order to deliver their children from the "cruel oppression of the Slave Power," are "bound in duty" to complete what they began.[10] Despite the passage of the Thirteenth Amendment, which the *Messenger* called a "dead letter," slavery was not entirely abolished.[11]

Organizers connected what they viewed as second-class status implicit in relations under a company union to conditions under slave labor, and a worker-organized union to rights accorded to free labor. The "overthrow of slavery," as

Eric Foner explains, "reinforced the definition of the contract as the very opposite of the master-slave relationship."[12] But Foner also reminds us that what freedmen desired was not just the contract but greater autonomy over the day-to-day organization of work.[13] By that standard, Pullman porters, maids, and many black workers fought, fifty years after the end of Reconstruction, for the freedom to negotiate their own economic contracts. BSCP organizers claimed the Pullman Company opposed their union because the company did not think the porter had any rights that the company was bound to respect. "So far as his manhood is concerned," the *Messenger* told its readers, "in the eyes of the Company, the porter is not supposed to have any."[14] The campaign for manhood was to claim "the humanhood of the Negro race," starting with a company that demanded of its porters and maids the "submersion of their manhood by making public beggars of them."[15] BSCP propaganda asked if porters and maids were "tired of being treated like children instead of men," and if so implored them to oppose the company union.[16]

The BSCP used the company union to raise questions related not just to porters and maids but the status and place of all African Americans. Slavery was not a metaphor for black Americans as it was for white Americans; it did not *represent* a condition or experience for black Americans; it *was* the state of having one's humanity reduced to what value it could command as a piece of real estate. Freedom, on the other hand, was employed and thought of metaphorically by black Americans, for it represented a state of possibilities, contingencies on a continuum that spread outward from slavery. Claiming manhood rights was to step out of the servant stereotype that cloaked the humanity of black Americans.[17]

More than suffrage, manhood rights included the right to equal economic opportunity and the right to a place at the bargaining table of labor. The Brotherhood implied that these rights were held by white Americans despite the fact that during the 1920s rights of many white workers were also limited by company unions. The Brotherhood's rhetorical flourishes are revealing not so much for what is *true* as for what they reveal about the perspective of those African Americans for whom the propaganda was targeted. Was the exclusion of black workers from the bargaining process open to white workers really a literal violation of citizenship rights? Were Pullman porters really slaves? The fact that many in the black community rallied around these interpretations suggests the degree to which slavery metaphors resonated with a population that felt excluded from full participation in American society.

The Brotherhood's campaign was infused with ideas about entitlements of American citizenship. The *Messenger* noted, not quite accurately, that the slaves were set free in 1863 and presumably given their rights as free Americans, yet they emerged five years later (the year when the Fourteenth Amendment was ratified) as "full-fledged citizens of the United States, *on the books* (emphasis in the original)."[18] Organizers told porters, maids, and the public that "though the Federal Government calls the so-called Negro a citizen, it classifies him as an alien, or rather something betwist and between, . . . being still a slave, to a certain degree, of the white man." Black people were considered 100 percent citizens when it was to the "white man's benefit," for example, "when it comes to paying taxes, to service in the draft, to defense of the country." But "in those things that makes for his own benefit, he is only a Negro." The battle for manhood rights and the right to compete on an equal footing with white workers in the job market would bring black workers closer to enjoyment of full citizenship.[19]

The Brotherhood said it was building "upon the spirit and work" started during Reconstruction, when Isaac Myers and other black workers "banded themselves together into unions of their own as well as sought to join with their white brothers."[20] Myers, a caulker from Baltimore and president of the Colored National Labor Union (CNLU) formed in 1869, told the CNLU that "American citizenship is a complete failure if [black workers are] proscribed from the workshops of this country." And, he added, "if citizenship means anything at all, it means the freedom of labor, as broad and as universal as freedom of the ballot."[21] A black colleague of Myers, in a speech about interracial cooperation delivered before a white labor union, told the audience that black labor "did not come seeking . . . parlor sociabilities, but for the rights of manhood."[22]

Organizers insisted that these early black labor unions were concerned with more than just increased wages. They "fought for certain civil and social legislation . . . fighting hard to consolidate their civil status." The Brotherhood argued that when African Americans abandoned the economic program of Myers, replacing it with an emphasis on political reform, efforts to organize black workers failed. Nevertheless, the BSCP applauded the "considerable interest in organization" shown by black workers following the Civil War: collective organization was a step toward gaining a measure of power necessary when negotiating for greater economic opportunity, opening up workshops and the bargaining process to black workers.[23]

The influence of Randolph's formative years, shaped in part by the legacy of Reconstruction, was apparent in May 1926 when he extolled the participation of African Americans in the process of Reconstruction before a crowd of approximately 60,000 at the Sesqui-Centennial Exposition in Philadelphia. He proclaimed that "despite the cynicism of certain political historians on the reconstruction period of Negro history, an unbiased examination will reveal that black freedom gave to the South its first glimpse of democratic institutions."[24] Since Reconstruction, black workers "have fought nobly in the ranks of white workers in long industrial struggles." Not only could the "victims of slavery be the carriers and preservers of democracy," Randolph suggested, but "the Negro's next gift to America will be in economic democracy."[25] Randolph implied the mantle had been handed to the BSCP to carry forward the work begun during Reconstruction.[26]

Randolph advanced his positive view of Reconstruction at a point when the era was characterized as the darkest page in American history. Much of the "wisdom" of the time portrayed freedmen and women as childlike, unprepared for responsibilities of citizenship and freedom, and engaged in misrule and corruption.[27] Randolph's remarks, delivered to an overwhelmingly white audience, eulogized African Americans who helped build an interracial, democratic society during Reconstruction. Nearly a decade later, in 1935, W. E. B. Du Bois published his pathbreaking *Black Reconstruction*, arguing at the end of his book that the study of the Reconstruction era was historically flawed because most scholars "cannot conceive of Negroes as men."[28]

The Brotherhood liberally laced its discourse with images and references to slavery. One organizer compared "that shot from the South Carolina fortress" that was " 'heard round the world' and marked the beginning of the Civil War" with the shot "fired on August 25, 1925, by the Pullman porters." The porters' cannon fire, he declared, would "result in the direct emancipation of 12,000 Negro Pullman porters and maids from a condition of slavery but little removed from that of their forebears."[29] Randolph reminded porters and maids that white people thought that black people were "still slaves in mind if not in body. And it is a matter of common knowledge that if one thinks as a slave, he will act as a slave." Thus, the Pullman Company, Randolph warned, "really believes that you should not desire to do the things white workers seek to do. This notion is expressed in the saying the 'The Negro should keep in his place,' wherever that is."[30]

The *Messenger* publicized the narrative of Silas M. Taylor, head of the Boston division of the BSCP, to illustrate themes central to the Brotherhood's message. Although parts of the story were most likely embellished, Taylor dramatized the journey from slave to "essential humanhood," despite forces that decreed black people should "be the eternal footstool of a supposedly strong, pure and virile white race." Born near Appomattox, Virginia, Taylor remembered leaving "one form of human slavery" and beginning another when he found work in a Virginia tobacco factory. Taylor and his co-workers struck their employer for better working conditions. Although the group won the strike, they did not know how to proceed since they were leaderless. The result was the "lash of the master." After a few more years, Taylor went to work for the Pullman Company, first as a car cleaner and finally a Pullman porter, a position he held for almost forty years.[31]

When the Brotherhood of Sleeping Car Porters was launched, Taylor "entered the struggle with the same zest and fervor that characterized his activities in the early days of his freedom on the tobacco plantation in Virginia." The Brotherhood was carrying on where black activists of the Reconstruction era left off. After he joined the BSCP, Taylor, considered among the more militant members of the Brotherhood, was "retired" without pension. He had no regrets, for, he observed, "they can withhold my pension," for "I am not old. I was born when the Brotherhood of Sleeping Car Porters was born." He planned to stand by the union. "Lincoln's Emancipation Proclamation freed my people and me," he concluded. But when the "shackles fell from our limbs, Lincoln's son [Robert Todd Lincoln became president of the Pullman Company following George Pullman's death in 1897][32] girdled again our loins with a new form of slavery." His final wish was to live long enough to see porters and maids freed from servile relations and take their "place in the world of men to do an honest day's work and receive honest wage for the same, rather than to depend upon tips."[33]

Citizenship, freedom, and slavery were themes addressed on a regular basis in the local black press.[34] Douglass, for example, was remembered for his relentless, militant agitation for civil and political rights gained through Emancipation and Reconstruction.[35] When Randolph, Webster, and other BSCP organizers discussed full-fledged Americanism and citizenship, they used the terms to question just what progress had been made and on whose terms. A company union denied the porters and maids a fundamental right to organize and choose one's leaders. In a similar fashion, black leaders were usually chosen by white patrons who controlled the decision-making process for allocation of resources.[36] All black Americans, according to Brotherhood philosophy, had to assert their manhood rights to first-class citizenship by changing the racial status quo. For that reason, the BSCP argued that developing "a labor union background," a prolabor point of view, was the task of "the Negro public, too."[37]

The Fourteenth Amendment and Full Citizenship

At the first Negro Labor Conference in January 1928, the BSCP invoked the historical memory of the Fourteenth Amendment to shape a prolabor point of view in black Chicago. Randolph utilized a letter he wrote to ex-governor

Frank O. Lowden of Illinois, reprinted in the *Chicago Defender*, as a rhetorical tool to connect citizenship and the right to organize in the workplace. He asked Lowden, at the time a potential candidate for the Republican nomination for president, where he stood on the question of enforcement of the Fourteenth Amendment.[38] Randolph probably wrote Lowden, a son-in-law of George Pullman, because his close connection to the Pullman Company made it easy to connect his Fourteenth Amendment question to discrimination by the Pullman Company toward its black employees. He praised Lowden for his advocacy of "organization of, by and for the farmers," but noted that the Pullman Company honored the organization of its white conductors, while refusing to meet with the BSCP. "Do you think it fair for the company to co-operate with, recognize and deal with the conductors' union and fight and refuse to meet the porters' union? If you grant that farmers have the right to organize, conductors have the right to organize, the engineers have the right to organize, haven't porters, the lowest paid of all the transportation workers, a right to organize also?"[39] The exclusion of black workers from the bargaining process open to white workers was, in Randolph's mind, a violation of the Fourteenth Amendment and full citizenship rights that it guaranteed.

The original intent of the Fourteenth Amendment flowed from a desire on the part of Republicans supporting the Amendment in 1866 to make plain the new status of former slaves and was meant, in part, to remedy the lack of a "citizenship" clause in the original Constitution.[40] For newly emancipated slaves and their descendants, this was the amendment that overturned the *Dred Scott* decision, which had decreed that a black person could not be a citizen of the United States.[41] The amendment clarified for all Americans the citizenship question, which had remained mired in ambiguity during the antebellum period.

But the Fourteenth Amendment was also linked to free labor. Reconstruction Republicans introduced the Fourteenth Amendment, in part, as a way to defend black workers against a recurrence of state legislation like the Black Codes, which W. E. B. Du Bois called a "plain and indisputable attempt on the part of the Southern states to make Negroes slaves in everything but name."[42] It was thought by Radical Republicans that only an amendment could restrain the South from subjecting freedmen and women to permanent servitude. Freedom meant little without enfranchisement, Du Bois noted, if ex-masters could whip ex-slaves and throw them back into slavery when freedmen were "caught" exercising the freedom to chose a new employer and were declared, thus, in a state of vagrancy while between jobs.[43] Although largely a civic ideology "grounded in a definition of American citizenship," Reconstruction radicalism, as Eric

Foner explains, possessed an economic agenda derived from the free-labor ideology that declared freedmen and white workers were entitled to the same economic opportunities.[44] One of the framers of the Fourteenth Amendment, William Lawrence, representative from Ohio, acknowledged that "it is a mockery to say that a citizen may have a right to live, and yet deny him the right to make a contract to secure the privilege and the rewards of labor."[45] Experiences during Reconstruction led freedmen and women to understand American citizenship in terms of the freedom to be able to negotiate the conditions under which they worked, free from white supervision, which was compared with the oppression of working in gangs under slave drivers.[46]

The BSCP solution was to "build the mightiest economic Movement among Negroes in the world" for "the liberation of a large group of Negro workers in particular and the race in general."[47] But the movement had to be built by and for black people, which created conflict with many black businessmen and women, professionals, scholars, clergy, and politicians who harbored, by the 1920s, varying interpretations of just what social and political means were appropriate for claiming and securing Fourteenth Amendment rights of citizenship. Despite conflicts over means, there was widespread agreement on the goal.

The demand for rights of American citizenship continued to drive the reform agenda among black American leaders into the twentieth century.[48] The question of black citizenship "like Banquo's ghost . . . will not down," historian Charles H. Wesley noted in *Opportunity* in 1924.[49] The *Messenger* pressed the issue of the Fourteenth Amendment and reminded its audience that "Chief Justice Taney [in the *Dred Scott* decision of 1857] said that a Negro had no rights that a white man was bound to respect." The author posed the question, "How true is this statement today?" While the Fourteenth Amendment granted citizenship based on certain rights and responsibilities, the problem was that while "the Negro had laid his allegiance upon the altar of his country in every war and every clime," the question remained, "what will America do in return to give him that protection in life, liberty and the pursuit of happiness that he so earnestly desires?"[50] Implicitly, the answer was not much. Randolph was aware that the courts did not endorse his interpretation of the Fourteenth Amendment. "By the subtle manipulation of shrewd, highly paid lawyers," Randolph wrote, the Fourteenth Amendment "has become the bulwark of property rights instead of Negro rights."[51] The interpretation of the Fourteenth Amendment embraced by black Americans must be understood not in terms of what it had become, but as holding high what Vincent Harding calls the "best egalitarian traditions" of American democracy.[52]

The labor conferences also fused full citizenship demands with a reawakening of race consciousness that emphasized neither complete assimilation nor segregation. The interpretation of "race consciousness" promoted by the BSCP conferences was compatible with Du Bois's analysis of black identity: a "twoness—an American, a Negro; two souls, two thoughts, two unreconciled strivings." The solution was based on adopting what Du Bois's biographer David Levering Lewis called "affirming" a state of "permanent tension," a state of "enduring hyphenation," a place somewhere between assimilation and segregation.[53] Race consciousness implied that African Americans would determine their place in American society. The concept was infused with a belief in self-determination and active participation in the process of claiming rights embedded in American citizenship. Race consciousness and race solidarity, as practiced by the new crowd, never meant withdrawal from mainstream society.

The BSCP thought cultivation of a pro–organized labor perspective, what organizers referred to as the "labor viewpoint," was a key component for change. It believed the "labor movement is the only school, the only crucible in which such a consciousness can be developed."[54] By reinvigorating race consciousness and linking it with labor organization, the labor conference could increase the power of the black worker, who was "exploited as slave, as peon, and now becomes the underpaid, the first to be laid off and employed in the most undesirable phases of northern and southern industries." A labor movement would develop organizational skills needed to claim first-class status and raise the standards for all African Americans through effective organizations, just as white workers have done. As Webster noted, the "porters want to be self-respecting citizens . . . the Pullman Company want them to be serfs."[55]

But labor organization was also a tool for developing "self-reliance," by which the Brotherhood meant independence from white control. Self-reliance was developed from the experience of facing "tremendous odds and a withering fire of opposition," learning through trial how "to reform its ranks when shattered and rise up when beaten down."[56] Through the "process of self-organization and self-struggle, Negro workers will develop the necessary labor view-point, sense of responsibility, a labor union morale and technique." Developing a black labor movement would mark "the beginning of the period when the Negro earnestly begins to help himself instead of merely looking for his friends to help him."[57]

"Legislating for the economic welfare of the porters," Randolph wrote, carried "immeasurable" significance for the race. With the "recognition of our economic rights, privileges and power, will develop the initiative and ability to write our own economic contracts." That accomplishment was connected in his mind with ushering "the Negro into the final cycle of race freedom. It is our next step as a group of workers and as a race, oppressed, outraged and exploited. It is the final road to freedom of all oppressed peoples." He told union porters and maids that "in the Brotherhood, you have built the agency with which to approach this new task. Ours now is the big problem of rationally and constructively handling this instrument which invests us with a new power."[58]

Nurturing a prolabor point of view was far more than making union porters out of company men. Civil rights were inextricably fused to the labor agenda of the BSCP. This is an area where Randolph and the Brotherhood's outlook differed from Du Bois's. The BSCP invested the process of developing a prolabor point of view with the task of finishing work left undone in 1877—that of granting black Americans the same civil rights assumed by white Americans. Although Du Bois strongly suggested that a labor-oriented perspective was important for black workers, he nevertheless believed into the 1920s that gaining political power should be emphasized first. Upon observing the situation in the New South before World War I, as Lewis observes, Du Bois thought "economic power would come once political power had been regained." After the horrific East St. Louis race riot of 1917, Lewis argues, Du Bois sustained an "antiunion hostility for years to come," for the American Federation of Labor offered "no hope of justice" for African Americans.[59] While Du Bois invested the "talented tenth" with the responsibility of challenging Jim Crow institutions, Randolph, Webster, the Brotherhood, and others were laying the foundation for a coalition of activists that would use a labor movement to make claims for full civil rights.

The Brotherhood's message at the first labor conference was designed to mobilize support for the union by shaming what it called the "mis-leaders" of black Americans, those who union activists claimed did not work for the interest of the group and who identified with individual white employers or politicians to whom they must be eternally grateful. This was part of the Brotherhood's attempt to destroy the myth that "only white men are supposed to organize for power, for justice and freedom."[60] Uncle Tom was portrayed as "an individualist" who believed he was, like Jesse Binga, different.[61] Individualism precluded Uncle Toms from raising a voice against the powerful interests of the dominant society, a problem depicted in the *Messenger* in the form of a dialogue between old and new porters. The new porter said: "White folks are no different from any other kind of folks, pop. It all depends on how much *power* you got, and you can't get power unless you are *organized*. You know the old joke about the farmer not bothering *one hornet* because of fear of the *rest* of the *hornets standing behind him*. Well, that's all we porters got to do. That's all the

Negro race has got to do—*stick together*; be *all for each and each for all*" (emphasis in original).[62] In order to adopt the Brotherhood's outlook it was necessary to shift from an individual perspective to that of a collective consciousness, a shift that proved to be harder for some than others. Robert S. Abbott and even Claude Barnett eventually endorsed many of the tactics and strategies that emerged from the Brotherhood's perspective; Jesse Binga never did.

The June Movement

Between January and June 1928, the Brotherhood stretched its wings in two directions, as a labor union and a social movement, in embryo, for all black Americans. The two purposes were not reconciled until after the "June Movement," as the *Chicago Defender* called the BSCP's attempt to strike against the Pullman Company, had passed. The crisis of the proposed strike brought the BSCP to a fork in the road when the strike vote tactic failed to impress the Pullman Company, reinforcing the importance of gaining the allegiance of the larger community by making the BSCP primarily a community-based social movement with a labor agenda.

In April, by a vote of 6,053 to 17, porters and maids voted to strike.[63] The scenario that followed is well documented: the Pullman Company stalled operations of the mediation board, the body charged with ruling on the validity of the porters' grievances and whether they warranted the attention of the president of the United States; the company housed and fed strikebreakers in Pullman Company yards and added new men to the payroll; and the company reinforced Pullman's security at all railroad stations with the help of local police.[64] When the BSCP canceled the impending strike, many historians declared the "failed" strike vote tactic the catalyst that led to poor morale, dramatic decrease in memberships, the demise of the *Messenger*, and a union that was a shadow of its former self.[65]

What failed was the dual agenda, which the BSCP had pursued for several months.[66] It has been suggested that Randolph went against the wishes of the generally militant porters when he called off the strike, which may be true. But it is also true, as William Harris argues, that it is not entirely clear just how the decision to postpone was reached.[67] What is clearer is that hopes that the BSCP could succeed by following strategies used by white labor were dashed. Webster, clearly more militant in terms of labor tactics than Randolph, was more than a little impatient with his leader, even mocking Randolph for placing publicity higher on the union's agenda than calling a strike.[68] But Webster was also aware that the union was extremely weak in terms of support on this issue from the larger community. Shortly after the strike vote was announced, the Chicago Citizens' Committee suggested it was not willing to stand behind the porters and maids in a nationwide strike.[69] Without the support of the Citizens' Committee in Chicago, where so many Pullman porters lived, Webster and Randolph understood the difficulty they faced trying to mobilize significant portions of black Chicago to join in a strike by union porters against the Pullman Company. Citizens' Committee members may not have felt the time was right to take on the Pullman Company, which had the power to crush the BSCP. Pullman had strikebreakers and access to other resources that black middle-class support could not influence or counter. It was only within the last several months that the Citizens' Committee and BSCP organizers had gained support from the *Defender* and launched the first Negro Labor Conference. While the Citizens' Committee was willing to publicly declare allegiance to the BSCP as a movement for manhood rights, perhaps it was not prepared to support a strike against the Pullman Company where so many black men were employed in Chicago. As pioneers in the Brotherhood's movement, the Citizens' Committee could gauge better than most the forces of opposition arrayed against the fledgling union. What is certain is that the strike threat revealed that the BSCP as a community-wide movement was in its infancy. When the *Defender* assessed the June movement, it felt the "public sentiment" had not been sufficiently awakened to support the union.[70]

It humbled many organizers, such as Webster, to realize the union could not operate as a traditional labor union. Disappointed though Webster may have been, he gained a new appreciation for the value of publicity. Immediately after the strike was postponed, he devoted more time to broadcasting the Brotherhood's message to the larger community. Pullman denied "these men the right to select representatives of their own choice," Webster reminded black Chicago as he connected workers' rights with interests of black citizens.[71] Speaking before the Chicago Forum Council at Waukeegan, Illinois, attended by "all the big Negroes and so-called best people," Webster tried to win support for the Brotherhood's movement.[72]

By the fall of 1928, the *Messenger* had folded and Webster reported the first signs of dwindling memberships in Chicago. The Brotherhood reevaluated its campaign on two fronts.[73] BSCP goals had not changed, but the strike issue emphasized to the Brotherhood that while it did not have the power to pull off a strike, its movement would "rest upon its power solely" with the porters, Citizens' Committee, and networks in the community. This period etched firmly in both Randolph and Webster's thinking the lesson that for Pullman porters and maids, as well as for all black people, "salvation must and can only come from within." The theme—salvation from within, a movement "for the self-expression and interest of Negroes by Negroes for Negroes"—remained the basic principle behind the movement until well into the late 1940s.[74] This emphasis on independence from white control contained the seeds of what Randolph and Webster thought of as the self-assertive new crowd of black Americans leading the protest against the racial status quo. In the aftermath of the June Movement, Webster told Randolph that he felt the Chicago branch was "much stronger" as a result of the strike vote. "We might proceed on the premises that this is the public's fight as well as the porter's fight."[75]

As a social movement in the vanguard of the black freedom struggle in Chicago, the BSCP had laid down roots within black neighborhoods. Allegiance within the black community for the Brotherhood's approach would increase over the next five years, exhibiting an inverse relationship to the decrease in paid memberships in the union. The alliances forged through the labor conferences expanded the agenda of the Brotherhood and directly challenged the culture of black politics. As the struggle increasingly focused on winning the hearts and minds of black Chicagoans, BSCP networks branched out into the community through the Negro labor conferences.

Labor Conferences Promote a Civil Rights
Agenda Anchored in Labor Organization

African Americans, Randolph and Webster agreed in the summer of 1928, "will no more permit white people to select their leaders than will white people permit Negroes to select theirs." This right to choose their own leaders was "as fundamental as the right of life itself."[76] Whereas Randolph's relationship to patronage politics was unambiguous, Webster's was more complicated, reflecting the multiple positions that shaped many leaders within the black community. After Webster was fired from the Pullman Company, he was largely dependent upon his patronage position as a ward heeler for the Republican Party, along with rent from two apartment buildings, for income.[77] In 1924 Bernard Snow, chief bailiff of the municipal court, secured a job for Webster as an assistant bailiff and also helped him study the law.[78] Coming shortly after Webster was "let go" by Pullman after working as a porter since 1906, the job must have looked especially attractive.[79]

In the spring of 1928 Webster wrote Randolph that "the big Negro boss in Chicago has got this axe on my head because I would not be stampeded into supporting his stool pigeon candidate for legislature." Although he knew he would be out of a job if he did not follow party bosses, it was increasingly difficult for Webster to buckle to the wishes of a political machine, more interested in maintaining itself than working for the good of African Americans.[80] By May, Webster's political boss let him know that "pressure was being brought to bear upon him" from Pullman Company connections to force Webster to choose between the BSCP and politics.[81] The ultimatum made him feel "rather elated because they [Pullman Company] would not bring pressure on anybody if they were not feeling the effects of the [Brotherhood's] program."[82]

Webster kept his patronage job until 1930, but tried to use his position to further the Brotherhood's movement. Perhaps more than any other organizer, Webster understood that the Brotherhood's movement was just as much about organizing middle-class citizens as it was about Pullman porters and maids. Without attacking the politics of the black machine, there never could be a black labor movement in Chicago. The "role that Webster played will perhaps never be understood by those on the outside," reflected BSCP organizer Benjamin McLaurin in 1981, because "Webster was a politician."[83] Although Webster would periodically lash out at the "big Negroes," the "high-brows," and the "big shots," who he felt tried to show white folks that "the best thinking Negroes are not with us," he realized how important it was to win their allegiance. He attempted to " 'get a ring-side seat' on the inside in the Republican party" at the state level to push a prolabor point of view and convince the " 'high-brow' Negroes" that they had to represent the interests of black workers as well as the elite. The extent of anti-Brotherhood sentiment in high places within black society dismayed Webster even as it illuminated the enormity of the task the Brotherhood challenge had unleashed.[84] Enmeshed in the politics of a labor movement, Webster spoke from both his head and his heart when he connected the labor agenda of the BSCP to civil rights embodied in the Constitution.

The chief place for integrating the public's and the porter's fight was the labor conference, which focused on creating cross-class alliances within the community to make demands for basic rights of citizenship. Much work needed to be done, for, as the *Chicago Defender* explained it, a "strange mixture of ignorance and indifference" characterized "the attitude of the Race toward problems in the field of industry and industrial relations."[85] The process was slow and marked by fits and starts, for inclusion in a political machine and the recognition that came from playing by the rules of that machine continued to have an appeal. The *Chicago Whip*, the Appomadox Club, and the Reverend L. K. Williams represented a few of the people and institutions that, along with Jesse Binga and loans from Binga State Bank, continued working against the

Brotherhood's movement. By 1930, the BSCP had won the support of many members of the community who once had rejected collective organization and labor unions as a vehicle for gaining rights. Appeals to first-class citizenship and racial solidarity, made through the labor conferences of the BSCP, challenged the political culture of the status quo. Slowly, the Brotherhood's network helped pave the way for a politics based not just on the ballot box and good intentions of white patrons but on strategies challenging the fundamental tenets of patronage politics.

The large turnout at the labor conferences and other meetings arranged by the Brotherhood within the black community suggests the impatience people felt with the politics of the status quo.[86] By January 1929 close to 2,000 teachers, businessmen and women, social workers, porters, and maids listened to discussions about mobilization for economic power, housing, and the health of workers at the BSCP's three-day labor conference. The network reached out to the future business and professional class with the participation of the Intercollegiate Club, which represented the young, educated elite, whose members liked to think of themselves as representing the "New Negro"—a seeker of opportunity rather than philanthropy, a "lover of world brotherhood" who "supports human principles." These young college graduates, who prided themselves in advancing cross-class alliances, told students they ought to "quit criticizing workers and get in harmony with them." Frederic Robb, president of the Intercollegiate Club, spoke at several Brotherhood mass meetings, advocating that churches "foster a labor psychology."[87] Frankie Adams, industrial secretary of the South Parkway Branch of the Young Women's Christian Association (located in the black belt), addressed the topic of black women in industry. Jessie Bond, president of the Colored Women's Economic Council, discussed activities of the women's auxiliary to the BSCP in "developing the moral spirit of the members of the Brotherhood." When representatives of the National Negro Business League spoke at the Negro Labor Conference, Webster was pleased because he considered them a "hardboiled bunch," that is, not easy to win over to the Brotherhood's side.[88]

Another important addition to the Brotherhood network was the Reverend Harold M. Kingsley, pastor of the Church of the Good Shepherd with its largely white-collar members. In his sermons he emphasized the virtue and value of labor.[89] It was at the 1930 National Negro Labor Conference that Reverend Kingsley used his influence to persuade other clergy to reexamine their relationship to organized labor and the black worker. He compared the black church of the late 1920s with the Russian church before the Russian Revolution of 1917, which was particularly blind to the needs of workers. "The Church is the one institution that gets more of the people together than any other institution," he said, but it needed to be "educated up to the economic conditions of the workers."[90] In the past, the church often told black workers whom to vote for; Kingsley was suggesting that workers educate the clergy, who had a responsibility to workers. Not all clergy who spoke at the labor conference promoted the same approach. Dr. Norman B. Barr of Olivet Institute talked on "Work, Wages, and Worship," urging workers to depend more on worship to solve their industrial problems, differing considerably from the spirit of the Brotherhood's interpretation of self-reliance.[91]

The front pages of the *Chicago Defender* captured part of the central message of the 1930 National Negro Labor Conference in a large, political cartoon, which it centered beneath a one and a half inch headline announcing the conference. The Brotherhood, proclaimed the cartoon, was awakening "our workers" from slumber while an alarm rang out the necessity for "organization." Through the bedroom window, workers are marching into the sunrise of "economic freedom."[92] BSCP propaganda often used the term "awaken" to describe the process it tried to unleash through its movement.[93] The labor conferences stressed the importance of awakening a cross-class alliance in Chicago. Acknowledging that 98 percent of black Americans are "workers of hand and brain who depend upon jobs and wages for life," the conference called upon the middle class—"the student, minister, doctor, lawyer, teacher, and business man"—to unite in support of the "struggle of the black workers for the right to organize."[94]

Labor conferences made a pioneering effort to connect issues of labor with those for basic citizenship rights, bringing together citizens from all walks of life around the basic right of all Americans to pick their leaders. The BSCP's effort to focus on standing tall as a group and claiming a first-class place in society through collective organization, beyond the pay of a white politician, turned the labor conferences into a protest network, challenging the political status quo, and by extension any black leadership dependent on white patronage. The new crowd that gathered at the conferences was engaged in a community education project aimed at redefining how politics and power were understood. It was, as the *Chicago Defender* put it, one of the "most ambitious efforts to influence race thinking," a "movement to stir interest in serious economic problems and to educate the Race in channels of thought where there hadn't been much thought before."[95]

Even as the Brotherhood protested the approach of those it often referred to as "misleaders," the status quo was dealt a blow after Jesse Binga's Binga State Bank crashed in 1930. Binga State Bank, one of the largest black banks in the

United States with deposits of $1,465,266.62, just before it failed, was financially dependent upon the largesse of Samuel Insull, a white utilities' magnate. Insull was so preoccupied with the maintenance of his financial empire in 1930 that he was unable or unwilling to help, making Binga State Bank the first in Chicago to fall after the stock market crash. When Binga was later arrested for embezzlement of bank funds, the *Defender* flooded the city and its nationwide readers with headlines documenting how Binga released funds to save himself when "his back was against the wall" and appealed to Samuel Insull for help.[96] The bank failure reminded the community about the fragility of the patron-client relationship. After 1930 Binga was no longer invited to speak at Pullman Company Union functions. Another leader, Bishop Archibald J. Carey, fell from grace that spring when he was charged with irregularities connected with the administration of civil service examinations.[97] With no Sam Insull to help Binga and Bishop Carey's post in the civil service commission in question, the argument for gratitude toward white benefactors lost some of its punch and diminished the stature of these two leaders who had thrived in the culture of patronage politics. The old-guard leaders were losing support, partly, because they could no longer deliver prized patronage positions.

From 1928 to 1933, between 2,000 and 3,000 people attended and participated each year in BSCP labor conferences as the labor-oriented approach for claiming basic rights of citizenship reached far into black neighborhoods on the South Side. Perhaps the best gauge of the success of the labor conferences in launching a social movement was a public meeting held in the spring of 1932 at the Metropolitan Church. Those attending the meeting, a joint effort of several churches in black Chicago, women's clubs, and social and civil groups, demonstrated their support of the Brotherhood by giving a considerable amount of money to the BSCP. Randolph called that meeting a "significant turning point to the economic life of the race." He, along with other organizers and representatives from the Citizens' Committee, told the gathering they were grateful to the community for its endorsement of the Brotherhood's movement and for awakening their groups to the "basic need and value of labor organization to develop power to bargain and fight" for justice.[98]

The BSCP continued to sponsor labor rallies, labor institutes, and mass meetings to mobilize the community.[99] By the early 1930s, its message was reinforced by that of other networks formed within the community advancing the necessity of organization and making demands on the state. Scholars have called the years 1928 to 1933, when membership plummeted, the dark days in BSCP history. In 1933, although the Chicago division was down to 250 members from its high of 1,150 members in 1928, it had won the support of a large cross section of the black middle class.[100] And while concentrating on gaining community support may have contributed to the low membership in the BSCP as a labor union, the Chicago division of the BSCP had a large and significant following from a cross section of the community for its labor-oriented, civil rights agenda. By the early 1930s, tactics and strategies in many circles focused on using interclass alliances in protest networks to make demands rather than relying on limitations of conventional political structures. This multipositional approach to politics and power was shaped, in part, through the process of labor organizing by the BSCP. As a window on the political culture in Chicago, the Brotherhood's movement revealed that a strong current galvanizing the spirit of black Chicago was the desire to be free of white control and second-class citizenship. When the BSCP's challenge to patronage politics and a company union tapped into this current, the Brotherhood steadily gained support and recognition.

President A. Philip Randolph delivering Presidential Address on "Constitution Night" at the Second National Negro Congress, Philadelphia, 1937. Behind Randolph is a giant banner with a picture of Abraham Lincoln and the words: "All men are created equal." (SC-CN-83-0164. Courtesy of Photographs and Prints Division, Schomburg Center for Research in Black Culture, The New York Public Library, Astor, Lenox and Tilden Foundations.)

Portrait of Ida B. Wells-Barnett. (Photograph by Oscar B. Willis, Chicago, n.d. SC-CN-84-0154. Courtesy of Photographs and Prints Division, Schomburg Center for Research in Black Culture, The New York Public Library, Astor, Lenox and Tilden Foundations.)

Left: Walter Francis White, executive secretary of the NAACP during the 1930s. White helped guide the civil rights association through one of its more challenging decades. (Photograph by Gordon Parks. LC-USF-34-13343. Courtesy of the Prints and Photographs Division, Library of Congress, Washington, D.C.)

Below: A. Philip Randolph carrying sign "If Negroes must fight . . . ," demonstrating for civil rights in the military. (SC-CN-97-051. Courtesy of Photographs and Prints Division, Schomburg Center for Research in Black Culture, The New York Public Library, Astor, Lenox and Tilden Foundations.)

BULLETIN

OUR ECONOMIC FREEDOM VICTORY DASH

Vol. I   "Ye shall know the truth and the truth shall make you free"   No. 8

"Douglass Fought For The Abolition Of Chattel Slavery And Today We Fight For ECONOMIC FREEDOM".

"The Time Has Passed When A Grown-up Black Man Should Beg A Grown-up White Man For Anything."

A. Philip Randolph.

Ye Brotherhood men, hold high your banner of solidarity. Remember that a **quitter** never wins and a **winner** never quits. Remember that he who would be free must himself first strike the blow. Let us stand firm and be unafraid. Pay your dues and assessment. The Mediation Board will call us soon. If we fight and faint not, we shall reap our just reward in due season.

Your faithful servant,
A. PHILIP RANDOLPH,
General Organizer.

(By courtesy of the
Pittsburgh Courier)

WITH APOLOGIES TO CARL AKELEYS SCULPTURE "THE CHRYSALIS"

THE CHRYSALIS

THE BROTHERHOOD OF SLEEPING CAR PORTERS

2311 Seventh Avenue   New York City

The cover of the *Bulletin*, a BSCP publication, comparing economic freedom with freedom from slavery, and invoking the name of Frederick Douglass. (*Bulletin*, 1:8 [1926]. Courtesy of The Newberry Library, Chicago.)

Brotherhood of Sleeping Car Porters meeting at Webster's office at 4231 South Michigan Avenue in 1943. *Left to right*: A. R. Dailey, G. C. Garron, Henry T. Yates, E. J. Bradley, C. L. Dellums, Milton P. Webster, A. Philip Randolph, Ashley L. Totten, T. T. Patterson, Benjamin Smith, John Mills, J. C. Bell, and Benoit. (Photograph by Harrison, Chicago, 1943. Item CHS:ICHi-21658. Courtesy of the Chicago Historical Society.)

A mass meeting sponsored by the BSCP that took place in a Chicago auditorium. The BSCP Citizens' Committee helped break down resistance to its union in the community in Chicago. (Photographer unknown, n.d. From G1980.0169, box 1, folder 4, item CHS:ICHi-25673. Courtesy of the Chicago Historical Society.)

A Pullman sleeping car porter, standing to the right of women boarding a train, waits to serve their needs, while a Pullman conductor collects tickets and money from the passengers. (Photographer unknown, Chicago, ca. 1915. Item ICHi-26271. Courtesy of the Chicago Historical Society.)

The Reverend Junius C. Austin, pastor of Pilgrim Baptist Church, and member of the BSCP Citizens' Committee, Chicago. Reverend Austin, a supporter of Marcus Garvey in the early 1920s, used his pulpit to mobilize support for the BSCP and rallied Chicago in support of Angelo Herndon in the early 1930s. (Photograph by Woodard Studio, Chicago, n.d. Item ICHi-30755. Courtesy of the Chicago Historical Society.)

Milton P. Webster, head of the BSCP Chicago division from its beginning in 1925 and a former porter. (Photographer unknown, n.d. From G1980.0169, box 1, folder 6, item CHS:ICHi-30759. Courtesy of the Chicago Historical Society.)

Left: The Reverend Archibald J. Carey, who announced job openings for Pullman porters from the pulpit of his church in Chicago. (Photograph by Melvin H. Sykes, n.d. Item CHS:ICHi-30756. Courtesy of the Chicago Historical Society.)

Below: Irene McCoy Gaines, secretary of the BSCP Citizens' Committee, sitting at her desk under a picture of Abraham Lincoln. (Photograph by Adams' Fotos, Chicago, n.d. Item ICHi-30757. Courtesy of the Chicago Historical Society.)

A. Philip Randolph, head of the Brotherhood of Sleeping Car Porters and President of the National Negro Congress, who organized African Americans to March on Washington for economic rights of citizenship in 1941. (Photograph by Electric Studio, Chicago, n.d. Item ICHi-12255. Courtesy of the Chicago Historical Society.)

A dinner for defense workers, sponsored by the St. Louis unit of the March on Washington Movement, at the Pine Street YMCA in St. Louis, 1942. (Photograph by Young. Item ICHi-24991. Courtesy of the Chicago Historical Society.)

Thyra Edwards, journalist, whom the brotherhood sponsored on her trip to Denmark in the early 1930s. After returning to Chicago, she lectured on labor and civil rights issues for the BSCP's Citizens' Committee. (Photographer unknown. From G1980.0213, box 1, folder 5, item ICHi-30758. Courtesy of the Chicago Historical Society.)

Daisy Lampkin, regional field secretary for the NAACP during the 1930s. Lampkin often used her position as an organizer for the National Association of Colored Women to reach recruits for the NAACP. (From box lot, x61980, box 1, folder 1, n.d., item ICHi-26897. Courtesy of the Chicago Historical Society.)

Forging Alliances

New-Crowd Protest Networks, 1930–1935

> Any man who does not want freedom is either a fool or
> an idiot, and if to want freedom is to be a Communist, then I am
> a Communist, and will be till I die.
> REV. JUNIUS C. AUSTIN, Pilgrim Baptist Church and
> BSCP Citizens' Committee, September 1934

The severity of the Great Depression jolted the nation. Black and white Americans suffered as unemployment reached about 25 percent of the national labor force by 1933 and an estimated 20 million Americans sought public and private relief.[1] Despite the hardships, African Americans continued migrating north, pushing black unemployment rates to over 50 percent, substantially above white workers, and intensifying hard times for black urban dwellers.[2]

Known as the "dark days," the early Depression hit the BSCP particularly hard. The Brotherhood, too weak in 1928 to carry out a strike against Pullman, was weaker still in 1930 as a labor union. A severe decline in travelers on Pullman sleeping cars meant fewer jobs for porters and fewer tips for working porters. BSCP memberships plunged: some porters dropped out because they were unemployed; some because they were disappointed in the failure of the BSCP; and some because they feared reprisals from Pullman supervisors intent on destroying what was left of the union. Chicago area memberships dropped to 300 in 1932, from 1,150 in 1928. In 1933, when national memberships were at their lowest at 658, Chicago carried the nation with 250, compared to only 40 members in New York City.[3] After five years of struggle with few concrete results, the times were hardly auspicious for reenlisting the support of porters.

Yet, by 1935, memberships soared, with 1,100 in Chicago and 4,165 nationally. This was due, in part, to New Deal labor legislation.[4] As C. L. Dellums, head of the Oakland branch of the BSCP, observed, "Roosevelt came along, started the

New Deal, and they started passing laws."[5] The BSCP finally forced the Pullman Company to negotiate with the union for a labor contract in 1937. When the BSCP again vigorously pressed forward as a labor union, a prolabor point of view mobilized the larger black community behind the BSCP.

During the dark days, the BSCP network reached deeper into the community to mobilize black Chicago around a labor-oriented approach to citizenship, intensifying its efforts as a social movement. Between 1930 and 1935, the Brotherhood helped forge alliances around issues such as the nomination of Judge Parker to the U.S. Supreme Court, organization of black, female domestic and industrial workers, and the plight of Angelo Herndon. Mobilization around the restricted freedom of all black Americans fueled the formation of cross-class alliances and strengthened the development of protest networks operating outside political channels traditionally used to address grievances.

As activities of protest networks overlapped, a new crowd of leaders emerged, challenging the politics of civility that permeated old-guard relations in black Chicago. New-crowd leaders, impatient with tactics that assumed black Americans should appeal for rights by working within structures created and controlled by white Chicago, sought to gain a measure of greater power through the use of direct, collective action for making demands. The new crowd opposed tactics that placed black Chicagoans in deferential poses and leaders who made requests in a cautious manner in order to avoid direct conflict with white leaders and liberals. Protest networks active during the early Depression years included the labor conferences of the BSCP, the Brotherhood's Citizens' Committee, the local Scottsboro defense committee, and the industrial committee of the South Parkway Branch of the Chicago Young Women's Christian Association (YWCA).

Bridging the Gulf between Labor and Civil Rights Groups

In March 1930 President Herbert Hoover announced the appointment of Judge John J. Parker of the Fourth Circuit Court in North Carolina to the U.S. Supreme Court. Both organized labor and civil rights organizations opposed the appointment and launched national campaigns to protest Parker's confirmation. Neither group, however, wanted to connect its protest with that of the other. The NAACP opposed Judge Parker because he had declared, while campaigning in North Carolina in 1920, that he opposed political participation by black Americans, either as voters or officeholders. The American Federation of Labor (AFL) fought the confirmation of Judge Parker because he supported "yellow dog" contracts, in which, as a condition of employment, a worker agreed not to remain in or join a union.[6] While the NAACP limited its concern to Parker's stand on political freedom, "the fact that the judge's economic views were of direct concern to thousands of wage-earning Negroes," was, as scholars Sterling Spero and Abram Harris noted, "ignored by the association."[7] Organized labor, on the other hand, was silent on the issue of Parker's racism.[8]

The Brotherhood pursued a third path when it tried to link Parker's attitudes toward labor *and* black civil rights in protests it initiated. In the pages of the *Black Worker*, the new official organ of the Brotherhood, the BSCP endorsed a joint attack against Parker "for the Negro is essentially a worker and should ever join hands with labor in its struggle against economic oppression."[9] Rather than diminishing the role of the NAACP, as the Communists were doing at the time, the BSCP elevated the importance of the NAACP in the campaign while reminding the organized labor movement of its responsibility to assist black Americans on civil rights issues. The Brotherhood may have hoped to draw the national office of the NAACP closer to its movement, for despite official endorsement of the BSCP, the NAACP did not, during the early 1930s, believe that unions had much of a role to play in improving the overall position of black Americans. In January 1930, for instance, the NAACP advised the American Fund for Public Service, known as the Garland Fund, against funding organizations advocating the cause of black workers. Both the BSCP and the American Negro Labor Congress, led by the Communist Party, were attempting to receive money at the same time from the fund. The NAACP warned the Garland Fund that to "put money into the salaries of union organizers . . . would be like pouring money down a sink." Neither labor group received any funds. Although it is not likely that the Brotherhood knew about the NAACP's advice to the Garland Fund, Randolph was aware that the NAACP's support for black workers was lukewarm at best.[10]

Within days of the Parker nomination, the Chicago branch of the Brotherhood began organizing protests, petition drives, and mass meetings against the nomination. Parker's labor and civil rights agenda, argued the BSCP, violated the "constitutional rights" of African Americans. To protest this violation, the union urged Chicagoans to write to their senators urging them to fight Parker's confirmation with petitions.[11] Irene McCoy Gaines orchestrated a multipronged attack against Parker, drawing from the BSCP Citizens' Committee alliance and her base as president of the Women's Republican Clubs of Illinois. First, she led the statewide convention of Republican women in a petition campaign to educate the president of the United States and the senators from Illinois about Parker's record on labor and civil rights issues. Second, the Republican women advised voters at the local and state level to let Illinois senators know a vote for Parker's confirmation was a vote against their reelection. Third, as secretary of the BSCP Citizens' Committee, Gaines organized mass meetings of black Chicagoans to protest Parker's nomination.[12]

Ida B. Wells-Barnett used her club network, along with the pages of the *Defender*, to link the protest against Judge Parker to the protection of basic rights, which she reminded her readers were guaranteed in the Fourteenth and Fifteenth Amendments. Wells-Barnett credited Parker's defeat to the organized efforts of "the Race," working "in its own behalf," with the result that despite President Hoover's support for Parker, Parker's nomination was defeated by two votes. Collective organization captured the attention of Illinois's senators, who, she maintained, "saved the day." The strategies adopted by Gaines and Wells-Barnett highlight the fact that new-crowd protest politics did not preclude a fusion of tactics, some taken directly from the pages of old-guard lobbying efforts used by such people as Walter White, executive secretary of the NAACP. There was certainly room within the broad definition of politics that was emerging from the new crowd for lobbying, letter writing, and even personal appeals to people in places of power. But, as Wells-Barnett pointed out, it was collective organization that saved the day.[13]

The Communist Party (CP) had been trying unsuccessfully to establish a foothold in Chicago since the 1920s. In the early 1930s, it had still not resolved what Cyril Briggs of the African Black Brotherhood in Harlem called the problem of chauvinism or white racism within the party. Examples of chauvinism cited by Briggs included not paying black Communist organizers, unwillingness to accept black leadership, opposition to working with black comrades, hesitancy to fight the color bar in unions, and failure to champion, without reservation, the plight of black Americans. Finally, Briggs pointed out that party ideology was handed down to black Americans, detached from their experiences.[14]

At this stage of its struggle the Communist Party focused largely on revolution and class conflict between employers and employees. Issues such as first-class citizenship were not often discussed, nor did white comrades fully understand how African Americans assessed certain figures in American history, such as Abraham Lincoln, who was dismissed by the Chicago Communist Party.[15] In addition, black Americans did not always feel they were being treated as equals by their leftist colleagues, a fact that emerged at some party-sponsored social functions. Certain white ethnic groups, active within the party in Chicago, displayed ambivalent attitudes toward black Americans, which, in turn, led many black recruits to keep their distance from the party. At least once in 1932, at a meeting of the local Unemployed Council, black Chicagoans charged that white comrades had not come to the defense of black comrades when police and a white mob had harassed and attacked them.[16]

That notwithstanding, the party's campaign to erase racism from its rank and file was increasingly successful. At the same time, many middle-class members of the black community who had been active participants in the BSCP's movement—particularly ministers, teachers, clubwomen—opened their minds to a perspective sympathetic to labor and working-class issues. In this sense, the Brotherhood's labor conferences, particularly between 1928 and 1933, helped to pave the way for alliances between the middle-class and black Communist organizers that took place in the mid-to-late 1930s. In Chicago, the Communists became more active in the community, especially by winter and spring of 1931 through its Unemployed Council, which directly addressed problems facing thousands of black Chicagoans. Communists used the councils to struggle against landlords who evicted unemployed black Americans; in the process, hundreds of non-Communists were introduced to collective action tactics through opposition to the eviction process.[17]

The issue of eviction for failure to pay rent created enormous interest within black neighborhoods. Young black radicals, organized into "flying squadrons" and led by the Unemployed Council, gathered large groups of people to replace furniture removed to the streets by landlords and resist the force of police. An old spiritual, "I shall not, I shall not be moved," often accompanied the resistance.[18] At one gathering on August 3, 1931, close to 2,000 people, led by the Unemployed Council, protected the furniture of seventy-two-year-old Diana Gross, an unemployed resident of the South Side. When the police received word of this gathering, several men were arrested. Eventually the police fired into the crowd, killing three black men. An estimated 5,000 to 8,000 people joined a funeral procession, led by the Unemployed Council and Communists through the heart of black Chicago, while many thousands more looked on.[19]

After the shooting, a coalition of leaders from black Chicago met with city officials to discuss ways to prevent bloodshed in the future. Rev. J. C. Austin and Rev. Harold L. Kingsley, activists in the Brotherhood's labor conference and Citizens' Committee alliance, informed the officials that they could not talk religion to men with empty stomachs; the appeal of the Communists would grow until the problem of hunger was taken care of. Austin and Kingsley wrote a statement with others to that effect. In addition the city adopted a resolution, written by Austin and Kingsley, declaring a temporary moratorium on evictions, and state agencies provided additional funding for unemployment relief.[20]

Although the Communist Party gained influence in black Chicago after the conflict, the main focus of attention was the Unemployed Council.[21] Branches of the councils may have been under the overall supervision of the Communist Party, but operations at the local level in black Chicago were carried out by an eclectic group, which included Republicans, Democrats, black fraternal orders, and some ex-members of the all black, Eighth Infantry Regiment.[22] As Paul Young has argued, the diverse background of black activists within the councils located in black neighborhoods "prevented the Party from exerting hegemony over Council branches." Party leadership even criticized the Chicago district for "following rather than leading" mass demonstrations in the black community.[23] The party's success with black Chicago was directly related to its ability to build upon traditions and experiences germane to African Americans in Chicago.

Communist organizers may have received their best education on how to approach the Chicago black community by visiting Washington Park, located on the edge of black Chicago. Washington Park established a public, open-air "forum," a favorite political spot for anyone who wanted to speak—black radicals, interracial activists, Zionists, and others. Longtime Chicago resident Dempsey J. Travis describes Washington Park as a place where someone could get "a liberal education . . . by simply moving from one bench speaker to another."[24] Reverend Austin, who spoke several times in Washington Park, exemplifies the several points on the political compass that were interacting to propose new directions for black Chicago during the early thirties.

The Depression presented the Chicago branch of the NAACP with an opportunity to expand its constituency. Like the Communists, the NAACP had few members in the twenties. During the summer of 1930, the Chicago NAACP, under the direction of A. Clement MacNeal, began participating with the *Chicago Whip* in a "Don't Buy Where You Can't Work" campaign. MacNeal, who was also managing editor of the *Chicago Whip*, had hoped to win support for the "Don't Buy" campaign from middle- and working-class black Chicagoans. What support the NAACP won did not translate into increasing memberships, but the campaign signaled a shift in leadership within the branch into the hands of a group that wanted to pursue a more activist role for the local association.[25]

The boycott targeted a Woolworth's Five and Ten on the South Side because it was the only major national chain in Chicago that did not employ black clerks in stores located in black neighborhoods. MacNeal chose a confrontational tactic—a boycott with picketing, propaganda, and public meetings—rather than a strategy based on conciliation, and acted without the support of the national board of the NAACP as well as many branch members.[26] What is not clear is why the "Don't Buy Where You Can't Work" campaign did not win more converts. Although the boycott opened up a few hundred white-collar jobs, an achievement in the midst of the Depression, some members of the middle class kept their distance, fearing that the tactics might produce a back-lash in job losses. Others, like Harold Kingsley, probably saw the boycott taking attention away from organizing around the interests of black factory workers, which was the issue that kept the Communists from supporting the campaign.[27] As a Communist journalist wrote in the *Crisis*, "what has this to do with the hundreds of thousands of Negro workers in the coal, iron, steel, oil, automobile and packing industries, in the basic industries of America?"[28]

Although the alliances formed by the BSCP network against Judge Parker, of the Unemployed Council against evictions, and of the *Whip*-NAACP leaders in the "Don't Buy Where You Can't Work" campaign often did not overlap in the early thirties, all of these groups endorsed confrontation, relied on the power of collective action, and organized around issues of importance to black workers.[29] Finally, these activities were led by people interested in using aggressive tactics to make claims for rights black Americans were entitled to, rights that had framed the agenda of the Brotherhood labor conferences during the 1920s and early 1930s.

Entangling Alliances: New-Crowd Citizens in Action

The South Parkway Branch of the Chicago YWCA placed the interests of black female industrial workers high on its agenda in the early 1930s. Thelma McWorter, who had just received her masters degree from Case Western Reserve, was hired in 1931 as South Parkway's industrial secretary, a position that included community outreach and education. McWorter, born on July 29, 1907, in Hadley Township, Illinois, came from a family with a long history of protest. Her great-grandfather, Free Frank McWorter, had purchased his freedom, along with that of sixteen family members, from slavery between 1817 and 1854. Free Frank and his wife, Lucy, settled in Illinois in 1831.

Two years after arriving in Chicago, Thelma McWorter married Allen James Kirkpatrick, a postal employee whose brother worked as a Pullman porter during the 1930s and was a member of the BSCP. After the death of Kirkpatrick in 1948, she married William McKinley Wheaton, a Pullman porter and a member of the BSCP.[30] Wheaton, recalling life in the early thirties in Chicago, considered her job—teaching and training female workers about labor laws, social problems, housing, and coping on the job—a plumb for a young, highly educated person.

Wheaton worked with both industrial and domestic-service workers. "Most of these women were full-time industrial workers who were very glad to have their jobs," she recalled. "Their normal work day was ten hours." Because money was scarce, they "loved overtime; they needed the job; they desired any work they could get." Wheaton's boss, Arnetta Dieckmann, the metropolitan industrial secretary of the Chicago YWCA, encouraged a progressive approach to social and economic issues. In that context, Wheaton broadly interpreted her responsibility as teacher and mentor. Although she pointed out that the Y's approach did not advocate joining any particular union, it did teach "the value of the unions. How you get in and participate." Wheaton did not want workers joining unions and shying away from participation because the women did not know the procedure for negotiating and conducting business meetings. Wheaton's message, coming from a member of the educated elite who also promoted labor unions, probably carried weight. But the most important thing Wheaton recalled trying to teach the industrial workers was self-confidence. "We tried to teach the women to learn to speak up" for themselves.[31]

Very few household and industrial workers, according to Wheaton, "even knew they had rights." In order to encourage a fresh look at their role as both citizens and workers, she not only taught about labor laws but put laws and rights into historical context by introducing the women to labor history, the history of women workers, and problems women workers faced in various occupations. The Chicago YWCA supplemented its labor education program by selecting a few potential leaders each year and sending them to Bryn Mawr's Summer School in Pennsylvania. A larger group attended the University of Wisconsin School for Workers. She recalled that as a community organizer she was aware of the significance of her work, for trade unions were making "no effort to get the women to join."[32]

The women Wheaton worked with were not especially adverse to the idea of unions, but they also had not "realized that there were benefits in belonging." Some of the women were workers in the garment factory jobs at the Sopkins apron and dress plants on the South Side. Once they understood the benefits unions offered in terms of increased control and security over jobs for black workers, the next hurdle was overcoming the fear most of her students felt over losing their jobs. To allay that fear, the other component of her curriculum emphasized rights and entitlements, which was backed by building trust among the group and teaching the importance of collective action. The process of winning converts and overcoming fear moved forward after a few joined unions. Those who were union members "were so energetic and so understanding of the value of the union, that they were able to persuade others to join."[33]

Wheaton worked closely with the BSCP, which also promoted organization among black female domestic and industrial workers. The efforts of the two organizations fused in 1932 when Irene McCoy Gaines, secretary of the BSCP Citizens' Committee, brought Wheaton into her community-wide cooperative effort to advance the interests of black workers. At the time, Gaines also included Helena Wilson, president of the Colored Women's Economic Council, in her alliance. Activists from the BSCP Citizens' Committee as well as Randolph and Webster discussed problems black labor faced in a discriminatory economic marketplace. From that base, the Wheaton and Citizens' Committee networks branched out further into the community. Meetings were held and neighborhoods canvassed as more women were drawn into the process of educating black Chicago about the utility of labor organization—for both men and women—as a tool to advance civil rights. Strategy sessions were often held at BSCP headquarters in Chicago.[34] Wheaton expanded her network to include the Women's Economic Council of the BSCP between 1933 and 1935. She lectured on Saturdays and Sundays to the Women's Council about labor laws and women's rights as workers. She recalled that the wives of BSCP members were "very conscious" of the meaning of unions.[35]

Participation in labor schools was another avenue for expanding a prolabor perspective. Wheaton's industrial committee raised money to cover expenses for students selected for labor schools. To be eligible, one had to have at least three years of wage-earning experience in factory work, shopwork, or household work, and have completed at least the eighth grade. Despite the setback in fund raising caused by the Depression, South Parkway continued to send black women to Bryn Mawr and Wisconsin by intensifying its own efforts and pooling resources with other organizations interested in training future female labor organizers.[36] The South Parkway YWCA relied upon assistance from networks established by the BSCP's Citizens' Committee when it held benefits to raise money for those attending labor schools. The relationship was mutually beneficial, for by helping Wheaton with interested volunteers, the BSCP's networks were able to act upon their interest in promoting black women in the role of labor organizer. Key members of the local board of Wheaton's industrial committee—Mrs. Estelle Webster McNeal, sister of Milton P. Webster; the wife of Charles W. Burton, president of the BSCP Citizens' Committee; and Mrs. Milton Webster—illustrate the collaboration that developed.[37]

In addition to Bryn Mawr and Wisconsin, South Parkway YWCA sent students to Camp Grey, located in Saugatuck, deep in the woods of northern Michigan. The camp was sponsored by the Regional Industrial Conference of the YWCA and drew the largest participant group from South Parkway. Students, between twenty and thirty-five years of age, were introduced to other workers from the South Side as well as other parts of the city, while taking classes from faculty who often had taught at other labor schools throughout the country. Camp Grey had teachers from Brookwood Labor College in New York and the Worker's Education Project in Atlanta. For Thelma Wheaton, also a lecturer at Camp Grey, the summer school offered an opportunity to plan strategies with other activists from the Chicago area.[38]

Labor schools, located on college campuses or country farms, were designed to remove workers from the responsibilities and distractions of jobs and families for several weeks. Labor educators hoped that women would explore ideas in history, politics, labor, and economics, speak their minds freely, and develop the confidence to go back to their neighborhoods and disseminate what they had learned.[39] Wheaton gave one of the YWCA's scholarships to Katheryn Williams, who attended Bryn Mawr Summer School in 1936. After studying at the labor college, Williams returned to Chicago and became an organizer for the Upholsterers International Union of the AFL. Williams recalled, in 1937, the importance of building trust when organizing black workers. When she approached workers on the street with pamphlets, they might avoid her. But "they will talk," she said, "in their homes." Indeed, "most of our work has been done in the homes. It slows the progress but is quite effective."[40] Although the process was slow, overlapping educational networks helped spread the idea of workers' rights.

Yet Wheaton understood well that, as the educator of both industrial and domestic workers, not all workers' issues and interests were the same. Separate classes for household workers addressed the special context of their experience as domestic workers. Neva Ryan, a schoolteacher, struggled in 1932 to establish a Domestic Workers Union. Although it took several years to establish the organization, the educational work carried out by Ryan and Wheaton introduced domestic workers to their rights as Americans; often students taught by Wheaton became members of Ryan's union.[41]

The life of Thyra J. Edwards, a social worker, community organizer, and journalist, who directed the Lake County Children's home at Gary, Indiana, during the 1920s, was transformed through her alliance with the Brotherhood and other new-crowd networks in the Chicago area in the thirties. In 1931 Edwards's activities as a social worker with the Abraham Lincoln Center, an educational community organization under the auspices of the Illinois Emergency Relief Commission, first brought her in contact with Wheaton and the BSCP's Citizens' Committee.[42] In 1932 Edwards entered Brookwood Labor College at Katonah, New York, where she studied until early in 1933. From there, she spent several months in the mining district of southern Illinois, studying conditions among black and white miners.[43] When she returned to the South Side, BSCP Citizens' Committee officials, Irene Gaines and Charles Burton, honored her at a gathering that included Sophia Boaz Pitts, an attorney and a member of the industrial committee of South Parkway YWCA and A. L. Foster, executive secretary of the Chicago Urban League.[44]

The Brotherhood recommended Thyra Edwards for a fellowship in 1933, which allowed her to attend a folk school in Elsinore, Denmark, where she studied the cooperative movement of Scandinavia. From there she spent several months traveling to the Soviet Union to study the Communist approach to social welfare policies.[45] Edwards developed her talent as a journalist during this period, writing articles and essays on the economic and social status of black Americans, which appeared in the *Crisis*, *Opportunity*, the *Chicago Defender*, and the *Daily Worker* and were distributed widely through the Associated Negro Press. By the time she arrived back in the United States, she had developed a reputation as a labor activist that went far beyond Chicago.[46]

A constant theme in her writings was the search for black manhood. Being a black person was a "dual challenge," Edwards argued. "One must first struggle to recognize one's status as one of the genus man. And secondly come the peculiarities of one's status as a particular race, that is as a Negro." Because, as she asserted, there was a "trend" to "accentuate the Negro as a particular species rather than one of the human race," the special challenge to black Americans was "the task of recognizing his own status as that of man."[47] Through her travel abroad, Edwards broadened her understanding of black manhood as well as the place of black people in world affairs. As she wrote a colleague from Europe, "To the powerful white nations . . . we blacks are only so much machine power for crude labor. . . . To the 'liberal' philanthropists of these groups we are objects of charity—tolerantly conceded the right to exist. No where in the world are we recognized as one of the species of man kind. This we must win with our own dark hands."[48]

Edwards remained active as a community organizer and popular lecturer for the Brotherhood on issues of labor and manhood rights throughout the thirties.[49] In the summer of 1933, she helped form the Abraham Lincoln Center Interracial Group to address, through collective action, problems "dealing with discrimination in housing, restaurants and attempted discrimination in bathing beaches." She organized a diverse group of activists that included Claude Lightfoot and Mary Dalton of the League for Struggle for Negro Rights, an organization for young Communists; BSCP Citizens' Committee member Lulu E. Lawson; and A. L. Foster of the Chicago Urban League. Foster spoke about discrimination at the beaches on Lake Michigan at the first meeting. Even the Chicago branch of the NAACP cooperated with Edwards, reflecting the broad-based coalitions that were emerging.[50]

The NAACP at a Crossroads

The NAACP, both locally and nationally, stood at a crossroads in the early thirties, largely a result of the considerable deficit in contributions from branch memberships—considered the lifeline of the association and its chief source of funding—during the Depression.[51] Roy Wilkins, assistant secretary of the NAACP, thought it was "perfectly obvious that the branches we have now are not reaching all the people who could be interested in the Association."[52] That criticism applied to the Chicago branch when it ignored the interest demonstrated in the Scottsboro case. The Scottsboro Committee of Chicago, formed in 1931 under Communist tutelage, brought to the local level a national debate between the CP and the NAACP over strategies for defending nine black men accused of raping two white women in Scottsboro, Alabama.[53] As the Scottsboro case caught the nation's attention, the Communist-led International Labor Defense (ILD)—taking the battle against Jim Crow justice into the court of public opinion—struck a chord with a population the NAACP had not been able to reach. The Communists' militant approach raised questions about appropriate strategies for challenging racial inequities in a justice system embedded in a racist social context. It did so at a point when the NAACP was particularly vulnerable to sagging membership contributions.[54]

Daisy Lampkin, regional field secretary for the NAACP between 1933 and 1939, understood the threat Scottsboro posed. She confided to Walter White, the association's executive secretary, that "the NAACP is being openly criticized by its own members, some frankly saying that the NAACP is less militant" than it used to be. Moreover, friends of the NAACP asked her whether she thought "the NAACP has outlived its usefulness and that the time has come for it to give away to another organization with a more militant program." Her advice in 1933 was to initiate a more aggressive program in order to meet the "onslaught of the Communists."[55]

Locally, the *Defender* supported legal assistance from the Communists and called for a united front to "bring these young men out of a sentence to die." The glory, warned Abbott, was not in "who is closest to the power . . . or even what organization is proper to raise funds or conduct an appeal to the country," but in rescuing "nine young men caught and undone by the clutch of circumstances."[56] When the ILD held a meeting to elicit support for the Scottsboro case, the *Defender* reported that 182 organizations, including eighteen churches, pledged support.[57] How many of those organizations were anchored in the black community was not clear, but the Chicago branch of the NAACP kept its distance, initially, from the more radical ILD. When Dean William Pickens, field secretary of the NAACP, spoke in Chicago a month later to raise money for the convicted youths, he charged the ILD with "intimidating methods" that put "the entire state of Alabama, the governor, the judge in the case and in fact both the jury and the prosecuting attorneys on the defensive." Agitators, reported to be ILD members, responded by disrupting the meeting for over thirty minutes. The NAACP program was able to continue only after the local branch called the Chicago police to arrest the ILD members.[58]

When the Chicago branch attempted to broaden its agenda to include a boycott against Sears Roebuck in June 1933, NAACP headquarters declared the Chicago branch a problem. The "problem" was its proposed nationwide boycott against Sears Roebuck, orchestrated by A. C. MacNeal, the new branch president. MacNeal attempted his boycott at the same time Walter White made a personal appeal to William Rosenwald, son of Julius Rosenwald, who founded Sears, for a special contribution to the NAACP.[59]

The boycott was aimed at Sears for discriminating against "prominent women" from Chicago's black neighborhoods when they tried to buy shoes and clothing from the department store. The local NAACP directed its grievances to Lessing J. Rosenwald, brother of William Rosenwald and chairman of the board of Sears Roebuck, whose stock initially funded the Rosenwald Fund, a major contributor to projects benefiting black Americans.[60] MacNeal questioned whether Sears Roebuck subscribed to Jim Crow policies. Sears denied discriminating in a letter to MacNeal that carried no signature. In late June, William Rosenwald informed White that the Chicago branch had sent his brother a letter which was "couched in so unpleasant a tone that he did not think it worth the trouble of attempting to answer it." Moreover, "your Chicago branch does not have a very good reputation . . . that they are not personally know [sic] by some citizens in Chicago who take a leading interest in negro work. Upon hearing of this situation, I felt certain you would want this called to your attention, as you doubtless wish to uphold the reputation of your Organization."[61] To Rosenwald, MacNeal had violated a code prescribing the behavior expected of black citizens when negotiating with liberal patrons for reforms.

Walter White told MacNeal to curtail all protest activity against Sears Roebuck. Rosenwald, he explained, "has already taken up, as he promised, the matter of the charges of discrimination in the Sears Roebuck store at Chicago." Roy Wilkins informed MacNeal that the NAACP and Rosenwald had a "gentleman's agreement" to correct the misunderstanding. In fact, Rosenwald put the matter in the hands of someone who was "highest in authority," someone, it turned out, who was unable to attend to the matter immediately because he was traveling; there would be a slight delay until "he will be in a position to handle the matter."[62]

Before White's gag order arrived, however, the Chicago branch released a story to the *Chicago Defender*, outlining plans for a nationwide protest and boycott against Sears.[63] MacNeal reluctantly canceled the Sears protest, but not before telling White he hoped the $2,500 William Rosenwald gave each year to the association was not influencing his policy directives.[64] By then matters had escalated, for the National Association of Colored Women (NACW) also condemned Sears Roebuck for its discriminatory policy.[65] MacNeal begged White and Wilkins to allow Chicago to continue publicizing the Sears Case, arguing that the branch's "reputation" was at stake if it did not follow through and instead stayed "in the back ground while other organizations push the fight."[66] To complicate matters, Daisy Lampkin added to the tension between the NAACP branch and the national office when she failed to visit the Chicago branch while attending the NACW convention. MacNeal felt slighted by Lampkin and complained to White about her behavior. Lampkin was running for vice president of the NACW, which strongly endorsed the resolution against Sears and urged "wide spread publicity on the matter."[67] Was Lampkin trying to disassociate herself from the NAACP's compromising stance toward Rosenwald in the Sears case? That seems likely; she was seeking the vice presidency of an organization that not only was among the first national organizations to support the BSCP in the 1920s but had gone on record against the NAACP's passive approach to reform. Lampkin defended her behavior to White by reminding him that it was because of her influence in the "largest organization of colored women in America" that she was important to the staff of the association. The public was well aware, she said, of her "many other interests in addition to the NAACP." Those interests "account to a very large degree for the success I have in getting people to work with me in campaigns for the NAACP."[68]

The agenda of the national NAACP lagged behind other protest networks in Chicago as well. While the NAACP met for its 24th Annual Convention in Chicago during the summer of 1933, 1,500 female employees, many of them African Americans, of B. Sopkins and Sons Co., manufacturers of aprons and house dresses, struck the company in protest over low wages and long hours. By the time the association convened for its convention on June 29, the strike had escalated as police beat what the *Chicago Defender* called "wage-starved girls." That headline appeared while the NAACP was still in session, yet the association maintained its distance from the conflict. Meanwhile, several South Side community leaders, including Congressman Oscar DePriest, Junius Austin of the BSCP Citizens' Committee and the Pilgrim Baptist Church, Alderman William L. Dawson, and Mrs. Elizabeth Lindsay Davis of the Illinois Federation of Colored Women's Clubs, investigated police brutality and offered assistance to strikers. Although Sopkins complained of Communist influence in turning the "girls'" heads toward unionism, middle-class African Americans who came to help thought the workers were acting out of their own interests. One of the demands was "equal pay for equal work," to correct discrimination in pay for black and white workers.[69] "These girls are entitled to organize and peacefully picket the Sopkins plant," the *Chicago Defender* argued, connecting that right to constitutional guarantees, much like the Brotherhood had done at its labor conferences.[70] Yet another supporter of the strike was Arnetta Dieckmann of the Chicago YWCA. She knew that more than communism had influenced the walkout, for many of the black women had learned about unionism from Wheaton through the South Parkway Y, where black garment workers were taught "to speak up."[71]

Strikers at Sopkins did just that. They rejected an agreement worked out by Congressman DePriest and Alderman Dawson, demanded better terms, and the addition of James W. Ford, a black Communist, at the negotiating table. Sopkins had tried to lock Ford out of the labor discussions, but the strikers valued his advice and wanted his input to resolve the labor conflict.[72] The Needle Trades Industrial Union, a Communist Party union, was hoping to gain recognition as the bargaining agent for the garment workers. The Communists influenced the outcome of the 1933 Sopkins strike by helping the women get organized, but the Needle Trades Industrial Union was not recognized and the party cadre was disappointed when very few women joined the party. One Communist organizer noted that although black garment workers were ready for a strike and a union, the local Communist Party structure was "not built sufficiently" to direct the strike and "consolidate organizationally in the shops" in order to build the party. Organizing was carried on, according to a scholar writing at the time, "entirely by word of mouth under the leadership of a woman organizer who understood factory conditions and who had been trained in a workers' school." While it is likely, although not clear, that the organizer was a Communist Party member, it is questionable whether the CP could have made inroads with the garment workers had Thelma Wheaton not paved the way by educating female industrial workers about their rights. The strike succeeded for garment workers when the grievances of 1,500 women were recognized with wage rate increases of 17 percent, a provision for equal pay for equal work, and no discrimination against black workers.[73]

Although the number of recruits to the Communist Party was small, party members increasingly worked alongside new-crowd leaders in protest networks. As activities of protest networks began to overlap, new leaders emerged and new strategies were employed to protest racial inequities. New-crowd activists supported militant action against prime targets, such as landlords and employers. But they sought inclusion in the American economic system in contrast to the Communists. Class issues were important within new-crowd networks, but race was at the core of the agenda connecting the new alliances. When the black elite worked under the umbrella of the Communist Party, there was, according to St. Clair Drake, a contemporary observer, "no great opprobrium . . . in Chicago . . . attached to being a Communist, and both the party and individual Communists were tolerated and cooperated with *on specific* issues of benefit to Negroes."[74] When issues of race were put in the foreground, Communists enjoyed their greatest success among African Americans, as they did with the case of the Scottsboro boys and Unemployed Councils.

Forging Alliances:
New-Crowd Networks with Communists

The BSCP continued focusing on manhood rights and citizenship while questioning the agenda and strategies of traditional leaders who eschewed workers' rights. During the summer of 1933, Milton Webster brought Congressman Fiorello H. La Guardia to Chicago to host a five-day labor conference. La Guardia condemned the Pullman Company because it refused to recognize the "rights of labor in the history of America." The Brotherhood's struggle, he suggested, was a pioneering effort in breaking the company union and resurrecting the "rights of self-organization," despite the fact that Pullman "persistently refused to recognize the rights of its Pullman porters and maids to organize a union of their own."[75]

Within a month the *Chicago Defender* reinforced the message of the BSCP labor conference by raising the issue of manhood rights and citizenship in response to an American Legion convention that brought over 30,000 to Chicago. The tone of its front-page editorial reveals something of the mood that permeated black Chicago. "On every tongue will be heard the word 'comrade,' and in every eye will be that gleam of happy welcome and recognition of a brother." But, the *Defender* warned, "with all this heartiness . . . will come a bitterness and a hatred more vicious than ever existed during the war." For "although black men were good enough to risk their lives in the common cause against the enemy, they are today more abused and more insulted than they ever were before the war. The very Germans we fought, many of whom have not bothered to take out citizenship papers, have more privileges in our country than we do."[76]

A series of "workers' mass meetings" in 1934, under the auspices of the Lincoln Memorial Congregational Church and the American Consolidated Trade Council, a Communist-affiliated organization, encouraged the process of forging new-crowd alliances. Communist Party sympathizers John T. Gray and E. L. Doty, at the initial meeting that united leaders from diverse groups around the issue of job discrimination, told the gathering that they wanted to organize the entire community to put "our people to work on all jobs, CWA, PWA, etc. or any public or private work." Other activists within this alliance included members of the BSCP Citizens' Committee, Junius Austin, and A. L. Foster, president of the Chicago Urban League.[77]

As new-crowd networks pooled resources, often combining efforts with the Communists, the *Chicago Defender* pointed out that it was "injustice, not Reds, stirring up workers." For "black men, like all other men, will find interest in any organization, whether it be red or blue, that promises them better opportunities for life and livelihood for themselves and [their] dependents." The problem, declared the *Defender* was that while the black man "believes in the American Constitution, . . . the American Constitution does not believe in the black man."[78]

It was this spirit that captured the attention of large segments of black America in 1934 over the case of Angelo Herndon, a black worker arrested in Atlanta for exercising his right of free speech. In 1932, Herndon was found guilty of insurrection for leading a biracial demonstration and passing "subversive" literature. The Communist Party defended Herndon, reinforcing its image as a champion of civil rights for black Americans, which it earned in the Scottsboro case.[79] The Chicago BSCP raised funds for Herndon's defense and discussed the case in public meetings in Chicago. "Herndon deserves the unstinted, definite, and aggressive moral and financial support of every Negro with any pride of race, regardless of his political philosophy," Randolph declared.[80]

Perhaps the most prominent and vocal supporter of Herndon in Chicago was Reverend Austin of the BSCP Citizens' Committee. In 1933 Austin set out to awaken the clergy of Chicago "to meet the demands of a new day." He called it a fight for "civic righteousness," supporting men and measures that "promote equal opportunity." It was an attempt to link the church to the issues that concern black people in Chicago "lost in the maelstrom of our modern problems, economic, political, social as well as religious."[81] In a sermon during that

summer, Austin discussed the slavery of second-class status and the need to
fight for "our New Emancipation."[82]

In 1934 Austin invited Herndon, on a national tour after his release from a
Georgia prison, to speak in Pilgrim Baptist Church, despite orders he received,
presumably from community leaders, "not to allow the International Labor
Defense to use his church for the Herndon meeting." Over 3,000 people
crowded into the church, filling every available seat and standing in the aisles
and on the platform by the pulpit listening as Herndon talked of his two years
in prison. But while the audience cheered Herndon, they "went wild" when
Austin declared, "any man who does not want freedom is either a fool or an
idiot, and if to want freedom is to be a Communist, then I am a Communist,
and will be till I die." From all I have learned, he added, communism "means
simply the brotherhood of man and as far as I can see Jesus Christ was the
greatest Communist of them all." Then he announced that his church would
always be open to "any group that stood for the universal brotherhood of man."
The *Defender* reported that deafening applause followed Austin's speech. "For
fully five minutes the crowd stood and cheered." The *Defender*'s front page
carried a banner headline exclaiming, " 'I'm a Communist,' Shouts Rev. Austin
As Herndon Tells of Prison Horrors."[83]

Austin's activism connected the BSCP Citizens' Committee network directly
with the Communists, reflecting the fusion of interests that united middle-class
groups with Communists by 1935. Austin used his church to hold meetings for
the BSCP Citizens' Committee, bringing together new-crowd networks, and his
position as a minister to distill Communist rhetoric for middle-class congregations, forging a link in the development of a new relationship between the black
community and Communists. The possibility for such fusion reflects, in part, a
new approach to the "Negro Question" within the Communist Party. The
activism of black radicals—inside and outside the party—forced the CP to place
black interests higher on its agenda if it wanted to be heard within the black
community. By the time of the Popular Front, roughly between 1935 and 1939,
the party also changed its position toward the NAACP and the black bourgeois,
making collaboration with the party easier.[84] Both the BSCP and the Communists were perceived by the mid-thirties as organizations emphasizing the importance of black independence from white control. When the Brotherhood
addressed the issue, it challenged leaders who approached white benefactors
with a posture of deference. Thelma Wheaton did not think it was strange that
the Communist Party was able to win the confidence of many black Americans
during the 1930s. She recalled many years later that "I never knew a Communist
who was not also a Christian. I'll bet over a third of my church was Commu-

nist." While that figure may be high, Wheaton claims it was the perception that Communists were independent of control by the dominant white culture that was the key issue.[85]

In 1935, at both the national and local level, the direction of black protest politics was not clear. The reputation of the national NAACP was tarnished by its timidity, raising probing questions about its approach and entire modus operandi. At the local level, the power base of old-guard Republican politicians was toppled when the Democrats finally seized control between 1932 and 1936. Leaders from the NAACP and Chicago Urban League worked with many of the new networks, helping chart a course not endorsed by conventional tactics and politics. Networks formed by the South Parkway YWCA and the BSCP focused on mobilizing the community around a labor-oriented, civil rights agenda. Many of the new-crowd alliances concentrated on organizing black Americans under the umbrella of the National Negro Congress, an organization formed in 1935 by Randolph and other new-crowd leaders to address the interests of the black working class.

The leaders emerging from new-crowd networks may have been in the vanguard, but a shift in power relations was far from complete. The tactics and agenda of new-crowd networks challenged traditional institutions and old-guard leaders to be more accountable to the interests of the working class. As the South Side new-crowd networks began organizing throughout the summer and fall of 1935 for the forthcoming National Negro Congress convention scheduled for February 1936, a new organization, the Chicago Council of Negro Organizations (CCNO), formed. Members of both the Chicago branch of the NAACP and the Wabash Avenue YMCA were part of the small group of men and women responsible for development of the CCNO, whose agenda did not address inequities in the economic arena.[86] The Communist Party was not part of the CCNO, nor was the Brotherhood of Sleeping Car Porters. At this stage the CCNO did not represent so much a rival organization as proof of the many positions represented in the political life of black Chicago at the end of 1935. As the next chapter suggests, the growing influence of the new-crowd networks in Chicago helped shape not only local protest politics, but contributed as well to reconfigure the range and direction of national protest politics.

New-Crowd Networks and the Course
of Protest Politics, 1935–1940

> True liberation can be acquired and maintained only when the
> Negro people possess power; and power is product and flower of
> organization—organization of the masses, the masses in the mills and
> mines, on the farms, in the factories, in churches, in fraternal
> organizations, in homes, colleges, women's clubs, student groups,
> trade unions, tenants' leagues, in cooperative guilds, political
> organization and civil rights association.
> A. PHILIP RANDOLPH, Second National Negro Congress,
> Philadelphia, 1937

On July 29, 1935, A. Philip Randolph, Milton Webster, and six other organizers walked into the Pullman Company headquarters on Adams Street in downtown Chicago to negotiate a contract.[1] When management sat down to discuss porters' wages and working conditions, they were under duress from the National Mediation Board, which had recently supervised a secret ballot to determine the bargaining agent preferred by porters and maids. Amendments to the 1934 Railway Labor Act forced the issue of representation, which for ten years the Pullman Company had ignored. The Railway Labor Act and the generally favorable climate of the New Deal brought porters back into the union. By 1935 membership was up to 4,165.[2] By the fall more success came when the American Federation of Labor presented the Brotherhood with the first international charter awarded to a union of black workers.[3] The company officially recognized the BSCP on August 25, 1937, and signed a contract that included a reduction in the work month from 400 to 240 hours and an annual wage package that increased porters' salaries by a total of $1.25 million. Porters and maids rejoiced, and Brotherhood memberships increased to 6,581 by 1938. The Brotherhood's victory marked the first time representatives from a major American corporation had negotiated a contract with a union of black workers.[4] The *Chicago Defender* called the contract "the largest single financial transaction any group of the Race has ever negotiated." It also pointed out that the Pullman Company had "never before capitulated to a group of its workers in a bona fide trade union—for the Pullman conductors secured their union during the World War when there was no opposition while railroads were under government control." Finally, they won "respect" for all African Americans because they succeeded without "begging"; by negotiating as "upstanding fighters for justice, the porters have pointed the way." In that respect, concluded the *Defender*, "race men have broken with a long established trait."[5] Winning a contract from the Pullman Company secured a place for Randolph and the union porters and maids in labor history.

But the Brotherhood also provided important preconditions for widespread unionization of black workers, which was its larger significance. The Brotherhood's manhood rights campaign, disseminated through its network of activists in labor conferences, the Citizens' Committee, clubwomen's networks, the YWCA, and other groups, prepared the way for the rise of trade unionism and a prolabor point of view within the black community. When the Congress of Industrial Organizations (CIO) began organizing black workers in mass-production industries in 1936, organizers relied on new-crowd networks formed during the previous decade to open doors in the black community. The new-crowd networks that overlapped with efforts of the BSCP's cadre of activists were not the only groups contributing to a new outlook toward labor, but the Brotherhood's struggle for manhood rights, aimed at gaining the confidence of middle-class leaders as well as workers, planted its labor rhetoric firmly in the soil of rights denied African Americans as citizens. Its appeal was grounded in the role it played as a social movement. Through the collective organization of labor, African Americans would gain greater control over the direction of their lives, for the process of labor organizing would be a tutorial for acquiring skills necessary to attain self-reliance and independence even as participants became more integrated within American society. Traditional labor unions, which in 1925 were judged on an individual basis—sometimes favorably, often not favorably—were not generally thought of as institutions for breaking down barriers to black inclusion into American society.[6] Yet, by the mid-thirties, unions were increasingly perceived as vehicles for the advancement of African Americans. The Brotherhood's appeal was grounded in the role it played as a social movement.

Pullman Company welfare workers or spies noted as much in several reports that commented on widespread influence of BSCP activities within Chicago's black neighborhoods.[7] During the later half of the thirties, the Brotherhood expanded its social agenda greatly as local actions of the BSCP Citizens' Com-

mittee and other new-crowd networks were increasingly linked to protest politics at the national level. Brotherhood activists were part of social, political, and
economic challenges hurled against the racial status quo through new organizations like the National Negro Congress (NNC), which threatened, for a time, the
prominence of the NAACP within the black community.

Throughout America, the economic upheaval of the Great Depression re-
strained the ability of institutions and organizations to serve their intended
memberships. While the NAACP was no exception, it suffered a double challenge during this period because it was under fire at the national and local levels
for dragging its feet over issues related to black workers. Despite the interest
demonstrated by many black Americans toward unions and economic issues,
the NAACP, as late as 1937, issued conflicting statements about the value of new
industrial unions and continued, according to Roy Wilkins, assistant secretary
of the NAACP, "refusing to adopt any suggestion for mass appeal with the single
exception of the anti-lynching buttons."[8] The NAACP relied largely on methods
and tools condoned by the dominant culture for making its protests. The
NAACP, for example, committed its resources to making appeals in courts on a
case-by-case basis and agitated by compiling facts and deluging government
officials with information. Collective organization within the larger black community of workers was not part of the gradual, legal approach that had been its
hallmark since 1909. Its appeal, as pointed out by scholars August Meier and
John Bracey Jr., was basically a moral one, "to reach the conscience of America."[9] The moderate approach of the old guard, represented by leaders who
wanted to maintain a somber, reformist stance when negotiating with the
dominant white culture, contrasted sharply with that of the more militant new
crowd: one relied on individual appeals or legal redress of individuals, the other
on collective demands; one deferred to the expectations of white allies and
patrons, whereas the other asserted rights by making direct demands. Nevertheless, it is important to remember that this was a period of both turmoil,
experimentation, and transition. There were NAACP staff members in both
"camps." But although some members of the NAACP did lobby for strategies
that placed the economic interests of the black majority higher on the agenda
and cultivated relationships intended to broaden the membership base, such
efforts were often overshadowed by increasing dependency on philanthropic
patrons.

New-crowd activists and leaders did not shun alliances with white people.
Many, including Randolph, often depended through the years on white allies
for the entre they offered into corridors of power. What new-crowd activists did

condemn was restricting tactics and strategies to the ground rules established by the dominant white culture when negotiating for equal access or greater economic opportunity. The gradual legal approach of the NAACP was criticized not because it was wrong but because it was not enough. From the perspective of the Brotherhood, the rub lay with petitioning the dominant society for rights won decades ago at the end of the Civil War. At issue was the willingness of the activists to abandon the etiquette of the politics of civility. In addition to legal briefs, it was time to apply direct pressure using the power of mass collective action, making demands to change the racial status quo.

Frustration with the gradual process of negotiation and the search for new strategies to address economic interests of the black working class was responsible, in part, for the formation of the NNC in 1935. Randolph, who served as president between 1936 and April 1940, was only one of several prominent leaders to shape the NNC's challenge to the limited reform agenda of the NAACP. Randolph used the BSCP local network in Chicago and elsewhere to mobilize African Americans in the NNC. Charles Burton, president of the BSCP's Citizens' Committee in Chicago, fused BSCP and NNC networks when he became head of the local branch of the NNC as well as a member of the national executive council of the NNC. Similarly, Thyra Edwards, organizer for both the International Ladies Garment Workers' Union (ILGWU) and the BSCP, was a member of the national executive council of the NNC.[10] All were aware that the foundation they had helped lay in Chicago required a broader infrastructure in order to carry the message of labor organization deeper into the community.

Two of the more prominent leaders of the thirties—Randolph and Walter White, executive secretary of the NAACP—exemplify the divide between new crowd and old guard. In the early thirties, they sometimes worked together as they did while protesting the nomination of Judge John Parker to the U.S. Supreme Court in 1930 and gathering evidence of discrimination against black workers for the June 1935 hearings of the AFL's Committee of Five on Negro Discrimination. Although the two men maintained a cordial relationship, Randolph and White moved in different directions: Randolph focused on mobilizing the masses to take charge and demand rights, whereas White concentrated his efforts on changing the perceptions and policies of the status quo. Their goals were similar: to attain a more secure place for African Americans. Nevertheless, by 1941 Walter White borrowed tactics used by the new crowd when he joined the United Auto Workers' call for collective action and actively supported striking workers at Ford's River Rouge Plant near Detroit. What led an old-guard leader like Walter White to change tactics?[11] By looking at interactions between the NAACP and the NNC at the national and local levels, we can access how challenges to the NAACP's agenda reshaped the direction of black politics nationally.

The Challenge from Within

"What is Wrong with the NAACP," asked W. E. B. Du Bois, member of the board of directors and editor of the *Crisis*, in a speech before the association's 1932 annual conference. His answer suggested the problem stemmed from a "program of negation" and the defensive posture and tactics used by the association. Rather than waiting for cases of discrimination, on a case-by-case basis, Du Bois urged the association to go on the offensive with a larger "positive program" for black advancement, using "a frontal attack on race prejudice."[12] In addition, a minority within the organization questioned the NAACP's priorities and tried to get the old guard to wean itself of its dependency on white patronage, calling for a new emphasis to address the primary problems facing black Americans—bread-and-butter issues. Both at the Amenia Conference in 1933 and in 1934–35 during discussions over the so-called Harris Report, they charged that the NAACP ignored issues central to the lives of the "masses."[13]

The 1933 Amenia Conference brought together thirty-three black intellectuals, men and women "who have been out of college only a few years," to make suggestions to the board of the NAACP about "how . . . the program (should) be changed or enlarged or shifted . . . toward certain ends." Convened and sanctioned by the NAACP board, the conference did not result in immediate changes in the NAACP agenda. But its recommendations included putting an end to reliance on white patronage for solving problems and encouraging the formation of alliances between middle-class leaders and working-class black Americans.[14]

Within one year of Amenia, Du Bois resigned from the NAACP board of directors because he felt his work inside the organization for "realignment" had "been almost absolutely unsuccessful." Reorganization, Du Bois reminded the board, was "the most gruelling of tests which come to an old organization." Although the NAACP had "succeeded so well that the program seemed perfect and unlimited," new circumstances called for "a positive program of construction and inspiration," a task they seemed incapable of performing. Thus, he found the association ossifying, without a workable strategy to cope with the changing circumstances of the Great Depression.[15]

Before leaving his post, Du Bois had cultivated alliances in local branches with those who shared his desire to reorganize the NAACP "root and branch." One of his allies, Abram Harris, a Marxist economist at Howard University, was recommended for membership on the board of directors by Du Bois. When the NAACP leadership ignored the recommendations proposed at Amenia, Harris used his position on the board and as chair of the NAACP's Committee on the Future Plan and Program in 1934–35 to attempt to restructure the NAACP's agenda.[16] Two issues foreshadowed the breach between the old guard and new crowd that ensued. The first issue involved Harris's request to invite A. C. MacNeal to represent NAACP branch interests, for, as he told White, the Chicago branch had "something on their chests that they should be given a chance to get off." The second issue was Harris's refusal to accept NAACP board chairman Joel Spingarn's invitation to work out the future direction of the NAACP at his country estate, Troutbeck, in Amenia, New York. "I don't see how the Committee can function," Harris confided to White, "while it is the guest of the Chairman of the Board. Discussion ought to be free and untrammeled. And I fear . . . there are certain proprieties that some people can't ignore."[17]

The venue for committee meetings was changed to New York City, but White managed to keep MacNeal off the committee. Nonetheless, the issue of distributing power to NAACP branches—to restructure what scholar B. Joyce Ross describes as a "closed corporation" operating out of New York City—was hardly moot.[18] The Harris Committee tried to diminish the role of the national office, the executive secretary, and the board of directors by transforming local branches into "permanent centers of economic and political education and agitation" supervised by a salaried regional secretary.[19] Under Harris's arrangement, the direction of the NAACP would be determined as much by the spokes of the wheel as the hub. In the final report, however, after editing by the board of directors, ultimate control remained with the old guard stationed at the hub.[20]

The board also eliminated the report's call for direct, mass-action tactics. Harris hoped branches would form workers' councils "not to be mere discussion groups." His desire was that "through actual participation in strikes, lockouts and labor demonstrations [the councils] will seek to protect the interests of Negro workingmen and to promote their organization and unity with white labor." That was changed to make branches "centers of education in the use of the ballot."[21]

Despite rhetorical flourishes in the final version that gave greater weight to economic issues and branch interests, the Harris Report, as scholars August Meier and John Bracey stress, "advocated such sweeping changes to the Association's organization that it foreclosed any possibility of being adopted."[22] Frustrated with his inability to alter substantially the NAACP's structure and agenda, Harris resigned from the board in March 1935.[23] White then declared

that a severe financial crisis made it impossible to implement the reform called
for in the Harris Report, including funding for hiring John P. Davis, a Harvard
lawyer and new-crowd leader of Harris's ilk.[24] The original Harris Report had
suggested that Davis, who had been investigating the severity of the Depression
and New Deal programs on black Americans for the Joint Committee on
National Recovery (JCNR), be hired as an economic adviser for the NAACP's
executive staff. The JCNR, formed in September 1933 with the help of the Rosenwald Fund and money from the NAACP, was chiefly under the direction of the
NAACP although fifteen other organizations were also named as sponsors.
Davis, charged with representing the special economic circumstances of black
Americans, carried out his mission, as Mark Solomon notes, with an "uncompromising assault upon New Deal racial policies," which apparently was one
reason White never fully trusted Davis.[25] There is also reason to believe White
wanted to keep Davis off the payroll of the executive staff in order to maintain
his personal control over the association's agenda. When Harris had suggested
that Davis replace Du Bois as editor of the *Crisis*, White countered by successfully campaigning for Roy Wilkins.[26] White suspected Davis of "personal
and political opportunism."[27] Whatever the basis for his suspicions, White no
longer had to contend with potential rivals for leadership within the association
after the departure of Davis, Harris, and Du Bois. The old-guard approach and
tactics of White strongly influenced the NAACP agenda after the Harris Report,
but those who remained on the staff did not always agree with White, nor do
they all fit the definition of old-guard leaders. Charles Houston, NAACP's chief
legal strategist, for example, sympathized with the new-crowd challengers, attended local National Negro Congress meetings in New York, and donated
money to the organization. Houston took part in Scottsboro marches, and in
1932 and 1933 he helped the ILD, as Genna Rae McNeil points out, by sending
financial contributions for the Scottsboro case. Houston, who shared neither
White's anticommunism nor his approach to the NNC, understood the symbi-
otic relationship between grass-roots activism and legal strategy. On one occasion he wrote White that, "with all due respect, we have not worked out a solution" to the current problems. Houston understood, as Patricia Sullivan notes,
that much more attention needed to be focused at the local level. "Take the Association home to the people," he urged the 1934 national NAACP convention.[28]

More was at stake for White than reordering priorities to appease dissident
voices. As a salaried officer of the association, he was charged with carrying out
policy directives of a board to which he owed his position. White was recommended to the board by Joel Spingarn when James Weldon Johnson resigned as

executive secretary in 1930. Spingarn reinforced the hierarchical nature of the relationship when, as Ross noted, he formulated an elaborate "network of checks and balances" to assure that "White would be answerable to the top-level leadership of the organization."[29] At the same time, White felt the need to meet the approval of liberal reformers outside the association. For that reason, White welcomed the endorsement of Edwin Embree, president of the Rosenwald Foundation, who told White that he agreed with his hesitations and concerns over the Harris Report.[30]

Having muffled the voices of protest against the structure and strategies of the NAACP for the moment, Walter White tried to restore the financial integrity of the association and his position as the best person to lead the NAACP by focusing on an antilynching campaign. The association believed antilynching was a good issue for fund raising, certainly better than pushing an economic agenda, and lobbying against lynching was White's forte.[31] He possessed all of the requisite skills for such work and had a network of liberal reformers and public officials that he drew upon to make his appeals to Congress and the New Deal administration for antilynching legislation.[32] The hope was that by high-lighting lynching the NAACP could not only force an antilynching bill through Congress, but match the appeal of the Scottsboro case and increase support from liberal whites, for the financial situation was dire.[33]

When the economic upheaval of the depression led to a 50 percent drop in membership contributions in the early 1930s, the financial committee of the board responded by decreasing the size of the staff and slashing the operating budget more than a third between 1930 and 1934. To make up the shortfall, Walter White and the board looked increasingly to large contributions from well-to-do benefactors, shifting the attention of the staff and board further from the concerns of the rank and file.[34]

William Rosenwald initiated fund offers in 1930 and 1932. The first offer, $1,000 for three-years, was matched by $1,000 each from Edsel Ford, Lieutenant-Governor Herbert H. Lehman (of New York), Mr. and Mrs. Felix M. Warburg, and Samuel S. Fels. By 1932, the NAACP could boast that the ten largest contributions, which included one from John D. Rockefeller, totaled $13,825, out of a budget of $50,000. Faced with the declining membership contributions, this money was appreciated.[35]

A new dependency flowed from these funding patterns. First, despite the NAACP's dependence during the 1920s on large contributions from people like Edsel Ford and John D. Rockefeller, member fees and branch contributions remained the largest source of funds.[36] Second, the Depression hit longtime, large contributors, creating the need to cultivate new contributors—part of the reason for Rosenwald's offers—as well as maintaining good relationships with older supporters. Philip Peabody, unlike Ford and Rockefeller, could not continue his contributions into the 1930s because economic "necessity knows no law." Still others who were financially sound in early 1930s had, by mid-1930s, been reduced to small or no donations. Mother M. Katherine of Philadelphia donated $2,000 in 1932 but had to reduce her contribution to $200 by 1937. Third, during the 1920s, a relatively small amount of staff time was required to secure funds. By contrast, Walter White noted during the spring of 1932 that he had sent out 3,500 letters to appeal for matching funds for William Rosenwald's offer.[37]

These new patterns also set in motion a growing volume of office work that took time from field work, which, in theory, would have developed branches and been attentive to membership needs.[38] Large contributions had a strong appeal, since White and his staff seemed to spend as much time cultivating a $25 contribution as a $500 or $1,000 contribution. Learning the job of executive secretary in the midst of national economic disaster made White dependent upon Rosenwald's support.[39]

Nevertheless, even the relative certainty of Rosenwald's generosity could not overcome the turmoil of the times that made financial planning something of a guessing game. For that reason, White and the board agreed that the association should also cultivate small, $5 to $100 donations, along with large $1,000 gifts.[40] But, as one NAACP study suggested, this decision may have strengthened the bond between white liberals and the organization. The finance committee of the board of directors was informed that one way to view the relationship between race and per capita contribution was to note that *less* than 1 percent of total members and contributors gave $25 or more in 1937, yet the 105 individuals who contributed $25 or more accounted for 31 percent of the total general funds that year; 93 percent of people in the $25 plus category were white Americans.[41]

Those financial ties were reinforced by White's identification with the basic assumptions espoused by New Deal liberals. Although White criticized the New Deal for its shortcomings in terms of black unemployment, he believed in the liberal reform philosophy of his friends Harold Ickes and Eleanor Roosevelt, who thought inclusion of black Americans in New Deal programs was the route to racial justice in society. Moreover, through his relationships with Ickes and Roosevelt, White became a major source within the Roosevelt administration for advice on the welfare of black Americans.[42] It was a position that accorded White a measure of control over the perceptions prominent white

Americans had of both the NAACP and black America's struggle for civil and political rights.[43]

The National Negro Congress:
A Window on Protest Politics in the Black Community

In May 1935 John P. Davis, along with Ralph Bunche, Randolph, and other new-crowd leaders who agreed with Abram Harris's assessment of the NAACP, thought the time had come to create a new organization. Although the organization of the National Negro Congress may have been inspired, partially, by the inability of the NAACP to change its agenda and approach, its program went far beyond that envisioned by the Harris Report. As president of the NNC, Randolph stated the intention was to "mobilize and rally power" in the community around "a social program" that all black Americans could endorse. But the "all" referred to the 99 percent of the "Negro peoples" who "win their bread by selling their labor power."[44] During the summer, fall, and winter of 1935, Davis, Randolph, and Bunche issued a call for founding the NNC, while Charles Burton, Thyra Edwards, and the BSCP network advertised the event in Chicago.[45]

In February 1936 more than 5,000 men and women—secretaries and social workers, labor leaders and preachers, politicians and doctors—responded by journeying to the first convention in Chicago. In his presidential address, Randolph cautioned the delegates against placing "their problems for solution down at the feet of their white sympathetic allies which has been and is the common fashion of the old school Negro leadership, for, in the final analysis, the salvation of the Negro, like the workers, must come from within."[46] Randolph extended his critique of Pullman's paternalism to relations between black and white Americans. The NNC alternative to the NAACP was to be based on mass demonstrations, "picketing, boycotting, mass protest, and mass distribution of propaganda literature."[47] Although John Davis, national secretary of the NNC, and Randolph were no doubt grateful for the degree of federal intervention ushered in by the New Deal, both believed it was necessary to harness the power of collective action in order to bring about meaningful, long-term relief from racial inequities. In short, as Randolph put it, the NNC would advance a "militant program," to challenge old-guard social relations.[48]

Davis, Randolph, and other BSCP organizers active in the NNC spoke in terms of creating a "united front" to shift the tenor of the reform agenda in the black community from moderate to militant, with an emphasis on working-class empowerment. As a BSCP organizer wrote in the *Black Worker*, "in terms of advantage and power for oppressed minorities, the principle of the united front is sound and should be developed." African Americans were weak "not due to a lack of numbers or of organization, but to the separate functioning of the organizations in relation to any basic demand."[49]

Newspaper editorials, letters to the editor, and news stories written after the first NNC congress from around the country agreed that "a new race leadership is in the making," that "older leaders [were] missing at the National Negro Congress," and that "it seems clear that the Negro masses are moving rapidly towards a definite break with the old leadership of the race." "Aha! a new leadership!" wrote Dr. Wilfred Rankin in the *Amsterdam News*, "Let the leaders be free of the inhibitions which have tended to distort the thinking or seal the lips of many of the older generation."[50] The *Chicago Defender* praised the NNC's new-crowd networks for relying on collective action rather than philanthropic foundations for challenging inequities.[51] Perhaps the most important thing the NNC did at the local level was provide an organizational base, bringing together various efforts and interests, which allowed new-crowd leaders to emerge.

Randolph's keynote address to the first NNC convention, which bore a re-markable resemblance to many he had given at Brotherhood events, mapped out the multiple issues the NNC hoped would mobilize black Americans. Evok-ing black history, he asked the crowd to draw upon the "fearless courage" of "black rebels and martyrs for human justice," citing Denmark Vesey, Harriet Tubman, Sojourner Truth, Frederick Douglass, and others. Similarly, resolu-tions of the Congress emphasized the need to "fight for the enforcement" of the Thirteenth, Fourteenth, and Fifteenth Amendments. The congress connected second-class status of African Americans to the plight of oppressed people in other parts of the world with its support for Ethiopia and creation of the American Association for the Aid of Ethiopia.[52]

Despite popular support for the NNC, this institution has often been regarded as a failure. Some scholars claim it failed because the NNC created divisions within the black community rather than uniting it. One division cited was that between the NAACP and the NNC.[53] It has been suggested that because the NAACP did not participate in the NNC's work, it did not "obtain the depth of support it needed, and functioned both nationally and locally largely as a paper organiza-tion." If it was just a paper organization, then why did Walter White consider the NNC a threat to the "preeminence of the NAACP in black protest activities"?[54] Other scholars suggest the NAACP was reluctant to join forces with the NNC, fearing Communist participation.[55] Yet when the NNC was organized—during the Popular Front, a phase when the Communist Party encouraged coalitions with liberals, socialists, and left-leaning New Deal personnel—Communists neither dominated nor controlled the NNC's agenda,[56] raising the question whether Walter White feared Communist influence in the NNC, grass-roots activism that he had not tapped, or alliances with a group defined as the class enemy of many NAACP benefactors.

Although during the 1920s Randolph had ranked among the more vocal skeptics and opponents of the Communists, by the early 1930s, he and many of his alliance within the new-crowd networks initiated or supported by the BSCP worked together with known Communists. Pressured from within by black Communists, the party had shifted its agenda and begun attacking white chauvinism within its ranks. By the time the NNC was formed, Randolph had watched the Communists gain a voice within the black community as they paid close attention to concerns of black workers.[57] In Chicago, as discussed in the previous chapter, the BSCP and its networks were closely entwined with Communists by the early and mid-thirties. As the interests of African Americans rose to the fore within Communist Party circles, many black Americans abandoned their previous hesitation and willingly collaborated with the Communists. Randolph may have shifted his position on this issue because he sensed political possibilities that could emerge from an alliance with the left. He also may have been persuaded by the simple argument that black Americans needed more allies, agreeing with Charles Houston, who praised the militant activities of Communists that inspired mass struggle.[58] What we do know is that by the time he was president of the NNC, Randolph and the Brotherhood had been collaborating with Communists in campaigns against injustice on several fronts. He was apparently persuaded that white chauvinism was no longer a problem.

Roy Wilkins, evaluating the role played by the Communists within the NNC, believed rumors that the congress was financed by Communists were "wholly without foundation." The NNC must be taken seriously, he thought, because "unquestionably, the congress was an expression of the willingness of masses of the people to sacrifice and fight." He called the democratic strategy, which appealed to the "working class" constituency at the first Congress, a major departure from the way organizations usually "select the delegates from the top," and suggested the NNC should not be viewed as an obstacle to the NAACP just because the congress "tends toward the left." He urged endorsement of the NNC by the NAACP as a way to counter the "wide-spread feeling among great numbers of people that the Association is not a true representative of the aspirations of the race and is not attacking the problems as vigorously as they should be attacked."[59] In 1936 Lester Granger of the National Urban League attributed the "inner significance of the Congress" partially to the "growing importance of labor leadership and . . . the power of the labor movement."[60]

Both observations suggest that the NNC became a thorn in the side of the NAACP because it was a vehicle for organizing black workers—just the folks the NAACP had often not reached.[61]

The Development of NNC Networks: The Case of Chicago

The Chicago NNC local, called the Chicago Council, was formed in 1936 by men and women from the ranks of organized labor, the Communist Party, and the BSCP's Citizens' Committee. With that as its base, the Chicago Council brought in churches, trade unions, and social organizations to work together around local issues such as economic discrimination and jobs for black Chicagoans. Most of its activities, while initiated by Charles Burton, its director, were managed through the labor committee and its secretary, Eleanor Rye.[62] As a member of the executive board of the Fur Workers Union, a friend of the Communist Party, an active participant in the Chicago Federation of Labor, and a supporter of the BSCP, Rye had established contacts within both white and black working-class communities of Chicago. Alliances were further extended when two other NNC organizers—Henry Johnson, a veteran of the Trade Union Unity League (TUUL) and James McDonald, of the Amalgamated Association of Meat Cutters and Butcher Workmen of North America—contacted more than 600 black organizations in Chicago and Gary, Indiana. Poro College, headquarters of Annie M. Malone's $2 million beauty college business and a favorite community meeting center during the 1930s, opened up a suite of four rooms, "fully furnished," for the NNC local office.[63]

Rye, Johnson, and McDonald collaborated with the Urban League, the Interclub Council of Chicago, South Side Garment Workers Club (members of the ILGWU), women's clubs, and several other groups. The Chicago Council joined with sociologists Horace Cayton of University of Chicago and other "prominent people" to raise funds to support their activities. Their efforts built upon work of other organizations and individuals active in black neighborhoods: Wheaton's work as a community organizer for the YWCA, for example, helped prepare many female industrial and domestic workers for the NNC message; John Davis understood the role Wheaton had played in the early thirties and suggested that Marion Cuthbert, member of the national board of the NAACP, the national YWCA, and the NNC, consult with Wheaton before she addressed the NNC Congress outlining its agenda on black female workers.[64]

Not only did the NNC local connect disparate new-crowd networks, it also developed a mutually beneficial relationship with the CIO. The support of the thousands of black workers in steel, auto, and meat-packing was crucial to the new industrial union federation. The CIO's campaign to organize industrial unions required black participation in basic industries, particularly in major industrial centers of the Midwest and South where black workers were concentrated. John Davis, Randolph, and other NNC activists introduced CIO organizers to the black community and connected them with new-crowd leaders and their organizations. Chicago was a center of the CIO drive because many of the industries it intended to organize were concentrated there.[65] To create the conditions for a favorable reception for the CIO, the NNC labor committee published and distributed leaflets to white and black trade unionists, established labor forums, worked with the ILGWU toward the organization of black women, used the Chicago Federation of Labor radio station, WCFL, to broadcast the NNC labor message, and wrote articles in the *Chicago Defender*.[66]

The first collaboration between the CIO and NNC grew out of mutual interests of the Steel Workers Organizing Committee (SWOC), organized in June 1936, and the NNC. A mutual dependency lay behind the merger: SWOC needed the support of black steelworkers to make industrial organization work;[67] John Davis and Randolph, on the other hand, needed the endorsement and backing of SWOC and the CIO to aid their plans to organize black workers. As Davis told Charles Burton, if the NNC could mobilize black and white steelworkers, "it will mean that we can secure large sums of money from the Steel Workers Organizing Committee to further organization work among Negro steel workers."[68] By mid-July, Davis convinced Van A. Bittner, midwest director of SWOC, to employ NNC organizers Henry Johnson, James MacDonald, and Eleanor Rye to work in the Great Lakes area.[69] For the next three years, joint efforts with the CIO became a major focus of both Davis and Randolph.[70] The NNC provided the SWOC with an important inroad into Chicago's South Side black community that proved indispensable in winning the support of black steelworkers to the union's cause. Through the NNC networks, the larger black community learned to trust white industrial unions. Thus did the NNC locals prepare the community for the CIO organizing drives.

Davis specifically recommended the services of Rye for the SWOC effort because she could work both sides of the street: not only could she effectively organize within the steel mills, but she could be of "endless value" organizing within the community, especially in the homes of steelworkers' wives, dealing with women's "fears and doubts in a convincing way." Van Bittner was aware of the obstacles SWOC organizers faced in Homestead and Clairton, Pennsylvania, where "emissaries of the steel companies" went "to the houses of Negro steel workers urging their wives to keep their husbands out of the Union."[71] Whether Davis or Van Bittner knew that steel company managers in the Chicago area considered hiring black "investigators" to interview black steelworkers about their feelings toward the CIO is not known. Claude Barnett of the Associated Negro Press suggested the plan to managers of industrial relations for United States Steel Corporation and Carnegie-Illinois Steel Corporation in the summer and fall of 1936.[72] What does seem clear is that all parties understood the importance of organizing not just the workplace but also the home and community.

Eleanor Rye selected Helena Wilson, president of the Chicago Women's Economic Council of the BSCP, to help her organize the Inland Steel Company in Indiana Harbor.[73] The two women worked with both black and white women's clubs and ministers, bringing group pressure on clergy still in the pockets of steel companies. At first they concentrated on discussions in private homes, in order to discuss unions and the power of collective organization away from the eyes and ears of company informants. From the home, they branched out to public interracial meetings. Their efforts paid off when they set up a NNC-SWOC women's auxiliary with a black vice president and treasurer, and gained the support of some of the black ministers.[74] One reporter estimated that 5,000 African American workers at Indiana Harbor (located in the Chicago metropolitan area), backed by the network NNC-SWOC had developed, signed up with the SWOC in 1937, and black steelworkers were active in serving on all committees of the SWOC.[75] Observers Horace Cayton and George Mitchell concluded that SWOC was lucky that the NNC and other union-minded folk were "in a position to challenge the leadership of the Negro community of the more conservative element."[76] The CIO rewarded the NNC local council with donations, including $50 every two weeks toward expenses of the labor committee, one-half rent on its office, and telephone service.[77] The efforts of Rye, Wilson, Johnson, and McDonald in Indiana Harbor illustrate how the NNC-SWOC network opened up opportunities for black steelworkers to gain a voice in workplace issues and mobilized the community around a labor agenda.[78]

The success of the NNC-SWOC collaboration led black packinghouse workers to expect the same kind of attention from the CIO. The Packinghouse Workers Organizing Committee (PWOC), as Roger Horowitz shows, built upon the "highly visible welcome extended to black steelworkers by the SWOC," when trying to win the support of black packinghouse workers, who made up 25 percent of the Chicago work force in that industry. PWOC hired Henry Johnson away from the NNC-SWOC campaign, making Johnson assistant director of the PWOC campaign.[79] Johnson's talent as an organizer was, according to fellow Chicago NNC organizer Ishmael P. Flory, "legendary, for he could work a crowd, both black and white, like few others."[80] He was also able to cross class lines, aided perhaps by his start in life as the son of a Texas sharecropper who went on to earn a bachelor's degree from City College of New York in 1934.[81]

Johnson, along with Thyra Edwards, extended the influence of the new crowd by belonging to both the NNC and a competing group, the Chicago Council of Negro Organizations (CCNO), which was formed late in 1935 by a group of middle-class leaders representing the Chicago NAACP, Chicago Urban League, and other civic, church, and fraternal groups. Eleanor Rye decided that the CCNO was "trying to steal the thunder from us."[82] But the Chicago Council of Negro Organizations worried about the influence of the Chicago NNC, which threatened its acceptance by the "masses." MacNeal, a member of the CCNO, wrote to Wilkins that "the NAACP must get going on some new 'techniques' or the Congress will have the field."[83] By belonging to both the NNC and the CCNO, Johnson and Edwards attempted to meld rank-and-file interests with those of the middle-class reformers.

Neva Ryan's Domestic Workers Association also showed that a degree of cross-fertilization had occurred.[84] By 1938, Ryan gathered old-guard leaders to support the domestic workers' union, which had about 150 black women members in the Chicago area. Claude A. Barnett of the Associated Negro Press, until recently an ally of benevolent managers,[85] and A. L. Foster of the Chicago Urban League, spoke of the interests of working-class domestics when they raised funds. Ryan, a member of the NNC's executive board, established a network crossing class lines, but united around workers' concerns. As members of Chicago's old guard accommodated themselves to the more radical new crowd, labor unions and interracial organizing gained acceptance in black neighborhoods and became part of the civic discourse.[86]

By 1938 over 200 middle-class Chicagoans joined in a march demanding more "bread and shelter" for black Chicagoans and an end to discriminatory practices by AFL trade unions. Scholars St. Clair Drake and Horace Cayton claimed that a more militant approach had become "respectable" in Chicago.[87] Thelma Wheaton's recollections support their claim. She remembered attending NNC meetings because there she could get "information . . . that would not go through the newspapers," and she felt the NNC was "independent" in a way that the NAACP was not.[88] By the late 1930s, Irene McCoy Gaines, a member of the BSCP Citizens' Committee during the 1920s, was elected president of the CCNO, carried her own union card, and yet still appeared on the society pages of black newspapers as the "charming wife of Representative Harris B. Gaines."[89]

Despite opposition from national headquarters, the Chicago branch of the NAACP joined the NNC in March 1938 to support a national antilynching conference. The Chicago Council brought together church, women's civic, and labor groups in a mass meeting in Chicago to endorse an antilynching bill pending before Congress. Henry Johnson, A. Philip Randolph, Alderman William Dawson, and the Chicago YWCA joined efforts to support the bill. Although the effort was backed by Senator Robert F. Wagner of New York and the NNC declared its desire to work with the NAACP in a joint antilynching effort, Walter White and Roy Wilkins felt that John Davis was "attempting in every way to cut in on our program," and they refused to collaborate. Instead, NAACP headquarters made an issue out of the fact that it was "appealing for funds" and the NNC was cutting into a potentially rich revenue source for the NAACP.[90]

The Financial Crisis and the Ambivalence of Walter White

The mass protests organized by John Davis and the NNC, White believed, employed tactics that threatened his bailiwick, the domain of antilynching. When the NAACP had taken up antilynching in 1935, it did so, as Robert Zangrando has shown, in the context of increased lynchings and "in anticipation that New Deal liberalism, the expansion of southern interracial activities, and recent Senate victories all augured well for the attempt."[91] White still believed between 1935 and 1939 that he could convince President Roosevelt, through individual lobbying of Congress and his special relationship with Eleanor Roosevelt, to back an antilynching bill.[92]

Nevertheless, as Nancy Weiss shows, "White was in a difficult position." While he wanted to believe Roosevelt would eventually push legislation through Congress, the "larger black community neither shared White's close ties to the First Lady nor was privy to her assurances that FDR intended to deal with the antilynching bill through the private political channels at his command." In some circles it was thought the NAACP was misleading black Americans by relying on its traditional individual lobbying tactics to combat lynching.[93] Not only did the Roosevelt administration fail to deliver an antilynching bill, but despite continued efforts, the NAACP's antilynching campaign brought forth few large contributions from liberal sources. Financial uncertainty seemed the major constant.[94] White and Wilkins were not yet prepared to abandon the politics of civility and moderation, which had been the model for the NAACP. MacNeal, president of the Chicago branch of the NAACP, needled them by asking:

> How are you so sure that the timid and sometimes tepid gestures which are of the nature of a compromise are not the very things that now operate

to prevent the Association from having a membership of 100,000? Will a scrutiny of your position reveal that the present leadership of the Association is now 25 years BEHIND [emphasis in original] the demands and wants of the people which it seeks to serve? Are you sure the refusal of the Association to take the positive and uncompromising stand ... [is not] the "hang-over" of the "Old Guard" psychology[?]"[95]

Wilkins acknowledged that "in some respects we have failed to sense the public pulse"; still he was "not convinced as yet" that MacNeal was correct.[96] Daisy Lampkin, on the other hand, told White that the Chicago branch "showed the possibilities of what a well set up local NAACP office can do."[97] MacNeal warned White that the NAACP was in danger of "real competition for the support of the beloved 'masses.'" Chicago, however, was not the only branch deviating from the direction of the national. Historian Cheryl L. Greenberg found that "foot-dragging of the NAACP" helped spur "new mass movements for black jobs" in Harlem.[98]

NAACP branches in Philadelphia, Baltimore, and Detroit, particularly between 1937 and 1940, joined protest activities initiated by NNC locals. Philadelphia's NAACP, against the national's wishes, cooperated with the NNC local in its antilynching campaign.[99] Lillie Jackson, Baltimore head, believed "the NAACP has got to get away from just the classes, the teachers and doctors and lawyers; we've got to have the masses." She worked with longshoreman leader Jefferson Davis and NNC-SWOC organizer Arthur Murphy.[100] In Detroit, the interests and needs of black workers increasingly shaped the discourse of the reform agenda in the black community through the combined efforts of the local chapter of the NNC, the Youth Division of the NAACP, and new-crowd leaders in the Detroit NAACP chapter. The secretary of the Detroit chapter was a founder and board member of the NNC local, a fact that helped, as Meier and Rudwick pointed out, dilute the impact of the pro–Henry Ford, old-guard NAACP leaders.[101] When the three largest NAACP branches—Chicago, Detroit, and Baltimore—worked with black workers, memberships increased. While correlation is not causation, we do know Daisy Lampkin was rewarded for her successes in Chicago and Detroit with an increase in salary, despite the NAACP's financial problems.[102]

Several events during 1937 persuaded White and Wilkins to change their position. They contemplated the new directions charted at the February meeting of the National Conference of Negro Organizations, sponsored by the NNC and attended by 350 black union delegates and community leaders.[103] At a time when support for the NNC was probably at an all-time high, White agreed to be a speaker at the Philadelphia NNC congress in October. Roy Wilkins put Randolph on the *Crisis* cover after the BSCP's victory over Pullman's company union. The issue included an article by George Schuyler attacking "old-guard" black leaders, who did little or nothing to assist black workers. Black labor's new position within the New Unionism Movement came about, he argued, despite the "indifference, hostility and open opposition" of the "old leadership."[104] When the Garland Fund failed to renew a $10,000 educational fund White had counted on, choosing instead to support the CIO's United Canning, Agricultural, Packing and Allied Workers of America, White concluded that labor organization was the "type of work that displaced our educational program."[105]

By 1939 White and Wilkins were convinced that they should alter the NAACP's agenda and tactics. Wilkins urged expanding the "association's program in a popular manner to reach the masses of the people" and noted that the "people" want to fight, and as long as we "fight they will be with us." White told Wilkins that it was probably true, "as you say, that 'our cautious conservatism has kept us standing still.'" White admitted to Houston that people were "demanding a leadership of uncompromising action instead of the temporizing of the past." Daisy Lampkin knew change was imminent when Wilkins confided that the "seriousness of the present situation" was going to bring some "radical revisions all down the line."[106]

By then, several changes within the association increased White's freedom to change the NAACP agenda. First, the death of president Joel Spingarn in 1939 left a void in NAACP's white liberal leadership that never was filled. Although Arthur Spingarn succeeded his brother as president of the association, the presidency reverted to a "largely honorary post," which it had not been since the tenure of Moorefield Storey.[107] Second, the Internal Revenue Service (IRS) inspired a major change in the NAACP's structure when it outlawed deductions of contributors on the grounds that NAACP funds engaged in propaganda and lobbying. The NAACP Legal Defense and Education Fund (LDF), a charitable organization designed to perform nonpropaganda, nonlobbying activities, rose out of this problem with the IRS in 1940. In the interim, several large contributions were canceled, increasing the pressure on White to look elsewhere for a solution.[108] Eventually, separation of legal and educational activities from other protest activities gave both White and Wilkins more freedom to explore mass-action strategies of a labor-oriented, civil rights agenda, no longer hobbled by opposition from contributors who favored a moderate approach using legal tactics.

Pushed by the decline of funding from liberal philanthropists and attracted by the large number of activists organizing around labor issues in northern cities, White made up for some funding lost from liberals with contributions from labor unions.[109] He also began laying the groundwork for future union support when he convinced the board to take over a $25,000 debt owed by the International Ladies Garment Workers Union to the Garland Fund. As an added inducement, White suggested that the NAACP "knock off $5,000" from the debt for the benefit of the ILGWU, thereby demonstrating its pro-CIO stance in a concrete way. By 1940 this strategy seemed to be paying dividends as several CIO unions gave substantial contributions to the NAACP.[110]

In January 1940 A. Philip Randolph was made a member of the NAACP board, four months before he resigned as president of the NNC. While Randolph's presence on the board represented a major endorsement of the NAACP by the person commonly known as Mr. Black Labor, it also sent a message to the black community about the association's interest in linking labor issues with civil rights. Randolph used the platform to expand the board's understanding of issues and tactics of union organizing.[111] But Randolph's acceptance of the board position also signaled a turning point in his collaboration with the Communists.

The NNC's united front within the black community cracked when the NNC hewed to the antiwar and anti-imperialist line ushered in after the Nazi-Soviet nonaggression pact in August 1939. By putting race issues low on its agenda and allegiance to the Soviet Union at the top, the NNC, Randolph charged, did not care about African Americans. Randolph believed the American Communist Party had defiled the independence and integrity of the NNC's previous opposition to fascism around the world when it made a pact with the Nazi Party; he resigned as president of the NNC in April 1940. The American Communist movement, as Komozi Woodard points out, "made a momentous mistake in interfering with the autonomous political development of the NNC on foreign policy issues."[112] When Randolph blasted the Soviet Union, charging that the Soviets were imperialist and profascist, many in the NNC audience, according to Ralph Bunche, were offended. In addition, Randolph raised the issue of black nationalism, not for the last time, to counter what he perceived was too much control by largely white interests over the direction of the NNC, pointing out that "where you get your money you also get your ideas and control."[113] As Mark Solomon suggests, an agenda placing revolutionary concerns over race interests, which "had hindered Communist aspirations in the black community" in the past, "had not gone away."[114]

Although Randolph's resignation weakened the NNC's claim to speak for the interests of black workers, many local NNC networks continued to retain a strong position in places like Detroit. Walter White, who modified his opposition to the NNC after Randolph joined the NAACP board, noted that voices from a new crowd had grown louder in Detroit by the end of the thirties.[115] Despite the appearance of loyalty many black industrial workers and prominent local leaders, including members of Detroit's NAACP, showed toward Henry Ford, the NAACP at the national level was impressed with new-crowd activities.[116] When collaborations between the NNC local and the Detroit branch of the NAACP formed around labor and civil rights issues, NAACP memberships increased. Between 1938 and 1939, for example, membership jumped from 3,283 to over 6,000.[117] That year the Detroit branch of the NAACP considered its work with the NNC important enough to highlight in an official report to headquarters. One black newspaper, not willing to let the NAACP rest on its recent success, pointed out that the branch might do even better if it stopped acting like a "mere club of the so-called upper crust of the town" leaving "the dispossessed masses . . . to feel ill at ease."[118] Meanwhile, the NNC local collaborated with the United Auto Workers (UAW-CIO), developed community-wide networks, and talked with black workers in small groups in their homes. Still, recruiting was not easy in a community that had depended on recommendations from ministers for access to jobs with Ford Motor Company.[119]

Walter White entered the contested arena in Detroit during the UAW-CIO Ford strike at River Rouge, which employed over 9,000 black workers, in April 1941, worrying about whether the UAW would deliver on its promise not to discriminate against black Americans. If they did not deliver, he said, "the NAACP and I are going to be on the spot." But he was willing to risk his reputation because he knew the Ford strike went beyond union representation. When White declared from the loudspeaker of a union sound truck that "Negro Ford workers . . . cannot afford to rely on the personal kindness of any individual when what the workers want is justice," he showed he understood that new circumstances demanded forging new relationships.[120] As he called for collective action, he also sought a place in the new crowd. From his chronicle of events during the strike against Ford at the River Rouge plant, it is clear that White hoped the large population of black autoworkers would notice his activities. He understood well the link between a union victory in Detroit, the NAACP's participation in that strike, and the credibility of the association in the eyes of black labor. For, as White observed, the Ford strike represented "the new order of things," in "the eyes" of African American Detroit.[121]

The new order of things was predicated upon a change in the relationship between old-guard leaders and new-crowd African Americans, fusing their interests and looking to the power of collective action to make demands. In shepherding the association from an organization that in 1933 largely ignored the interests of black workers to one that by 1941 had adopted a labor-oriented agenda and made demands by employing the power of collective organization, White had come a long way, and so had the association. The strike represented a turning point in terms of the protest politics of the major civil rights organization and marked the beginning of a new partnership between the NAACP and organized labor as well as between the NAACP and the demands of new-crowd leaders. Ella Jo Baker, who helped shape the Student Nonviolent Coordinating Committee (SNCC) in 1960, was hired as assistant field secretary for the NAACP in 1941. For the next five years she directed her talents as a grass-roots organizer to expanding the organization in the South, hoping to give branches more power and place "the NAACP and its program on the lips of all the people," as Charles Payne notes.[122] Thus, the legacy of new-crowd networks, such as those formed by the NNC at the local level, may lie as much in the influence they had reordering priorities of the old guard within the NAACP as in contributing to a realignment of power relations in black communities.

White changed his approach as a result of several influences, including the activism and success of people operating beyond the orbit of the NAACP's old guard. While the failure of the old guard to address the demand for a broader, more inclusive agenda inspired the formation of new-crowd networks, the interests of black workers that emerged from the process spurred the association to change its agenda and tactics. However, important as black workers were in transforming the NAACP agenda, White's participation in the Ford strike should not be viewed as merely opportunistic. When White looked beyond white liberal reformers and into the black community for support and solidarity, he not only revitalized the association and increased memberships;[123] his actions gave notice to white liberals that the balance of power in the larger black community had shifted. The old guard was no longer recognized as the sole guardian of the civil rights agenda in negotiations with the white community. Increasingly, decisions concerning the agenda and direction of protest politics would reside in the domain of new-crowd leaders. In the future when White approached the Roosevelt administration, as he did in June 1941 along with A. Philip Randolph, his voice was one among many threatening mass action. That threat to carry out a massive March on Washington to protest discrimination in defense industries carried the added weight of the NAACP's stand at River Rouge when it helped to mobilize the community around the interests of black workers.

We Are Americans, Too

The March on Washington Movement, 1941–1943

The struggle of the Negro for equitable and decent treatment in the
national defense program is another aspect of the race's continuing
battle for full manhood citizenship rights and privileges in America.
ROY WILKINS, *Crisis*, December 1940

We are simply fighting for our constitutional
rights as American citizens.
A. PHILIP RANDOLPH, "Let the Negro Masses Speak,"
Black Worker, 1941

No greater wrong has been committed against the Negro
than the denial to him of the right to work.
A. PHILIP RANDOLPH, *What the Negro Wants*, 1944

This order—executive order 8802—has given new meaning, new
vitality to the Emancipation Proclamation. Lincoln's proclamation
of 1863 freed us physically; Roosevelt's proclamation of 1941 is the
beginning of our economic freedom.
EARL B. DICKERSON, January 9, 1942, Chicago

Between 1941 and 1943, the new crowd increasingly determined the direction of
protest politics as the old guard's role as primary guardian of the civil rights
agenda and arbiter of relations between the black and white community faded.
Significantly, Walter White joined A. Philip Randolph and other BSCP organizers in 1941 in a call to march on Washington to protest discrimination in the
defense industries, forcing Franklin D. Roosevelt to issue Executive Order 8802
and form the Fair Employment Practice Committee (FEPC) to carry out the
order. With Executive Order 8802, the president prohibited discrimination in
defense industries and agencies of the federal government, acknowledging and,
in the words of Roosevelt, "reaffirming" rights black Americans thought were

first proclaimed shortly after Emancipation. The FEPC represented the first time since Reconstruction that race-related issues were the exclusive preoccupation of a federal agency.[1]

Randolph and White initially mobilized African Americans to march on Washington to demand an end to segregation in the armed forces and discrimination in the job market. Although the executive order did not address segregation in the armed forces, Randolph called off the march because the major demand for jobs was met and he regarded the order as a first step. The next step was to sustain and perpetuate the momentum generated for the threatened march, which was done through the BSCP's March on Washington Movement (MOWM). Strategically, the most provocative aspect of the MOWM was limiting membership to African Americans, a necessary tactic, Randolph believed, to develop and promote self-reliance and self-determination. Its program was designed to mobilize the power of collective action, not just to obtain jobs, but to advance the economic, political, educational, and social interests of black Americans. Organizing large numbers would give black Americans the power to demand and take their rights. "There are some things," Randolph declared, that "Negroes must do alone."[2] It was also important for white America to witness African Americans building a movement for themselves, using their own resources.

The march movement was not antiwhite, nor was it an expression of a desire to simply retreat into all-black institutions. It was a means toward the goal of equal treatment for African Americans, and it reflected the growth of a new black nationalist consciousness that was taking root in the urban North.[3] By World War II, many voices spoke of rights of citizenship that included the right, as Du Bois expressed it, to "establish a feeling of belonging—a feeling that [black Americans are] . . . an integral and participating part of American society."[4] But, as Komozi Woodard reminds us, the sentiment to claim full rights of participation within American society should not necessarily be equated with assimilation, understood as adopting the cultural patterns of the dominant culture. African Americans who migrated North "were definitely *not* assimilated into white America." They were "urbanized and modernized in a very separate manner" from other Americans.[5]

The tactics utilized to organize the March on Washington represented the culmination of struggle and community organizing at the local level through protest networks dating back to the 1920s. One focus of the Brotherhood's efforts in its early years in Chicago was to gain a measure of independence from white control. In 1925 the target was Pullman paternalism, challenging the deferential nature of a relationship in the private sector, which assumed black workers should rely on the goodwill of benevolent employers. In 1941, as attention shifted to the nation's policy of dual citizenship, the challenge was to move the discussion at the highest level of government beyond the politics of good intentions to the point of demanding an executive order mandating that defense industries cease discriminating against black workers. MOWM was an expression of African Americans making their own decisions about what strategies to follow to claim rights that were, in theory, granted decades ago. Independence from white control and self-reliance linked the BSCP in the 1920s and the MOWM in the 1940s; both were means for claiming citizenship rights, challenging the politics of civility, and shaping the black place within the American political economy.

Between 1941 and 1945, African Americans struggled on several fronts to break down barriers. The old guard–new crowd dichotomy was no longer useful in a climate better described by a melding of leadership agendas around the national citizenship campaign—the "Double V for Victory," victory over fascism at home and abroad. As the *Chicago Defender* warned shortly before Pearl Harbor, "we are not exaggerating when we say that the American Negro is damned tired of spilling his blood for empty promises of better days."[6] But for a year, between the summer of 1941 and summer of 1942, MOWM was the major vehicle uniting the African American community around equal citizenship. A March on Washington rally, attended by over 20,000 people in the summer of 1942 in New York City represented the pinnacle of MOWM's popularity. The alliance began to crack during the fall of 1942 when the MOWM reaffirmed its all-black membership policy, advocated nonviolent civil disobedience, and declared itself a permanent organization. Leaders in the NAACP and several other black advancement organizations opposed those policies and distanced themselves from the movement. The united front of the early war years began to fade.

Executive Order 8802

Slavery, as David Brion Davis notes, was more than a legal construct or an institution determining economic functions of people. Slavery also structured and shaped interpersonal relationships in society.[7] One impulse for the March on Washington scheduled for July 1, 1941, was to address the failure of American society to come to terms with economic and interpersonal relations inherited from slavery. The task remained, as A. Philip Randolph and BSCP organizers defined it, the need to overcome the second-class status reserved for black Americans. Randolph criticized the politics of a system that relegated black workers to the status of what he called Jim Crow "slaves."[8] In addition, the

March on Washington challenged the protocol and the assumptions that set the limits and boundaries in political dialogue between black individuals and the highest chamber of government. The March on Washington utilized a two-pronged approach to challenge two barriers—one economic and the other interpersonal—that held black Americans in an inferior position.

The major objective of the March on Washington Committee was to address directly the problem of high unemployment among black workers while defense plants discriminated with signs advertising "*Help Wanted*, White."[9] When the U.S. Employment Service inquired about the hiring policies of a number of defense industries, more than 50 percent responded that they would not hire black workers. According to the 1940 census, there were 5,389,000 black Americans in the labor force, 3,582,000 were men and more than 1 million were unemployed.[10] While unemployed white workers found employment by the millions in 1940, African American workers continued to stand in unemployment lines, despite the increased demand for labor to meet the challenge of the military buildup. In April 1940 black and white unemployment rates nationwide stood at 22.0 percent and 17.7 percent, respectively. By October 1940 employment had grown by 2 million and the unemployment rate among whites had fallen to 13.0 percent; black unemployment, however, declined by a mere one-tenth of 1 percent. Yet when the U.S. Employment Service, between January and March 1941, placed nearly 35,000 workers in foundry and forging, machine shop and machine tool, and metal processing industries, only 245 were black Americans. Proportionately fewer African Americans were placed in aircraft and electrical equipment industries. African Americans' employment gains in 1941 were in restaurant and hotel service work, janitorial services, and unskilled manual labor, areas recently vacated by upwardly mobile whites.[11]

The second objective, to attack servile social relations, has received less notice by scholars. By 1940 Randolph, along with others, argued that the status of black Americans in the twentieth century could be traced to expectations and mores of mainstream Americans, carried forward from nineteenth-century practices, which regarded black Americans as inferior participants in American democracy. Historian Charles H. Wesley wrote, in 1944, that the basic reason for second-class status was the "belief in the inferiority of the Negro, a concept based upon the master-slave psychology and past poor white-Negro relationships." It was a condition that Wesley thought was no longer "peculiarly Southern," because "custom limits the Negro in the North just as legislation and custom circumscribe him in the South." Wesley, raising the issue of servile relations in a manner similar to that of W. E. B. Du Bois in "No More Servants in the House" (see chapter 1), declared that the "presence of the Negro raises objection whenever he comes as an equal. As long as he is an inferior—a porter, a nurse, a sexton, a servant—he is tolerated."[12]

Randolph, whose career of protest against the racial status quo was inspired by his desire to equalize social relations between black and white Americans, wanted to negotiate with the federal government from a position of strength. He believed perpetuation of servile social relations was inherent in the old-guard approach—based on a politics of civility—for gaining first-class citizenship. By 1941 many agreed that the era of gratitude toward paternalistic white liberals for their good intentions in lifting black Americans out of second-class status was over.

Randolph understood the black freedom struggle as one of power, a belief he had articulated since his days in Harlem in the early twenties as an editor for the *Messenger*.[13] He maintained that black Americans would not be able to make good the promises inscribed in the Fourteenth and Fifteenth Amendments without struggling from a position of power.[14] But more than making demands was required, as a meeting in the White House between Randolph, T. Arnold Hill of the National Urban League, Walter White, and President Roosevelt in September of 1940 revealed. The three leaders of black America met with Roosevelt to discuss inclusion of black Americans in the armed forces after passage of the Selective Service Act. Although Roosevelt promised to investigate the matter, he issued a statement declaring that a segregation policy would be maintained in the military, intimating that the three leaders had agreed to the propagation of the racial status quo. All three leaders were denounced by George S. Schuyler, a journalist writing for the *Pittsburgh Courier*, who called such conferences a "fraud." White felt betrayed by Roosevelt, one reason he later joined the effort of Randolph to mobilize a mass, direct-action response to discrimination. White's friendship with Eleanor Roosevelt got the three leaders inside the Oval Office for the meeting with the president, but the conference yielded nothing positive for the black community. In addition, Hill, Randolph, and White had to endure Roosevelt's insults when he referred to "colored" men as "boys," reminded them that mess attendant was a good career track for African Americans and suggested that the Navy increase opportunities for black sailors by starting "a colored band on some of these ships, because they're darn good at it."[15] White tried once more to speak with the president on the issue of job discrimination in the defense industry. That attempt was equally frustrating, for Roosevelt responded by sending the associate director general of the Office of Production Management in his place. Randolph refused to be a party to this meeting.[16]

Before White joined forces with Randolph and the emerging March on Washington, he published an essay in *Saturday Evening Post*, "It's Our Country,

Too," demanding that black Americans be allowed to "Fight for It." He reminded the nation that black Americans "regard the United States as a country
which they helped to build"; black citizens were "hanging on to" their "faith in
democracy," determined to carry on their "shoulders a fair share of the burden
of its defense."[17] Yet, as he told John Temple Graves, a southern journalist, his
repeated requests to Roosevelt, asking him to "break his silence and to speak
out against this discrimination," were met with procrastination. Meanwhile,
"discontent and bitterness were growing like wildfire among Negroes all over
the country."[18] The Federal Bureau of Investigation noticed the increasingly
militant tone in the black press and the speeches of black leaders, which led it to
place many African Americans under surveillance.[19]

Between the two world wars a politics of civility prevailed in America, imposing limits on the degrees of freedom African Americans enjoyed socially and
economically. The negotiation process was controlled by the dominant culture.
So long as White spoke the language and used tools considered civil and reasonable by those in power, he could protest through petitions, exposés, and conferences. White could speak his mind, and even articulate radical ideas—but the
structure for discussing his ideas was controlled by an etiquette that prescribed
certain manners and prohibited others: consensus was rewarded and collective,
sustained protest was ruled contrary to the spirit of reasonable discourse.[20]
Although White was regarded as a spokesman from the black community, so
long as his words were not backed by activists willing to take action, they
carried little weight.

What was needed, according to Randolph, was a language of protest that
would "shake up white America."[21] When Randolph presented his March on
Washington idea to the black community, he portrayed the proposed demonstration in terms of "Let the Negro Masses Speak," linking mass protest politics
with an effort to make the voice of black Americans heard at the highest
chamber of government. Reduced to its simplest terms, mass-based demonstrations amounted to a new method for lobbying the federal government.
Black Americans have a "stake in National Defense. . . . It involves equal employment opportunities." But they were not being heard. "We are being pushed
around. . . . what do we get? . . . Polite promises."

It was time for America to listen to African Americans, he argued. Let 10,000
black Americans march down Pennsylvania Avenue in the nation's capital,
singing "John Brown's Body Lies a 'Mouldering in the Grave' " and "Before I'll
Be a Slave, I'll Be Buried in My Grave and Go Home to My Father and Be
Saved," Randolph declared. If black Americans want to be heard, then let them
mobilize large numbers of black people. "Negroes cannot stop discrimination

in national Defense with conferences of leaders and the intelligentsia alone. While conferences have merit, they won't get desired results by themselves." The battle was, as Randolph reminded black Americans, for "our constitutional rights as American citizens." The United States was "our own, our native land. . . . We are fighting for the right to work!" But the battle must be fought with new weapons in order to reach the "top powers of industry, organized white labor and government," which "has *not* yet felt the pressure of the Negro masses." White America was familiar with the language of "Negro leaders who are intelligent and well-meaning, pleading for Negro rights," but it has not "seen the Negro masses in action," speaking the language of mass protest.[22]

Threatening to deploy the power of "mass action," the MOWM demanded that the government "issue an executive order abolishing discrimination in all government departments, army, navy, air corps and national defense jobs." Randolph placed the demand for an executive order in the context of laying claim to basic Constitutional freedoms guaranteed in the Thirteenth, Fourteenth, and Fifteenth Amendments. Just as Abraham Lincoln had "issued the Proclamation of Emancipation for the freedom of Negro slaves and the preservation of American democracy," so "we call upon President Roosevelt . . . to follow in the footsteps of his noble and illustrious predecessor and take the second decisive step in this world and national emergency and free American Negro citizens of the stigma, humiliation and insult of discrimination and Jim-Crowism in Government departments and national defense."[23]

When first promoting the march idea in black communities, Randolph and the BSCP organizers spoke as organizers and participants in the new-crowd networks that had emerged from the upheaval of the 1930s. With the success of the Brotherhood's battle against the Pullman Company behind them, union porter organizers for the MOWM captured the attention of the larger black community. The executive order targeted the question of citizenship and recognition of black humanity, issues the Brotherhood had built its labor organization upon in Chicago. The language spoken by the MOWM organizers was familiar to communities steeped in the struggles for democratic rights for black Americans that had unfolded during the 1920s and 1930s.[24]

Between January and March 1941, chapters of the BSCP began organizing in railroad centers like New York, Detroit, Los Angeles, and Chicago.[25] There, according to Roi Ottley, a contemporary observer and journalist, "those efficient couriers—the Pullman porters—carried the word to Negro communities throughout the country." Most members of the black press and clergy promoted the march. Buses and trains were chartered to carry an estimated 50,000 African Americans to Washington, D.C., on July 1, 1941.[26] Randolph believed that "the administration leaders in Washington will never give the Negro justice until they see masses—ten, twenty, fifty thousand Negroes on the White House lawn!"[27] The Baltimore *Afro-American* told its readers that "one individual marching up and down Pennsylvania Avenue in front of the White House denouncing race prejudice is arrested as a crank. Ten thousand persons get respectful attention!"[28]

In New York City, Randolph, Benjamin McLaurin, a BSCP organizer, and other Brotherhood members, as Herbert Garfinkel has shown, took to the streets for "outdoor meetings, poster walks and similar forms of direct contract." Randolph claimed that he and others canvassed Harlem by "talking up the March by word of mouth . . . in all the beauty parlors and taverns and barber shops, etc."[29] In Chicago, Milton Webster relied largely upon Charles Burton, head of the BSCP Citizens' Committee in the 1920s and chair of the NNC local in Chicago during the 1930s, to mobilize people. The BSCP office in Chicago was the major site for organizing, and the majority of the funding came from Brotherhood dues. Webster used a subcommittee within the BSCP chapter to arrange activities for the March on Washington and make announcements about march activities. He told union porters that he looked with "justifiable pride" to the fact that the Brotherhood of Sleeping Car Porters was not only definitely and materially aiding porters, but that it was extending its benefits to other workers by helping to arrange the "mass protest in Washington, D.C., by Negroes from all over the nation."[30] The Brotherhood stressed the "credit" union porters deserved for the "March on Washington," which was "stretching its arm of good will throughout the land in an attempt to make a better place for our children yet unborn."[31] In Oakland, California, union porters canvassed the black community for support of the march; in Montgomery, Alabama, E. D. Nixon, head of the local BSCP and president of the NAACP local chapter, participated by organizing transportation to get participants to Washington. The Chicago BSCP drew upon the new-crowd protest networks, which they had helped shape, to mobilize black Chicago for the proposed March on Washington. One such network, the Chicago Congress of Negro Organizations, led by Irene McCoy Gaines, former BSCP Citizens' Committee secretary, was so well organized it was prepared to march to Washington in late March 1941.[32]

The sale of buttons at ten cents each helped financed march activities. In less than one week in early May over 15,000 buttons were sold in the New York metropolitan area. Button sales were supplemented with collections made in participating churches on special "March" Sundays. Bulletins explaining the main objectives of the movement appeared in beauty parlors, pool halls, churches, clubs, stores, selected black magazines and newspapers in at least eighteen cities. The "Statement of Purpose" that was circulated throughout the country during the spring said:

> We march in protest against the flagrantly cruel treatment that is being accorded us who are citizens of the United States Government. . . . We march by virtue of that article in the Bill of Rights of the Constitution which guarantees the right of assembly and petition to all American citizens. . . . We seek the unqualified and unrestricted opportunity to work in defense industries, on the same terms and under the same conditions as other Americans.
>
> We are citizens. We have won our citizenship by every test that can be applied. For this our country we have worked and in defense of this government we have offered our lives. We march as Americans seeking that equality of opportunity which is the boast of this democracy.
>
> We march to keep alive the spirit of Lincoln's government of the people, for the people, and by the people.[33]

In March 1941 Randolph's March on Washington Committee (the official title of the March movement before July 1941) broadened its base when it gained the support of Walter White, who by then was also supporting the UAW strike in Detroit.[34] Before the end of the month, Randolph and the March Committee also had Lester Granger of the National Urban League and Channing Tobias of the Young Men's Christian Association on board. By mid-May, the NAACP contributed money to the March on Washington and advised all its branches to cooperate with local march committees to organize marchers, distribute march buttons, and disseminate publicity.[35]

White demonstrated his new commitment to aggressive militant action when the steering committee of the march discussed what position it would take if the president did not issue an executive order. Granger and Tobias tried to direct the steering committee from taking a definite position. Tobias claimed that "demand" was too strong a word to hurl at the president because it is a "CP-copyrighted word," a reference to the Communist Party. Granger pointed out that the committee ought to give the president enough time to react to the demand. The president, he argued, faced "a fundamental principal of law and we should recognize that the President has to consult many of the department heads and weigh technicalities." Tobias wondered how Randolph and White could tell the president that they could not accept his word if Roosevelt "indicates that it is impossible to issue an overnight order and gives assurance that he will proceed along the lines we agreed to, to get this done." "Don't kid yourself," White replied. "The President's promises are not more than water, and soon forgotten because it is politically expedient." Randolph, agreeing with White, observed the "President is a shrewd politician. The Solid South is legislating Negro affairs in Washington. We won't accept a promise. His promises are political." After the discussion, the group agreed, unanimously, to march if no executive order was issued. In preparation for that possibility, White told the committee he had wired "all members of the Board of the National Association for the Advancement of Colored People for approval to cut short the Houston Conference [the annual NAACP convention scheduled for late June] so that they can come back to Washington for the demonstration."[36]

By early June, word had spread that 100,000 African Americans planned to march on Washington July 1 and carry out a "monster" demonstration at the Lincoln Memorial. The black press, even the *Pittsburgh Courier*, which had called the march a crackpot proposal, screamed out with banner headlines, "March to Washington Draws Nationwide Response" as "100,000" get ready to march.[37] The White House, which had been ignoring the threatened march all spring and denying repeated requests from Walter White to discuss the exclusion of black workers from employment, could no longer block out the numbers gathering force in the black community. Feeling hounded, Roosevelt turned to four people he thought African Americans trusted: Eleanor Roosevelt; Aubrey Williams, the head of the National Youth Administration; Mayor Fiorello H. LaGuardia, a friend of Randolph's; and Anna Rosenberg, regional director of New York City's Social Security Board. Roosevelt contacted Williams and told him to "Get the missus and Fiorello and Anna and get it [the march] stopped."[38]

While both Eleanor and Franklin Roosevelt feared the results of even 10,000 black Americans in segregated Washington, D.C., Eleanor approved of the principles of the march. Yet she worried that the timing was wrong because the demonstration "will set back the progress which is being made," unleashing "more solid opposition from certain groups than we have had in the past." Randolph and White stood firm, reminding the emissaries from the president that the march committee sought jobs, not promises. Randolph, who believed Eleanor Roosevelt was a "genuine friend of the race," rejected her advice because, as he explained to William Knudsen, head of General Motors and Roosevelt's Office of Production Management (OPM), he thought nothing had "gripped" the heart of black Americans since Emancipation like the "girding of our country for national defense without according them the recognition and opportunity as citizens, consumers and workers they felt justified in expecting." When the good intentions and friendly persuasion of trusted allies failed, Roosevelt invited Randolph and White to meet with him in the White House.[39]

The crucial meeting in the White House took place on June 18. The negotiations between Roosevelt, Randolph, and White reveal how Randolph, with White's assistance, managed to keep the exchange open while simultaneously defending the priorities of black America, ensuring that those priorities remained central to the negotiation process. In addition to Randolph and White, Roosevelt included Henry Stimson, secretary of war; Frank Knox, secretary of the navy; William Knudsen; Sidney Hillman of OPM; Aubrey Williams; and Anna Rosenberg.[40]

Roosevelt . . . embarked upon one of his favorite filibuster stratagems. But, finding he could not engage Randolph in small talk, he turned raconteur and started regaling his audience with old political anecdotes. Randolph, unfailingly well-mannered, allowed himself to be entertained. But the clock was running, the President's time was no doubt well budgeted. . . . So, with as much graciousness as he commanded, Randolph broke in: "Mr. President, time is running on. You are quite busy, I know. But what we want to talk with you about is the problem of jobs for Negroes in defense industries. Our people are being turned away at factory gates because they are colored. They can't live with this thing. Now, what are you going to do about it?"

"Well, Phil [A. Philip Randolph], what do you want me to do?"

"Mr. President, we want you to do something that will enable Negro workers to get work in these plants."

"Why," Roosevelt replied, "I surely want them to work, too. I'll call up the heads of the various defense plants and have them see to it that Negroes are given the same opportunity to work in defense plants as any other citizen in the country."

"We want you to do more than that," Randolph said. "We want something concrete, something tangible, definite, positive, and affirmative."

"What do you mean?"

"Mr. President, we want you to issue an executive order making it mandatory that Negroes be permitted to work in these plants."

"Well, Phil," Roosevelt replied, "you know I can't do that. If I issue an executive order for you, then there'll be no end to other groups coming in here and asking me to issue executive orders for them, too. In any event, I couldn't do anything unless you called off this march of yours. Questions like this can't be settled with a sledge hammer."

"I'm sorry, Mr. President, the march cannot be called off."

"How many people do you plan to bring?" Roosevelt wanted to know.

"One hundred thousand, Mr. President."

Roosevelt seemed torn between alarm and disbelief. Perhaps this was a bluff. He turned to Walter White, as if to a man whose word he could trust, looked White squarely in the eye for a few seconds, and asked, "Walter, how many people will really march?"

White's eyes did not blink. He said, "One hundred thousand, Mr. President." . . .

You can't bring 100,000 Negroes to Washington," Roosevelt said. "Somebody might get killed."

Randolph said that was unlikely, especially if the President himself came out and addressed the gathering.

Roosevelt was not amused. "Call it off," he said curtly, "and we'll talk again."

Randolph said he had a pledge to honor with his people, and he could not go back to them with anything less than an executive order. . . . Roosevelt suggested that Randolph and White confer with his presidential assistant over some way of solving the problem with defense contractors.

"Not defense contractors alone," Randolph broke in. "The government, too. The government is the worst offender."

Roosevelt . . . informed the president of the porter's union that it was not the policy of the President of the United States to rule, or be ruled, with a gun at his head.

"Then," Randolph replied, "I shall have to stand by the pledge I've made to the people."[41]

White's steadfast support of Randolph's lobbying tactics during the White House discussions marked the end of an era when black Americans were willing to rely on the promise of good intentions from white political leaders. Mary McLeod Bethune, an official in the National Youth Administration from 1935 to 1943, added power to the White House discussions by using the trust she had established with both Roosevelts as leverage to back Randolph's demands. As White looked Roosevelt in the eye from within the White House, declaring that indeed 100,000 black Americans would march if an executive order was not forthcoming, Bethune called upon the National Council of Negro Women, of which she was president, to meet in Washington, D.C., the day before the march, dramatizing its imminence. Bethune, one of the few black New Dealers who "openly supported" the March on Washington, was considered as close a confident to Eleanor Roosevelt as White.[42]

With White in the foreground and Bethune in the background, Randolph maintained control over the multiple drafts the executive order went through for the next six days. Many versions were rejected because the language was not forceful. Finally, Randolph approved a draft and Roosevelt signed Executive Order 8802 on June 25. White, who had flown to Texas for the NAACP conference, sent Randolph telegrams to boost his resolve during the week while he studied various drafts. As proof that the March on Washington had the backing of the country, he told Randolph that the National Baptist Sunday School convention, with more than 5,000 delegates, enthusiastically endorsed the march and pledged to participate and noted that Elmer Carter, editor of *Opportunity*, was certain that there were "huge delegations planning to go to Washington from Virginia and other seaboard and middle western states."[43]

The credibility of the march in the eyes of President Roosevelt may have hinged on the participation and endorsement of White and Bethune. Randolph's power as a leader of black labor may not have carried enough weight with Roosevelt had the two friends of the New Deal not stood beside him. Roosevelt was probably not surprised when Randolph pushed the march quid pro quo to its limit, but accounts suggest he was unprepared for White's response. Conversely, had White and Bethune requested an executive order as individuals utilizing channels of quiet communication established by dominant power brokers—without threatening collective, mass action—their complaint would have caught Roosevelt's attention but not action. The approach used by Randolph in gaining Executive Order 8802 exemplified the collective, mass-based strategy espoused by the new crowd. Rather than balancing interests and negotiating as individuals for the interests of all disenfranchised black Americans, Randolph, with the Brotherhood and the march committee, directly confronted discrimination using the threat of the "meaning of our numbers."[44]

The essence of Executive Order 8802 stated that:

> As a prerequisite to the successful conduct of our national defense production effort, I do hereby reaffirm the policy of the United States that there shall be no discrimination in the employment of workers in defense industries or government because of race, creed, color, or national origin, and I do hereby declare that it is the duty of employers and of labor organizations, in furtherance of said policy and of this order, to provide for the full and equitable participation of all workers in defense industries, without discrimination because of race, creed, color, or national origin.[45]

The executive order gained a measure of economic citizenship, one of the goals of the Brotherhood protest networks since the 1920s, and represented the most definitive break with past silence at the federal level over the issue of economic disenfranchisement based on color.[46] As Harvard Sitkoff argues, Randolph's leadership in the march issue contributed to "propelling civil rights to the fore as a national issue."[47] But Executive Order 8802 did much more when it expanded the definition of enfranchisement to include rights in the economic sphere. The order did not just put civil rights on the national agenda, it also introduced the idea at the national level that access to work was a civil right, giving legitimacy to the idea that the right to economic opportunity was embedded in citizenship. What Roosevelt "reaffirmed" in the executive order was, in the eyes of black America, a confirmation of rights won in the early years of Emancipation.[48]

Finally, when Randolph and White departed from the political etiquette normally employed when lobbying the White House, they broke a tradition whereby black leaders beseeched white leaders for the opportunity to participate fully as American citizens. "If the 'March on Washington' does nothing else," an editorial in the *Chicago Defender* declared, "it will convince white America that the American black man has decided henceforth and forever to abandon the timid role of Uncle-Tomism in his struggle for social justice."[49] Executive Order 8802 was as important in terms of the tactics used to extract the order as for the recognition and acknowledgment by the federal government that American democracy failed to grant equal economic opportunity to all its citizens. It was an attempt by black America to approach the negotiating table from a position of strength and remove a vestige of servile, patron-client relations. In this respect, the threatened march introduced black Americans to the use of a powerful tool for challenging the racial status quo.

The March on Washington Movement

The Fair Employment Practice Committee (FEPC), established to investigate violations of Executive Order 8802, lacked enforcement power, which was one reason Randolph turned the March on Washington *Committee* into the March on Washington *Movement* shortly after the executive order was issued.[50] MOWM was to be the "watchdog" over enactment of 8802, in an effort to put teeth into FEPC investigations.[51] Edwin Embree, president of the Rosenwald Foundation, described the March on Washington Movement as "mysterious," because it has "almost no organization, no big machine for promotion and publicity. Yet it grips the people's imagination and holds their loyalty."[52] The mystery surrounding the MOWM and its activities may have been a result of not understanding how grass-roots movements coalesce and sustain themselves.[53] While MOWM appeared to function as a spontaneous organization with its large rallies, held during the summer of 1942, the staying power of the MOWM was in its local activities, initiated in conjunction with units of the BSCP. News stories in the *Black Worker*, the monthly newspaper of the BSCP, documenting joint activities of the BSCP and the MOWM, showed the degree to which the organizations were fused between 1941 and 1943. Indeed, the connection between the organizing cadre of the BSCP and the MOWM was a point of friction in Chicago where veteran BSCP organizer Charles Burton, who led the Chicago branch of MOWM, was accused of controlling MOWM activities with an iron fist. Several younger, better-educated recruits appealed to Milton Webster and Randolph for Burton's resignation, suggesting as well that parliamentary procedures be enforced at the local level. Neither Burton nor Webster felt they had time for parliamentary procedures when what they were after was building a "movement."[54]

The exchange between the "young turks" and Randolph showed that despite the lack of internal democracy, communication could flow vertically within the movement. By comparison, many working-class activists often criticized the NAACP for its rigid procedures. Randolph felt the younger members meant well, but did not understand what it takes to build a movement. He planned to explain the value of Burton to the movement, somebody who could "withstand the pressure," to the dissident group.[55] But group dissension also reflected the active participation of members at the local level, which was also shown in the volume of letters in Randolph's files thanking those who voluntarily contributed to meetings and rallies.[56]

Dissension first emerged when Randolph "postponed" the July 1941 March. Several members of the youth division of MOWM, led by Richard Parrish and Bayard Rustin, felt Randolph had not pushed far enough with his demands. Randolph addressed postponement, in the *Black Worker*, by explaining that the primary objective of the march was gaining jobs for unemployed black workers in defense industries. Although discrimination in the armed forces was not addressed, African Americans "would have been placed in an untenable, absurd, and ridiculous position had it rejected [the offer] . . . on the grounds that we didn't get everything we wanted." Randolph settled for half a loaf, but rationalized the result by reminding the black public that the march was not an end in itself. As a means to a larger end, the march had a simple, clearly defined objective. "Without an issue which is clear, understandable and possible of realization, the masses cannot be rallied."[57]

Despite his emphasis on simple objectives, MOWM also had a spiritual, moral, and educational component, which was often invisible to outsiders.[58] But it was the less clearly definable aspect of MOWM that Bayard Rustin recalled years later. MOWM locals were incubators for teaching mass protest politics: how to mobilize people, determine goals at the local level, and utilize existing resources, especially talents of the local population. Rustin recalled his work with MOWM and Randolph as "one of the most important things I ever did because it prepared me for many of the other activities that I was to engage in over the years." Rustin, an organizer for Congress on Racial Equality (CORE) in 1942, worked with Martin Luther King Jr. in the Montgomery Improvement Association (MIA) in the 1950s and was a principal organizer for the 1963 March on Washington. MOWM taught Rustin "a great deal of practical experience in terms of . . . getting people in motion." Traveling around the country for MOWM, he learned that the most economical way to reach large numbers of people was to "piggyback on other peoples' meetings," not set up separate meetings. In some cities he would piggyback on Urban League meetings, in other cities the NAACP or women's groups. But while it was efficient for organizing new MOWM branches and gaining support, the method left few opportunities for records, increasing the mystery of the movement at the local level.[59] Between September and December 1941, Randolph and Webster also traveled cross-country, addressing some 25,000 people in Seattle and Spokane, Portland, Oakland and Los Angeles, Salt Lake City, Denver, Omaha, Kansas City and St. Louis, and Chicago, organizing local MOWM chapters, and dispensing the MOWM guide for "organization and structure."[60]

The next phase of MOWM activities focused on the U.S. entry into World War II after the attack on Pearl Harbor. Remembering the experience of World War I, African Americans were determined to take advantage of the context World War II provided for highlighting democratic rights and advancing black interests.[61] In January 1942, for example, the National Urban League, declared "that the Negro was 'not whole-heartedly and unreservedly' behind the government's program" for war against Japan and Germany. In March delegates from fifty black organizations informed a government official that "the Negro people were cool to the war effort and that there could be no national unity nor high morale among Negroes unless they were given their rights."[62] Rather than issuing a call to "close ranks" behind the administration as they did during World War I, black leaders wanted to use the very dependency of the government on cooperation from black Americans to increase demands for civil rights.[63] "If we don't fight for our rights during this war while the government needs us," wrote a leader from Harlem, "it will be too late after the war."[64] Walter White challenged the administration to "prove to us . . . that you are not hypocrites when you say this is a war for freedom. Prove it to us and we will show you that we can and will fight like fury for that freedom. But we want— and we intend to have—our share of that freedom!"[65]

Once the United States officially entered the war, Randolph and MOWM organizers linked the war for democracy in Europe and Asia to the war for democracy on the home front with the slogan, "Winning Democracy for the Negro Is Winning the War for Democracy." The phrase resonated with black America because, as philosopher Alaine Locke noted, black Americans were "now a touchstone the world over of our democratic integrity." The phrase grew out of the "Double-V" campaign which became popular during the winter of 1942.[66] The *Pittsburgh Courier* spread the idea to its readership when it launched its "Double V" effort, "a victory over our enemies at home and victory over our enemies on the battlefields abroad." The *Chicago Defender* began a similar campaign a few weeks later.[67]

Building on the Double-V campaign, Randolph announced in March plans "to stage a series of giant protest meetings in the key cities 'to win the democratic rights for Negroes now during the war.'"[68] The three cities designated for the massive rallies were New York, Chicago, and St. Louis. Randolph promoted the rallies as a show of black solidarity, declaring "the President will move, only when Negroes make him move. He is not going to take action on the Negro's problem unless he is compelled to."[69] The *Amsterdam News* helped perpetuate the link with a headline, "March-on-Washington to Garden on Tuesday, Randolph Reports Roosevelt Concerned over Rallies to Be Held in Key Cities."[70]

The first mass gathering of MOWM, in Madison Square Garden in New York City on June 16, used a two-hour blackout of Harlem, keeping Harlem "dark, dry, and silent," as a way to convey a sense of strength, direct action, and control. The blackout was to symbolize "the economic and political blackout through which our people still stumble and fall in their too-slow progress toward the light in half-free America," according to Randolph. MOWM generated support for the blackout from ministers, who encouraged cooperation from their pulpits, and social and civic organizations.[71] Considered a huge success, New York drew an estimated 20,000 people, with a mere "scattering of whites."[72]

The mass gatherings engendered a spirit of unity around the issue of citizenship through music, drama, and "oratory." In preparation, leaflets flooded the streets of black communities exclaiming: "WAKE UP NEGRO AMERICA! Do you want work? Do you want equal rights? Do you want justice? Then prepare now to fight for it! . . . STORM MADISON SQUARE GARDEN." Another widely circulated "press release" demanded that black Americans "JOIN IN THE GREATEST . . . GATHERING OF NEGRO PEOPLE FOR JUSTICE—DEMOCRACY—FREEDOM AND MANHOOD RIGHTS IN THE HISTORY OF THE WORLD!" Stamps sold by the BSCP local to raise money for the rallies proclaimed, "We are Americans!" Literature advertising the Chicago rally, dispersed by the BSCP division in Chicago, had a banner stating, "Fight or Be Slaves!" The program cover for the New York rally depicted a cross section of black Americans marching together as they carried the American flag. The five musical numbers at the New York rally included the songs, "Brown Soldier Boy" and "We Are Americans, Too." The latter, written by Andy Razaf and Eubie Blake, was popular in black communities throughout the country during the summer of 1942.[73]

Perhaps Mary McLeod Bethune best expressed the sentiment running through the crowd in New York and the country in her speech at the New York rally. She congratulated the crowd for its "militancy and resoluteness," reminding the audience that for more than 300 years in America "you have been regarded as the patient, submissive minority." After Emancipation and the Thirteenth, Fourteenth, and Fifteenth Amendments "took you out of the status of chattels . . . the pall of a slave experience still hung over the masses of our people." But "today—a New Negro has arisen in America. He is here in Madison Square Garden tonight." The New Negro had stopped "begging" and was now "insisting" on "full freedom, justice, respect, and opportunity." Finally, Bethune explained, "we have grown tied of turning the other cheek. Both our cheeks are now so blistered that they are too sensitive for further blows."[74]

All the rallies included several speakers and the presentation of a play written especially for the summer demonstrations by Dick Campbell, director of the Rose McClendon Players from New York. The play, "The Watchword Is Forward!" a slogan used by Randolph to close his letters, featured a monthly meeting of the Domestic Workers Association and the local draft board. Reports from all three cities claimed that audiences responded "wildly" when a young black man, called by his draft board, told the board: "Yes sir, I am against them Japs. I'm against them Germans, them Italians—and I'm also against them Negro hating crackers down South." At that point the response was described in terms of "screams, cheers and hand clapping" creating a "bedlam"; or the "pandemonium which greeted this declaration is indescribable."[75]

A large well-organized volunteer effort was required to carry out all of the details involved in producing these rallies, with approximately 12,000 attending in Chicago and 9,000 attending the August event in St. Louis. For the New York rally, over 200 individuals gave between $5 and $25, approximately fifty organizations contributed between $5 and $25, and some thirty organizations gave $25 or more to the MOWM. The meetings were financed largely by black individuals and organizations, with the financial strength of the BSCP backing the operation.[76] In Chicago, the MOWM coordinated its efforts closely with approximately twenty ministers from the South Side, who ended their strategy sessions by singing "John Brown's Body." The ministers set aside June 21 as MOWM Sunday in Chicago, donated the offering from that day to the Chicago rally, and promoted the rally in their sermons.[77]

The black press commented on the broad cross section from black communities participating in the rallies. The New York rally was described as having a "decidedly working class atmosphere."[78] Ellen Tarry, a newspaperwomen who covered the New York event, claimed that "Harlem was like a deserted village. Every man, woman, and child who had carfare was in Madison Square Garden."[79] In Chicago workers cheered along with professionals when White said, "We Negroes must fight for the right to fight to make the world safe for democracy." The St. Louis rally, held on August 14, was noted not just for the large numbers of workers but for the fact that about half the audience comprised women.[80]

To many, black protest politics had come of age during the summer of 1942. The *Amsterdam News* declared in the aftermath of the New York rally that "20,000 Storm Madison Square Garden to Help Bury Race's 'Uncle Toms'" and carried a cartoon with a caption, "Here Lies Uncle Tom, Died June 16, 1942, at Madison Square Garden," with an editorial, "Uncle Tom's Funeral."[81] Reading the pulse of African Americans for the Rosenwald Fund, Will Alexander, Edwin Embree, and Charles S. Johnson claimed that the nature of protest within the black community had changed. The "characteristic movements among Negroes are now for the first time becoming proletarian, as contrasted to upper class or intellectual influence that was typical of previous movements," they observed. The "present proletarian direction," they argued, reflected the "increasing general feelings of protest against discrimination" that emerged from war activities.[82]

Contemporary assessments agreed that a more militant impulse flowed from black communities and characterized the culture of protest politics endorsed in the crowds at the summer rallies. The *Pittsburgh Courier* claimed that African Americans no longer "made the mistake of relying entirely upon the gratitude and sense of fair play of the American people." The new crowd of activists had "neither faith in promises, nor a high opinion of the integrity of the American people, where race is involved." Instead, they noted that black Americans learned they "must rely primarily upon ... [their] own efforts."[83]

The coming of age of protest politics did not guarantee the success of the March on Washington Movement, for the organization still had not marched. In Chicago, Randolph promised that "If the President does not issue a war proclamation to abolish jim crow in Washington, the District of Columbia and all government departments and the armed forces, Negroes are going to march and we don't give a damn what happens." Furthermore, Randolph cried out, black Americans would "rather . . . die standing on our feet fighting for our rights than to exist upon our knees begging for life."[84] In St. Louis, Randolph again declared that the original idea of bringing 100,000 black Americans to march on Washington would be undertaken "sometime this fall" and announced "big mass meetings" for black Americans in Washington, D.C., in September.[85]

None of these promises were carried out, opening the door for critics to raise questions about the agenda and approach of the March on Washington movement. The *Pittsburgh Courier*, for example, accused Randolph of irresponsibility with his talk of "mass marches which never materialize."[86] Randolph probably sensed the fragility of the coalition the MOWM had inspired. By early July signs of a schism were apparent. The Chicago rally did not receive the full cooperation of black leaders that the New York event had. Mary McLeod Bethune, advertised in advance as a major speaker for the Chicago rally, declined to speak because, as she told Randolph, MOWM meetings threatened the war effort.[87] Randolph replied that the war effort would be helped if black citizens insisted on "their democratic rights of being permitted to play their part in the Army, Navy, Air and Marine Corps, defense industries, and the government as equals with the white people in this country."[88]

Walter White participated in the Chicago rally but not without reservations. He was increasingly concerned with the all-black clause in the constitution of the MOWM. The very success of the summer rallies in New York and Chicago created new tensions within black leadership groups and set the stage for splits in the alliance between the March on Washington Committee and the NAACP.[89] Transferring jurisdiction over the FEPC from the executive branch to Congress raised the question, Why continue the MOWM? If its role was to act as a watchdog by threatening mass-based collective action to lobby the executive branch, then how was the MOWM to use its bargaining power to lobby the War Manpower Commission funded by Congress? These issues forced the question of the purpose of MOWM, which led to a policy conference for September 1942 in Detroit.

Garvey's Revenge: The Detroit Conference of the MOWM

Two clear directives emerged from the Detroit conference that drove a wedge in the crack that had begun to divide the MOWM and NAACP. While both contributed to the demise of the MOWM in the 1940s, they also foreshadowed the direction of the larger civil rights struggles in the 1950s and 1960s. One directive emphasized using nonviolent civil disobedience as a tactic to attack Jim Crow in restaurants, hotels, buses, and movie theaters.[90] Randolph explained the strategy developed the "principle of repetition" to keep pressure on society, forcing the white public to recognize the liminal world of the half slave, half free in which most black Americans lived.[91] Black Americans, according to Randolph, had "the moral obligation to demand the right to enjoy and make use of their civil and political privileges." Without fighting for "our citizenship rights" the "Public will consider that we don't want them and should not have them." In the process of fighting for "these civil rights the Negro masses will be disciplined in struggle." When black citizens were put in jail, black Americans would have a "sense of their importance and value as citizens and as fighters in the Negro liberation movement."[92] Although Randolph was ahead of his time with his vision of disciplined nonviolent demonstrations modeled after Mohandas K. Gandhi, he introduced large numbers of black Americans to a concept that led to the upheaval, if not overthrow, of Jim Crow in the 1960s.[93]

The other directive reaffirmed limiting MOWM membership to African Americans in order to control better the direction of the protest agenda. The ongoing campaign to build up self-reliance and self-determination, to assure that black Americans "lead in fighting their own battle," continued. MOWM wanted to "insure against whites . . . dominating it in an unhealthy way."[94] In a letter to a MOWM organizer and BSCP member, Randolph said, "We don't want any white people in the March on Washington Movement. In fact we are not going to have any."[95] Collective organization among black Americans must come from within to be effective. "Now there is organization and organization," Randolph told the Detroit conference. Although black Americans are highly organized, traditional black "organizations are not built to deal with and manipulate the mechanics of power. . . . They don't seek to transform the socio-economic racial milieu," which was the ultimate aim of the MOWM through its "action program."[96] Even as the policy conference distinguished MOWM from other black advancement organizations, it added fuel to the fire of disunity smoldering in the NAACP.

The MOWM did not believe in "educating high government officials or in deals and horse-trading negotiations-kind of 'education,'" as one of its pamphlets read. It favored "bolder, more direct action than other Negro organizations do," inviting comparison with the NAACP.[97] The Detroit delegates said the MOWM did not intend "to be a rival organization to any established agency already functioning to advance the interests of the Negro," but the NAACP's reaction to Detroit resembled its earlier response to the formation of the NNC in 1936. White declined Randolph's invitation to attend the Detroit conference, and the NAACP board of directors, of which Randolph was still a member, voted to sever its close relationship with the MOWM during its September meeting.

The NAACP's previous endorsement of the MOWM, it pointed out, was with the understanding that the March on Washington Movement was not a permanent organization.[98]

Although White thought the idea of excluding white people was a way to reduce the "possible danger of the Comrades trying to capture the march," he was uncomfortable with a strategy that discriminated against white participation to make a statement "about discrimination in the defense program." Charles H. Houston, who had opposed the all-black clause since the MOWM was first formed, saw little value in excluding white participants in order to eliminate the possible "charge of Communism," reminding Randolph not to forget that "there are Negro Communists as well as whites." But Houston's major reason for opposition to exclusion of white people was that he did not "believe the Negroes can win the battle for integration and citizenship by themselves. What success Negroes have had in the past has been due in large part to their ability to interest and enlist other persons in their cause."[99] Randolph disagreed not with Houston's long-run analysis, just with collaboration with white America in the short run. During the first year, the issue of racial exclusivity did not limit NAACP support and participation in MOWM activities. The all-black issue in conjunction with making MOWM a permanent entity led the NAACP to draw a line against further collaboration.[100]

That Randolph persisted in maintaining the all-black membership clause was portrayed as contradictory by some contemporaries. Critics of MOWM's tactics called Randolph a "Negro isolationist" and a "racist" who espoused, according to one journalist, "Ku Kluxism in reverse." The black press portrayed Randolph as a bundle of contradictions for advocating interracial unions in the 1920s and a racially exclusive MOWM in the 1940s.[101] Yet Randolph built his career by using an all-black union to attain long-range inclusion within the organized labor movement.[102] Others who linked the all-black qualification with Marcus Garvey, despite Randolph's attempts to persuade the public otherwise, may have been closer to the mark.[103] His steadfast allegiance to the principle of self-determination and self-reliance and his movement away from white control over black leaders and institutions—the very foundation of the MOWM philosophy—was a reflection of his black nationalism. So was Randolph's resignation from the NNC in 1940. Despite Randolph's collaboration with known Communists in the NNC, his tolerance for the NNC decreased with the increased attention to the demands of a white radical agenda. It was not that the NNC was dominated by Communists in 1940 so much as it was dominated by white labor activists—whether they were radicals, socialists, or Communists—who increasingly placed needs and interests of black workers on the back burner. When he resigned, he played the red card, as the consummate publicist that he was, for practical reasons: to place some distance between Communists and the BSCP new crowd in order to reduce the troubles faced by those labeled "black and red." That was for mainstream public consumption.

But the issue for Randolph was larger than just communism, as Houston's remark pointed out, and as Randolph's policy in the MOWM demonstrates. An all-black membership does not exclude black Communists, but does exclude white socialists, white liberals, and white Communists. Randolph, very likely, was expressing agreement with a belief stated by Hubert Harrison, his mentor from the early Harlem days. When Harrison severed relations with the Socialist Party, he protested the "colorline" honored by its platform. Harrison had problems with a party, he protested, that said that when working people struggle for jobs, self-preservation comes naturally to the fore. The Socialist Party rationalized racism when they claimed that "Race feeling is not so much a result of social as biological evolution."[104] Had Randolph grown tired of negotiating the racism of white liberals and radicals, including that ostensibly benign variant which manifests itself in the form of good intentions, during his nearly three-decade-long struggle for black freedom? If he had, he was in good company. Poet Claude McKay explained that he had moved toward a black nationalist position after spending years "beating" his brains out "against the walls of [white] prejudice."[105] Winston James, pointing out the remarkable number of former opponents of Marcus Garvey from the 1920s who moved toward more black nationalist positions in the 1930s and 1940s, suggests there may be an "unwritten law of tendency in the United States which states that because of the racism of the labor movement and its organizations, black socialists are almost inexorably pushed to a black nationalist position." He calls the tendency Garvey's Revenge, because Garvey managed to "wreck revenge upon his erstwhile black socialist opponents by diminishing their belief in and commitment to alliances across racial lines for radical transformation."[106]

Randolph carefully explained that the MOWM, while all-black, was not black nationalism, but that was to distinguish MOWM from the "so-called 'Back to Africa Movements.' "[107] He was not trying to adopt racial exclusiveness to win a mass following but to continue to challenge social relations between black and white America. Randolph continued to seek the advice of white professionals as long as he controlled the working relationship. The movement was "not anti-white, anti-American, anti-labor, anti-Catholic or anti-Semitic. It's simply pro-Negro." Although "white liberals and labor may sympathize with the Negro's fight against Jim Crow . . . they are not going to lead the fight. They never have and they never will." Building self-esteem and self-reliance was directly related to the all-black policy. In order to nurture the development of self-reliance, Randolph and the MOWM cadre believed they first had to eradicate certain myths that sometimes immobilized black Americans. Bennie Smith, an organizer for both the BSCP and the MOWM in the Midwest, called it a fear of an all-black movement. Randolph, agreeing with Smith, said too many black Americans "want some white people hanging around to whom they may run as though they were their parents when they get into difficulties."[108]

Randolph's strategy for an all-black organization was part of his larger, long-term goal to remove vestiges of servile relations that held both black and white citizens hostage to stereotypes of each other. The stereotype white people often held of black citizens was embedded in a system that was still coming to terms with accepting black Americans as the moral equals of white citizens. Custom and practice had so conflated African Americans with slave status in the eyes of white America that seventy-five years after the end of the institution black Americans continued to be identified as second-class citizens. Thus, MOWM tactics were designed to change the outlook white citizens had of black Americans as much as they were to alter black self-esteem.

The all-black tactic was designed to do much more than keep out the Communists, as some have suggested, and it was also designed to do more than borrow from Marcus Garvey.[109] Randolph's contribution in the MOWM was to use black nationalism as a tool to shatter barriers—social, economic, political—that barred African Americans from full participation in American society. For Randolph, the motivation for excluding white participation grew out of his preoccupation with removing the stigma of the servant class from black Americans. The MOWM was designed to be not just a national organization but the means to form local networks, where the experience of building the MOWM at the local level would be in the hands of African Americans. In order to avoid situations where white Americans could impose boundaries in interracial strategy sessions as a way to control the decision-making process, black Americans had to formulate their own agenda and tactics based on the interests of the black community; they had to be free of the politics of civility that tried to channel dissent away from protest and toward moderation.

"We Are Americans, Too"

The Detroit conference revealed shortcomings of the MOWM as solidarity over key issues broke down. By the spring of 1943, as the MOWM prepared for a national conference in Chicago, called "We Are Americans, Too," division within the black community regarding appropriate tactics had widened. The

MOWM continued to emphasize the battle on the home front against the "de-struction of our American democratic institutions, ideals, faiths and values," but black leaders in the NAACP grew wary of the backlash black militancy inspired. Black despair and frustration were expressed through the aggressive politics of men and women who had "come to maturity and . . . [wanted] to be free to walk as a man . . . no longer a child of the human race begging that some self-appointed savior take his hand and lead him."[110]

New-crowd protest politics was not received well by whites who wanted to maintain the racial status quo. Black Americans engaged in at least 242 racial confrontations in forty-seven cities during 1943.[111] The NAACP wished to curb the excesses and refused to join the MOWM's campaign to expose, during the spring of 1943, the "War's Greatest Scandal: The Story of Jim Crow in Uniform." MOWM distributed a sixteen-page booklet exposing the treatment black soldiers had to endure as "servants and laborers" without the chance to serve as officers; it told of black soldiers "forced to march at the tail end" of a parade "behind garbage trucks," and of a lynching of a black soldier.[112] The NAACP also declined to support the call for the proposed MOWM meeting in Chicago in June, creat-ing more distance between the two organizations. By the summer of 1943, even Adam Clayton Powell Jr., a member of the executive committee of the MOWM, thought the organization had run its course. He attributed its demise to the mistake of excluding white Americans.[113]

When the "We Are Americans, Too" convention was finally held in Chicago between June 30 and July 4, MOWM decided to sponsor a march on Washington, but the timing was left to Randolph's discretion. Rather than one large march, the emphasis shifted to having a number of smaller marches on city halls and state capitals. There was much discussion about requiring all-black member-ship, and delegates voted 55 to 2 to exclude white citizens. The Metropolitan Community Church, the first church in Chicago to open its doors to Pullman porters, hosted the convention the first three nights. The attendance averaged close to 600 each evening, reaching over 2,000 people the final night.[114]

The goals of MOWM were similar to those that drove the manhood rights campaign in the 1920s. As Randolph told the 1942 March on Washington Move-ment conference in Detroit, the objective was to break up servile social relations that were kept alive when black Americans relied "on white people for direction and support." It was a situation that "inevitably" happened "in mixed organiza-tions that are supposed to be in the interest of the Negro." A "march on Washington" was "evidence to white America that black America is on the march for its rights and means business," and that black Americans were setting the terms for conducting negotiations.[115]

MOWM received a serious blow when, only ten days before the "We Are Americans, Too" convention, the worst race riot of 1943 erupted in Detroit, Michigan. Thirty-four people were killed, twenty-five of them black Detroiters. A committee appointed by the governor of Michigan blamed the civil war, in part, on "the positive exhortation by many so-called responsible Negro leaders to be 'militant' in the struggle for racial equality."[116] The violence of the summer of 1943 dampened the spirit of militancy that had fueled the resolute determination to lay claim to what was granted with emancipation. The fear was physical reprisals from whites who were impatient with black activism. Increasingly, white liberals in alliance with moderate black leaders advised the more militant activists to go slow, inspiring many African Americans to adopt more moderate positions.

Although events in Detroit testify to the break down of solidarity between the MOWM and the NAACP at the national level, there is reason to believe there was cross-fertilization between the two groups at the local level. When Walter White appointed Ella Baker as national director of branches in April 1943, she pushed her populist approach with its emphasis on developing strong local leaders. Because Baker's approach and agenda were compatible with the MOWM, a synergy—what Bayard Rustin, organizing for the MOWM, referred to as "piggy-backing"—may have evolved between them at the local level.[117] Nevertheless, MOWM never recovered the momentum and interest it generated during the summer of 1942 and dissolved into the Council for a Permanent FEPC and then was declared defunct, by Randolph, in 1946.[118]

August Meier and Elliott Rudwick claimed that MOWM was "a key inspiration for CORE," the Congress on Racial Equality formed in 1942, which also stressed direct action but, unlike MOWM, was interracial.[119] Some of MOWM tactics, which were used later in the civil rights movement, were carried forward by CORE. Randolph's spree of black nationalism illustrates that aspects of the black power movement of the sixties grew from soil tilled during the forties. Similarly, the energy and enthusiasm reflected in the MOWM rallies were a forerunner of the civil rights movement: having reached a point where the status quo was no longer tolerable, people found a way to change their daily lives in the actions they could take together.

Finally, Executive Order 8802 helped change public policy by expanding government's understanding of citizenship rights. When the order suggested that access to work was a civil right, the issue of economic rights of citizenship was placed on the political agenda at the highest level of government. The struggle carried out by African Americans for full inclusion in the economic life of the nation expanded how the nation thought about citizenship and served as a benchmark in future campaigns waged by other Americans to claim rights of citizenship.

Early in 1944 the president raised the question of citizenship rights when he presented his Economic Bill of Rights in the State of the Union Address. "True individual freedom cannot exist without economic security and independence," Roosevelt declared. The rights to a job, decent housing, a good education, medical care, and protection from unemployment were basic components of rights of citizenship, regardless of race, color, or creed, he explained. Raising the issue of social citizenship in the State of the Union Address, Roosevelt also raised the hope that such a fundamental change in the nation's perception of citizenship rights might help African Americans win the war on the home front.[120] That did not happen, and the larger task remained unfinished. But MOWM underscored the value of collective mass action to checkmate the dominant culture's ability to keep African Americans in an inferior place, which was its most significant contribution.

Protest Politics Comes of Age

Today the Negro stands on the porch and knocks on the door. He
clutches the receipts for three centuries of slave labor for which our
fathers never paid him. "Let me come in," he asks. "Let me sit by the
fire and join the talk. I helped to build this house." There are some men
who slam the door with a curse. There are others who send him
around to the rear for a handout of old clothes and leftovers in a paper
sack. "I am your friend," they tell him. "My father never abused you
and neither do I. After the war I will find a way to help you. Go back to
the cabins and tell them to sing." The Negro turns away in bitterness.

THOMAS SANCTON, February 1943

The prominence of the March on Washington Movement faded after 1942 as the
movement tried to transform itself into a permanent entity. But as the MOWM
formalized structure withered, the polices and tactics taught by the march
movement continued to guide activists, particularly in the labor movement.
MOWM had tapped into the assertiveness that emerged when the national effort
to arm the world for democracy put few black workers in defense plants. Within
one month of Executive Order 8802, black workers in Detroit were in the vanguard demanding equal opportunity on the shop floor, utilizing tactics that
challenged the control of management and local union officials. African Americans viewed the executive order as a legitimation of protest politics: by expressing grievances through means not condoned by mainstream power brokers,
black citizens had opened up new possibilities for improving their status in
society.[1] The lesson—power begets power—encouraged using mass demonstrations as a tool for challenging power relations. Once the genie was out of the
bottle, black workers drew from the formula to demand changes in race relations, particularly within the CIO. When management, government, or union
officials dragged their feet over issues involving discrimination in workplaces,
black workers expressed their impatience by initiating wildcat strikes and work
stoppages, applying the lessons of new-crowd protest politics on the shop floor.[2]

Randolph had announced at the Detroit policy conference in September 1942 that black America wanted the "full works of citizenship with no reservations."[3] Reservations continued. New-crowd efforts to claim economic rights within the broader labor movement in Detroit and in FEPC hearings throughout the country illustrate how protest politics widened the sphere of struggle even as it circumscribed the role Randolph played in the emerging civil rights movement.

"Now Is the Time! Here Is the Place!": New-Crowd Strategies Invade the Workplace[4]

The promise of Executive Order 8802 and the Fair Employment Practice Committee (FEPC) reconfirmed the conviction in the hearts and minds of black Americans that they were engaged in a long-overdue crusade. Although black workers in the United States had been actively fighting for economic rights of citizenship since the 1860s, the march for greater opportunity had accelerated considerably during the years between World War I and World War II. As soon as the executive order was issued, many black workers in defense operations who were overlooked for upgrading during the production buildup for World War II took matters into their own hands. New-crowd protest politics infused labor negotiations in Detroit during the early years of the war when black workers were restricted to unskilled jobs and locked out of training programs, funded by federal tax dollars, to which white unskilled and semiskilled workers had easy access. Although black protest yielded enormous gains in terms of entrée to diverse industrial jobs, African American workers were rarely promoted and remained locked out of higher-paying, better-skilled craft positions in the auto and other industries.

Just two months after Roosevelt issued Executive Order 8802, the Bureau of Employment Security reported that over half of the openings expected to occur in selected war plants during the period September 1941 to February 1942 barred black workers as a matter of policy. "The greater the skill involved, the higher the degree of exclusion," even in industries traditionally open to black workers.[5] Robert Weaver, head of the Negro Employment and Training Branch of Roosevelt's Office of Production Management (OPM), noted that the tragedy of the color line in labor was reflected in the nation's failure to employ "its total manpower resources for three long years." He called it the "most striking instance of the tenacity with which America has clung to its established color-caste system in occupations." During the early phases of the defense effort the black worker did not benefit much, if at all, "from the expanding needs for workers, nor was he permitted to prepare himself for future employment in

essential war industries."[6] Weaver documented hundreds of cases of industrialists hiring out-of-town white workers rather than employing local black
workers.[7] Skilled and semiskilled positions for black workers were usually won
after African Americans waged extensive battles on the home front.

The situation in Detroit is illustrative because the city was one of the most
important arsenals during the Second World War. Despite the presence of a few
black workers in skilled positions at Ford Motor Company where, in 1941,
approximately 12,000 black workers made up over 12 percent of the labor force,
on the eve of the war the majority of black employees at Ford worked in
foundries as "general laborers" or as janitors. The A.C. Spark Plug Company in
Detroit employed 23 black men and women as janitors and janitresses out of its
3,500 workers; Vickers, Incorporated employed about 90 black janitors and
stock handlers among its 3,000 employees.[8]

Converting industry to manufacture war material entailed changes in production with implications for the occupational future of black workers. Generally, management resisted introducing black workers on assembly lines because,
they alleged, white workers would not accept them. Although a few firms
honored the government policy against discrimination in defense employment,
it was clear to black workers that they must seize the opportunities for upgrading.[9] At times their challenge to the occupational status quo forced a face-off
between the rank and file and union officials, which led to walkouts, mass
demonstrations, work stoppages, and wildcat strikes, as black workers relied on
direct action to first secure, then to maintain new positions in industry.[10]

In July 1941 black workers at Dodge Truck in Detroit walked out of work
when neither their union nor management would transfer them to the assembly line. In August, African America workers at Dodge Main staged two work
stoppages to protest the transfer of white workers only from foundries at Dodge
to production jobs at the Chrysler tank arsenal. Both management and local
union officials justified the transfers on the grounds that only management
could make transfer decisions. Black workers had stopped work when their
grievance was dismissed, which led to an official investigation of racial bias by
the Office of Production Management (OPM), to which the Fair Employment
Practice Committee was attached. Although African American workers continued working in the Dodge foundry, the investigation persuaded the international leadership of the UAW that it ought to pressure the local union to follow
the governmental edict lest the UAW-CIO lose support within the black community.[11] The pattern of restricting black workers to unskilled and foundry work
was broken because they were willing to challenge a prerogative—transfers and
upgrading—that management had claimed was its own. Only after black work-

ers acted did the international representatives, according to Weaver, admit "the need for firmer control over locals."[12] Direct action in the form of work stoppages and threatened strikes was one factor that inspired R. J. Thomas, UAW president, to create an interracial committee, designed to settle "racial issues," chaired by Walter Hardin, a black organizer and member of the UAW international staff.[13]

UAW union locals were often the problem, not the solution, as African Americans sought their share of the widespread upgrading of workers to higher-paying, more desirable jobs. Absent confrontation by black workers, the staff of the UAW international was unlikely to oppose racist hiring and job assignment practices. During the winter of 1942, black workers expanded their protests to housing when they joined a community-wide network demanding that the federal government uphold its commitment to house black Detroiters at the Sojourner Truth Housing Project. That effort successfully mobilized support from UAW's top leadership, forging an alliance between Detroit's black advancement organizations, particularly the NAACP, and the UAW.[14]

New-crowd leaders who directed action against the government's exclusion of black citizens from Sojourner Truth organized daily picketing of City Hall and the Detroit Housing Commission in February 1942. Some leaders like the Reverend Charles Hill, minister at the popular Hartford Avenue Baptist Church, a founder of the Detroit chapter of the National Negro Congress, and a member of the NAACP, represented the militancy that emerged from new-crowd alliances in the late thirties; others were active in the UAW. Still others were NAACP stalwarts, like the local chapter's president James McClendon, who had been encouraged to utilize protest politics by Hill, Walter White, and others during the UAW strike against Ford Motor Company in 1941. The Sojourner Truth Citizens Committee, formed by Hill, the Reverend Horace White, McClendon, and LeBron Simmons, a young lawyer who also helped start the Detroit NNC chapter, reflects the degree to which new-crowd politics shaped the political arena. The committee drew support from practically every major institution in the black community as well as several white liberals, leftists, and unionists. Forces opposing black occupancy of Sojourner Truth Homes included white workers, white residents from the neighborhood, and some mid-level union leaders pressured by white constituents. Although the federal government switched its position several times, militant pressure from the black community forced the government to keep the housing project open to black workers.[15] The message to the larger white community was that new-crowd African Americans were not going to accept the racial status quo in housing, even when the power reinforcing local patterns was that of the federal government.

But the Sojourner Truth controversy was also a sign of social change in terms of a new direction that relations between black and white Detroit would take in the postwar world. White community groups, utilizing many of the tactics employed by new-crowd activists within the black community, began to form neighborhood improvement associations and carry signs demanding "Our Rights to Protest, Restrict and Improve Our Neighborhood."[16] As Thomas Sugrue has shown, battles over housing that took place in postwar Detroit, drew from the "potent political language of rights that they developed during the public housing debates," such as the battle over Sojourner Truth during the war.[17] Black Detroiters were not the only group organizing around civil rights: as protest politics came of age in the black community, portions of the white community co-opted some of the tactics utilized in new-crowd protests.

After Sojourner, black new-crowd community leaders, who now came increasingly from the ranks of the labor movement, pledged themselves to combat discrimination at the workplace and in housing. The Sojourner Truth committee was transformed by Hill into the Citizens Committee for Jobs in War Industries in an alliance with progressive black workers in the UAW Ford local 600.[18] Within a year, as the rank and file continued its push for immediate access to new jobs, labor-union officials became increasingly impatient with the assertive independence exhibited by the black rank and file. Walter Hardin, as chair of the UAW's interracial committee, found it increasingly difficult to represent the needs of the black rank and file during the spring of 1943.

Powerless to fight individual grievances or resolve crisis situations, Hardin announced that he wanted to quit his "job with the UAW-CIO and go back into the shop unless some of the Negro's labor problems are solved."[19] In April, exasperated with the inability of both management and UAW locals to control hate-strikes against black upgrading, Hardin decided to increase community pressure on industrialists and union officials by mobilizing the black community in an alliance with Hill's Citizens Committee for Jobs in the War Industry. More than 10,000 black and white citizens took part the mass rally and march at Cadillac Square protesting continued discrimination in war plants. McClendon, Hill, and Walter Reuther, UAW vice president, gave speeches, and a "Cadillac Charter" declared "that all industry participating in the war effort treat all labor alike, regardless of race, color, creed, religion, or national origin, in hiring, upgrading and training of men and women, fully observing Executive Order 8802."[20]

The mass demonstration at Cadillac Square not only symbolized the commitment of the black community to job equality and the spirit and principles inscribed in Executive Order 8802 but marked a turning point in protest politics in Detroit. In the process of carrying out a successful protest rally, Hardin was criticized by several local NAACP members and UAW directors for his assertive independent style. After old NAACP hands who felt that he had slighted them in staging the rally rebuked Hardin, he resigned from his position on the NAACP's labor committee. Simultaneously, UAW's directors lost confidence in Hardin, even as UAW leaders and the NAACP branch grew closer together.[21]

These tendencies grew stronger in the wake of the upheaval at Packard one month later. A protest that began as white workers opposed the upgrading of 3 black men to the aircraft assembly line and the hiring of black women led to a black walkout, which closed the foundry for three days. Management, government, and the union appealed directly to black insurgents to get the foundry back in operation. Black workers returned, but only after the 3 men were placed in their new jobs. The situation then escalated when 25,000 white workers, refusing to obey an order of the War Labor Board to work with the 3 black men, walked off and shut down the entire plant. Only after Thomas flew to Washington seeking help and the WLB got involved a second time did the Packard employees return to work. The WLB suspended 30 black and white ringleaders. Although the majority of leaders returned to work, Colonel George E. Strong, a government contract compliance officer called in by Thomas to settle the strike, told black union steward Christopher Alston that if he did not modify his position, he would be drafted.[22] He not only lost his job but also his draft deferment, despite the fact that he was thirty-one years old with dependents. The action was interpreted as a message to those who protest and do not play by the rules of organized labor: not only were uniformed police present in many plants, but draft boards often canceled deferments for militant workers.[23]

By June 1943 the patience of UAW officials had worn thin with what was termed "march" behavior, a reference to the assertive approach of the MOWM exhibited by UAW rank-and-file activists who, rather than follow union procedure, took matters into their own hands, using the language of protest politics.[24] Operating beyond the boundaries of conventional union politics, such behavior demonstrated contempt for union authority. But it also made a mockery of the no-strike pledge agreement between union leadership and the government, which placed Thomas and Reuther in the position of curbing workers' insurgency in exchange for a "modified union shop" and dues check off.[25] Thomas and Walter Reuther apparently rationalized this awkward position between the interests of workers and those of management and government by claiming that only by demanding a policy of self-restraint could the union be spared assault from the right.[26]

Thomas dissolved the UAW interracial committee soon after the strikes in

June 1943 and dismissed Hardin from the international staff of the UAW a year later.[27] Dominic Capeci argues that UAW officers feared an autonomous interracial body that was capable of "outstepping their gradualism and alienating their constituencies."[28] There was too much "march" behavior in Hardin's approach, too much independence as he attempted to broker relations between the black rank and file and UAW top management.[29]

Confidential correspondence to Walter White in May 1943 suggests that Thomas and Reuther were developing special measures to control rank-and-file politics before the massive Packard walkout. Leslie Perry, a staff member in the NAACP's Washington, D.C., office, alleged that Reuther and Thomas were "very much concerned about the race situation in Detroit" because it appeared that black workers were in a position to "close down three or four shops there." Their concern was not just the fact that "such action tears down whatever work they have done to get Negroes into the shops," but over the "much more personal reason that stoppages or wildcat strikes will hurt UAW." Reuther and Thomas assumed work stoppages and wildcat strikes were inspired by the March on Washington Movement, which encouraged "the wrong type of racial consciousness." In an effort to control the situation, the UAW leaders, according to Perry, had decided to tell Randolph "that he has got to tone it [the MOWM] down and make it interracial."[30]

As Perry explained, the "UAW feels so strongly about this thing [the aggressive nature of MOWM-style tactics] that they our [sic] entirely willing to wreck the March if they can." On the other hand, the UAW was also willing to put money into the MOWM if "Phil will get in line." Reuther and Thomas suggested they could "give him [Randolph] a real boost by having Hardin and Townsend [Willard Townsend, head of the United Transport Service Employees of America-CIO] invite you [White], Lester Granger and others to a pre-MOW Chicago Conference [a reference to the June 1943 'We Are Americans, Too' conference] creating in the public mind endorsement of the movement and conference."[31]

Although Perry's allegations have not been corroborated, a column by George McCray, a labor reporter for the *Defender*, also pointed to growing impatience of UAW-CIO leaders with methods encouraged by MOWM's protest politics. McCray claimed CIO leaders had chased "Randolph all over the East finally" catching up "with him in Chicago." There they told Randolph the CIO "would like to support MOW [many people referred to MOWM simply as MOW] if Randolph and Webster would 'go along' with a program to build better interracial labor relations." The leaders told Randolph and Webster that in several instances, black followers of MOWM in Detroit had become "so unreasonable and troublesome that race relations were being seriously endangered; that prejudice was being intensified; and that the whole fight of the union to uproot job discrimination is being jeopardized." McCray concluded that the CIO leaders "got absolutely no place with the chief of the MOW," who "dismissed the whole matter."[32]

By contrast, the relationship between Walter White and top UAW officials was friendlier than ever. During a NAACP conference on the "Status of the Negro in the War for Freedom" in early June in Detroit, Thomas and Reuther enthusiastically endorsed the bond between labor and the NAACP. Black workers were urged to "become full fledged members of organized labor on a basis of equality with all other workers." However, when the conference, one of the largest national gatherings of the NAACP in several years, tried to praise the no-strike policy of the UAW-CIO, the action was defeated after much "heated debate," reflecting the influence militant black workers had within the Detroit NAACP, the largest in the country.[33]

At the same time, although Randolph and White collaborated occasionally, they often worked through different networks, applying new-crowd tactics in different arenas. White was concerned increasingly with how the behavior of black workers during the war was going to affect their status after the war. Writing in the *Chicago Defender*, White blamed the bad behavior and "thoughtlessness" of a small percentage of black workers for management's reluctance to employ black workers, claiming "we must admit that a lot of the trouble is our own."[34] The Detroit branch of the NAACP condemned "unauthorized strikes" by workers who did not understand union procedures and took matters into their own hands.[35]

The labor–civil rights collaboration between the UAW and the NAACP had begun to take precedence over the democratic aspirations of insurgent black workers. Yet, despite the setbacks that black workers experienced in the early stages of World War II in terms of racism in both hiring and upgrading, by 1943, in Detroit and nationwide, real progress was occurring in the workplace. UAW shop steward Alston may have been packed off to fight the war abroad, but wildcat strikes and work stoppages continued to plague production at Packard and other factories.[36] When black foundry workers staged a walkout in November 1943 to protest lack of transfers, Packard quickly upgraded 200 by the end of the month; by the end of 1943, Packard had transferred nearly 500 out of the foundry to production jobs previously held only by white workers. Militancy paid off and continued to the end of the war and beyond.[37] Many influences account for the gains from 1943 forward: the presence of MOWM protest politics and publicity from FEPC, an ever tightening labor market, and the fact that unions like the UAW did begin to make real concessions when pushed to do so by the militancy of black workers. As Robert Korstad and Nelson Lichtenstein have shown, Reuther may have denounced proposals for an African American seat on the executive board of the UAW as "reverse Jim Crow," but he also advocated civil rights, not so much because the UAW executives "expected to win black political support," but because the rapid growth of a "quasi-autonomous black movement had made militancy on civil rights the sine qua non of serious political leadership in the UAW" by the end of the war.[38]

At the same time, the militant "assertiveness" of black Americans engendered a backlash from the larger white community, particularly after the Detroit riot of June 20, 1943. It was CIO leadership, alone among the city's influential whites, who came to the defense of black citizens. Many Detroit police were especially brutal toward black insurgents, killing seventeen blacks, but no whites.[39] Although incidents often centered on white fears of black economic competition, the rub was white intolerance with African Americans who stepped out of place and challenged the racial status quo. There was a white walkout in Philadelphia when the city hired eight black Americans as trolley operators, and a group of black citizens were driven from a Louisiana town that had set up a welding school for black workers. Those who opposed the school did not want "the colored folk to learn to be anything but sharecroppers and servants."[40] As a *New Republic* article put it, throughout the South a black man in uniform symbolized someone "not knowing his place." The situation encouraged many white Americans to increase their efforts to keep black Americans in "their place."[41] After the race riots black Americans were increasingly suspected of disloyalty for not hewing the line and controlling their resentment, leading some to declare that "the more they get the more they want."[42] Black demands for equal rights were often portrayed as the behavior of "uppity, out of line Negroes."[43]

The defining issue of new-crowd politics—challenging the protocol and decorum prescribed by the status quo for negotiations between the races—and the rights consciousness that justified the militancy and assertiveness of protest politics were certainly used against black America. White resistance to Sojourner Truth expanded in the wake of the summer of 1943 to include keeping African Americans from moving into predominantly white neighborhoods. Sugrue notes that white Detroiters began viewing "home ownership as a prerequisite of citizenship," using the threat of imminent violence against black Detroiters as a tool to gain leverage in housing debates.[44] The problem was, and still is, the perception that civil rights for black Americans were only being won at the expense of white rights. Rights for black Americans were OK, but only in the abstract. "Not in my backyard" became the watchword in the white neighborhood associations, formed during World War II, that were dedicated to racially segregated housing.

By the summer of 1943, several factors appeared to weaken the power of protest politics as a means for winning democracy for African Americans on the home front. The intense negative reactions of white workers and citizens to the battle waged by African Americans for a measure of economic opportunity stunned white liberals, which in turn pushed the issue of interracial collaboration to the fore. Just when it seemed as though leaders like Randolph and White had come together as new-crowd leaders united in their commitment to assert rights to break the culture of dependency, their paths began to diverge. Meanwhile, as Randolph remained committed to all-black membership, the nonviolent civil disobedience tactic he espoused was called "dangerous demagoguery" by the *Pittsburgh Courier* during the spring of 1943 and stripped of credibility in mainstream black and white liberal circles after the violence of the summer of 1943. In this milieu, Walter White was drawn for practical reasons to more moderate political tactics and the NAACP advised its branches to concentrate on challenging inequality through the courts and the voting booth.[45] Although scholars argue that these efforts led to diluting black militancy and "reinforcing the tactics of cooperation over confrontation, legalism over disruption," possibilities for advancing the citizenship rights of African Americans lay along several coordinates and black leaders followed different paths to carry forward the struggle.[46]

White turned his attention during this period in other directions. He joined Edwin R. Embree, president of the Julius Rosenwald Fund, along with Dr. Robert Weaver, Horace Cayton, Dr. Charles S. Johnson, Mary McCloud Bethune, and Willard Townsend, to look for a "widely accepted program of practical action by the Negro group."[47] The NAACP also worked closely with black workers in Detroit standing up against city government over issues such as police discrimination against black citizens. In the aftermath of the Detroit riot, Walter White did not slide back into the politics of civility of an earlier era, but the synthesis he fashioned included channeling black militancy into the political arena and away from the shop floor.[48] Walter White accepted mass protest as a legitimate tactic for making claims, but he also valued interracial alliances pressing for reform of society from within its institutional framework. Although he harbored a suspicion of black working-class radicalism, which surfaced from time to time, he also was sensitive to the interests of African American workers who provided significant funding for NAACP activities through NAACP memberships. White, who helped forge the bond with unions, particularly between the UAW and the NAACP, promoted a labor-oriented civil rights agenda, thereby attempting to integrate the urban black worker into the NAACP. The merger transformed the NAACP in places like Detroit, where 12,356 members in 1942 made it the largest branch and among the more diverse chapters.[49]

In addition, the war at home to claim basic rights of citizenship was perceived through a wider lens by the end of World War II, and black Americans increasingly viewed their situation within a global context. Contemporary sociologist Horace Cayton wrote that African Americans had awakened to the exploitation suffered by "all the world's peoples," placing the problems they found on the home front in "a new and larger frame of reference."[50] Penny Von Eschen argues that as United States involvement in the Second World War increased, leaders such as Walter White came to "share the language of imperialism with leftists" and view the international arena as a site for continuing to raise issues of freedom and equality. What Von Eschen calls the politics of diaspora reinforced the urgency of the struggle for full equality for leaders like White.[51]

The issue that distinguished new-crowd activists, transgressions against traditional protocol, continued to tweak white power brokers, and Walter White often did his part to keep the disrespect for authority alive. Within the Roosevelt administration, the methods and modes used by both White and Randolph to address racial inequities were sometimes reduced to a question of proper or improper behavior. Presidential assistants Jonathan Daniels and Will Alexander, southern liberals who advised the administration on racial issues, criticized White and Randolph in reports they filed on the racial situation. Daniels thought that a letter from White smacked of dictating "the policies of this Administration" at the same time that he was also one of the "sharp critics" of the administration. Alexander reviewed a speech Randolph made to a Cleveland gathering of the Federal Council of Churches and concluded, after hearing Randolph remind the audience that Roosevelt "did not create the [President's] Committee [on Fair Employment] until the Negroes forced him to and that he has done nothing to support it since," that his speech was "straight anti-administration and anti-Roosevelt."[52]

Patricia Sullivan attributes the "far-reaching social and political implications" of FEPC hearings in Birmingham, Alabama, to transgressions of southern tradition. She cites the example of black FEPC committee members Earl Dickerson and Milton Webster questioning white witnesses, challenging them in ways that "breached southern racial practice."[53] By breaching southern mores at the Birmingham hearings, Dickerson and Webster aroused the southern bloc in Congress. Soon several publications, including the *Saturday Review of Litera-*

ture, the *Atlantic Monthly*, the *Virginia Quarterly Review*, and *Reader's Digest*, criticized radical African Americans for raising the ire of southern racists.[54]

FEPC hearings nationalized the citizenship issue as they questioned authority and exposed the hypocrisy of industrialists and many union representatives proclaiming patriotism for war against fascism abroad while supporting racial discrimination at home. Despite the lack of direct authority, interracial efforts of the Fair Employment Practice Committee did, in many instances, pressure companies to hire black workers. William Harris argues that even when black workers did not receive fair treatment, as in the contentious West Coast ship-yards, they did make "major inroads into a previously closed job market."[55] Although the forces against FEPC hearings were strong, the black community could still attempt to hold the agency hostage by the weight of bad publicity through collective action, as they did when FEPC hearings on the railroad industry, scheduled for late January 1943, were canceled. New-crowd networks across the country mobilized black Americans, who flooded the White House with telegrams and letters. A committee of about forty activists met with War Manpower Commissioner Paul McNutt, who had canceled the hearings, de-manding an explanation. McNutt refused to discuss the reasons for his decision and failed to answer any of the groups' questions, treating them like children.[56] The FEPC survived conservative attacks and lack of financial and political com-mitment from the White House largely because of the power of organized protest and, as Merl Reed suggests, "because work as a civil right had become a moral issue too powerful to ignore."[57]

Despite the forces arrayed against the FEPC, changes and improvements did occur. As Weaver argued, much of what happened between 1940 and 1945 represented a departure from older practices, resulting in greater industrial and occupational diversification than had occurred for black workers in the preced-ing seventy-five years. It was the first chance many had to perform basic skilled and semiskilled jobs in a wide range of industries and plants, and it gave black and white workers an opportunity to work alongside each other on the "basis of industrial equality."[58] When black working-class activists seized the "window of opportunity" that the war presented for assaulting Jim Crow, their efforts mobilized the larger community and politicized the home front, reinforcing strategies pioneered by the new crowd.[59]

The coming of age of protest politics did not finish the task of gaining full citizenship. African Americans, as Randolph declared in Rayford Logan's *What the Negro Wants*, were not free because they were "not equal to other citizens within the national framework of the laws, institutions, customs and practices of our so-called democratic government."[60] The manhood rights campaign initiated by Randolph and the BSCP was for equality in all social relations. Although its goals remain unfulfilled, the manhood rights campaign spawned the growth of protest politics between the wars, which led to the upheaval of Jim Crow in the years that followed.

By the end of World War II, Randolph's star had dimmed, and so had much of the militant activism on the home front. But by that time black workers were part of the mainstream labor movement, having made unprecedented gains securing more jobs at better wages and in more diversified occupational and industrial categories than ever before.[61] Although the fire of militancy may have waned, the resolve to attain recognition of human rights of citizenship was still very much alive.

Victory in Europe did not win the war for democracy on the home front, which had a profound influence on the next generation of activists. Some were black veterans who returned fighting, to become, in the words of John Dittmer, the "shock troops of the modern civil rights movement."[62] Others, like James Boggs, a Detroit autoworker, took note of the contradictions exposed in the "Double-V for Victory" and utilized that knowledge to arm themselves in the next phase of struggle.[63] Rosa Parks and E. D. Nixon, shaped by the March on Washington Movement, were leaders of the Montgomery Bus Boycott in 1955. Still later, in 1968, African American sanitation workers in Memphis expressed their grievances with the words, "I *am* a Man!" striking against the racial status quo to claim dignity and self-respect as human beings, which was, as Randolph had declared some forty years before, the unfinished task of emancipation.

The rise of protest politics was as significant for the *experience* black Americans gained trying out new strategies for taking control of their destiny, on their own terms, as for the changes it engendered in the racial status quo. Lessons African Americans had learned by 1945 shored up the next generation of activists. Among those lessons was an awareness that America, to paraphrase Langston Hughes, was still not all she could be.[64] New-crowd activist Thelma Wheaton observed, many years later, that World War II was the last time African Americans still had faith in American democracy.[65] Nevertheless, the struggle was carried forward into the fifties and sixties by Wheaton and others who understood, as Randolph had in 1944, that "a militant fight" by African Americans for equality may yet "save the day for the democratic way of life" in America.[66] Despite the inability of the nation to deliver on its promise to African Americans, the politics they unleashed enlarged the vision of what America could be, saving the idea of democracy for future generations to ponder.

NOTES

Abbreviations

In addition to the abbreviations found in the text, the following source abbreviations are used in notes.

ALUA	Archives of Labor and Urban Affairs, Walter Reuther Library, Wayne State University, Detroit
APRP	A. Philip Randolph Papers, Library of Congress, Washington, D.C.
BSCP Chicago	Brotherhood of Sleeping Car Porters Papers, Chicago Historical Society, Chicago. Microfilm, University Publications of America
BSCP-LC	Brotherhood of Sleeping Car Porters Papers, Library of Congress, Washington, D.C.
CABP	Claude A. Barnett Papers, Chicago Historical Society, Chicago
CHS	Chicago Historical Society, Chicago
CMS	Carnegie-Myrdal Study of the Negro in America Papers, microfilm, Library of Congress, Washington, D.C.
FBI Archives	Federal Bureau of Investigation, Archives, Washington, D.C.
IBWP	Ida B. Wells Papers, Special Collections, Joseph Regenstein Library, University of Chicago, Chicago
JFP	John Fitzpatrick Papers, Chicago Historical Society, Chicago
NAACP-NYC	National Association for the Advancement of Colored People, New York City Branch
NAACP Papers	Papers of the National Association for the Advancement of Colored People, Library of Congress, Washington, D.C.
NNBL	National Negro Business League
NNC Papers	Papers of the National Negro Congress, Schomburg Center for Research on Black Culture, New York
OHC-CU	Oral History Collection of Columbia University, New York
PCP	Papers of the Pullman Company, Newberry Library, Chicago
PCP-UPA	Records of the Brotherhood of Sleeping Car Porters (Chicago Historical Society holdings) and Pullman Company relations with the BSCP from Pullman Company Papers, Newberry Library, microfilm, University Publications of America
TEP	Thyra Edwards Papers, Chicago Historical Society, Chicago
VGHC	Vivian G. Harsh Collection of Afro-American History and Literature, Carter Woodson Regional Library, Chicago Public Library, Chicago

Introduction

1. Wright, *Black Boy*, 283; see also Wright, *Black Boy (American Hunger)*, 212–303.

2. Referring to the same experience depicted by Wright and numerous other black men and women, Thomas Holt describes that "special alienation that separates one not only from the world . . . but from one's very own being." This encounter with one's racialized self, Holt argues, is a moment of "traumatic confrontation with the Other that fixes the meaning of one's self before one even has had the opportunity to *live* and *make* a self more nearly of one's own choosing." See Holt, "Marking: Race, Race-Making," 2.

3. My understanding of social relations and race as a social construction draws from Barbara Fields's work. See especially "Slavery, Race and Ideology" and "Ideology and Race in American History."

4. Wright, *Black Boy (American Hunger)*, 453; see also the introduction by Jerry W. Ward Jr., especially xiii. For biographies of Randolph, see Jervis Anderson, *A. Philip Randolph*, and Pfeffer, *A. Philip Randolph, Pioneer*.

5. Harding, *There Is a River*, xxiv.

6. A. Philip Randolph, "A New Crowd—a New Negro," *Messenger* 2 (May–June 1919), 26–27; "New Leadership for the Negro," ibid., 9–10.

7. See Kornweibel, *No Crystal Stair*, 25; Huggins, *Voices from the Harlem Renaissance*, 3–11.

8. Arnesen, " 'Like Banquo's Ghost, It Will Not Down,' " 1633. For the growing literature on the currency of "whiteness" to the self-esteem of the white working class, see Roediger, *The Wages of Whiteness*. On race and citizenship, see Mink, "The Lady and the Tramp"; Collomp, "Unions, Civics, and National Identity"; Glickman, "Inventing the 'American Standard of Living.' "

9. Eric Foner, *Nothing But Freedom*, 110.

10. For the work culture of Pullman porters, see Perata, *Those Pullman Blues*, and Santino, *Miles of Smiles*. I am grateful to Barry Tompkins for suggesting that I examine these sources. The BSCP also organized maids employed by the Pullman Company. Although the organizing campaign of the Brotherhood was aimed at *both* porters and maids, this study focuses largely on Pullman porters. While there were between 8,000 and 12,000 porters employed during the years 1915–30, the number of maids was about 200.

11. Halpern, *Down on the Killing Floor*, 44–72; Grossman, *Land of Hope*, 209–45; Trotter and Lewis, *African Americans in the Industrial Age*, 1–3, 105–9; Franklin and Moss, *From Slavery to Freedom*, 2:381–82.

12. David Lewis, *W. E. B. Du Bois*, 579.

13. David Lewis, *When Harlem Was in Vogue*, 23 (quotation), 17–24; Franklin and Moss, *From Slavery to Freedom*, 2:347–52; Reich, "Soldiers of Democracy."

14. From the *Kansas City CALL*, quoted in David Lewis, *When Harlem Was in Vogue*, 24. For a few of the many works on Garvey and protest movements in the early twenties, see Cronon, *Black Moses: The Story of Marcus Garvey*; Garvey, *Garvey and Garveyism*; James, *Holding Aloft the Banner of Ethiopia*; Martin, *Race First*; Stein, *The World of Marcus Garvey*; Vincent, *Black Power and the Garvey Movement*.

15. Stein, *The World of Marcus Garvey*, 58 (quotation), 58–59.

16. Potter, *The Impending Crisis*, 145.

17. See Wilson, *Tearing Down the Color Line*, 25.

18. For a scholarly history of the Brotherhood of Sleeping Car Porters, as a labor

union, see Brazeal, *The Brotherhood of Sleeping Car Porters*, and Harris, *Keeping the Faith*.

19. A. Philip Randolph, "Pullman Porters Need Own Union," *Messenger* 7:8 (August 1925): 290.

20. A. Philip Randolph, "The Pullman Company and the Pullman Porter," *Messenger* 7:9 (September 1925): 312.

21. Du Bois, *The Souls of Black Folk*, 85, 86.

22. For Wells-Barnett's account, see *Crusade for Justice*, 47–52; "Southern Horrors"; and "A Red Record," especially 78–82. See also Shaw, "Black Club Women," 10; Gilmore, *Gender and Jim Crow*, 31–89; Schechter, "Unsettled Business: Ida B. Wells against Lynching," 292–317.

23. Wells, *Crusade for Justice*, xix. For Wells-Barnett's direct responsibility in forming the Chicago Wells Club, see Holt, "Lonely Warrior," 56.

24. Deborah White, "The Cost of Club Work, the Price of Black Feminism," 247–69, especially 249–50.

25. For an exploration of these gender tensions within the Brotherhood of Sleeping Car Porters, see Chateauvert, *Marching Together*.

26. Trotter and Lewis, *African Americans in the Industrial Age*, 109.

27. A. Philip Randolph, "The Indictment," *Messenger* 8:4 (April 1926): 114.

28. For strategies used to protest exclusion from citizenship in black communities in Texas during and after World War I, see Reich, "Soldiers of Democracy."

29. The best treatment of Randolph and his years with the *Messenger* is Kornweibel, *No Crystal Stair*. Kornweibel refers to "servility" on p. 238; see also 220–75. For discussion of Randolph as a "new-style" leader, see Pfeffer, *A. Philip Randolph, Pioneer*, 6–44. For quotation, see A. Philip Randolph, "The Crisis of the Negro and the Constitution," in Meier, Rudwick, and Broderick, *Black Protest Thought*, 206.

30. Chafe, *Civilities and Civil Rights*, 7–8. See also Chafe, "Epilogue from Greesboro."

31. In her graduate seminar and critique of earlier drafts of this study, Elizabeth Blackmar first pushed me to think harder about the concept "community." I also found Brown's "Negotiating and Transforming the Public Sphere" very helpful.

32. Earl Lewis, "To Turn as on a Pivot," 783; see also Earl Lewis, "Connecting Memory, Self, and the Power of Place."

33. Important studies that may have pushed harder on the question of independent protest within the black community, had they been written in a different national political climate, include, Fishel, "The Negro in the New Deal Era," and Wolters, *Negroes and the Great Depression*. It should also be noted that these contributions asked different questions than the present endeavor.

34. I have Lawrence S. Wittner to thank for turning the spotlight on the local councils of the NNC and noting the vigorous grass-roots support for the NNC during the first years of existence. See Wittner, "The National Negro Congress." For works that add significantly to our understanding of the importance of the NNC to black history, see Streater, "The National Negro Congress"; Alvin Hughes, "Toward a Black United Front"; Griffler, "What Price Alliance?"

35. Kelley, *Hammer and Hoe*.

m36. For details on the broad expansion of rights the Civil War and Reconstruction inspired, see Eric Foner, "Rights and the Constitution in Black Life." For the framers' understanding of civil rights embedded in the Thirteenth and Fourteenth Amendments, see Kaczorowski, "To Begin the Nation Anew."

37. As Eric Foner has demonstrated, ex-slaves interpreted emancipation in terms that drew from definitions of freedom "shared among white Americans—self-ownership, family stability, marketplace equality, political participation, and economic autonomy." See Foner, "The Meaning of Freedom," 458.

38. The literature touching on black protest politics in the 1920s is growing. The sources include the vast literature on the Garvey movement's protest and civil rights histories that, correctly, are pushing the chronology of black protest back to the 1920s and 1930s. For a few of the many important works, see sources on Garvey cited in note 14, and Dittmer, *Local People*; Payne, *I've Got the Light of Freedom*; Morris, *The Origins of the Civil Rights Movement*; Chafe, *Civilities and Civil Rights*; Lawson, "Freedom Then, Freedom Now"; Meier and Rudwick, *CORE*; Carson, *In Struggle*; Korstad and Lichtenstein, "Opportunities Found and Lost." Patricia Sullivan finds the "roots of the twentieth century civil rights movement" in the 1930s, in "Southern Reformers, the New Deal, and the Movement's Foundation," 82; see also her *Days of Hope*; Sitkoff, *A New Deal for Blacks*; Glen, *Highlander: No Ordinary School*; Dalfiume, "The 'Forgotten Years' of the Negro Revolution"; Fairclough, *Race and Democracy*.

39. Douglass, "The Significance of Emancipation in the West Indies," 204.

Chapter One

1. Husband, *The Story of the Pullman Car*, 155.

2. Brazeal, *The Brotherhood of Sleeping Car Porters*, 2. For the company's position that it hired black men out of concern for their welfare, see Harris, *Keeping the Faith*, 3. Perata, *Those Pullman Blues*, xv.

3. For use of plantation culture on Pullman sleeping cars, see Perata, *Those Pullman Blues*, xvii–xviii.

4. For assessment of Pullman Company profits at the beginning World War I, see Commission on Industrial Relations, *Final Report*, 10:9663–80. For the quotation, see Jervis Anderson, *A. Philip Randolph*, 159.

5. For images of Pullman porters, see Reiff and Hirsch, "Pullman and Its Public," 102; for Martin Turner's story as a veteran film Pullman porter, see *Detroit News*, April 9, 1941, 18.

6. This film is discussed by Santino in *Miles of Smiles*, 118.

7. Santino interviewed more than twenty retired Pullman Porters between 1978 and 1984. He said the term "George" was associated with the days of slavery; see *Miles of Smiles*, 125.

8. Kempton, *Part of Our Time*, 259, 240–42.

9. Jervis Anderson, *A. Philip Randolph*, 160; Harris, *Keeping the Faith*, 15.

10. Ottley, *The Lonely Warrior*, 136–39; Gosnell, *Negro Politicians*, 101.

11. Spear, *Black Chicago*, 114–15, 184–85; Lochard, "Negro Press," 573; Ottley, *The Lonely Warrior*, 138–39; Grossman, *Land of Hope*, 78, and "Blowing the Trumpet," 86.

12. Ottley, *The Lonely Warrior*, 136–37; I am grateful to James Grossman for the reference to John W. Crawford, "A Brief History of Some Negro Newspapers in the United States with Special Reference to the *Chicago Defender*," student paper (1924), Robert E. Park Papers, box 1, folder 11, Regenstein Library, University of Chicago; Grossman, "Blowing the Trumpet," 85–86; Randolph to Mrs. Lula Slaughter, August 18, 1927, BSCP Chicago.

13. Cited in Jervis Anderson, *A. Philip Randolph*, 160.

14. For comparison of the porter's role to the black minstrel, see Mergen, "The Pullman Porter: From 'George' to Brotherhood," 235.

15. Benjamin McLaurin, interview by Greg LeRoy, January 22, 1981, CHS.

16. I found Holt's essay, "Marking: Race, Race-Making, and the Writing of History," very useful for thinking about the power of "marking" in the remaking of race.

17. Perata, *Those Pullman Blues*, 4.

18. Arnesen, *Brotherhoods of Color*. For more on a comparison of Pullman's innovations with those of his contemporaries, see Rae, *Westward by Rail*, 51; John H. White, *American Railroad Passenger Car*, 203–60; Maiken, *Night Trains*, 8–11; Holbrook, *The Story of American Railroads*, 317–28.

19. Husband, *The Story of the Pullman Car*, 32–33. See also Lindsey, *The Pullman Strike*, 22.

20. Buder, *Pullman*, 10.

21. For a history of the early years of George Pullman and the Pioneer, see ibid., 3–16; Lindsey, *The Pullman Strike*, 19–37; Jervis Anderson, *A. Philip Randolph*, 155–58; and Husband, *The Story of the Pullman Car*.

22. Buder, *Pullman*, 15–17; Jervis Anderson, *A. Philip Randolph*, 159–64; Husband, *The Story of the Pullman Car*, 155–56.

23. Harris, *Keeping the Faith*, 3. See also Colin Davis, *Power at Odds*.

24. For testimony submitted by Pullman Company officials appearing before the Commission on Industrial Relations, see *Final Report*, 10:9546–47, 9558–60. In 1967, porters-in-charge were promoted to conductor after a successful lawsuit brought by retired porter Earl A. Love against the Pullman Company. See *New York Times*, February 23, 1976, 18.

25. For the long-run implications of Pullman's racial divisions of labor, see Reiff and Hirsch, "Pullman and Its Public," 103; *New York Times*, February 23, 1976, 18; Posadas, "The Hierarchy of Color," 356, 361. There were, according to Sterling Spero and Abram Harris, approximately 400 Mexicans employed on Pullman cars that serviced Mexico at the end of the 1920s and a "few dozen Japanese and Chinese who were placed on club cars." See Spero and Harris, *The Black Worker*, 430.

26. Commission on Industrial Relations, *Final Report*, 10:9553.

27. Perata, *Those Pullman Blues*, xix, 55.

28. For Pullman Company officials testifying before the commission, see *Final Report*, 10:9553.

29. H. N. Hall, "The Art of the Pullman Porter," 333.

30. Porters' stories about tipping are reported in Jervis Anderson, *A. Philip Randolph*, 162.

31. Charles Anderson, *Freemen Yet Slaves*, 20, 30–31.

32. For "Uncle Tomming," see Perata, *Those Pullman Blues*, xxviii; Commission on Industrial Relations, *Final Report*, 10:9654–55.

33. For a detailed discussion of the tipping system from the perspective of retired Pullman porters, see Santino, *Miles of Smiles*, 72–74, 94–98, especially 96.

34. Commission on Industrial Relations, *Final Report*, 1:76.

35. Ibid., 10:9667–68.

36. Ibid., 9677–78.

37. Ibid., 9667–68.

38. Ibid., 9561.

39. Ibid., 9669.

40. For the number of porters during World War I era, see Harris, *Keeping the Faith*, 2; for Pullman's hiring of best-educated black men, see ibid., 15 and fn. 38. Harris received the information about Seldon from George E. Brooks Sr., a classmate of Seldon's at Dartmouth and teammate of his on the Dartmouth debating team.

41. Mays, *Born to Rebel*, 61–63.

42. Harris, *Keeping the Faith*, 15; Santino, *Miles of Smiles*, 7–8.

43. Commission on Industrial Relations, *Final Report*, 10:9553; Harris, *Keeping the Faith*, 2; Santino, *Miles of Smiles*, 7.

44. Grossman, "Blowing the Trumpet," 82–96.

45. Santino, *Miles of Smiles*, 15.

46. Levine, *Black Culture and Black Consciousness*, 226.

47. Harris, *Keeping the Faith*, 15; Santino, *Miles of Smiles*, 13.

48. Information on occupational status of black workers in Chicago is from Spear, *Black Chicago*, 30–34.

49. Frazier, *The Negro Family in Chicago*, 108.

50. Spear, *Black Chicago*, 23, n. 29; Drake and Cayton, *Black Metropolis*, 235–37, 506–10, 769–770; Jervis Anderson, *A. Philip Randolph*, 160.

51. The author compiled a sample of 309 names from 1,076 names on BSCP membership "B" list for 1927 found in BSCP Chicago. The 309 members were found in the 1928–29 *Chicago City Directory*, located in the Newberry Library. The goal was to create a random list, but there were times when I was forced to select from the BSCP membership list the next name that also appeared in the *City Directory*. The Matching sample consisted of 268 entries, which included the following variety of occupations: "waiter," "driver," "maid," "operator at Sopkins and Sons," "janitor," "laborer," "carpenter," "factory hand," "chauffeur," "carrier," "musician," "elevator operator," "decorator," "Post Office clerk," "artist," "truck driver," "presser," "dressmaker," "cleaner," "shademaker," "accountant," "barber," "chef," "bricklayer," "salesman," "stockman," "tailor," "printer," "auto mechanic," "foreman," and "physician." Of the 107 who called themselves "laborer," 29 percent said they were "householders," and 70 percent said they were boarders.

52. For changes in occupational status of black workers in Chicago, see Estelle Scott, *Occupational Changes among Negroes*, 174–216; Drake and Cayton, *Black Metropolis*, 510–11. Earl Lewis points out the "importance of place" in understanding urban history. Until we sift out the meaning of place, we cannot expect to understand how the new residents of Chicago, for example, constructed their identities. See Lewis, "Connecting Memory, Self, and the Power of Place," 347–71. Others who confirm the migration process as an act of individual and collective empowerment include Trotter, *Black Milwaukee*; Grossman, *Land of Hope*; and Gottlieb, "Making Their Own Way."

53. These statistics were reported in an unpublished seminar paper, Canaan, " 'Part of the Loaf,' " 8. My thanks to Gareth Canaan for sharing his research with me. See also Dieckmann, "The Effect of Common Interests on Race Relations in Certain Northern Cities: A Preliminary Study of Industry," 10, Dieckmann Papers; Greene and Woodson, *The Negro Wage Earner*, 265.

54. Estelle Scott, *Occupational Changes among Negroes*, 176–202; Drake and Cayton, *Black Metropolis*, 233–34. For the "Negro as Servant," a classification that included Pullman porters, waiters, headwaiters, valets, butlers, chauffeurs, see Drake and Cayton, *Black Metropolis*, 232–35. See also Frazier, *The Negro Family*, 109.

55. Memo for President E. F. Carry [president of the Pullman Company] from Claude A. Barnett, July 30, 1925, box 278, folder 4, CABP. It is interesting to note that the date of

this memo was just a few weeks before the formation of the Brotherhood of Sleeping Car Porters in New York City on August 25, 1925. While Barnett may be guilty of benefiting from the plight of the Pullman porters to acquire steady backing for his *Heebie Jeebies*, the thirty-two-page news magazine he said he would transform into a Pullman porter special with Carry's approval, he initiated this proposal before the BSCP was publicly organized.

56. Drake and Cayton, *Black Metropolis*, 304; Estelle Scott, *Occupational Changes among Negroes*, 192; Rick Halpern, *Down on the Killing Floor*, 51.

57. Horowitz, *"Negro and White, Unite and Fight,"* 63–64.

58. Estelle Scott, *Occupational Changes among Negroes*, 233, 236, 237, 239, 242, 244; Horowitz, "Negro and White, Unite and Fight," 64; Spero and Harris, *The Black Worker*, 432.

59. Chicago Commission on Race Relations, *The Negro in Chicago*, 371; Spear, *Black Chicago*, 157.

60. Trotter, architect of the proletarian approach to the migration process, discusses the making of the black working class in *Black Milwaukee*, 264–77. Also, see Trotter, "Black Migration in Historical Perspective," 1–21.

61. Memo for President E. F. Carry from Claude A. Barnett, July 30, 1925, box 278, folder 4, CABP.

62. Du Bois, *Darkwater*, 113.

63. Ibid., 114–15.

64. Ibid., 115.

65. Drake and Cayton, *Black Metropolis*, 220.

66. Du Bois, *Darkwater*, 115.

67. Ibid., 119.

68. Ibid., 116.

69. Ibid., 120.

70. Du Bois, "Close Ranks," *Crisis* 16 (July 1918): 111; Tuttle, *Race Riot*, 217. If the June 1918 editorial by Du Bois is placed next to the better-known, more controversial July 1918 editorial, a more powerful picture emerges of the impact of the war on reviving the ongoing struggle for first-class citizenship in America. In June, Du Bois forecast that "out of this war will rise, too, an American Negro, with a right to vote and a right to work and a right to live without insult." *Crisis* 16 (June 1918): 60. Despite disagreement over tactics, there was general agreement around the issue of making gains as a result of World War I. See Jordan, " 'The Damnable Dilemma' "; Ellis, " 'Closing Ranks' and 'Seeking Honors' "; and David Lewis, *Du Bois*, 551–60. See also Reich, "Soldiers of Democracy"; Stein, *The World of Marcus Garvey*.

71. See *Chicago Defender* May 24, 1919, 1, and *Broad Ax*, May 24, 1919.

72. Quotation from Tuttle, *Race Riot*, 218; see 217–219; *Chicago Defender*, July 28, August 25, September 22, October 13, November 19, December 22, 1917; January 5, August 10, 1918; February 22, 1919.

73. "Returning Soldiers," *Crisis* 18 (May 1919): 13–14.

74. Tuttle, *Race Riot*, 208–22; Kennedy, *The Negro Peasant Turns Cityward*, 135–40; Grossman, *Land of Hope*, 161–80.

75. *Broad Ax*, September 6, 1919, quoted in Kerlin, *Voice of the Negro*, 24.

76. Ibid., 24–25.

77. Ibid., 33.

78. Ibid., ix–xii.

79. David Lewis, *When Harlem Was in Vogue*, 47; the quotations are from Chicago Commission on Race Relations, *The Negro in Chicago*, 647, 650–51.

80. Quotation from the *Planet*, October 25, 1919, cited in Kerlin, *Voice of the Negro*, 80.

81. *Chicago Whip*, August 9, 1919, quoted in Kerlin, *Voice of the Negro*, 66–67.

82. Quotation from *Kansas City Call*, cited in David Lewis, *When Harlem Was in Vogue*, 24.

83. *Crusader*, October 1919, quoted in Kerlin, *Voice of the Negro*, 25.

84. Jervis Anderson, *A. Philip Randolph*, 113; Kornweibel, *No Crystal Stair*, 3–41.

85. I am grateful to Eric Arnesen for sharing his work on African American railroad workers in the World War I era with me. This quotation, from *Chicago Whip*, July 25, 1919, is in his "Charting an Independent Course," 289.

86. For the World War I–era history of Pullman porters' unionization efforts, see Brazeal, *The Brotherhood of Sleeping Car Porters*, 8–12; Harris, *Keeping the Faith*; Spero and Harris, *The Black Worker*. For previous struggles, see Frank Boyd, "Previous Struggles of the Pullman Porters to Organize," *Messenger* 8:10 (October 1926): 303, 306, 319. For the co-optation of the Brotherhood of Sleeping Car Porters Protective Union, see Ashley L. Totten, "Pullman Soothing Salve," *Messenger* 8:1 (January 1926): 13.

87. Brazeal, *The Brotherhood of Sleeping Car Porters*, 13.

88. Spero and Harris, *Black Worker*, 432.

89. Brazeal, *The Brotherhood of Sleeping Car Porters*, 13.

90. Totten, "Pullman Soothing Salve," 13, 28.

91. For Totten's characterization of welfare workers, see *Black Worker*, October 1930, 2; Spero and Harris, *Black Worker*, 440.

92. William Harris, *Keeping the Faith*, 33–35; Brazeal, *Brotherhood of Sleeping Car Porters*, 18–19.

93. William Harris, *Keeping the Faith*, 34–35.

94. A. Philip Randolph, "The Brotherhood's Anniversary," *Messenger* 8:9 (September 1926): 263.

95. For examples of other issues, see Ashley L. Totten, "An Expose of the Employee Representation Plan," *Messenger* 8 (May 1926): 151, 152, 156; Frank Boyd, "Previous Struggles of the Pullman Porters of Organize," ibid. (September): 283–84; (October): 303, 306, 319.

96. The concept of place used here is tied to that of diaspora—the movement of a people, as Penny Von Eschen aptly put it, from "one place to another." See Von Eschen, "African Americans and Anti-Colonialism," 9. My concept of place, therefore, operates in tandem with a view of the Great Migration as a transforming experience. What ultimately was transformed were power relations both within the black community and between the black community and the larger political economy. Power relations were transformed as actors assumed new positions and operated out of new understandings of their place in American society. For more on the connections between place and power, see my note 52.

97. Kornweibel, *No Crystal Stair*, 25; Jervis Anderson, *This Was Harlem*, 187.

98. Editorial, "The New Negro—What Is He?" *Messenger* 2 (August 1920).

99. Kornweibel, *No Crystal Stair*, 27–29. For Randolph's recollection of learning "manhood" from his father, see A. Philip Randolph, interview, *Reminiscences*, 68–80, OHC-CU.

100. A. Philip Randolph, interview by Robert Martin, New York City, January 14, 1969, 2 (quotation), 8–9, transcript in the Civil Rights Documentation Project, Moorland-

Spingarn Research Center, Howard University, Washington, D.C. For a solid biography of Randolph's early political schooling at his father's knee, see Jervis Anderson, *A. Philip Randolph*, and Kornweibel, *No Crystal Stair*, 27–29.

101. Jervis Anderson, *A. Philip Randolph*, 36, 29–30.

102. Eric Foner, *Freedom's Lawmakers*, 215–16.

103. Henry McNeal Turner quote is from Jervis Anderson, *A. Philip Randolph*, 29, 30 (quotation), 41.

104. Quoted in ibid., 98–99.

105. Jervis Anderson, *A. Philip Randolph*, 39. Quotation in A. Philip Randolph, interview, *Reminiscences*, 73, OHC-CU.

106. A. Philip Randolph, interview, *Reminiscences*, 18, 80, 72, OHC-CU.

107. Du Bois, *The Souls of Black Folk*, 87, 86.

108. Jervis Anderson, *A. Philip Randolph*, 31–52.

109. A. Philip Randolph, interview, *Reminiscences*, 75, 78 (quotation), OHC-CU.

110. Jervis Anderson, *A. Philip Randolph*, 46–47, 52.

111. Du Bois, *Souls of Black Folk*, 88.

112. Jervis Anderson, *A. Philip Randolph*, 61–62; Kornweibel, *No Crystal Stair*, 3–33.

113. For this analysis of Randolph's early years in New York, see Spero and Harris, *The Black Worker*, 388–92; Korweibel, *No Crystal Stair*, 26–33; and Jervis Anderson, *A. Philip Randolph*, 62–63. For the Rand School, see James, *Holding Aloft the Banner of Ethiopia*, 163.

114. James, *Holding Aloft the Banner of Ethiopia*, 126; see also 127.

115. Jervis Anderson, *A. Philip Randolph*, 80.

116. For this analysis, see Spero and Harris, *Black Worker*, 390.

117. James, *Holding Aloft the Banner of Ethiopia*, 125–28.

118. Hubert Harrison, *When Africa Awakes*, quoted in James, *Holding Aloft the Banner of Ethiopia*, 128.

119. Harrison quoted in Jervis Anderson, *A. Philip Randolph*, 121.

120. A. Philip Randolph, interview, *Reminiscences*, 153–54, quoted in James, *Holding Aloft the Banner of Ethiopia*, 130.

121. *Amsterdam News*, December 28, 1927, quoted in James, *Holding Aloft the Banner of Ethiopia*, 133–34.

122. Cronon, *Black Moses*, 35–38, 71–72, 170–72; Stein, *The World of Marcus Garvey*, 128–52.

123. For the considerable cooperation among black radicals of the left in Harlem in the early 1920s, see James, *Holding Aloft the Banner of Ethiopia*, 270–71. For discussion of delegates to the Versailles Peace Conference, see Jervis Anderson, *A. Philip Randolph*, 123–26; Stein, *The World of Marcus Garvey*, 48–51; *New York Times*, December 3, 1918.

124. *Messenger*, September 1921, 248–52.

125. Spero and Harris, *The Black Worker*, 390–91; Jervis Anderson, *A. Philip Randolph*, 120.

126. For more on this tension, see Pfeffer, *A. Philip Randolph, Pioneer*, 55–78.

127. Quoted in Jervis Anderson, *A. Philip Randolph*, 128; Stein, *The World of Marcus Garvey*, 128–52.

128. Debs quoted in Draper, *American Communism*, 316. For the Randolph quotation, see Jervis Anderson, *A. Philip Randolph*, 149; for socialism not catching on with the black community, see Spero and Harris, *The Black Worker*, 391.

129. Quotes are from James, *Holding Aloft the Banner of Ethiopia*, 180–181, which also

has an excellent discussion of the relationship of black radicals to the Workers' Party and the Communist Party, especially as it relates to the question of white chauvinism within local chapters of the Communist Party.

130. Alain Locke, "Harlem: Enter the New Negro," *Survey Graphic* 53:11 (March 1, 1925): 631, 634.

131. David Lewis, *When Harlem Was in Vogue*, 117–18.

132. For the economic, social, and political environment that favored the development of welfare capitalism, see Montgomery, *The Fall of the House of Labor*, 453–57; for the "hostile stance of the state toward labor's demands," see p. 453.

133. Joel A. Rogers, "What Are We, Negroes or Americans?," *Messenger* 8:8 (August 1926): 237–38.

134. Spero and Harris, *The Black Worker*, 398; Kornweibel, *No Crystal Stair*, 195.

135. Solomon, *The Cry Was Unity*, 55; also see 52–67.

136. Quoted in Jervis Anderson, *A. Philip Randolph*, 227.

Chapter Two

1. For history of the Pullman strike of 1894, see Carwardine, *The Pullman Strike*; Lindsey, *The Pullman Strike*.

2. Wright, *Black Boy (American Hunger)*, 307–8.

3. The Pullman Company began contributing to the "welfare" of black Chicago years before the proliferation of welfare capitalism during the 1920s.

4. A. Philip Randolph to Milton P. Webster, September 26, 1926, BSCP Chicago.

5. Lindsey, *The Pullman Strike*, 22.

6. For a history of the Pullman Palace Car Company, see ibid., 19–37; Buder, *Pullman*, 15–27.

7. Lindsey, *The Pullman Strike*, 19–37, 61–89; Buder, *Pullman*, 28–45; and Adelman, *Touring Pullman*, 1–2.

8. Buder, *Pullman*, 44.

9. Jervis Anderson, *A. Philip Randolph*, 153–86; Buckler, *Doctor Dan*, 73–84; Spear, *Black Chicago*, 98; A. Philip Randolph, interview, *Reminiscences*, 257, OHC-CU. The number of Pullman Company maids employed during the 1920s and 1930s was small. The BSCP put the total number of maids in the entire country at around 200. Historian M. Melinda Chateauvert's figures suggest that about 100 Pullman maids worked in the Chicago region. Of those 100, 43 paid union dues during the twelve-year struggle for recognition. See *Pullman Porter* (issued by BSCP) 1926, 7, 06/01/04, box 17, file 490, PCP; Chateauvert, *Marching Together*, 40.

10. Pullman's power within the black community of Chicago has largely been eclipsed by attention paid to meat-packers. For more on the influence of Swift, Armour, and others within black Chicago, see Halpern, " 'Black and White Unite and Fight,' " 127–98; Horowitz, "The Path Not Taken," 183–281; Tuttle, *Race Riot*, 108–56.

11. It is also important to note that wealthy white donors were not the only source of funds that carried the hospital project forward. Many black individuals and organizations gave money, equipment, and time; community volunteerism was always an important factor in opening and sustaining the facility (see Krieg and Cooksey, *Provident Hospital*, 4). Moreover, George and Florence Pullman were not the only large donors. Philip D. Armour, Marshall Field, and H. H. Kohlsaat also donated (see Wood, *The Negro in Chicago*, 16–17).

12. Buckler, *Doctor Dan*, 66–84; Wood, *The Negro in Chicago*, 17–18; Spear, *Black Chicago*, 97–98; Drake, "Churches and Voluntary Associations in the Chicago Negro Community," 102, VGHC.

13. Buckler, *Doctor Dan*, 70–71.

14. Ibid., 82–83.

15. Krieg and Cooksey, *Provident Hospital*, 4; Buckler, *Doctor Dan*, 83–84.

16. "Pullman Porters in Session at Y.M.C.A.," *Chicago Defender*, November 21, 1925, 9.

17. Grossman, *Land of Hope*, 200; George Arthur, "The Young Men's Christian Association Movement," *Opportunity* 1:3 (March 1923): 17; *Chicago Defender*, October 14, 1922; Strickland, *History of the Chicago Urban League*, 34–36; Spero and Harris, *Black Worker*, 142.

18. Spear, *Black Chicago*, 46; Ida B. Wells-Barnett, letter to the editor, *Record-Herald*, January 26, 1912, cited in Spear, *Black Chicago*, 47.

19. Spear, *Black Chicago*, 97–100, 151; Arthur, "The Young Men's Christian Association Movement," 17; *Chicago Defender*, October 14, 1922; Tuttle, *Race Riot*, 101; Grossman, *Land of Hope*, 200.

20. Arthur, "The Young Men's Christian Association Movement," 17.

21. Eric Halpern, " 'Black and White Unite and Fight,' " 162–63.

22. *Chicago Defender*, December 5, 1914, 1; September 27, 1924, 4; *Pullman Porter Review*, March 1916, 9; September 1916, 51; July 1919, 59; October 1919, 40–41; May 1920, 28. For George Arthur addressing porters, see "Annual Convention of the Pullman Porters Benefit Association of America, November 16–20, 1926," Chicago, 06/01/01, box 4, PCP.

23. Chicago Commission on Race Relations, *The Negro in Chicago*, 147–48; Arthur, "The Young Men's Christian Association," 18; Tuttle, *Race Riot*, 101; Rick Halpern, "Race, Ethnicity, and Union in the Chicago Stockyards," 45.

24. Arthur, "Young Men's Christian Association Movement," 17.

25. Tuttle, *Race Riot*, 151; William L. Evans, "The Negro in Chicago Industries," *Opportunity* 1 (February 1923): 15–16. See also Barrett, *Work and Community in the Jungle*, 213.

26. Grossman, *Land of Hope*, 203–4, 238–40; Arthur, "The Young Men's Christian Association Movement," 17; *Chicago Defender*, October 14, 1922; Strickland, *History of the Chicago Urban League*, 34–36; Spero and Harris, *Black Worker*, 141–42; Tuttle, *Race Riot*, 148.

27. Grossman, *Land of Hope*, 142; Tuttle, *Race Riot*, 99–101; The Chicago Urban League wanted to plot a course between management and organized labor, but usually came down on management's side because "unions did not lower their color bars, and Chicago's large industries could provide immediate opportunities for the migrants." See Tuttle, "Labor Conflict and Racial Violence," 427; Strickland, *History of the Chicago Urban League*, 48, 50–51, 56–68, 70–74.

28. *Chicago Defender*, May 12, 1923, 5; Ottley, *The Lonely Warrior*, 101, 109. Spear described Avendorph as an "assistant" to the president of the Pullman Company, *Black Chicago*, 66; St. Clair Drake said: "Julius Avendorph was a respected private messenger for the officials of the Pullman Company, and enjoyed high status in the Negro community, partially because of his wide contacts with prominent white persons." In "Churches and Voluntary Associations in the Chicago Negro Community," 108, VGHC.

29. *Broad Ax*, December 26, 1925, 6; Gosnell, *Negro Politicians*, 111; LeRoy, "The Founding Heart of A. Philip Randolph's Union," 25; Drake, "Churches and Voluntary Associations in the Chicago Negro Community," 108, VGHC. For specific information

on the Appomattox Club, see *Simms' Blue Book and Directory*, 114, CHS; and Proceedings: Seventh Annual Convention, Pullman Porters Benefit Association of America, November 15–18, 1927, 50, 06/01/01, box 4, file 85, PCP.

30. Logsdon, "The Rev. Archibald J. Carey and the Negro in Chicago Politics," 7–11, 17–18, 43, 79–80; Grossman, *Land of Hope*, 230. For Carey's support of Wright, see Branham, "Transformation of Black Political Leadership," 85. It is interesting to review a study conducted for Atlanta University in 1903 on the black church. One of the most common complaints from laymen was that ministers could not manage money. One said, "I think the greatest need of our churches is good business management of funds." This stereotype may explain why Reverend Carey captured the attention of Pullman and other industrialists such as Swift and Armour; quotation from Du Bois, Miller, and Terrell, *The Negro Church*, 91.

31. Logsdon, "The Rev. Archibald J. Carey," 15–16; *Chicago Defender*, April 5, 1913, 5, and January 17, 1914, 2; Rev. S. A. Bryant, interview, February 2, 1934, folder 5, box 89, Burgess Papers, Manuscripts Division, Joseph Regenstein Library, University of Chicago; Branham, "The Transformation of Black Political Leadership," 36, 66–67. For population statistics, see Grossman, *Land of Hope*, 127; U.S. Bureau of the Census, *Negroes in the United States, 1920–1932*, 55.

32. Logsdon, "The Rev. Archibald Carey," 16–18; Drake, "Churches and Voluntary Associations in the Chicago Negro Community," 6–12, VGHC; Branham, "The Transformation of Black Political Leadership," 37; Spero and Harris, *The Black Worker*, 308–9; *Heebie Jeebies* 2:41 (September 4, 1926): 18, CHS.

33. Branham, "The Transformation of Black Political Leadership," 36, 66–67; Anabelle Carey, interview by Joseph A. Logsdon, August 26, 1960, in Logsdon, "The Rev. Archibald J. Carey," 13–18.

34. Arnesen, "Following the Color Line of Labor," 53–87; Tuttle, "Labor Conflict and Racial Violence"; Bontemps and Conroy, *Anyplace But Here*, 140; Philip Foner, *Organized Labor and the Black Workers*, 104–5; William Harris, *The Harder We Run*, 41–42; Salvatore, *Eugene V. Debs*, 227; Grossman, *Land of Hope*, 208–45.

35. Arnesen, " 'Like Banquo's Ghost, It Will Not Down.' " Also see Spero and Harris, *The Black Worker*, 284–315; U.S. Bureau of Labor Statistics, *Monthly Labor Review*, November 1924, 161; William Harris, *The Harder We Run*, 38–48.

36. Tuttle, "Labor Conflict and Racial Violence," 418; Chicago Commission on Race Relations, *The Negro in Chicago*, 430–32; *Pullman Porters' Review*, April 1916, 18, cited in LeRoy, "Scandalized, Analyzed, Paternalized," 14–15.

37. Kempton, *Part of Our Time*, 242–43.

38. Washington, *Up From Slavery*, 83, and "The Negro and the Labor Unions"; Meier, *Negro Thought in America*, 104–5; Harlan, "Booker T. Washington and the Politics of Accommodation," 1–18.

39. Ida Mae Smith, interview by Joseph A. Logsdon, July 10, 1960, in Logsdon, "The Rev. Archibald Carey," 79–80.

40. *Chicago Whip*, March 29, 1924. Quoted in Spero and Harris, *The Black Worker*, 135.

41. Logsdon, "The Rev. Archibald Carey," 15–18; Drake, "Churches and Voluntary Associations in the Chicago Negro Community," 6–12, VGHC; Branham, "The Transformation of Black Political Leadership," 36–37; *Chicago Defender*, January 17, 1914, 2; April 5, 1913, 5.

42. Minutes from Employee Representative Conference, March 20, 1924, 5–6, micro-

film, pt. III, reel 9, PCP-UPA; *Chicago Evening Journal*, October 31, 1921, in 12/00/01, box 33a, PCP.

43. H. N. Hall, "The Art of the Pullman Porter," 334–35; the John Ford quotation is taken from Harris, *Keeping the Faith*, 15; Mays, *Born to Rebel*, 61–63; *Chicago Defender*, May 8, 1926; October 31, 1925; Minutes from Employee Representative Conference, March 20, 1924, 5–6, microfilm, pt. III, reel 9, PCP-UPA.

44. For "problems confronting the family," see Minutes of Employee Representative Conference, March 22, 1924, 3, microfilm, pt. III, reel 9, PCP-UPA; J. T. Parrell, J. P. Young, H. T. Pelkey to F. L. Simmons, supervisor of Industrial Relations, the Pullman Company, November 7, 1932, 06/01/01, box 4, folder 84, PCP. For "brothers" who had "wandered from family circle," see Memo from Pullman Porters Benefit Association of America, Chicago, to management of Pullman Company, September 9, 1927, 1, 06/01/01, box 4, folder 84, PCP. For the Pullman Company as an embodiment of George Pullman, see Santino, *Miles of Smiles*, 22.

45. *Heebie Jeebies* 2:41 (September 4, 1926): 18.

46. Report of President Carry of the Pullman Company, 1922, PCP. For quotation, see LeRoy, "Scandalized, Analyzed, Paternalized," 43.

47. Information on these educational programs was contained in two press releases by the Associated Negro Press, 1926; see all four pages, box 278, folder 5, CABP. See also Report of President Carry of the Pullman Company, 1922, PCP.

48. For bands performing at Pullman Porters' picnics, see Webster to Randolph, August 10, 1928, BSCP Chicago. For special quartets singing throughout the country, see *Chicago Defender*, June 5, 1926, pt. 2, p. 1; *Messenger* 8:1 (January 1926): 28.

49. Report of President Carry of the Pullman Company, 1922, *Pullman News* (November 1925): 221, PCP; *Heebie Jeebies* 2:41 (September 4, 1926): 18; Spero and Harris, *Black Worker*, 440.

50. See *Pullman News*, PCP, and BSCP Chicago. Although most storekeepers were white workers, there were several black men who held positions as storekeepers for the company's linen and supplies, Pullman Company Memo, August 1925, PCP.

51. For statistidcs on Pullman maids, see n. 9 above. See *Pullman Porter* (issued by BSCP) 1926, 7, 06/01/04, box 17, file 490, PCP; Chateauvert, *Marching Together*, 40.

52. *Pullman Porters' Review* 9:11 (August 1921): 365–94, especially 372 and 378, 06/01/04:17:489, PCP. Compare with *Pullman News* (December 1925): 252–78, and (July 1935): 16–33, BSCP Chicago.

53. "Lest We Forget," by Henry Pope Jr., porter from Nashville, 06/01/04, box 17, file 493; Constitution and By-Laws of the Pullman Porters' Benefit Association of America (amended 1922–23), 4–5, PCP; Spero and Harris, *Black Worker*, 440–41.

54. A. Philip Randolph, "Pullman Porters Need Own Union," *Messenger* 7 (August 1925): 289.

55. Spero and Harris, *Black Worker*, 441–442; The Pullman Company, Stock Purchase Plan for Employees, 1926, and Memo: Pullman Company to Employees of the Pullman Company, December 28, 1925, BSCP Chicago; *Pullman Porters' Review* June 1916, 41–42, PCP.

56. For a firsthand account of attempts at organization in the early twentieth century, which includes a discussion of the tipping system, see Charles Anderson, *Freemen Yet Slaves*, 3, 20–22. For further discussion of early porter efforts at organization, see Mergen, "The Pullman Porter," especially 225, 229.

57. *Messenger* 8 (September 1926: 283–284; Brazeal, *The Brotherhood of Sleeping Car Porters*, 7.

58. *Broad Ax*, April 24, 1915, 4.

59. Spero and Harris, *The Black Worker*, 124–26, 430; Brazeal, *The Brotherhood of Sleeping Car Porters*, 9–10.

60. Brazeal, *The Brotherhood of Sleeping Car Porters*, 8; see also 9. For more on Pullman porters and organizing during the World War I era, see Arnesen, "Charting an Independent Course," 288–90.

61. Harris, *Keeping the Faith*, 18; Brazeal, *Brotherhood of Sleeping Car Porters*, 11.

62. Brazeal, *Brotherhood of Sleeping Car Porters*, 11–12; Spero and Harris, *The Black Worker*, 441–44; Harris, *Keeping the Faith*, 17–18, 80.

63. Harris, *Keeping the Faith*, 18, 80; A. Philip Randolph to John Mills, August 19, 1926, 2, Milton Webster to Randolph, November 10, 1926, BSCP Chicago; Spero and Harris, *The Black Worker*, 441, 443.

64. Henry Pope Jr., "Lest We Forget," 5, 06/01/04, box 17, folder 493, PCP.

65. Edward F. Carry to F. L. Simmons, April 2, 1924, PCP.

66. Spero and Harris interviewed employee representatives on the ERP sometime between 1925 and 1930 and found that "almost every important objection which [BSCP] raised against the plan [ERP] has also been made in private by employee members of both local and zone committees." See Spero and Harris, *The Black Worker*, 443.

67. Ibid., 441; Brazeal, *Brotherhood of Sleeping Car Porters*, 12–13; Harris, *Keeping the Faith*, 17–18; Fred Powell to O. P. Powell, February 4, 1926, O. P. Powell to Fred Powell, February 5, 1926, Perry Parker to J. S. Seese, District Superintendent, February 15, 1926, F. L. Simmons to Fred Powell, June 29, 1926, BSCP Chicago; "The Pullman Porters Benefit Association of America," box 4; there were 950 black mechanics and laborers in Pullman Repair Shops by December 1928; most were employed in the Chicago area; 06/01/01, box 2, PCP.

68. Ashley L. Totten, "An Expose of the Pullman Porters Benefit Association of America," *Messenger* 8 (September 1926): 268–270, 285; "PPBA of America," box 4, folder 84; Proceedings of Seventh Annual Convention of PPBAA, November 1927, box 4, folder 85; "Loyal Pullman Porters' Club," November 8, 1927, box 4, folder 71; Parker to Management of Pullman Company, September 9, 1927, all in 06/01/01, PCP.

69. Press Release, Perry Parker and PPBAA Convention, 1925, Negro Press Association, box 279, folder 2, CABP; *Chicago Defender*, November 26, 1927, 3.

70. "P.P.B.A.A. Convention Hears of Progress and Reelects Directors," *Pullman News*, December 1925, 261, BSCP Chicago; Pullman Porters Benefit Association of America, Proceedings of Seventh Annual Convention, November 15–17, 1927, Memo to Management of Pullman Company from Board of Directors of PPBAA, September 9, 1927, 06/01/01, box 4, folder 84, PCP; *Messenger* 8:1 (January 1926): 13, 17; Press Release, Perry Parker and PPBAA Convention, 1925, Negro Press Association, box 279, folder 2, CABP.

71. Webster to Randolph, March 29, 1927; Webster to Randolph, January 4, 1928, BSCP Chicago. Binga quote re: "service" from *Chicago Defender*, November 26, 1927, 3.

72. Binga speech in Proceedings of Seventh Annual Convention, November 15–18, 1927, 50, 06/01/01, box 4, folder 85, PCP.

73. Spero and Harris, *The Black Worker*, 443.

74. Randolph to John C. Mills, August 19, 1926, 1–2, BSCP Chicago; *Messenger* 8:1 (January 1926): 30.

75. Webster to Randolph, August 4, 1926, BSCP Chicago; Annual Convention of the

P.P.B.A. of A., box 4; "Statement in Regard to the Plan of Employee Representation" (1930), 06/01/01, box 2, PCP.

76. Randolph, "Pullman Porters Need Own Union," *Messenger* 7 (August 1925): 289; Randolph, "The Pullman Company and the Pullman Porters," *Messenger* 7 (September 1925): 312–14, 355–56; R. W. Dunn, "Company Unions a la Pullman," *Messenger* 7 (December 1925): 394–95.

77. Harris, *Keeping the Faith*, 20.

78. Unfortunately for scholars, issues of the Chicago *Bee* for 1925–35 are largely extinct, making it difficult to verify claims that the *Bee* did not oppose the BSCP. The most that I can find is the suggestion of favorable reporting based on the fact that Chandler Owen, former editor of *Messenger* with Randolph, wrote for the *Bee* during the early years of BSCP organizing in Chicago. The author has searched every archive for issues and consulted experts on the history of black Chicago only to discover no complete runs. There are not even "incomplete" runs. The only citations in this study to Chicago *Bee* come from stories clipped from the *Bee* that were found in someone's papers. I consulted Margaret T. Burroughs, Charles R. Branham, James R. Grossman, Archie Motley, and Dempsey J. Travis.

79. ANP News Release, 1926, box 278, folder 5, CABP.

80. Harris, *Keeping the Faith*, 20, 48.

81. Hogan, *A Black National News Service*, 57.

82. See press releases, Associated Negro Press, box 278, folders 4 and 5, CABP.

83. See correspondence between Claude Barnett and E. F. Carry and James Keeley, assistant to the president of Pullman, and Perry Parker of the PPBAA, especially Barnett to James Keeley, April 26, 1926, and "Memo to Mr. K," (undated 1926), Associated Negro Press, box 275, folder 5 and box 278, folders 4 and 5. Barnett proposed his magazine just before the BSCP began organizing in Chicago. He told E. F. Carry (July 30, 1925) that his magazine would contain "worthwhile stories of the achievements of Pullman men" which would be broadcast through his Associated Negro Press, "In this way, public opinion among the porters and their communities would" be favorable. "Enlightened public opinion drives away opportunity for spreading discontent and proselyting by influences which are of disadvantage to the men and the service." Barnett pointed out that although the company "should pay printing bills," it should "not seem to be interested" in the publication. CABP.

84. Wright, *Black Boy*, 312.

85. Wright, *12 Million Black Voices*.

86. Logsdon, "The Rev. Archibald J. Carey," 28, 34, 39; Ralph Bunche, "The Thompson-Negro Alliance," *Opportunity* 7:3 (March 1929):78; Gosnell, *Negro Politicians*, 11, 50–51.

87. The Republican Party in Chicago, unlike in most other cities, was split into two factions—a reform-minded group and a machine group, based on patronage and powerful organization. Part of the explanation of relative black progress in Chicago can be attributed to the dependence of the patronage-reward, machine-oriented group on black votes to beat the other faction within the Republican Party. See Gosnell, *Negro Politicians*, 37–62; Chicago Commission on Race Relations, *The Negro in Chicago*, 79 .

88. Thompson utilized the playground in political speeches over the years as a symbol of the relationship that was cemented with Carey and black citizens on the South Side during his first campaign for alderman. See Logsdon, "The Rev. Archibald Carey," 38; Gosnell *Negro Politicians*, 50; *Chicago Defender*, February 5, 1927.

89. Quotations in *Chicago Defender*, September 20, 1913, 1; September 18, 1915, 1. Of

the 430 seamen who took part in the encounter at Put-in-Bay on Lake Erie, 109 were black Americans. Logsdon, "The Rev. Archibald J. Carey," 19–20, 35–39, 49, 51–52; Branham, "Transformation of Black Political Leadership," 70; Gosnell, *Negro Politicians*, 39, 49–51. The Republican primary vote for the city was: Olson, 84,825; Hey, 4,283; Thompson, 87,333. In the second ward: Olson, 1,870; Hey, 47; Thompson, 8,633. For these figures, see Gosnell, *Negro Politicians*, 40–41.

90. For understanding the "question," see Tuttle, *Race Riot*, 188–89. Reverend Carey was on the motion-picture censorship board at the time when Thompson publicly backed Carey's successful fight to suppress circulation of *Birth of a Nation* (Logsdon, "The Rev. Archibald J. Carey," 24–25). For appointing black citizens to patronage jobs, see *Chicago Defender*, April 5, 1919; *Chicago Tribune*, April 5, 1919.

91. Tuttle, *Race Riot*, 190–91; Bright, *Hizzoner Big Bill Thompson*, 87–88; *Broad Ax*, September 18, 1915.

92. Gosnell, *Negro Politicians*, 55; Robinson, "The Negro in Politics in Chicago," 184.

93. Robinson, "The Negro in Politics in Chicago," 214–16; Bunche, "The Thompson-Negro Alliance," 79.

94. Branham, "Transformation of Black Political Leadership," 160. *Chicago Defender*, August 7, 1915; Chicago *Daily News*, July 21, 1915;

95. Gosnell, *Negro Politicians*, 55–56; *Chicago Defender*, August 7, 1915.

96. Charles Branham notes that black politicians were "isolated from the [white] community's social, cultural, religious and charitable leadership." An "insular and individualistic pattern of political advancement that had characterized early political adaptation continued through the migration era." Branham, "The Transformation of Black Political Leadership," 52; see also 457–63. For further discussion, see Katznelson, *Black Men, White Cities*, 98, 102–3; Martin Kilson identified "clientage" politics as the fundamental "linkage" between black and white political leadership, in "Political Change in the Negro Ghetto, 1900–1940's," 172–74; Gosnell, *Negro Politicians*, 58, 96–97; Logsdon, "The Rev. Archibald Carey," 10–11, 16, 19, 72–73; and Spear, *Black Chicago*, 64.

97. Charles Branham summarizes the patterns this way: "The reality of black politics is that group advancement was retarded by the individualistic and competitive pattern of black political advancement which vitiated greater racial representation through concerted action." See Branham, "Transformation of Black Political Leadership," 53, 462–63. See also Bunche, "The Thompson-Negro Alliance," 78.

98. See *Chicago Defender* 1918, 1919; Meier, *Negro Thought in America*, 86, 121–38; Katznelson, *Black Men, White Cities*, 98.

99. Randolph to Webster, January 8, 1927; Randolph to union members, January 13, 1927; both in BSCP Chicago; Drake and Cayton, *Black Metropolis*, 391, 728, 731.

100. Tuttle, *Race Riot*, 130–32; Kennedy, *Negro Peasant*, 132–33; Sandburg, *The Chicago Race Riots*, 31–35.

101. Chicago Commission on Race Relations, *The Negro in Chicago*, 79, 106. According to the Census Bureau method of estimating natural population increases, the black population of Chicago—without migration—would have been 58,056 in 1920 (ibid., 79).

102. Brody, *Butcher Workmen*, 85; Spero and Harris, *Black Worker*, 271.

103. Tuttle, *Race Riot*, 151.

104. Tuttle, *Race Riots*, 134–41; Graham Taylor, "An Epidemic of Strikes in Chicago," *Survey Graphic* 62 (August 2, 1919): 645–46; William L. Evans, "The Negro in Chicago Industries," *Opportunity* 1:2 (February 1923): 15.

105. Tuttle, *Race Riot*, 109–11, 141–42, 153–54, 156. Tuttle quotes Ray Stannard Baker,

who noted that during the summer of 1919 in Chicago "labor is more closely organized, more self-conscious, more advanced in its views in Chicago than in any other American city" (141).

106. Rick Halpern, "Race, Ethnicity, and Union in the Chicago Stockyards," 25–58, especially 52–53, and *Down on the Killing Floor*.

107. Dilliard, "Civil Liberties of Negroes in Illinois," 610–11; Chicago Commission on Race Relations, *The Negro in Chicago*, 152–230.

108. The Grand Boulevard district was described by the Kenwood and Hyde Park Property Owners' Association as extending from Thirty-ninth to Sixty-third streets, and from Michigan Avenue to Cottage Grove Avenue. Quotations are from Chicago Commission on Race Relations, *The Negro in Chicago*, 115–22; *Chicago Defender*, March 1, 1919. See also Bontemps and Conroy, *Anyplace but Here*, 175.

109. Chicago Commission on Race Relations, *The Negro in Chicago*, 590.

110. One speaker seemed to voice the collective view of the group at a property owners' meeting when he proclaimed, "I am not nor ever have been in favor of bringing about in any way the social and political equality of the white and black race." Ibid., 106–10, 119 (quotation), 120–22.

111. For the quotation from *Chicago Defender*, see Tuttle, *Race Riot*, 235. For more on the mounting tension between the black and white communities, see *Chicago Defender*, June 8, 27, August 3, September 21, October 19, November 2, and December 28, 1918.

112. Bontemps and Conroy, *Anyplace but Here*, 179–80; Tuttle, *Race Riot*, 4–7, 241.

113. Quoted in Tuttle, *Race Riot*, 242.

114. Harry Haywood described Chicago as a "besieged city." He said it reminded him of battles in France from which he had just returned. And he also noted that "blacks fought back." See his *Black Bolshevik*, 3.

115. Tuttle, *Race Riot*, 232; *Chicago Defender*, July 6, 1918; Chicago Commission on Race Relations, *The Negro in Chicago*, 490; Gosnell, *Negro Politicians*, 250; Spear, *Black Chicago*, 35–36.

116. Chicago Commission on Race Relations, *The Negro in Chicago*, 551.

117. Wright, *Black Boy*, 312.

118. See Meier, *Negro Thought in America*, 121–38; Spear, *Black Chicago*, 53–54; Gaines, *Uplifting the Race*.

119. *Chicago Defender*, August 2, 1919; Ottley, *The Lonely Warrior*, 182–83.

120. Quoted in Branham, "Transformation of Black Political Leaders," 183.

121. Chicago Commission on Race Relations, *The Negro in Chicago*, 647, 650–51.

122. Quoted in Branham, "Transformation of Black Political Leaders," 188–89, n. 2.

123. For the quotation from Wright, see ibid., 186. This quotation appeared in an article in the *Chicago Daily News*, September 26, 1919.

124. The phrase, "biting the hand that feeds you," appeared in newspapers, in Brotherhood correspondence, and was mentioned by Drake and Cayton in *Black Metropolis*. It was commonly used by both black and white politicians as a way of reminding patrons about the terms of the social contract. See Drake and Cayton, *Black Metropolis*, 370. See also Frank L. Hayes, writing on the Chicago division of the BSCP for the *Chicago Daily News*, November 5, 1929, BSCP Chicago. Hayes quotes Webster on the problems that follow when black workers try to organize. Webster told Hayes that "influential people and publications" in black communities "immediately spring forth an avalanche of propaganda: 'Watch your step,' and 'Don't bite the hand that's feeding you,' " when black workers start organizing.

Chapter Three

1. Jervis Anderson, *A. Philip Randolph*, 221.

2. *Chicago Defender*, November 27, 1926, pt. 1, p. 3.

3. Leaders of the black community in Chicago often evaluated political questions by using a cost-benefit analysis. Leaders, generally, were not so much antiunion as against economic immobility and lack of opportunity. Thus, the Reverend L. K. Williams tried to determine what was in the best interests of the black community. During the 1920s, he thought the costs of opposition to Pullman were higher than the benefits that would flow from unionization of porters. Similarly, Warren Whatley, writing about the history of African American strikebreaking between the Civil War and the New Deal, cites the importance of community-based constraints, which grew out of open debate regarding the costs and benefits of strikebreaking. He found that "neither workers nor middle classes were unanimous in their opinions. Each interested party assessed the situation, sometimes deciding against strikebreaking, sometimes deciding in favor, but always acting in their own interest." Whatley, "African-American Strikebreaking," 546. For Pullman's success in defeating unions, see Carwardine, *The Pullman Strike*, 38–46; Buder, *Pullman*, 178–201.

4. Duncan and Duncan, *Negro Population of Chicago*, 24; Drake and Cayton, *Black Metropolis*, 77–97; Gosnell, *Negro Politicians*, 16.

5. I consciously use the term "clubwomen" because that was the noun used by the *Chicago Defender* to signify black women active in the Chicago women's club movement. See *Chicago Defender*, March 16, 1929, 7, or any issue during the 1920s and 1930s.

6. Some African American men had tried earlier, unsuccessfully, to challenge the Republican machine; see Branham, "Transformation of Black Political Leadership," 82–86.

7. Jervis Anderson, *A. Philip Randolph*, 183.

8. Ibid., 171.

9. *Messenger* 8:1 (January 1926): 24; Jervis Anderson, *A. Philip Randolph*, 171.

10. "Stool Pigeons," in "Bulletin," a BSCP Publication, 06/01/04, box 17, file 492, PCP. *Messenger*, 8 (October 1926): 294; (November 1926): 325; 9 (March 1927): 68.

11. Pullman supervisor, J. A. Kouper, report in secret memo to the Pullman Company on a BSCP meeting held in St. Louis, October 24, 1926. Similar connections between Pullman stool pigeons and slaves were made to the gathering, pt. III, reel 9, PCP-UPA. Benjamin McLaurin, interview by Greg LeRoy, January 22, 1981, tape 1, CHS.

12. Webster to Wells-Barnett, September 15, 1926; Randolph to Webster, September 26, 1926, BSCP Chicago.

13. Wells, *Crusade for Justice*, 47.

14. Wells-Barnett, "Southern Horrors," 35; Wells, *Crusade for Justice*, 47–52.

15. Tucker, "Wells and Memphis Lynching," 115; Wells, *Crusade for Justice*, 47–52.

16. Wells-Barnett, "Southern Horrors," 36; Wells, *Crusade for Justice*, 48.

17. Wells-Barnett, "Southern Horrors," 37.

18. Wells-Barnett, "A Red Record," 143.

19. Ibid., 143–44.

20. Ibid., 150–57.

21. Wells-Barnett, "Southern Horrors," 33.

22. Ibid., 28.

23. For what lynching really was, see Wells, *Crusade for Justice*, 64.

24. Wells-Barnett, "Southern Horrors," 42. A proposed lynching did not occur, she noted, in Jacksonville in 1892 because "men armed themselves." It is interesting to speculate whether this incident in Jacksonville is the same one Randolph's father took part in during the early nineties. See A. Philip Randolph, interview, *Reminiscences*, 68–70, OHC-CU.

25. My discussion of Ida B. Wells on manhood and civilization relies on the excellent discussion by McMurry, *To Keep the Waters Troubled*, 156–68. For further discussion of manhood and civilization, see Bederman, " 'Civilization,' the Decline of Middle-Class Manliness"; Carby, " 'On the Threshold of the Woman's Era.' "

26. Wells, *Crusade for Justice*, 70. For uses of civilization and manhood to denounce lynching, see McMurry, *To Keep the Waters Troubled*, 165–66.

27. Wells, *Crusade for Justice*, xix, 79, 128. See also Thompson, *Ida B. Wells-Barnett*, 38–39; Angela Davis, *Women, Race, and Class*, 132; Brown, "Womanist Consciousness"; Deborah White, "The Cost of Club Work." For the historical context of the idea of "the brotherhood of man," as understood by middle-class African American men and women, see Higginbotham, *Righteous Discontent*, and Gilmore, *Gender and Jim Crow*, 100.

28. Wells, *Crusade for Justice*, xix; Thompson, *Ida B. Wells-Barnett*, 47; McMurry, *To Keep the Waters Troubled*, 267; Holt, "The Lonely Warrior," 56.

29. McMurry, *To Keep the Waters Troubled*, 238–39.

30. *Broad Ax*, January 9, 1915, 4; February 13, 1915, 4; April 24, 1915, 4.; Wells, *Crusade for Justice*, xxv, 297.

31. For information on the Women's Second Ward Republican Club and quotation, see McMurry, *To Keep the Waters Troubled*, 304.

32. Williams, "The Alpha Suffrage Club," 12; Hendricks, *Gender, Race, and Politics*, 89–90.

33. *Chicago Daily Tribune*, March 4, 1913, 3.

34. Quotation in Wells, *Crusade for Justice*, 345; for Illinois enfranchisement of women, see Hendricks, "Wells-Barnett and the Alpha Suffrage Club," 270–71.

35. Williams, "The Alpha Suffrage Club," 12.

36. Wells, *Crusade for Justice*, 346. Wells-Barnett and the Alpha Suffrage Club were not the first to set out to elect a black man to City Council. For previous attempts, see Stovall, "The *Chicago Defender*"; Gosnell, *Negro Politicians*, 163–74; Spear, *Black Chicago*, 122–23; Pinderhughes, *Race and Ethnicity*, 25–26; Hendricks, *Gender, Race, and Politics*, 97–100.

37. *Chicago Defender*, February 21, 1914, 1.

38. Williams, "The Alpha Suffrage Club," 12.

39. *Broad Ax*, February 21, 1914, 2; February 28, 1914, l.

40. For population data on the second ward, see Spear, *Black Chicago*, 15, 122 (for 1915 statistics). For influence of competing political approaches, see Hendricks, *Gender, Race, and Politics*, 102–3.

41. *Broad Ax*, March 7, 1914, 1.

42. Wells-Barnett said Cowen was only 167 votes shy of a win for the primary nomination; see *Crusade for Justice*, 346. The *Broad Ax*, a black newspaper in Chicago, put the figure closer to 300, February 28, 1914, 1; the *Chicago Defender*, said that Cowan needed only 265 taken from Norris, February 28, 1914, 4.

43. Wells, *Crusade for Justice*, 346.

44. As Wanda Hendricks shows, not all the activism by newly enfranchised African

American women agreed with the ASC either before or after the February 1914 primary. Another suffrage organization was organized during the spring of 1914 by supporters of Hugh Norris. Hendricks, *Gender, Race, and Politics*, 102.

45. Wells, *Crusade for Justice*, 346–47.

46. For an excellent, more extensive, analysis of the Alpha Suffrage Club, see Hendricks, *Gender, Race, and Politics*, 96–111.

47. For biography of Oscar DePriest, see Gosnell, *Negro Politicians*, 163–95; Spear, *Black Chicago*, 78–79. For documentation regarding a motion to expel any member who supported a white candidate, see Thompson, *Ida B. Wells-Barnett*, 105.

48. *Alpha Suffrage Record*, March 18, 1914, box 5, folder 2, IBWP.

49. Terborg-Penn, *African American Women in Struggle for Vote*, 124–25.

50. This news editorial was reprinted in *Alpha Suffrage Record*, March 18, 1914.

51. Branham, "Transformation of Black Political Leadership," 150–53; Hendricks, *Gender, Race and Politics*, 97–100.

52. In addition, as Wanda Hendricks notes, "gender conflict was suppressed, and a male-female alliance was created that kept in check the resistance of the Republican machine to the leadership of African Americans over their own people." See, *Gender, Race, and Politics*, 110.

53. Deborah White argues that a "sense of real equality with black men made the black woman's club movement qualitatively different from the white woman's club movement of the period, even though black and white women seemed to be doing and saying the same things and embracing the same philosophy of womanhood." It grew out of the "knowledge that black women, just like black men, had endured incredible hardships during slavery and that neither sex had gained any advantage in the nearly two and a half centuries of enslavement." White, "The Cost of Club Work," 251–52. Also see Angela Davis, *Women, Race, and Class*, 135–48, who points out the support black clubwomen and suffragists received from black men, and Higginbotham, "In Politics to Stay," 200–202.

54. For an excellent discussion of the political poetics of Frances E. W. Harper, see Boyd, *Discarded Legacy*, especially 126–29, 221–27. For the role of African American women in the fight for the Nineteenth Amendment, see Terborg-Penn, "African American Women and Suffrage," 153–55.

55. Wells, *Crusade for Justice*, 397–404; Spear, *Black Chicago*, 190, 198; Branham, "Transformation of Black Leadership," 241–44; Waskow, *From Race Riot to Sit-In*, 121–74.

56. Percival Pratis to Claude Barnett, August 8, 1928, box 333, folder 4, CABP. Robb, "Survey of Negro Life," in *Negro in Chicago*, 27; Wells-Barnett was chair of Republican women against the machine candidate, Mrs. Ruth McCormick, *Chicago Defender*, October 19, 1929, 9; April 20, 1929, pt. 2, p. 6. Paula Giddings suggested that Wells-Barnett "had managed to run afoul of almost everyone with her strident independence and refusal to compromise her principles" by 1924. See Giddings, *When and Where I Enter*, 180. While that may have been true especially at the national level, she was able to command enough respect to carry weight within activist networks and circles in Chicago until her death in March 1931.

57. *Chicago Defender*, December 19, 1925, pt. 2, p. 4; Randolph spoke to the women of the Chicago and Northern District Federation of Women's Club on December 7, 1925, at Herman Baptist Church. The club appears through the years under a couple names. By 1932 it is known as the Chicago and Northern District Federation of Colored Women's

Clubs (*Chicago Defender*, March 1932); and by 1937, as the Chicago and Northern District Association of Colored Women (see letter from A. L. Foster, secretary of Chicago Urban League, to Irene McCoy Gaines, president of the Chicago and Northern District Association of Colored Women, July 29, 1937, box 1, Irene McCoy Gaines Papers, CHS).

58. S.W.O. 193, report on the Woman's Forum, Dec. 21, 1925, file: History of BSCP, box 10, APRP.

59. Ibid.

60. See brief history of Ida B. Wells' Club, *Chicago Defender*, December 5, 1934, 22.

61. Milton P. Webster to Ida Wells-Barnett, September 15, 1926, BSCP Chicago.

62. Quotation from a circular for BSCP meeting, October 30, 1926, Los Angeles, pt. III, reel 9, PCP-UPA. See also Webster to Dad Moore, May 16, 1926; Randolph to Webster, August 3, 1926; Randolph to John C. Mills, August 3, 1926; Randolph to Webster, January 28, 1927, 2; Randolph to Webster, n.d. (though it appears to be a September 1927 letter); BSCP Chicago.

63. Deborah White, "The Cost of Club Work," 249–50.

64. McMurry, *To Keep the Waters Troubled*, 339.

65. For another perspective on manhood, see Chateauvert, *Marching Together*, whose focus is activities of the women's Auxiliary of the BSCP and the relationship of the women's auxiliary to the BSCP. She argues that while the "Brotherhood's demand for manhood rights evolved from both African American protests and those of white working men," they were, nevertheless, "fundamentally gendered. They were the rights granted by the polity to the head of the patriarchal family. In both European and African political traditions, manhood rights served as the foundation of the nation-state" (4). Male supremacy within the union contributed, she argues, to diminishing respect for women and led to efforts to curtail the work of the auxiliary of the BSCP (54), 66.

66. "Civil Rights and the Negro," *Messenger* 8:3 (March 1926): 73–74.

67. For interpretation of this extant copy of *Chicago Whip*, October 11, 1919, see Spear, *Black Chicago*, 186. For comparison of the *Defender* and *Whip*, see Chicago Commission on Race Relations, *The Negro in Chicago*, 557–60.

68. *Chicago Whip*, June 24, December 13 1919; Spear, *Black Chicago*, 186, 197–98.

69. Unfortunately for scholars, issues of the *Chicago Whip* for this period do not exist. The interpretation given here is suggestive at best and constructed from scant evidence that exists in contemporary secondary sources.

70. "A Reply to Joe D. 'Bibb,'" *Messenger* 8 (December 1925): 378.

71. *Chicago Whip*, May 15, 1926, cited in Spero and Harris, *The Black Worker*, 137.

72. *Messenger* 7 (December 1925): 378–79.

73. William Harris, *Keeping the Faith*, 44–45; *Messenger* 8 (February 1926): 48–49.

74. See Chandler Owen, "The Neglected Truth," *Messenger* 8 (January 1926): 5, 6, 31; "The Neglected Truth," pt. 3, ibid. (March 1926): 83–85.

75. Owen, "The Neglected Truth," 83.

76. *Messenger* 8 (June 1926): 177.

77. LeRoy, "The Founding Heart of A. Philip Randolph's Union," 30–31.

78. Claude Barnett wrote a memo to a Pullman Company official in 1925 making reference to the *Whip*'s dependence on Sam Insull's Utilities. Some years later, Horace Cayton and George S. Mitchell further substantiated the relationship between Pullman and the *Whip* when they published an interview they had conducted in 1933 with an anonymous source connected with the *Whip*. Cayton and Mitchell were told that, "Yes,

after 1925 there was a change in the policy of the *Whip*. It came about in this way. To save the stockholders who had invested in the *Whip* we made a deal with Insull. In this deal Insull took over about $22,000 worth of stock. Then this necessitated the changing of our policy. Later when Insull's lawyer became the lawyer for the Pullman Company we had to change our policy toward the Pullman Porters' union. Before, we had been favoring it and we just had to pick out something and fight it. We just had to make a reason for being against it. There was an expose in the *Messenger*, but it was only half the truth. They never did know the whole story." Cayton and Mitchell, *Black Workers and New Unions*, 396.

79. See, for example, *Chicago Defender*, August 20, 1927.

80. *Messenger* 8 (January 1926): 15.

81. *Pittsburgh Courier*, May 1, 1926, 1.

82. For a discussion of the inability of racial uplift ideology to keep pace with forces of change, see Gaines, *Uplifting the Race*, 234–60.

83. For Dr. Cook's support of BSCP, see *Messenger* 8:1 (January 1926): 24; Jervis Anderson, *A. Philip Randolph*, 171. A. Philip Randolph's appearance at the Metropolitan Community Center was before the Sunday Evening Club, *Chicago Defender*, December 19, 1925, pt. 2, p. 4.

84. Webster to Wells-Barnett, September 15, 1926; Randolph to Webster, September 26, 1926, BSCP Chicago.

85. LeRoy, "The Founding Heart of A. Philip Randolph's Union," 27.

86. Analysis of Cook's People's Church is based on information gathered under the auspices of the Work Projects Administration, "The Peoples Community Church of Christ," by Ann Williams and Josephine Copeland, 1–7, box 047, folder 21, Illinois Writers' Project, VGHC; Robb, *The Negro in Chicago*, 68; *Chicago Defender*, July 11, 1914; October 9, 1920; April 2, 1921; September 29, 1923; LeRoy, "The Founding Heart of A. Philip Randolph's Union," 27. For Ida B. Wells-Barnett's support of Metropolitan Community Church, see *Crusade for Justice*, xxx.

87. For the Pittsburgh phase of Austin's activism, see Trotter, *River Jordan*, 120–21.

88. "Twentieth Century Churches (Chicago): Pilgrim Baptist Church," pp. 1–2, box 17, folder 25, Illinois Writers' project, VGHC; *Pittsburgh Courier*, December 26, 1925, 1; Robb, *The Negro in Chicago*, 163, 167.

89. Webster to Randolph, March 26, 1927; Randolph to Webster, March 28, 1927; Webster to Randolph, March 28, 1927, BSCP Chicago. Report, "Meetings Held with Ministers in an Attempt to Secure Their Cooperation in the Interest of Community Welfare," August 1920, box 25, JFP.

90. Harris, *Keeping the Faith*, 20; Logsdon, "The Rev. Archibald J. Carey," 79–80; *Black Worker*, November 15, 1929; Robb, *The Negro in Chicago*, 171; Drake, "Churches and Voluntary Associations in Chicago," 183, VGHC; LeRoy, "The Founding Heart of A. Philip Randolph's Union," 27; Spear, *Black Chicago*, 177–78, 186; "Meetings Held with Ministers in an Attempt to Secure Their Cooperation in the Interest of Community Welfare."

91. Harris, *Keeping the Faith*, 20; *Black Worker*, November 15, 1929; Robb, *The Negro in Chicago*, 171; Drake, "Churches and Voluntary Associations," 183, VGHC; LeRoy, "The Founding Heart A. Philip Randolph's Union," 27; Spear, *Black Chicago*, 177–78, 186; Chicago Law and Order League, Hyde Park Protective Association Newsletter, December 21, 1925, box 2, section 12, folder 11, CABP; "Meetings Held with Ministers in an Attempt to Secure Their Cooperation in the Interest of Community Welfare"; Grossman, *Land of Hope*, 156, 230.

92. Canaan, "'Part of the Loaf,'" 30. For more on the 1920s, see Kornweibel, "An Economic Profile of Black Life in the Twentieth Century."

93. Drake and Cayton, *Black Metropolis*, 78–83; Scott, *Occupational Changes among Negroes*, 217–28.

94. But the ambivalence is significant, too, as a way of measuring the pulse of church-goers. Du Bois noticed at the turn of the century that it was the preacher who followed "the standard of his flock, and only exceptional men dare seek to change this." The "moral standards are therefore set by the congregations." Du Bois, *The Philadelphia Negro*, 205–6. Drake and Cayton suggested the pattern—ministers as followers of the flock—continued in the 1920s in Chicago. Drake and Cayton, *Black Metropolis*, 412–29.

95. Logsdon, "The Rev. Archibald J. Carey," 17–18, 80.

96. Gosnell, *Negro Politicians*, 163–71; Branham, "Transformation of Black Politicians," 246.

97. Furthermore, as Ira Katznelson pointed out, symbolic recognition must not be confused with group power. See *Black Men, White Cities*, 98, 103–4.

98. Milton P. Webster to Ida Wells-Barnett, September 15, 1926, BSCP Chicago.

99. *Chicago Defender*, March 16, 1929, 7; May 4, 1929, pt. 2, p. 6; on the topic of community work and black clubwomen, see Lerner, *The Majority Finds Its Past*, 83–93; other sources on the black women's club movement include Giddings, *When and Where I Entered*; Angela Davis, "Black Women and the Club Movement," in *Women, Race, and Class*; Salem, *To Better Our World*; Jacqueline Jones, *Labor of Love*, 190–95; Frederick Douglass League of Women Voters was listed with headquarters at the home of Mrs. Irene Goins, "List of Newspapers and Organizations on the South Side," box 345a, folder 1, CABP; Hendricks, *Gender, Race, and Politics*, 29.

100. I am grateful for the work of Evelyn Brooks Higginbotham, who pointed out the interest in citizenship by Chicago and Illinois clubwomen. See "In Politics to Stay," 213–14.

101. Henry, *The Trade Union Woman*, 75; Philip Foner, *Women and the American Labor Movement*, 311–13. *Chicago Defender*, March 16, 1929, 7; Grossman, *Land of Hope*, 220; Halpern, *Down on the Killing Floor*, 52.

102. Philip Foner, *Women and the American Labor Movement*, 470–75.

103. Webster, "Sidelights on the National Negro Labor Conference," *Black Worker*, March 1930, 1.

104. Webster to Randolph, September 8, 1926; Randolph to Webster, September 21, 1926; Webster to Randolph, September 24, 1926, BSCP Chicago. See September 21, 1926, letter for deconstruction of text for posters advertising the October 3, 1926, meeting. Randolph suggested that the term "economic mass meeting," which Webster favored, did not mean anything to the average person, that it was too high brow. "You will have much greater effect if you make your wording simpler, such as, for instance, Victory Dash Rally, etc."

105. Webster to Randolph, October 9, 1926, BSCP Chicago.

106. "Speech by Mary McDowell," Sunday, October 3, 1926, Chicago, reprinted in the *Messenger* 8 (December 1926): 375.

107. Memo to L. S. Hungerford from J. A. Rittenhouse, Superintendent, re: "relative Mass Meeting of so-called Brotherhood of Sleeping Car Porters," October 26, 1927, file 209104, Propaganda sent out by the BSCP, pt. III, reel 9, PCP-UPA.

108. Dr. Cook's church must have been packed considering the nose count was over

2,000 people at the mass meeting. Webster to Dad Moore, November 8, 1927, BSCP Chicago.

109. *Chicago Defender*, November 19, 1927.

110. Ottley, *The Lonely Warrior*, 263–65; Frazier, "Chicago: A Cross-Section of Negro Life," 71.

111. Webster to Randolph, October 3, 1927, 2; Webster to Dad Moore, November 8, 1927; Webster to Randolph, November 11, 1927; Randolph to Webster, November 15, 1927; BSCP Chicago.

112. Brazeal, *The Brotherhood of Sleeping Car Porters*, 53.

113. Harris, *Keeping the Faith*, 47.

114. *Messenger* 8 (January 1926): 17.

115. Harry Kletzky, "Porter Brotherhood's Power Forces Negro Paper to Change Front," *Federated Press*, December 28, 1927, box 25, JFP.

116. Ottley, *The Lonely Warrior*, 266.

117. Ibid., 138–39; Gosnell, *Negro Politicians*, 101.

118. Frazier, "Chicago: A Cross-Section of Negro Life," 71.

119. Webster to Randolph, October 3, 1927, 2; Webster to Dad Moore, November 8, 1927; Webster to Randolph, November 11, 1927; Randolph to Webster, November 15, 1927; BSCP Chicago.

120. See Ottley for Robert Abbott's concern over what was best for the "race," *The Lonely Warrior*, 13–16, 109, 265.

121. *Chicago Defender*, December 17, 1927, 1–2.

122. Randolph to Webster, November 22, 1927; Webster to Fitzpatrick, December 1, 1927; BSCP Chicago.

123. Webster to Randolph, December 17, 1927, BSCP Chicago.

124. See entries in "Datebook," Irene McCoy Gaines, for January 13, 17, 25, 29, 1921, box 8, Irene McCoy Gaines Papers, CHS.

125. Advertising Circular, January 1928, BSCP Chicago.

126. Webster to Randolph, December 17, 1927, 2; Webster to Randolph, January 4, 1928; Circular for Mass Meeting, August 4, 1929; BSCP Chicago.

127. Robb, *The Negro in Chicago*, 120; Webster to Randolph, December 17, 1927, BSCP Chicago.

128. Larch-Quinn, *Black Neighbors*, 142–44.

129. *Messenger* 8:9 (September 1926): 265; *Black Worker* (July 1935): 2.

130. For more on the activities of the Women's Economic Council, see Chateauvert, *Marching Together*, especially, 40–70 (the quotation is from 52). See also Pfeffer, "The Women behind the Union."

131. Webster to Randolph, June 1, 1927; Webster to Randolph, February 18, 1927; Webster to Randolph, February 19, 1927; Webster to Randolph, February 28, 1927; Webster to Randolph, March 25, 1927; Program from Mass Meeting, June 30, 1929, New York, all in BSCP Chicago.

132. Hendricks, *Gender, Race, and Politics*, 90.

133. "Extensive Work of Dr. G. C. Hall," *Broad Ax*, February 17, 1912, 3; obituary on Hall, *Chicago Defender*, June 21, 1930, 1, 12, 14; Strickland, *History of the Chicago Urban League*, 28.

134. Spear, *Black Chicago*, 73, 87–89; *Broad Ax*, December 31, 1904; February 17, 1912, 3; *Crisis* 6 (May 1, 1913): 38–39; Boris, *Who's Who in Colored America, 1928–1929*; Strickland, *History of Chicago Urban League*, 28.

135. Spear, *Black Chicago*, 228.

136. Robert Park, introduction to Gosnell's *Negro Politicians*. See also Katznelson, *Black Men, White Cities*, 102–3; Branham, "The Transformation of Black Political Leadership," 462–63.

137. Randolph to Webster, January 8, 1927; Randolph to union members, January 13, 1927, BSCP Chicago; Drake and Cayton, *Black Metropolis*, 391, 728, 731. *Chicago Defender*, February 23, 1918.

138. Waskow, *From Race Riot to Sit-In*, 74; Chicago Commission on Race Relations, *The Negro in Chicago*, 652; *Chicago Defender*, June 21, 1930, 1.

139. Greg LeRoy says that Milton Webster attributed the lack of support from the Chicago Urban League to Barnett. LeRoy, "The Founding Heart of A. Philip Randolph's Union," 29.

140. Pullman asked the Chicago branch if Jones spoke for them. After the Chicago League explained to Pullman that the National did not control policies of the local, Pullman made its contribution. See Spero and Harris, *Black Worker*, 141–42. In 1939, Abram Harris wrote Horace Cayton that in 1925, "about the time that Mr. [T. Arnold] Hill [of Chicago Urban League] resigned to go to New York, the endorsement by Mr. Kinckle Jones of the Pullman Porters' movement caused an unfavorable reaction among contributors to the local Chicago league. As a matter of fact, I was present during a conversation in which a certain member of the Board questioned the wisdom of Mr. Jones' position. Mr. Foster [A. L. Foster, executive secretary of Chicago Urban League] was not a party to this conversation." In "Correspondence re: ""Black Workers and the New Unions,'" 1939–40, letter from Harris to Cayton, November 20, 1939, ser. 4, box 2, National Urban League Papers.

141. Drake, "Churches and Voluntary Associations in the Chicago Negro Community," 125, VGHC.

142. Webster to Randolph, November 29, 1927; Webster to Randolph, January 4, 1928, BSCP Chicago.

143. Josephine Copeland, "The History of Lincoln Memorial Congregational Church," 2, June 18, 1941, box 47, VGHC.

144. Report: "Meetings Held with Ministers in the an Attempt to Secure Their Cooperation in the Interest of Community Welfare"; "Labor and Civil Rights," JFP. My thanks to James Grossman for this citation.

145. David W. Johnson to John Fitzpatrick, January 28, 1928, BSCP Chicago; C. E. Thompson to John Fitzpatrick, January 24, 1928, and Bulletin of Lincoln Industrial Health Bureau and Employment Service, box 25, JFP.

Chapter Four

1. Milton P. Webster to A. Philip Randolph, November 11, 1927; Randolph to Webster, December 1, 1927; Webster to John Fitzpatrick, December 1, 1927; BSCP Chicago.

2. Sullivan, *Days of Hope*, 14; see also 13–15. For other scholars who have commented on the power of memory and tradition in African American history, see Harding, *There Is a River*; Higginbotham, *Righteous Discontent*; Brown, "Negotiating and Transforming the Public Sphere," 107–46.

3. Branham, "The Transformation of Black Political Leadership," 457.

4. For a discussion of independence from white control, see Eric Foner, *Reconstruction*, 60–123, especially 78. For oral histories of former slaves in the 1930s by the Works

Progress Administration, which show us how vivid were recollections of Reconstruction, see Rawick, *The American Slave*, 9, pt. 3:30, 80–81, pt. 4:41–42; suppl., ser. 1, 6:134,
7:568; suppl., ser. 2, 1650, 4015. Also Escott, *Slavery Remembered*, 153; Eric Foner, *Reconstruction*, 610–11, and "The Meaning of Freedom," 457–58; Naison, "Black Agrarian
Radicalism," 52–55.

5. Quoted in Philip Foner, *Life and Writings of Frederick Douglass*, 4:430. For more on
Frances E. W. Harper, see Boyd, *Discarded Legacy*; for Ida B. Wells, see Giddings, *When
and Where I Enter*; McMurry, *To Keep the Waters Troubled*; for influence of black women
on post-Reconstruction politics, see Brown, "Negotiating and Transforming the Public
Sphere."

6. Philip Foner, *Life and Writings of Frederick Douglass*, 4:413.

7. For Douglass's interpretation and promotion of the liberating spirit of humanism,
see Waldo Martin, *The Mind of Frederick Douglass*, 118, 119, 122.

8. For Douglass's thoughts on power, see ibid., 124–25.

9. "Posters, handbills, propaganda of the BSCP," pt. III, reel 9, PCP-UPA.

10. *Messenger* 8:4 (April 1926): 114.

11. *Messenger* 9:6 (June 1927): 207.

12. Eric Foner, "The Meaning of Freedom," 459–60.

13. Eric Foner, *Reconstruction*, 124–75, especially 164–75.

14. *Messenger* 7:8 (August 1925): 312.

15. Frank W. Crosswaith, "Toward the Home Stretch," *Messenger* 8:7 (July 1926): 196.

16. *Messenger* 7 (September 1925): 336, 314; (November–December 1925): 384.

17. This idea has a long history. See, for example, references in Robertson, *American
Myth, American Reality*, 97–99; Harding, *There Is a River*, 260–61; Eric Foner, *Reconstruction*, 77–88, and "The Meaning of Freedom," 457–59.

18. That the Emancipation Proclamation did not free slaves in union states and
exerted little immediate influence over those in confederate territory does not negate the
conviction harbored by many African Americans that they were free and equal American
citizens in 1863.

19. Joel A. Rogers, "What Are We?," *Messenger* 8:8 (August 1926): 237–38.

20. *Messenger* 9:8 (August 1927): 256.

21. Quoted in Philip Foner, *Organized Labor and the Black Worker*, 25. On the unions
and organization among black workers following the Civil War, see Spero and Harris,
The Black Worker, 16–35; Philip Foner, *Organized Labor and the Black Worker*, chaps. 2
and 3; Harris, *The Harder We Run*, 7–28; Bettye Thomas, "Black Operated Shipyard";
Rachleff, *Black Labor in Richmond*, 55–69.

22. Quote from Spero and Harris, *Black Worker*, 26.

23. Editorial, "The Need of a Labor Background," *Messenger* 9:8 (August 1927): 256.

24. Randolph, "The Negro Race Faces the Future," speech, Sesqui-Centennial Exposition at Philadelphia, May 31, 1926, reprinted in *Messenger* 8:7 (July 1926): 201–3 (quotation from 202).

25. Ibid., 202, 203.

26. Editorial, "The Need of a Labor Background," 256.

27. By the early 1920s, the William Dunning School and the John W. Burgess School
had reduced the period of Reconstruction to a power struggle between Radical Republicans and Andrew Johnson with no room left for the freedmen and women. Dissenting
voices questioning this narrative included survivors of Reconstruction and a small
group of black historians. For more on the historiography of Reconstruction, see Du

Bois, *Black Reconstruction*; Taylor, "Historians of the Reconstruction"; Beale, "On Rewriting Reconstruction"; Franklin, "Whither Reconstruction Historiography"; Weisberger, "The Dark and Bloody Ground of Reconstruction"; Eric Foner, "Reconstruction Revisited," and *Reconstruction*, xix–xxvii.

28. Quoted in Eric Foner, *Reconstruction*, xxi.

29. Frank R. Crosswaith, "A Year of History Making," *Messenger* 8:9 (September 1926): 281.

30. A. Philip Randolph, "To the Brotherhood Men," *Messenger* 8:11 (November 1926): 325.

31. Frank R. Crosswaith, "An Ex-Slave," *Messenger* 8:9 (November 1926): 330.

32. Robert Todd Lincoln was the second president of the Pullman Company from 1897 to 1911, Husband, *The Story of the Pullman Car*, 157.

33. Crosswaith, "An Ex-Slave," 330.

34. See most any issue of *Chicago Defender* or *Broad Ax* published close to Lincoln's birthday, February 12, or Douglass's, February 14, for example, *Defender*, February 11, 1933, 17.

35. See *Broad Ax*, January 9, 1926, 1.

36. Branham, "Transformation of Black Leadership," 456–57.

37. Editorial, "The Need of a Labor Background," 256.

38. "Chicago's First Negro Labor Conference," sponsored by "A Committee of Chicago Citizens and BSCP," January 23, 1928, BSCP Chicago; *Chicago Defender*, January 7, 1928, pt. 1, p. 2.

39. *Chicago Defender*, January 7, 1928, pt. 1, p. 2.

40. For a discussion of the Fourteenth Amendment and its original intent, see Eric Foner, *Reconstruction*, 256–57, who agues that the Amendment's central principle remained constant, "despite the many drafts, changes, and deletions." It was intended to be "a national guarantee of equality before the law." See also Abraham, *Freedom and the Court*, 31; Kaczorowski, "To Begin the Nation Anew."

41. Black newspapers document the enduring nature of the legacy of the Fourteenth Amendment. See, for example, *Chicago Defender*, 1920–28; Berry and Blassingame, *Long Memory*, 301–2, who point out that Paul Laurence Dunbar wrote in his "The Colored Soldiers" in 1896, that black Americans felt military service should guarantee their rights; Wesley, "The Historical Basis of Negro Citizenship."

42. Du Bois, *Black Reconstruction*, 167, 329–30.

43. Du Bois on vagrancy laws, ibid., 167; also 128–81. See also Jaynes, *Branches without Roots*, 16–18, 303; Eric Foner, "Rights and the Constitution in Black Life," 880; Kaczorowski, "To Begin the Nation Anew," 47.

44. Eric Foner, *Reconstruction*, 233, 235.

45. Quoted in Kaczorowski, "To Begin the Nation Anew," 55.

46. For background on the understanding freedmen and women had of free labor, see Berlin et al., "The Wartime Genesis of Free Labor."

47. *Messenger* 8:3 (March 1926): 68.

48. David Lewis, *W. E. B. Du Bois*, 258, 396, 421.

49. Wesley, "The Historical Basis of Negro Citizenship," 356.

50. Harold Eustace Simmelkjaer, "Civil Rights," *Messenger* 8:3 (March 1926): 74.

51. *Messenger* 6:11 (November 1924): 340.

52. For the history of fusing the Declaration of Independence with definitions of

manhood rights and suffrage, see Eric Foner, *Reconstruction*, 114–15, and "Rights and the Constitution in Black Life"; Harding, *There Is a River*, 242–57.

53. Du Bois, *Souls of Black Folk*, 45; David Lewis, *W. E. B. Du Bois*, 281.

54. *Messenger* 9 (March 1927): 83.

55. Webster, "Labor Must Organize," 189.

56. "The Labor Viewpoint," *Messenger* 9:3 (March 1927): 83.

57. Editorial, "The Need of Labor a Background," 256.

58. A. Philip Randolph, "State and Policy of Brotherhood," *Messenger* 8:4 (April 1926): 186.

59. David Lewis, *W. E. B. Du Bois*, 393, 546.

60. Brotherhood quote, *Messenger* 9 (January 1927): 17.

61. J. A. Rogers, "Who Is the New Negro, and Why?," *Messenger* 9 (March 1927): 68.

62. A. Philip Randolph, "Dialogue of the Old and New," *Messenger* 9 (March 1927): 94.

63. Spero and Harris, *The Black Worker*, 453.

64. Edwin P. Morrow's report to Mediation Board, June 5, 1928, discussed by Harris in *Keeping the Faith*, 109, n. 79, maintained that the company had enough employees in the wings, on reserve, to replace all striking porters. Brazeal, *The Brotherhood of Sleeping Car Porters*, 78; Spero and Harris, *The Black Worker*, 453.

65. *Chicago Defender*, June 16, 1928, 1; Harris, *Keeping the Faith*, 111–14; Brazeal, *The Brotherhood of Sleeping Car Porters*, 77–85; Spero and Harris, *The Black Worker*, 453–60; Kornweibel, *No Crystal Stair*, 270.

66. For a fuller discussion of the proposed strike vote in the context of the literature, see Bates, "Unfinished Task of Emancipation," 196–208.

67. Harris, *Keeping the Faith*, 110–14; Philip Foner, *Organized Labor and the Black Worker*, 185; Marable, "A. Philip Randolph," 222.

68. Harris, *Keeping the Faith*, 106.

69. Randolph to Webster, March 30, 1928, BSCP Chicago.

70. *Chicago Defender*, September 1, 1928, pt. 2, p. 2.

71. Webster to Randolph, June 8, 1928; Webster to Randolph, June 14, 1928; BSCP Chicago. Harris argued that "APR [A. Philip Randolph] probably convinced MPW [Milton P. Webster] to go along with the decision of June 8 by promising that the strike would come at a later date." Harris, *Keeping the Faith*, 115, fn. 108. While Webster believed the strike had just been postponed, not canceled, Webster's actions and responses must be put into the context of his emphasis on "publicity," the value of a strike vote before the event, and his insistence that, indeed, on June 8, 1928, conditions were not favorable for a strike. What constituted correct conditions must be gleaned from the sum of the written record between Randolph and Webster. This is a union in the process of redefining what a labor union could mean for the black community.

72. Randolph to Webster, June 16, 1928, BSCP Chicago.

73. First signs of dwindling memberships in the Chicago Division of the BSCP showed up in late September 1928. See Webster to Randolph, September 26, 1928, BSCP Chicago.

74. This quotation, often repeated through the years, is from Randolph; see Randolph to Webster, August 27, 1928, BSCP Chicago. Webster had his own longer version. To compare, see Jervis Anderson, *A. Philip Randolph*, 151.

75. Webster to Randolph, June 11, 1928, Webster to Randolph, June 14, 1928, BSCP Chicago.

76. Randolph to Webster, August 27, 1928, BSCP Chicago.

77. LeRoy, "The Founding Heart of A. Philip Randolph's Union," 24.

78. Harold Gosnell pointed out that Bernard W. Snow was bailiff from 1924 to 1930 as part of the Harding-Crowe-Thompson Republican machine. When a Democratic was elected bailiff in 1930, Webster, along with twenty-seven other deputy bailiffs appointed by Snow, lost his job. Webster was originally appointed deputy bailiff because of his political activities in the sixth ward where he was a section chief. Gosnell, *Negro Politicians*, 204.

79. Memo: F. L. Simmons to G. A. Kelly, General Solicitor for Pullman Company, February 19, 1933; memo: Simmons to Kelly, February 15, 1933; report on service record of former porter Milton Price Webster; service record included an entry for February 2, 1921: "Discovered he was holding meetings during layover talking against Pullman Porters' Association"; 06/01/04, 17, PCP.

80. Webster to Randolph, April 7, 1928, p. 3, Webster to Dad Moore, April 14, 1928, BSCP Chicago.

81. Robinson, "The Negro in Politics in Chicago," 184.

82. Webster to Randolph, May 1, 1928; Randolph to Webster, May 4, 1928, BSCP Chicago.

83. Benjamin McLaurin, interview by Greg Le Roy, January 22, 1981, CHS. McLaurin was a BSCP organizer in Chicago from 1925 to 1930, who then was transferred to New York City.

84. Webster to Randolph, August 8, 1928; Webster to Randolph, June 14, 1928, BSCP Chicago.

85. *Chicago Defender*, January 25, 1930, 1.

86. Drake and Cayton, *Black Metropolis*, 365–74; Branham, "Transformation of Black Political Leadership," 241–45.

87. Robb, *Negro in Chicago*, 73. In addition, the BSCP's Citizens' Committee expanded to include prominent figures such as Lula E. Lawson, executive secretary of the South Parkway YWCA from 1922 to 1929, and part of the BSCP Citizens' Committee into the 1930s. Lawson brought to the BSCP Citizens' Committee a wide network of colleagues with influence in both working-class and middle-class circles: *Chicago Defender*, March 2, 1929, 7; pt. 2, p. 6.

88. For Adams and Bond, see Robb, *The Negro in Chicago*, 69, 72; for NNBL, see Webster to Randolph, Aug. 20, 1928, BSCP Chicago.

89. Herbert Morrisohn Smith, "Three Negro Preachers in Chicago," master's thesis, University of Chicago, 2–5, box 17, VGHC.

90. Robb, *The Negro in Chicago*, 71. The official title for BSCP Labor Conference became National Negro Labor Conference in 1930.

91. *Chicago Defender*, January 25, 1930, 9; Robb, *The Negro in Chicago*, 71.

92. *Chicago Defender*, January 25, 1930, 1.

93. See *Black Worker*, November 15, 1929, 4; January 15, 1930, 4.

94. Jeanette Smith, "Address Delivered Before National Labor Conference," by Jeanette Smith, *Chicago Defender*, February 1, 1930, 18; Robb, *The Negro in Chicago*, 198; Webster to John Fitzpatrick, April 25, 1930, BSCP Chicago; Bulletin, The National Negro Labor Conference, Second Annual Session, January 19 to 23, 1931, 06/01/04:17, box 497, PCP.

95. *Chicago Defender*, January 25, 1930, 1.

96. Cayton and Drake, *Black Metropolis*, 465; Spear, *Black Chicago*, 227; Childs, "Samuel Insul," I–III; "A Negro Bank Closes Its Doors," *Opportunity* 8 (September 1930): 264;

Du Bois, "Binga," *Crisis* 37 (December 1930): 425–26; *Chicago Defender*, March 7, 1931, 1, 6; June 10, 1933, 16; June 24, 1933, 1; Dawson, "Insull on Trial," 611–13.

97. *Chicago Defender*, February 1, 1930, 8; *Black Worker*, November 15, 1929, 4.

98. *Chicago Defender*, March 19, 1932, 5.

99. See *Chicago Defender*, August 19, 1933, 5; August 26, 1935, 13; September 7, 1935, 5.

100. William Harris points out that BSCP membership plummeted from its peak of 4,632 before the aborted strike in 1928 to 771 in 1932, and eventually to 658 in 1933; see *Keeping the Faith*, 152–82, especially 162; Spero and Harris, *Black Worker*, 460. For membership figures between 1925 and 1943, see Brazeal, *The Brotherhood of Sleeping Car Porters*, 221–22.

Chapter Five

1. Trotter, *River Jordan*, 123; Kirby, *Black Americans in the Roosevelt Era*; Leuchtenburg, *Franklin D. Roosevelt*; Harris, *Harder We Run*, 95–122; Sitkoff, *A New Deal for Blacks*, 34–57.

2. Trotter and Earl Lewis, *African Americans in the Industrial Age*, 169–75.

3. For membership figures, see Brazeal, *The Brotherhood of Sleeping Car Porters*, 221–22.

4. Ibid., 221–22; Spero and Harris, *The Black Worker*, 456–60; William Harris, *Keeping the Faith*, 161–62; Jervis Anderson, *A. Philip Randolph*, 205–15.

5. Quoted in Jervis Anderson, *A. Philip Randolph*, 216.

6. For background on the Judge John J. Parker confirmation protest, see Spero and Harris, *The Black Worker*, 463–64; Bernstein, *The Lean Years*, 406–9; Watson, "Defeat of Judge Parker"; Harris, *Keeping the Faith*, 166–68. Organized labor opposed Parker for ruling, in the Red Jacket case of 1927, that the United Mine Workers Union was illegal. See Watson, "The Defeat of Judge Parker."

7. Spero and Harris, *Black Worker*, 464.

8. Walter White, *A Man Called White*, 106. See also, Harris, *Keeping the Faith*, 167.

9. For linking of the two issues, see Harris, in *Keeping the Faith*, who pointed out that Randolph connected the rights of "black people and labor as oppressed groups" (168). For the Brotherhood's interpretation of the anti-Parker campaign, see "A.F.of L. and NAACP," *Black Worker* 2:8 (May 1, 1930): 1.

10. Memo: to the Directors of the American Fund for Public Service, May 28, 1930, 2, file: "American Fund for Public Service," I-C-196, NAACP Papers. William Harris also discusses this memo and the "superficial" nature of support from the NAACP for the BSCP in *Keeping the Faith*, 164–66.

11. "Opposing Judge Parker," *Black Worker* 2:8 (May 1930): 4; *Chicago Defender*, April 5, 1930, 13.

12. For Republican women protesting Judge Parker, see *Chicago Defender*, April 26, 1930, 19. See also Webster to John Fitzpatrick, April 25, 1930, JFP.

13. For Wells-Barnett's comments, see *Chicago Defender*, May 10, 1930, 4.

14. For an excellent discussion of the problem of chauvinism within the Communist Party in the twenties and very early thirties, see Solomon, *The Cry Was Unity*, 129–46, for Cyril Briggs's analysis, see 131–32.

15. Pullman Company informants noted, in a report they made of a Communist Party meeting on November 26, 1929, that a speaker raised doubts about Abraham Lincoln as a

friend of black Americans. "Confidential report on Communist Meeting, Nov. 26, 1929," 06/01/04, box 17, folder 491, PCP.

16. Solomon, *The Cry Was Unity*, 135–36; *Pittsburgh Courier*, August 27, 1932.

17. Gosnell, *Negro Politicians*, 329–31, including excerpt from *Chicago Whip*, July 25, 1931; Drake and Cayton, *Black Metropolis*, 85–87. For more on the history of the Unemployed Council, see Rosenzweig, "Organizing the Unemployed"; Leab, " 'United We Eat' "; Christopher Reed, "A Study of Black Politics and Protest," 50–54, 173–74.

18. For a reference to "We Shall Not Be Moved" as a "transliterated spiritual," see Drake, "Churches and Voluntary Associations in the Chicago Negro Community," 261–62, VGHC. For the overlap of spiritual and labor protest songs, see Reagon, "Songs of the Civil Rights Movement." Reagon argues that lyrics of traditional black religious songs evolved and were adopted for other forms; "We Shall Not Be Moved" was one of these songs, which began within the black community as a traditional spiritual, then was put to use in other struggles (64). My thanks to Pete Seeger for telling me about this dissertation and educating me on the history and connections of songs of struggle; telephone interview by author, January 1989. Drake and Cayton, *Black Metropolis*, 85–86; Lasswell and Blumenstock, *World Revolutionary Propaganda*, 20–36.

19. *Defender*, August 8, 1931; Christopher Reed, "A Study of Black Politics," 182; Haywood, *Black Bolshevik*, 443; Lasswell and Blumenstock, *World Revolutionary*, 73, 203. There is much dispute about the numbers of those who actually marched. The *Chicago Tribune*, August 9, 1931, said "several thousand"; Haywood claimed 30,000; the *Chicago Defender*, August 15, 1931, estimated between 5,000 and 8,000.

20. Solomon, *The Cry Was Unity*, 158; *Chicago Tribune*, August 6 and 7, 1931; *Pittsburgh Courier*, August 8, 1931; Pliven and Cloward, *Poor People's Movements*, 62–63.

21. Christopher Reed, "A Study of Black Politics," 182.

22. Ibid., 174.

23. My thanks to Paul Young for sharing his research findings on the Chicago Unemployed Council with me. See Young, "Race, Class, and Radical Protest," 11–12.

24. Quoted in ibid., 6; Ishmael P. Flory, interview by author, July 14, 1995. Cayton and Drake, *Black Metropolis*, 603.

25. Spear, *Black Chicago*, 198–99. See Christopher Reed, "Study of Black Politics and Protest," 151.

26. Will Herberg, "Shall the Negro Worker Turn to Labor or to Capital?" *Crisis* 38 (July 1931): 227, and (November 1931): 393; T. Arnold Hill, "Picketing for Jobs," *Opportunity* 8 (July 1930): 216; Memo: Walter White to Branches, October 30, 1931, I-C-321, NAACP Papers; Bontemps and Conroy, *Anyplace But Here*, 185–86; Christopher Reed, "Study of Black Politics," 146–56; Drake and Cayton, *Black Metropolis*, 84–85, 743; Meier and Rudwick, "The Origins of Nonviolent Direct Action," 17, 331.

27. Christopher Reed, "A Study of Black Politics and Protest," 152–56.

28. Herberg, "Shall the Negro Worker Turn to Labor," 227.

29. Christopher Reed, "A Study of Black Politics and Protest," 167–77.

30. The biography of Thelma McWorter Kirkpatrick Wheaton is drawn from interviews of Thelma Wheaton by the author in Chicago, between September 1, 1994, and January 5, 1995. I also relied on information provided by historian Juliet E. K. Walker in "The Afro-American Woman: Who Was She?"

31. My thanks to historian Rima L. Schultz for clearing up the many misspellings of "Dieckmann" that appear in texts found in various Chicago archives. *Chicago Defender*,

June 24, 1933, 4; July 1, 1933, 1, 3, 4; July 15, 1933, 4; Gosnell, *Negro Politicians*, 334; Wheaton interview, September 1 and 14, 1994.

32. Wheaton interview, September 14, 1994.

33. Wheaton interviews, September 1 and 14, 1994.

34. "Women Civil Leaders Hold Labor Confab," *Chicago Defender*, March 12, 1932, 2.

35. Wheaton interview, January 5, 1995. See also, "Women's Council to Present Program," *Chicago Defender*, March 25, 1933. Thelma Wheaton remembered working with Gaines but did not recall, when interviewed in 1995, working in the community with Helena Wilson. That the Women's Economic Council was, under the leadership of Wilson, concerned and committed to understanding problems related to female industrial and domestic workers seems apparent by the presence of Wheaton as speaker on labor issues. This interest was encouraged by Wilson, BSCP organizers, the BSCP's Citizens' Committee, and community activists like Wheaton. Wilson played a prominent role in community-wide efforts at labor organizing in the second half of the 1930s (see chapter 6). See also Chateauvert, *Marching Together*, 61–66.

36. Three women attended summer school for industrial workers at Bryn Mawr in 1926 and 1927, and one attended summer school at the University of Wisconsin each year. See Robb, *The Negro in Chicago* (1927), 151, VGHC.

37. "Scholarship for Women in Industry Given by YWCA," *Chicago Defender*, March 18, 1933, 20; April 15, 1933, 21.

38. "YWCA Activities," *Chicago Defender*, July 14, 1934, 15; "Scholarship for Women," 20; Wheaton, interview, September 14, 1994.

39. Kessler-Harris, *Out to Work*, 243–44. See also the testimonials, descriptions, and evaluations of students sent to Hudson Shore Labor School, University of Wisconsin School for Workers, and Summer Institute for Social Progress by Ladies Auxiliary, BSCP, 1949, pt. II, reel 10, BSCP Chicago PCP-UPA.

40. Katheryn Williams, interview by Robert Davis, August 6, 1937, box 34, folder 3, VGHC.

41. Handbill, written by Neva Ryan, announcing Domestic Workers' Association meeting for August 18, 1934, to John Fitzpatrick, box 25, JFP; *Chicago Defender*, December 8, 1934, 19.

42. Information on Thyra Edwards, from Thelma Wheaton, interview, January 5, 1995. Information verified through interviews by author with Ishmael P. Flory, a coworker with Edwards in the Chicago branch of the National Negro Congress, by author, August 31, 1994, and January 7, 1995. See also "Professional History," box 1, TEP.

43. "Lecturing: Thyra Edwards," *Chicago Defender*, April 1, 1933, 20; "Friends Gather at Poro College," *Chicago Defender*, April 22, 1933, 21. Rima L. Schultz helped me understand the larger context within which Thyra Edwards circulated.

44. "Lecturing: Miss Thyra Edwards," 20; "Friends Gather at Poro College," 21. Thelma Wheaton recalled the importance of Poro College to the history of the South Side: Poro College, owned by Annie M. Malone, head of a $2 million beauty college business, which manufactured and distributed a hair preparation, known originally as the "Wonderful Hair Grower." Poro College's business headquarters, a large mansion and several other buildings where Malone taught courses on beauty techniques, doubled as a multipurpose community facility. "Inside the house," there were "huge rooms—living room, dining room, and so forth," Wheaton remembered. Upstairs walls had been knocked out to create large conference rooms. "On the third floor," there was a ballroom. Meetings for schools and classes for the community were held in the same

building. "Malone, as long as she lived, supported the community by letting groups meet there. In the summer time many of the meetings were held outdoors on the lawn." Throughout the 1930s, newspapers and bulletins noted meetings by mainstream groups as well as Communists at Poro College. Wheaton, interview, January 5, 1995; *Heebie Jeebies*, February 19, 1927, 2, 12–17, box 131, folder 4, CABP.

45. "Eulogy of Thyra Edwards Gitlin," Saint Philips Church, July 12, 1953, by Bernard Ades, box 137, folder 5, CABP; Resume of Thyra Edwards, box 1; Thyra Edwards to Perrin H. Lowrey, December 19, 1942, box 1, folder 4, TEP.

46. Chatwood Hall, "Thyra Edwards makes 'Inspection' Tour of Soviet Russia: Noted Labor Student Seeks First-Hand Information on New Order," *Chicago Defender*, June 16, 1934, 2; "Pullman Porters to Hold Anniversary Celebration," *Chicago Defender*, August 25, 1934, 2; Edwards, "Essay on Being a Negro" (1934?), box 1, TEP.

47. "On Being a Negro" (1934?), box 1, folder 1, TEP.

48. Thyra Edwards to Ishmael Flory, April 11, 1934, box 1, folder 1, TEP.

49. For the popularity of Thyra Edwards as a speaker and lecturer, see Ishmael P. Flory, interview by author, April 11, 1995.

50. "Near South Side Gets Interracial Committee," *Chicago Defender*, June 3, 1933, 4.

51. Gunnar Myrdal called the NAACP branches the "lifeline of the Association," adding that "The national Office is constantly struggling to maintain them in vigor and to found new branches, especially in recent years." Myrdal, *An American Dilemma*, 2:822; Ralph J. Bunche, "Programs, Ideologies, Tactics," 52, CMS.

52. Roy Wilkins to Daisy E. Lampkin, March 23, 1935, I-C-80, NAACP Papers.

53. *Chicago Defender*, May 9, 1931, 14; May 30, 1931, 6.

54. For Scottsboro case, see Carter, *Scottsboro*; Hugh Murray Jr., "The NAACP versus the Communist Party"; Kelley, "Memory and Politics," 353; Meier and Bracey, "NAACP as a Reform Movement," 18; Martin, "The International Labor Defense and Black America," 171–72. For the relationship of the Scottsboro case to community protest activity in Alabama, see Kelley, *Hammer and Hoe*, 78–87. The NAACP, upset when the ILD stepped up activities exposing racial injustice in the South, and especially Alabama, used the Communist interference—the "wild talk and threats against the governor of Alabama"— to appeal for contributions to the NAACP's Scottsboro fund. A printed mailing to potential contributors stressed that the NAACP "believes that the only way to go about this case is in an orderly manner with a firm appeal to the regular courts of law" (Financial Papers, November 1931, I-C-145, NAACP Papers). Later, in 1932, after the ILD controlled the case, the NAACP had to refund several donations that had been made to the NAACP to help with the Scottsboro case; Walter White to Arthur Spingarn, April 4, 1932, I-C-78, NAACP Papers.

55. Daisy Lampkin to Walter White, March 13, 1933, I-C-67, NAACP Papers.

56. "The Scottsboro Victims," *Chicago Defender*, May 9, 1931, 14.

57. "Chicago Pledges Support to Scottsboro Victims," *Chicago Defender*, May 30, 1931, 6; June 27, 1931, 12.

58. "Arrest Reds after Making Threats to DePriest, Pickens," *Defender*, June 20, 1931, 1, 2.

59. This particular contribution was earmarked to pay Roy Wilkins's salary. Joel Spingarn to Walter White, June 7, 1933; White to J. E. Spingarn, June 8, 1933; Spingarn to White, June 9, 1933, I-A-27; "Dean" Pickens to White, June 6, 1933, I-G-51; White to William Rosenwald, June 8, 1933, I-C-78, NAACP Papers. See also discussion of these

issues and White's mention of Rosenwald monies to help pay Wilkins's salary by Ross, *J. E. Spingarn*, 135–37.

60. David Lewis, *When Harlem Was in Vogue*, 100–102.

61. A. C. MacNeal to "the Manager, Sears-Roebuck," June 12, 1933, Press Release, June 13, 1933, Memo: Case reported June 8, 1933, Mrs. Susie Myers, Mrs. Hazel Murray, Mrs. Ouida Smith, Sears, Roebuck & Co. to A. C. MacNeal (no signature of any individual; no accountability), June 16, 1933, I-G-51; William Rosenwald to White, June 28, 1933, I-C-74, NAACP Papers. The Rosenwald correspondence to White also intimated, strongly, that the NAACP might "improve its effectiveness by concentrating on important issues, only." What counted as "important" was left unclear.

62. A. C. MacNeal to Walter White, July 3, 1933; White to MacNeal, July 7, 1933; telegram, White to MacNeal, July 12, 1933; MacNeal to White, July 17, 1933; White to MacNeal, July 19; Roy Wilkins to MacNeal, August 3, 1933, I-G-51, NAACP Papers.

63. *Chicago Defender*, June 24, 1933, 12; July 8, 1933, 4.

64. For comments on the "$2500" connection to policy directives, see MacNeal to White, July 3, 1933, I-G-51. For MacNeal's warning that White not fall into a "trap" by agreeing to a truce with Rosenwald, see MacNeal to White, July 17, 1933, I-G-51. Rosenwald reminded White of the personal interest he took in all facets of NAACP work on other occasions. He often censored NAACP press releases, for example, and he told White explicitly that he thought "patient cooperation" was a much better approach than "widespread publicity." For interference from Rosenwald, see William Rosenwald to White, September 1, 1933; Rosenwald to White, November 1, 1933, I-C-74, all in NAACP Papers.

65. "Women Protest Sears-Roebuck," *Chicago Defender*, August 5, 1933, 24.

66. MacNeal to White, July 29, 1933, I-G-51, NAACP Papers. See also MacNeal to Roy Wilkins, September 13, 1933, I-G-51; White to William Pickens, October 25, 1933, Memo: White to Charles Houston, July 13, 1938, I-C-79, all in NAACP Papers.

67. MacNeal to White, July 29, 1933; MacNeal to White, July 29, 1933 (second letter with same date), I-G-51, NAACP Papers.

68. Daisy Lampkin to White, October 22, 1936, I-C-68, NAACP Papers. On the relationship between the NAACP and the NACW, see Salem, *To Better Our World*, 145–78.

69. *Chicago Defender*, June 24, 1933, 4, 12; July 1, 1933, 1, 3, 4; July 15, 1933, 4.

70. "The Sopkin Case," *Chicago Defender*, July 1, 1933, 14.

71. Gosnell, *Negro Politicians*, 334; Wheaton, interview, September 1, 14, 1994.

72. *Chicago Defender*, July 1, 1933, 3.

73. *Chicago Defender*, July 1, 1933; Wheaton, interview, September 1, 14, 1994; Gosnell, *Negro Politicians*, 334–36, with "Mistakes in the Sopkins Strike," *Workers' Voice*, quoted on 336; Solomon, *The Cry was Unity*, 251.

74. Drake, "Churches and Voluntary Associations in the Chicago Negro Community," 263, VGHC.

75. "N.Y. Congressman Addresses Pullman Porters Here," *Chicago Defender*, August 26, 1933, 13.

76. *Chicago Defender*, September 30, 1933, 1.

77. Solomon, *The Cry Was Unity*, 268; "Workers Plan Mass Meeting," *Chicago Defender*, February 17, 1934, 2.

78. Editorial, "Injustice, Not Reds, Stirring Up Workers," *Chicago Defender*, June 16, 1934, 14.

79. *Nation* 139 (August 1, 1934): 127–28; Sitkoff, *A New Deal for Blacks*, 150–51.

80. *Chicago Defender*, July 6, 1935, 4.

81. "Leader in War for Civic Betterment," *Chicago Defender*, July 22, 1933, 4.

82. *Chicago Defender*, June 16, 1934, 2.

83. *Chicago Defender*, September 22, 1934, 1, 2.

84. Solomon, *The Cry Was Unity*; Woodard, *A Nation within a Nation*, 27.

85. Wheaton interview, January 5, 1995.

86. Eleanor Rye, "Toward a National Negro Congress," *Chicago Defender*, June 15, 1935, 18; *Chicago Defender*, November 30, 1935, 2.

Chapter Six

1. Jervis Anderson, *A. Philip Randolph*, 220–21.

2. For fuller analysis of the Railway Labor Act, see Harris, *Keeping the Faith*, 185–208, who also notes the BSCP was the "first union to invoke a nationwide jurisdictional election" (204). For membership figures, see Brazeal, *Brotherhood of Sleeping Car Porters*, 222.

3. Harris, *Keeping the Faith*, 209–16.

4. Brazeal, *Brotherhood of Sleeping Car Porters*, 217; Harris, *Keeping the Faith*, 209–16; Jervis Anderson, *A. Philip Randolph*, 224–25.

5. "We Doff Our Hats to Pullman Porters," *Chicago Defender*, editorial, September 18, 1937.

6. Whatley, "African-American Strikebreaking from Civil War to New Deal."

7. For surveillance of BSCP, see internal memos for Champ Carry, box 633-A, especially, G. M. Zimmer, District Superintendent to Carry, March 29, 1931; Special memo, April 30, 1937; letter from company spy Mrs. M. Butler to E. M. Graham, May 9, 1937, for Pullman Protective Association; special memo, October 12, 1937, reporting reception Randolph received when he addressed several thousand steelworkers in the Calumet steel district, PCP.

8. Quotation in memo: Roy Wilkins to Walter White, March 11, 1939, p. 2, I-C-80, NAACP Papers. Drake and Cayton, *Black Metropolis*, 83–89; Meier and Rudwick, *Black Detroit*, 57–58; Bunche, "Programs, Ideologies, Tactics," 51, CMS; Ross, *J. E. Spingarn*, 222–41. The ambiguity of the NAACP's stand toward labor emerged at the June 3, 1935, hearings of the American Federation of Labor's Committee of Five on Negro Discrimination. Publicly White and the NAACP were strong supporters of this hearing. Charles Houston, dean of Howard University Law School and staff member on legal affairs for the NAACP, gave freely of his time and talent during the hearings. White, however, did not seem to give the hearing top priority and his resolve to orchestrate evidence revealed a lack of strong commitment. Roy Wilkins wrote to Charles Houston in frustration that he had received at the very last minute a memo from White requesting data on cases on discrimination by black workers needed for the hearing; see Randolph to Walter White, July 3, 1935, I-C-414; Roy Wilkins to Charles Houston, July 8, 1935, I-C-80, NAACP Papers. Moreover, although in 1935 Walter White congratulated John L. Lewis when the Committee for Industrial Organization was initially formed and the 1936 NAACP National Convention called the CIO the "greatest hope to black and white workers," in 1937 the convention rejected praising the CIO. Roy Wilkins to Charles Houston, July 8, 1935, I-C-80; Randolph to White, July 3, 1935, I-C-414; Walter White to John L. Lewis, November 27, 1935, I-C-413; "Tentative Draft of Suggested Resolution . . . Detroit Conference,

June 29, July 4, 1937," and "Resolutions Adopted by the Twenty-Eight Annual Conference . . ." I-B-14, NAACP Papers; *Crisis* 44 (August 1937): 246.

9. From the NAACP's tenth annual report, quoted in Meier and Bracey, "The NAACP
as a Reform Movement," 6.

10. Names and Addresses of Members of the NNC's National Executive Council, reel
11, NNC Papers, Schomburg Center for Research on Black Culture.

11. I do not mean to imply that "new strategies" or tactics dropped out of the sky.
Strategies tried out in the 1930s often had roots in the history of African American
communities. Many African Americans learned to look, for example, within their communities for solutions and leadership during Reconstruction. Peter Rachleff discusses
efforts of Richmond African Americans with "collective self-help," a strategy they used
to try to improve their economic conditions. Rachleff, *Black Labor*, 38, 34–54. Randolph
was aware of resistance and protest that ran through African American history; see
chapter 1.

12. Du Bois, "What Is Wrong with the NAACP?," speech given at the NAACP Annual
Conference, Washington, D.C., May 18, 1932, file: Annual Conferences, I-B-8, NAACP
Papers. See also excerpts from conference speeches, *Crisis* 39 (June 1932): 218. Ross
analyzed this speech in *J. E. Spingarn*, 159–60. Harold Cruse argued that a white liberal
bloc "aimed at reorienting the association's legal direction" was bypassing Du Bois
before he critiqued the overall program of the NAACP. By 1934, he claimed, the NAACP
was on the "verge of disintegration"; Cruse, *Plural but Equal*, 101.

13. As found in text of Amenia Conference file, "Findings," August 1933, I-C-229,
NAACP Papers; Ross, *J. E. Spingarn*, 180. The term "masses" is used to include all
members of the African American community who are below middle class, referring to
the 1930s understanding in northern cities. Concern over the sensitivity of the NAACP
to the masses appears to have been a relatively common issue during the thirties. For a
contemporary view, see Bunche, "Programs, Ideologies, Tactics," 142–55, CMS; for an
evaluation in a southern state, see Fairclough, *Race and Democracy*, 46–73.

14. Memo to All Those Invited to the Amenia Conference, May 27, 1933; Roy Wilkins
to George S. Schuyler, July 15, 1932; "Findings: Second Amenia Conference," August 18–
21, 1933, Amenia Conference File, I-C-229, NAACP Papers.

15. Minutes of the Board of Directors, July 9, 1934, pp. 3–4, I-A-3, NAACP Papers. See
also comments that Du Bois made regarding failure of black betterment organizations to
meet the challenges of everyday life for African Americans in letter from Du Bois to Dear
Friends, February 5, 1934, printed February 21, 1934 in *Amsterdam News*. Thomas Holt
believes "the resonance between philosophical differences and political animosities best
explain Du Bois's decision to resign," stating that the struggle was really for the soul of
the NAACP; see "The Political Uses of Alienation," 323, fn. 46.

16. Wolters, *Negroes and the Great Depression*, 219–29, 302–52; Ross, *J. E. Spingarn*,
218–41; Kirby, *Black Americans in the Roosevelt Era*, 176–77. On Du Bois cultivating allies
in local branches, see Holt, "The Political Uses of Alienation," 317; Du Bois to Abram
Harris, January 16, 1934, for "root and branch"; Abram Harris to Du Bois, January 6,
1934, Du Bois Papers, reel 42, frames 425, 427, Butler Memorial Library, Columbia
University. My specific reading of the Harris Report comes from the version called
"Future Plan and Program of the NAACP," I-A-29, NAACP Papers.

17. Abram Harris to White, July 28, 1934, file: "Future Plan and Program," July–August
1934, I-A-29, NAACP Papers. Ross pointed out that although the committee, appointed
by Spingarn, represented a split of three new-crowd members and three old-guard

thinkers, Spingarn specifically added both himself and Walter White as ex-officio members of the committee, presumably to counter the weight of the new crowd. Ross, *J. E. Spingarn*, 205, 219.

18. Wolters noted that when deciding on a meeting place, White "doubtless welcomed the restraining hand of President Spingarn," in *Negroes and the Great Depression*, 313. White tried to persuade Harris to reconsider his decision; White to Harris, July 30, 1934, "Personal and Confidential," I-A-29, NAACP Papers. For the "closed corporation" comment, see Ross, *J. E. Spingarn*, 235, also 221–22.

19. Preliminary draft of Report of the Committee on Future Plan and Program, I-A-29, NAACP Papers.

20. Minutes, Board of Directors' meetings, September 25, October 8, November 13, 24, 1934; March 11, April 8, June 10, 1935, I-A-3; comparison of drafts of Report of the Committee on Future Plan and Program, I-A-29, NAACP Papers.

21. Minutes, Board of Directors, September 25, October 8, 1934, and June 10, 1935, especially p. 2, I-A-3, NAACP Papers. Walter White had trouble with modified term, "workers' education." He wrote that "we have just got to find a better name," in Walter White to Benjamin Stolberg, August 30, 1934, I-A-29, NAACP Papers.

22. Meier and Bracey, "The NAACP as a Reform Movement," 17–18.

23. Minutes, Board of Directors, March 8, 1935, I-A-3, NAACP Papers.

24. Minutes, Board of Directors, November 11, 1935, I-C-150, NAACP Papers; Charles Houston was very upset when, during the trying financial crisis, Walter White hired Juanita Jackson as an addition to his staff. Houston told White, "if the Association really believes in the economic program that we have worked out, it will have to use more and more of its resources . . . [to] execute that program." Cited in Wolters, *Negroes and the Great Depression*, 327, 332.

25. Sullivan, *Days of Hope*, 49–50; for the relationship between Davis and White, see Solomon, *The Cry Was Unity*, 235–37.

26. Abram Harris to Walter White, July 18, 1934, I-A-29, NAACP Papers.

27. John Kirby pointed out that Walter White used much of the data compiled by Davis to carry out his critique of New Deal programs, suggesting White thought highly of his work. Kirby, *Black Americans in the Roosevelt Era*, 166 (quotation), 177. Wolters and Zangrando agree with Kirby that White's suspicions of John Davis stemmed from White's fear that Davis's economic projects would divert control away from White and the board. See Wolters, *Negroes and the Great Depression*, 315–34; Zangrando, *The NAACP Crusade against Lynching*, 110.

28. Charles Houston to White, May 23, 1935; see also Houston to John Davis, December 26, 1935, I-C-383, NAACP Papers. For Houston's deviation from Walter White's approach toward the NNC, see McNeil, *Groundwork*, 108. For Houston on focusing attention at local level, see Sullivan, *Days of Hope*, 84–91, 87 (quotation).

29. William Pickens to W. E. B. Du Bois, June 16, 1934, Board of Directors Correspondence, I-A-22, NAACP Papers; Ross, *J. E. Spingarn*, 126–30 (quotation from 129).

30. For relationship between White and Embree, see Kirby, *Black Americans in the Roosevelt Era*, 182.

31. Wolters, *Negroes and the Great Depression*, 337; Zangrando, *The NAACP Crusade against Lynching*, 110.

32. Weiss, *Farewell Party of Lincoln*, 97–99; Kirby, *Black Americans in Roosevelt Era*, 176–77.

33. Zangrando, *The NAACP Crusade against Lynching*, 98–165.

34. Information from Board of Directors, November 8, 1932; Minutes, Board of Directors, September 12, 1933, November 13, 1933, I-A-17; White to Philip G. Peabody, November 11, 1931; White to Fanny T. Cochran, November 11, 1931; White to E. Lewis Burnham, November 18, 1931; Roy Wilkins to Joseph Prince Loud, November 27, 1931, Financial Papers, I-C-145. For ten years between 1921 and 1931, a total of $406,058 was raised by the branches for the general fund, which contrasted with $161,566 from other sources. That average was around $40,000 per year during the 1920s as compared with around $20,000 for 1932–34. Board of Directors file, Annual Reports, I-A-21, I-A-25, I-A-17, NAACP Papers; Ross, *J. E. Spingarn*, 131–32.

35. For important discussion on finances, see Ross, *J. E. Spingarn*, 130–38. Board of Directors, Annual Reports, December 31, 1932, I-A-25; General Financial Papers, April 1933, I-C-147; White to Philip Peabody, November 11, 1931, I-C-145; all in NAACP Papers.

36. Ross, *J. E. Spingarn*, 105–6, 273, fn. 6.

37. Philip G. Peabody to Walter White, November 25, 1931, I-C-145; Walter White to William Rosenwald, April 8, 1932, I-C-78; Mother M. Katherine to Walter White, May 24, 1937; financial records, May 20–31, 1937, I-C-151, NAACP Papers. On memberships and contingent offers in the 1920s, see B. Joyce Ross, *J. E. Spingarn*, 131 and fn. 42.

38. "Supplementary Report of the Department of Branches," December 12, 1932, January–February file, I-A-21; a voluminous correspondence in the NAACP files documents the energy, time, and tenacity that Walter White put into appeals to potential donors. See, especially, Board of Directors, I-A-22; Board of Directors, Committee Correspondence and Reports, I-A-26; Finance Committee, 1933–39, I-A-27; Finance Committee, I-C-145–150, NAACP Papers.

39. White, for example, had appealed to Rosenwald with special financial problems in June 1933 when Spingarn threatened to reduce Wilkins's salary. White to William Rosenwald, June 8, 1933, I-C-78, White to J. E. Spingarn, June 8, 1933, J. E. Spingarn to White, June 9, 1933, Board of Directors file, I-A-27, NAACP Papers. See discussion of relationship between White and Spingarn in Ross, *J. E. Spingarn*, 135–37. Ross also argues that J. E. Spingarn was the "key formulator" of the association's financial policy during the most critical phase of the Depression from 1930 to 1933 and continued to influence financial decisions during the period 1931–38, with the possible exception of 1935 (*J. E. Spingarn*, 132).

40. Memo, Walter White to Board of Directors, May 8, 1933, I-C-147, NAACP Papers.

41. These tabulations, broken down by race, are rare in the files of the NAACP. My figures are based on computing figures from "Plan of Campaign," November 17, 1938, "Contributions List Submitted by Miss Marvin to Finance Committee for Conference with Villiard," December 30, 1938, Finance Committee, Board of Directors, I-A-27, and Minutes of December 13, 1937, meeting, Board of Directors, I-A-18, NAACP Papers.

42. Kirby argues that it was White's "personal desire to be seen as the administration's main source of information and advice concerning the welfare of black people and his promotion of the NAACP as the leading organization in the civil rights field that, as much as anything, determined White's response to racial and political events in the 1930s and 1940s." Kirby, *Black Americans in the Roosevelt Era*, 181; see also 178–84.

43. Walter White to Edward L. Bernays, June 16, 1934; Edward L. Bernays to Walter White, June 19, 1934; Walter White to Edward Bernays, June 20, 1934; George S. Schuyler to Edward Bernays, June 21, 1934, I-C-322; Walter White to J. E. Spingarn, November 26, 1935; Walter White to Felix Frankfurter, March 24, 1938; Memo: Walter White to Charles Houston and Thurgood Marshall, March 25, 1938; Walter White to William H. Hastie,

April 12, 1938; Walter White to William H. Hastie, April 15, 1938; Walter White to Felix Frankfurter, September 26, 1938; Walter White to Eleanor Roosevelt, November 13, 1935; Walter White to Eleanor Roosevelt, November 22, 1935; Walter White to Eleanor Roosevelt, November 27, 1935; Walter White to Eleanor Roosevelt, December 16, 1935; Walter White to Eleanor Roosevelt, September 30, 1938, I-C-79, NAACP Papers.

44. Randolph, address to NNC, Chicago, February 14, 1936, 8, copy, box 34, APRP. Randolph did not dismiss the professional class, but he clearly wanted "propaganda" to be aimed at a working-class audience. See Randolph to John P. Davis, September 4, 1936, box 7, NNC Papers.

45. *Chicago Defender*, February 15, 1936, 1, 8.

46. Quote from Randolph's speech delivered at the NNC, February 14–16, 1936. Lester Granger, "National Negro Congress," *Opportunity* 14 (May 1936): 151–52; Richard Wright, "Two Million Black Voices," *New Masses* 18 (February 25, 1936): 15.

47. Randolph, address for NNC, Chicago, February 14, 1936, p. 11, box 34, APRP.

48. *Black Worker*, September 1, 1935, 3.

49. "United Front," *Black Worker*, September 1, 1935, p. 3.

50. See *Chicago Defender*, February 22, 1936, 1; *Amsterdam News*, February 29, 1936, 12, 1.

51. *Chicago Defender*, October 23, 1937, 16.

52. "Randolph's Speech," *Chicago Defender*, February 22, 1936, 2, 17.

53. The NNC has been the subject of a great deal of investigation. Some have viewed the NNC as a Communist front; see Record, *The Negro and Communist Party*, and *Race and Radicalism*. Sitkoff with some justification accused the NNC of seeking "many of the same goals in many of the same ways," as the NAACP; Sitkoff, *A New Deal for Blacks*, 259. Zangrando suggested that the NNC "posed nothing but trouble for the Association" from the beginning; see *NAACP Crusade against Lynching*, 137. Pfeffer argued that the NNC had a "problem forging a coalition of black organizations from its inception" and saw the "reluctance of the NAACP to become a sponsor" a problem for the NNC; see Pfeffer, *A. Philip Randolph, Pioneer*, 37. Wolters considered in some detail the split within the NAACP and concluded that the NNC did not represent a significant threat to the NAACP because the Congress lost support after 1937 "from Negro professional and civil groups, and especially from businessmen"; see *Negroes and the Great Depression*, 363–64. On the other hand, Wittner turned the spotlight on the local councils of the NNC, by pointing out the healthy grass-roots flavor imparted to the NNC during the first years of existence. The interpretation in this book builds on his findings. While Wittner focused on the impact that local councils of the NNC had on community affairs, my interest is in the impact that black working-class mobilization had over the direction of protest politics and, in turn, the NAACP's agenda. See Wittner, "The National Negro Congress." Compare with Kirby's argument that the NNC failed to develop fully because Davis and the NNC "shifted to class rather than race alliances" in order to gain financial backing from the Communists, in *Black Americans in the Roosevelt Era*, 168–69. Kirby suggested that the purpose of the NNC was to develop black political independence.

54. Quotes from Meier and Rudwick, *Black Detroit*, 29. Both Wolters and Wittner raised important questions regarding the relationship between the NAACP and the NNC, and documented the broad base of support the NNC received through endorsements. See Wolters, *Negroes and the Great Depression*, 364–65, and Wittner, "The National Negro Congress," 884.

55. Wittner, "National Negro Congress," 887; Wolters, *Negroes and the Great Depression*, 364–67; Pfeffer, *A. Philip Randolph, Pioneer*, 32–40.

56. Pfeffer, *A. Philip Randolph, Pioneer*, 39; Wolters, *Negroes and the Great Depression*, 368–70; Meier and Rudwick noted that the NNC was "accorded considerable respect by black moderates during the 'Popular Front' period," and that it was not until 1940 that "communist influence became more evident"; see *Black Detroit*, 29.

57. For Randolph becoming convinced that "cooperation with Communists was possible," see Solomon, *Cry Was Unity*, 274.

58. McNeil, *Groundwork*, 99, 121.

59. See Memo: Roy Wilkins to Board of Directors, March 9, 1936, pp. 5–6, I-C-383, NAACP Papers.

60. Granger, "National Negro Congress: An Interpretation," *Opportunity* 14 (May 1936): 152.

61. Roy Wilkins reported to the board of the NAACP that William Hastie, a prominent black, New Deal lawyer, an assistant solicitor in the Interior Department, and longtime adviser to Walter White, stated "affiliation will give us an opportunity to expose our work and our history and philosophy to large groups of people who are now either totally ignorant of it or who have been misinformed about it." Memo to Board of Directors, March 9, 1936, p. 6. See also Charles Houston to White, February 29, 1936, both in I-C-383, NAACP Papers.

62. Charles Burton to residents of Chicago, May 12, 1936; Eleanor Rye to John Davis, May 13, 1936; Davis to Rye, March 26, 1936; Davis to Rye, May 18, 1936, box 7, NNC Papers.

63. For Rye as a "friend of the Communist Party," see author's interview with Ishmael Flory, a colleague of Rye in the 1930s, August 29, 1994. John Davis to Van A. Bittner, July 14, 1936, box 4, NNC Papers; Chateauvert, "Marching Together," 148, 159. For role of Poro College within community, see chapter 5, note 44; Thelma Wheaton, interview by author, January 5, 1995; and *Light and Heebie Jeebies*, February 19, 1927, 2, 12–17, box 131, folder 4, CABP.

64. See note 70 and Randolph to Davis, August 11, 1936; Eleanor Rye to Davis, March 15, 1936; Rye to Davis, October 3, 1936; Rye to Davis, n.d. (September 1936 ?); Rye to Davis, November 1936, box 7; Wheaton, interview by author, September 1 and 14, 1994. John Davis to Marion Cuthbert, January 18, 1936, box 4, NNC Papers, mentioned his concern regarding organizing black female industrial and domestic workers and suggested that Cuthbert contact Mrs. Kirkpatrick in Chicago. Mrs. Thelma Kirkpatrick later changed her name to Thelma Wheaton. For Marion Cuthbert's affiliation with the NAACP, see Memo: Roy Wilkins to Board of Directors, "National Negro Congress," March 9, 1936, p. 3, I-C-383, NNC file, NAACP Papers; for her other affiliations, see reel ll, NNC Papers.

65. Henderson, "Political Changes among Negroes," 545.

66. Bunche, "Programs, Ideologies, Tactics," 343, CMS; Eleanor Rye to John Davis, October 3, 1936, box 7; John Davis to A. Philip Randolph, June 6, 1936, box 7, NNC Papers; *Pittsburgh Courier*, July 31, 1937. See, for example, *Chicago Defender*, September 12, 1936, 4.

67. Zieger, *The CIO*, 37; Irving Bernstein, *Turbulent Years*, 92–94, 196–99, 369–72; Cayton and Mitchell, *Black Workers and the New Unions*, 190–224; Brody, *Steelworkers in America*; Brody, *Labor in Crisis*, and "The Origins of Modern Steel Unionism," 13–29; Dickerson, *Out of the Crucible*, 119–49.

68. John Davis to Charles W. Burton, July 11, 1936, box 4, NNC Papers.

69. J. Davis to Van A. Bittner, July 14, 1936; Bittner to Davis, July 18, 1936, box 4, NNC Papers.

70. John Davis to W. Gertrude Brown, July 11, 1936, box 4; John Davis to Charles W. Burton, July 11, 1936, box 4; John Davis to James H. Baker Jr., July 10, 1936, box 4; Van Bittner to John Davis, July 13, 1936, box 4; John Davis to Robert Evans, July 10, 1936, box 5; John Davis to Van Bittner, July 14, 1936, box 4, NNC Papers. I argue that Randolph was very involved with the NNC during his three years as president. Randolph and other BSCP organizers did what Randolph himself called "double duty" during the 1936 to 1939 NNC period. When Randolph stopped in Chicago for BSCP business, he also campaigned for the NNC local. Brotherhood organizers followed this same pattern in other cities, such as Omaha and Jacksonville, building NNC locals upon the BSCP base. See Memo from Pullman Company spy, November 15, 1937, box 633-A, PCP. Benjamin McLaurin, field organizer for the BSCP, rode the rails up and down the East Coast setting up local councils of the NNC while he continued to organize for the BSCP. Martin Richardson to U. Simpson Tate, January 22, 1936; Randolph to John Davis, November 15, 1935, box 7, NNC Papers.

71. John Davis to Van Bittner, July 14, 1936, box 4, NNC Papers. Similar relationships between the CIO and the NNC were developed in Cleveland and Pittsburgh. See Dickerson, *Out of the Crucible*, 136–37.

72. J. Carlisle MacDonald, assistant to chairman, United States Steel Corporation, to Claude A. Barnett, July 27, 1936; John A. Stephens, manager of industrial relations, Carnegie-Illinois Steel corporation, to Barnett, July 28, 1936; Barnett to John A. Stephens, August 1, 1936; John Stevens to Barnett, August 20, 1936; Barnett to J. Carlisle MacDonald, October 31, 1936; Memo: Barnett to J. Carlisle MacDonald, October 31, 1936; box 280, folder 1, CABP.

73. Rye and Wilson understood the need for secrecy. See reports from Pullman Company supervisors on BSCP mass meetings; report by J. A. Chapel to A. V. Burr, October 24, 1926, on Randolph's meeting with BSCP in St. Louis; report by Chapel to Burr, September 19, 1927, on Randolph's meeting with BSCP in St. Louis, all in PCP.

74. Eleanor Rye to John P. Davis, October 3, 1936, Rye to Davis, September Report on Inland Steel, 1936, Rye to Davis, August 27, 1936, box 7, NNC Papers.

75. Stated by George S. Schuyler, *Pittsburgh Courier*, July 31, 1937, 14; Cayton and Mitchell reported black workers joining the SWOC in greater proportion than whites in Chicago. Cayton and Mitchell, *Black Workers and the New Unions*, 202.

76. Cayton and Mitchell, *Black Workers and the New Unions*, 205.

77. Eleanor Rye to John Davis, August 12, 1936, box 7; Eleanor Rye to John Davis, October 6, 1936, "Resolutions of the Chicago Council of the NNC," n.d. [October 1936], box 10, NNC Papers.

78. For a different interpretation of the black middle class and its organizing ability within the black community during the 1930s, see Cruse, *Plural but Equal*, 201–3.

79. Eric Halpern, " 'Black and White Unite and Fight,' " 257–350; Rick Halpern, *Down on the Killing Floor*, 137–38; Zieger, *The CIO*, 80, 83. On contribution to PWOC's campaign, see Horowitz, "*Negro and White, Unite and Fight!*" 71.

80. Ishmael P. Flory, interview by author, August 31, 1994.

81. Brier, "Labor, Politics, and Race," 416–21; Horowitz, "The Path Not Taken," 241–49.

82. Eleanor Rye to John Davis, May 13, 1936, box 7, NNC Papers. See Drake and Cayton, *Black Metropolis*, 738; *Chicago Defender*, November 5, 1935, 22.

83. A. C. MacNeal to Roy Wilkins, March 1936, I-G-53, NAACP Papers.

84. Neva Ryan, a member of the executive committee of the NNC, gained support for domestic workers from the NNC, the Women's Trade Union League, and the YWCA of Chicago.

85. Claude Barnett, while on the payroll of the Pullman Company, produced the *Light and Heebie Jeebies*, a Chicago magazine that attacked the BSCP. See LeRoy, "The Founding Heart of A. Philip Randolph's Union," 29–30; Harris, *Keeping the Faith*, 43, fn. 67.

86. "Agenda of Conference on Domestic Service Workers," May 19–22, 1938; Neva Ryan to John Davis, May 14, 1938, with Citizens' Committee listed on the masthead, box 12, NNC Papers.

87. John Davis to Eleanor Rye, May 18, 1936, box 7, NNC Papers; Drake and Cayton, *Black Metropolis*, 737–38.

88. Wheaton, interview by author, September 14, 1994.

89. Copy union membership card, State, County and Municipal Workers of America, Local no. 30, Chicago, September 1937, folder: 1937–38; clipping, Chicago *Bee*, January 26, 1929; *Chicago Whip*, May 4, 1929, box 1, Irene McCoy Gaines Papers, CHS.

90. Chicago Council of the National Negro Congress to All Organizations, February 26, 1938; White to Charles D. Murray, March 10, 1938; White to "Organizations Cooperating on the Anti-Lynching Bill and NAACP Branches," March 14, 1938, I-C-383, NAACP Papers. For the quotation, see Roy Wilkins to William Pickens, April 19, 1938, I-C-80, NAACP Papers. For efforts by Davis, Randolph, and other NNC officials to gain cooperation from NAACP for antilynching activities, see Wilkins to Davis, February 3, 1938; A. C. MacNeal to White, January 18, 1936; Davis to White, January 29, 1936; Randolph to White, January 25, 1936; Davis to White, June 8, 1937; White to L. Wray Choat, April 2, 1938; White to Gertrude B. Stone, "personal and confidential," April 5, 1938; Memo: presidential delegation re antilynching bill, April 12, White to Staff Files, April 7, 1938; White to Arthur Huff Fauset, April 18, 1938; Davis to White, November 28, 1938, I-C-383, NAACP Papers. Davis to White, April 15, 1938, box 15; Davis to Dr. Albert E. Forsythe, February 24, 1938, box 13; James W. Ford to Randolph, February 1, 1938, box 13, NNC Papers.

91. For the quotation see Zangrando, *The NAACP Crusade against Lynching*, 106. See Wolters's discussion of Zangrando for another assessment in *Negroes and the Great Depression*, 351, n. 48. Compare with Gertrude B. Stone, "personal and confidential," where White says that there was "no doubt that what John [Davis] plans to do is take over lock, stock and barrel, the entire fight for the bill." In letter of April 5, 1938, I-C-383, NAACP Papers.

92. Kirby, *Black Americans in Roosevelt Era*, 182; Weiss, *Farewell to the Party of Lincoln*, 110–19.

93. Weiss, *Farewell to the Party of Lincoln*, 110–11; Kirby, *Black Americans in the Roosevelt Era*, 182–83.

94. Board of Directors, I-A-17, I-A-18, NAACP Papers.

95. A. C. MacNeal to Roy Wilkins, April 4, 1936, I-G-53, NAACP Papers.

96. Roy Wilkins to A. C. MacNeal, April 13, 1936, I-G-53, NAACP Papers.

97. Daisy Lampkin to Walter White, December 5, 1936, I-C-68, NAACP Papers.

98. A. C. MacNeal to Roy Wilkins, March 1936, Branches, I-G-53, NAACP Papers. Greenberg, *Or Does it Explode?*, 120. Brunn uncovered a similar situation in St. Louis where the NNC stepped into a void created by the "non-involvement" of "key black community organizations such as the N.A.A.C.P."; Brunn, "Black Workers and Social

Movements," 562–63; in Milwaukee, the old-guard leaders in the NAACP branch "conducted separate Scottsboro activities before joining broader efforts." Those broader efforts united leaders from middle-class institutions with black workers and the CIO, according to Trotter, *Black Milwaukee*, 163–66, 215–17.

99. Arthur Huff Fauset, local president of NNC, and Harry J. Greene, local president of NAACP, issued a joint call to Philadelphia citizens to support antilynching and Scottsboro campaigns; see handbill, March 23; Fauset to Davis, March 25, 1938, box 13, NNC Papers.

100. Skotnes, "The Black Freedom Movement in Baltimore," 422–37; Baltimore *Afro-American*, August 15, 29, 1936; October 3, 22, 1936.

101. Robert Evans was elected branch secretary of Detroit NAACP in 1938, while continuing to play an active role in the local NNC. Robert J. Evans to Davis, April 25, 1936; Evans to Davis, May 6, 1936; Davis to Evans, May 9, 1936; Davis to Evans, May 18, 1936; Davis to Evans, August 10, 1936; James B. Washington to Evans, November 6, 1936, box 4, NNC Papers. Meier and Rudwick, *Black Detroit*, 80.

102. For example, a report of Daisy E. Lampkin's activities as field secretary between October 1 and November 30, 1938, finds her addressing a NNC forum, as field secretary of the NAACP, in Baltimore, October 7, 1938; Lampkin to Walter White, December 27, 1938, I-C-69, NAACP Papers. Robin Kelley noted a similar correlation in Birmingham, Alabama, between increased militancy on the part of the local chapter and increased popularity of the NAACP. See "Hammer n'Hoe: Black Radicalism and the Communist Party," 522–23. For Lampkin's salary increase, see Lampkin to Walter White, December 27, 1938, I-C-69; see also Lampkin's itinerary in her correspondence with Walter White, I-C-69, NAACP Papers.

103. Joseph W. Givens to Walter White, February 24, 1937; White to Givens, March 2, 1937; Memo, White to Roy Wilkins, March 2, 1937, I-C-322; "NNC Bulletin," 1937, I-C-383, NAACP Papers.

104. Meier and Bracey, "The NAACP as a Reform Movement," 18. *Crisis*, November 1937, 328; see also article by G. James Fleming, "Pullman Porters Win Pot of Gold," ibid., 332–33, 338, 346–47.

105. Walter White to Roy Wilkins, March 22, 1938, I-C-323, NAACP Papers.

106. Memo from Roy Wilkins to Walter White, March 11, 1939; Wilkins to White, May 1, 1939; Memo from White to Wilkins, March 24, 1939; White to Charles H. Houston, May 2, 1939; Wilkins to Daisy Lampkin, December 14, 1939, all in box 80, NAACP Papers.

107. Ross, *J. E. Spingarn*, 244.

108. White to William Rosenwald, September 26, 1939; White to Arthur B. Spingarn, October 5, 1939; White to Rosenwald, October 10, 1939; White to Rosenwald, November 22, 1939; White to Arthur B. Spingarn, October 5, 1939, re: cancellation of $1,000 contribution because of IRS ruling; all in box 80, NAACP Papers. See Greenberg, *Crusaders in the Courts*, 19–21, for background on NAACP-LDF.

109. Compare with Meier and Bracey, "The NAACP as a Reform Movement," 18.

110. White to Arthur Spingarn, March 3, 1939, reel 13; Labor file, April–June 1940, II-A-335; Memo from White to Spingarn, Hastie, Houston, Wilkins, Marshall, and Murphy, April 3, 1940, II-A-335; all in NAACP Papers.

111. Wilkins to Randolph, January 10, 1940, Board of Directors file, II-A-143, NAACP Papers. For Randolph taking stand for collective action with board, see Committee on Discrimination in Labor Unions, 1940–41, June 9, 1941, II-A-128, NAACP Papers.

112. Woodard, *A Nation within a Nation*, 29.

113. For Randolph's resignation speech from NNC, see Bunche, "Critique of the NNC," 357–59, Carnegie-Myrdal Study of the Negro in America Papers, microfilm, Library of Congress. Randolph, "Why I Would Not Stand for Re-election in the National Negro Congress," 24–25; *Black Worker*, May 1940; August 1940, 4; Pfeffer, *A. Philip Randolph, Pioneer*, 41.

114. Solomon, *Cry Was Unity*, 307.

115. Jervis Anderson, *A. Philip Randolph*, 232–38; Bunche, "Programs, Ideologies, and Tactics," 319–71, CMS; *Pittsburgh Courier*, June 24, 1944, 1, 4; July 1, 1944, 1, 4; September 16, 1944, 1, 4; September 30, 1944, 1, 4; Kirby, *Black Americans in the Roosevelt Era*, 155, 164, 166; Streater, "The National Negro Congress," 157.

116. Meier and Rudwick, *Black Detroit*, 5–22; Thomas, *Life for Us Is What We Make It*, 271–312.

117. Meier and Rudwick, *Black Detroit*, 79.

118. *Michigan Chronicle*, June 19, 1939, 10. Also see John Davis to Le Bron Simmons, June 7, 1938, box 15, NNC Papers. For NAACP Detroit branch membership figures, see *Crisis* 45 (December 1938): 400. Financial Statement for the Year Ending December 31, 1939, Detroit, Michigan Branch, p. 2, file: Branches: Detroit, I-G-98, NAACP Papers. For collaboration, see Snow Grigsby, interview, March 12, 1967, 5–6, ALUA.

119. Simmons, interview, 9–10, box 33, folder 15, Nat Ganley Collection, ALUA; Meier and Rudwick, *Black Detroit*, 6–10.

120. White to A. J. Muste, April 15, 1941, NAACP file: Ford Strike, II-A-333, NAACP Papers. See also NAACP Board minutes, April 14, 1941, NAACP-NYC; NAACP press release, April 5, 1941; White to James J. McClendon, April 5, 1941, II-A-333, NAACP Papers. The transcript from the sound truck is in White's Notes from Ford Strike, n.d., file: Ford Strike, II-A-333, NAACP Papers. The *Detroit Free Press* (April 10, 1941, 3) reported that Walter White, "speaking from a union sound car in front of Gate 4" at the River Rouge Ford Plant, advised workers to leave the plant in order to "best serve their own cause, and that of democracy." On understanding new circumstances, see Rev. Charles Hill, interview by Roberta McBride, May 8, 1967, 5, Oral History of "Blacks in the Labor Movement," ALUA; Meier and Rudwick, *Black Detroit*, 91–103.

121. White to James J. McClendon, April 12, 1941, II-A-334, NAACP Papers. For the link between union victory and the reputation of NAACP, see White to A. J. Muste, April 15, 1941, file: Ford Strike, II-A-333, NAACP Papers. White recorded his version of his role in the Ford strike in his autobiography, *A Man Called White*, 214–16.

122. Payne, *I've Got the Light of Freedom*, 88. See also Payne's excellent analysis of Ella Baker, 77–102.

123. Between 1940 and 1946, the NAACP grew from 355 branches and membership of 50,556 to 1,073 branches and a membership around 450,000. See Dalfiume, "The 'Forgotten Years' of the Negro Revolution," 99–100.

Chapter Seven

1. Copy of Executive Order 8802, June 25, 1941, FEPC: General, II-A-252, NAACP Papers; Merl Reed, *Seedtime*, 15; Sullivan, *Days of Hope*, 136.

2. Randolph, "Let the Negro Masses Speak," *Black Worker*, March 1941, 4.

3. Randolph, "March on Washington Movement Presents Program for the Negro," 154–55. Hirsch, *Making the Second Ghetto*. For an excellent historical overview of five

distinct phases of black nationality formation in the United States, see Woodard, *Nation within a Nation*, 10–34.

4. W. E. B. Du Bois, "A Chronicle of Race Relations," *Phylon* 5:3 (1944): 207.

5. Woodard, *Nation within a Nation*, 33–34.

6. Quoted in Sitkoff, *A New Deal*, 324.

7. David Davis, *The Problem of Slavery in Western Culture*, 30.

8. *Messenger* 9:6 (June 1927): 205–6.

9. Garfinkel, *When Negroes March*, 21.

10. Census figures reported in Ottley, *New World A-Coming* 289–95.

11. Weaver, *Negro Labor*, 18–20; Fusfeld and Bates, *Political Economy of the Urban Ghetto*, 45–46.

12. Wesley, "The Negro Has Always Wanted the Four Freedoms," 97.

13. Editorial, "Negro Leaders Compromise as Usual," *Messenger*, September 1919, 7.

14. From pamphlet found in box 29, APRP.

15. Garfinkel, *When Negroes March*, 6; for Roosevelt's references see brief transcript of the September 27, 1940, meeting in the Oval Office in Doyle, *Inside the Oval Office*, 12–17.

16. For White's feeling of betrayal, see Kirby, *Black Americans in the Roosevelt Era*, 181. For other attempts to speak with Roosevelt, see Bracey and Meier, "Allies or Adversaries?: The NAACP," 7; Wynn, *The Afro-American and the Second World War*, 44; Nash, *Great Depression and World War II*, 66–70; Merl Reed, *Seedtime*, 13.

17. Walter White, " 'It's Our Country, Too': The Negro Demands the Right to Be Allowed to Fight for It," *Saturday Evening Post*, December 14, 1940, reprint, 1–8 (quotation from 8); file: Legal Defense Fund, 1940–41, B-96, NAACP Papers.

18. Letter, White to John Temple Graves, quoted in Ruchames, *Race, Jobs, and Politics*, 15. In addition, see the list drawn up by Walter White of "Requests Made to President Roosevelt by NAACP: 1932–1943." The list is sixteen pages long, single-spaced. II-A-416, NAACP Papers.

19. For general surveillance of black leaders and activists, see Savage, *Broadcasting Freedom*, 71, 305, n. 28; Washburn, *A Question of Sedition*, 33. For surveillance on Randolph, see memo recommending "custodial detention" for A. Philip Randolph in "the event of a national emergency," from John Edgar Hoover, Director, FBI to L. M. C. Smith [Special Defense Unit], 12/1/41, 100-55616-2, Freedom of Information/Privacy Acts, FBI Archives, Department of Justice.

20. For the framework of the etiquette of civility, which my analysis builds on, see Chafe, *Civilities and Civil Rights*, 245–46.

21. Editorial, "Call to Negro America," *Black Worker*, May 1941, 4.

22. Randolph, "Let the Negro Masses Speak," *Black Worker*, March 1941, 4.

23. *Black Worker*, May 1941.

24. These connections were addressed in chapters 4 and 5.

25. Garfinkel, *When Negroes March*, 59.

26. Ottley, *New World A-Coming*, 291.

27. See both Ottley's report of this quotation in *New World A-Coming*, 291, and in Ottley, "Negro Morale," *New Republic* 105 (November 10, 1941): 614.

28. Ottley, *New World A-Coming*, 291; editorial, *Afro-American*, March 15, 1941, 4.

29. From A. Philip Randolph, interview by Herbert Garfinkel, July 22, 1955, in Garfinkel, *When Negroes March*, 59.

30. Minutes, Chicago division, BSCP, May 31, 1941, BSCP Chicago.

31. See, for example, letter from Ashley L. Totten, international secretary-treasurer of

the BSCP to fellow porters active in the March on Washington Movement, April 20, 1942, box 10, APRP.

32. Walter White to A. Philip Randolph, March 20, 1941, II, A-417, NAACP Papers; Brinkley *Rosa Parks*, 53–54.

33. "Suggestions for Developing Local Committee," Bulletin, May 22, 1941; "Minutes: subcommittee meeting on 'March to Washington,' NAACP office, April 10, 1941"; Statement of the March on Washington, and Memorandum, Spring 1941, file: MOWM, II-A-416, NAACP Papers.

34. Randolph to White, March 18, 1941, II-A-417, NAACP Papers.

35. Memo to Miss Crump from White, May 7, 1941; "To All Branches," May 12, 1941; Memo from White to Mr. Turner, May 13, 1941, requesting a check for $100 from NAACP toward the March to Washington, file: MOWM, II-A-416, NAACP Papers.

36. "Minutes of Local Unit of March-On-Washington Committee," YMCA, West 135th Street, New York City, file: MOWM, II-A-416, NAACP Papers.

37. For the news stories about the March, see *Pittsburgh Courier* and *Amsterdam News* June 7, 14, 21, 1941.

38. For Aubrey Williams's recollections, see Goodwin, *No Ordinary Time*, 250.

39. For Eleanor Roosevelt's concerns, see ibid., 250–51, for Randolph's comments, see ibid., 250; for perspective from White, see *A Man Called White*, 189–92; *Amsterdam News* and *Afro-American*, June 21, 1941.

40. For members of White House Conference, June 18, see Goodwin, *No Ordinary Time*, 251.

41. This particular reconstruction of the exchange between Randolph, White, and President Roosevelt is from Jervis Anderson, *A. Philip Randolph*, 257–58, which is the result of Anderson's interviews with Randolph and his research into the MOWM. Also see version reported in *Ebony* by Bennett, box 43, APRP, and Bennett, *Confrontation: Black and White*, 176–77; Goodwin, *No Ordinary Time*, 251; *Chicago Defender*, June 28, 1941, 2; *Amsterdam News*, June 28, 1941.

42. Kirby, *Black Americans*, 110–19; B. Joyce Ross, "Mary McLeod Bethune and the National Youth Administration," *Amsterdam News*, June 28, 1941, 1; Garfinkel, *When Negroes March*, 58.

43. Telegram, White to A. Philip Randolph, June 22, 1941, II-A-217, NAACP Papers.

44. Randolph's speech, August 28, 1963, Lincoln Memorial, Washington, D.C., is quoted in Jervis Anderson, *A. Philip Randolph*, 328.

45. Copy of text of Executive Order 8802, June 25, 1941, FEPC: General, II-A-252, NAACP Papers.

46. Myrdal, *An American Dilemma*, 1:416; Garfinkel, *When Negroes March*, 61.

47. Sitkoff, *A New Deal for Blacks*, 309.

48. Copy of Executive Order 8802, June 25, 1941, FEPC: General, II-A-252, NAACP Papers.

49. Editorial, "Crusade for Democracy," *Chicago Defender*, June 28, 1941, 14.

50. The transition of the March on Washington committee into the March on Washington Movement did not occur at one point in time, a fact that has led to some confusion. Yet, as early as December 1941, Randolph initiated the process to turn the March on Washington committees, scattered throughout the country, into entities with dues-paying members. Even when the letterhead still said "committee," the leaders and staff thought of the March as a movement by the spring of 1942. See correspondence in boxes 9 and 26, APRP, and box 130, BSCP Chicago.

51. *Amsterdam News*, July 5, 1944, 4; Kesselman, *The Social Politics of FEPC*, 3–24; Merl Reed, *Seedtime*, 16–21; Ruchames, *Race, Jobs, and Politics*, 22–23; Garfinkel, *When Negroes March*, 63; Pfeffer, *A. Philip Randolph, Pioneer*, 50–51.

52. Embree, *13 against the Odds*, 225.

53. For the argument that the MOWM was "a one-man organization," see Kesselman, *The Social Politics of FEPC*, 93–97. For an opposing view, see Garfinkel, *When Negroes March*, 62–96.

54. See correspondence between Webster, Randolph, and group of fourteen during spring and summer of 1942, box 9, APRP. Much has been made of this dispute in Chicago between factions within the MOWM. The major differences were between the BSCP cadre, those who had been with the BSCP, struggling for economic rights through its networks since the 1920s, and those who had no affiliation with the BSCP. See Randolph to Webster, September 3, 1942; Webster to Randolph, July 1, 1942; Webster to Randolph, August 27, 1942; Webster to Randolph, August 29, 1942; Randolph to fourteen members of MOWM in Chicago, September 2, 9; Box 9, APRP.

55. Randolph to Webster, Sept. 3, 1942, box 9, APRP.

56. For the scope of the participation in MOWM, see Garfinkel, *When Negroes March*, 84.

57. *Black Worker*, August 1941, 1–2.

58. Ibid., p. 2; Jervis Anderson, *A. Philip Randolph*, 259, and *Bayard Rustin*, 85–86.

59. *The Reminiscences of Bayard Rustin*, January 24, 1985, 39–40, in OHC-CU. Obituary, *New York Times*, August 25, 1987, A1, B8. Wittner, *Rebels against War*.

60. *Black Worker*, November 1941, 1. See also, *Black Worker*, October 1941, 1–2. "Organization and Structure: Present Organization," folder: MOWM: Principles and Strategies, box 26, APRP.

61. See Jones, "The Editorial Policy of Negro Newspapers"; Baltimore *Afro-American*, December 20, 1941, February 7, 1942; *Norfolk Journal and Guide*, March 21, 1942; "Now Is the Time Not to Be Silent," *Crisis* 49 (January 1942): 7; "The Fate of Democracy," *Opportunity* 20 (January 1942): 2; Dalfiume, *Desegregation of the Armed Forces*, 105–31, and, "The 'Forgotten Years' "; Sitkoff, "Racial Militancy"; Bennett, *Before the Mayflower*, 307, and *Confrontation Black and White*, 179–80; Ottley, *New World A-Coming*, 268–69.

62. Quotation in Garfinkel, *When Negroes March*, 77; Murray, *The Negro Handbook*, 1, 3; Ottley, *New World A-Coming*, 269.

63. Sitkoff, "Racial Militancy," 662.

64. Charles Williams, "Harlem at War," *Nation* 156 (January 16, 1943): 88.

65. Walter White, "The Negro Problem in America," 40.

66. Editorial, *Black Worker*, April 1942, 4; Locke, "The Unfinished Business of Democracy," *Survey Graphic* 31:11 (November 1942): 458.

67. *Pittsburgh Courier*, February 14, 1942; *Chicago Defender*, March 14, 1942. See also Ralph N. Davis, "The Negro Newspapers and the War," *Sociology and Social Research* 27 (May–June 1943): 373–80.

68. "March on Washington Movement Plans Giant Meeting," *Black Worker*, March 1942, 4.

69. *Amsterdam News*, April 11, 1942, 21.

70. For this reference, see Garfinkel, *When Negroes March*, 90. For the headline, see *Amsterdam News*, June 13, 1942, 1.

71. *Black Worker*, June 1942, 1.

72. Roy Wilkins, *Amsterdam News*, June 27, 1942, 7, reported 18,000; *Chicago Defender*, June 27, 1942, 6, reported 20,000.

73. Leaflets reprinted in Garfinkel, *When Negroes Marched*, 89. For the BSCP selling stamps for MOWM rallies, see *Black Worker*, July 1942, 3. "Mass Meeting" Program, MOWM, Madison Square Garden, New York City, June 16, 1942, box 6, folder 5, BSCP Chicago. On the popularity of "We are Americans Too," see Ottley, *New World A-Coming*, 321.

74. Speech of Dr. Mary McLeod Bethune, "The New Negro," in *Interracial Review: A Journal for Christian Democracy* 15:7 (July 1942): 106.

75. "The Watchword is Forward!" in "Mass Meeting" Program, June 16, box 6, folder 5, BSCP Chicago; "12,000 in Chicago Voice Demands for Democracy," *Chicago Defender*, July 4, 1942, 3; report, MOWM meeting, New York, in Roy Wilkins, *Amsterdam News*, June 27, 1942, 7.

76. "Mass Meeting" Program, MOWM; letter to *Pittsburgh Courier* from Randolph, April 4, 1942, BSCP Chicago. Randolph wrote in November that "in view of charges made that they [MOWM rallies] were subsidized by Nazi funds, it may not be amiss to point out that of the $8,000 expenses of the Madison Square meeting every dime was contributed by Negroes themselves, except for tickets bought by some liberal white organizations." *Survey Graphic*, November 6, 1942, fn. 489.

77. Chicago division, MOWM, meeting with "Negro ministers of Chicago," June 3, 1942, box 130, folder 4, BSCP Chicago. The Reverend Junius C. Austin, member of the BSCP's Citizens' Committee in 1920s, was one of the featured speakers at the Chicago Coliseum on June 26, 1942; see the flyer, "To Storm the Coliseum," file: MOWM, II-A-416, NAACP Papers.

78. Theophilus Lewis, "Plays and a Point of View," *Interracial Review* 15:7 (July 1942): 111.

79. Tarry, *Third Door*, 192.

80. *Chicago Defender* , July 4, 1942, 1, 3; Dona Blakeley, "Woman's Role in March on Washington Movement"; George F. McCray, *Chicago Defender*, August 22, 1942, 1, 3; "Negroes Threaten March on Washington to Demand 'Equality' in War Effort," *St. Louis Star-Times*, August 15, 1942; in St. Louis Scrapbook, BSCP Chicago.

81. For a discussion of this editorial and cartoon, see Garfinkel, *When Negroes March*, 92, 106.

82. Dalfiume, "The 'Forgotten Years,' " 100.

83. *Pittsburgh Courier*, September 12, 1942. For more on a "new spirit," see Dalfiume, "The 'Forgotten Years,' " 100, n. 49.

84. George F. McCray, *Chicago Defender*, July 4, 1942, 3.

85. "Negroes Threaten March on Washington."

86. *Pittsburgh Courier*, May 3, 1943; article from *Courier*, quoted in *Chicago Defender*, June 12, 1943.

87. Yet Bethune spoke at the earlier New York rally. "Huge Mass Meeting Is Set for June 26," *Pittsburgh Courier*, May 9, 1942, copy, box 130, folder 3, BSCP Chicago. Mary McLeod Bethune to Randolph, June 2, 1942, box 26, APRP.

88. Randolph to Bethune, June 8, 1942, box 26, APRP.

89. Roy Wilkins to Walter White, June 24, 1942. For more correspondence about the MOW Committee as a permanent organization, see White to Daisy Lampkin, April 6, 1942, Lampkin to White, April 7, 1942. All in file: MOW Committee, II-A-417, NAACP Papers.

90. Report: March on Washington Policy Conference, Lucy Thurman YWCA, Detroit, September 26–27, 1942, by Pauli Murphy to Walter White, pp. 7–8, submitted October 6, 1942, file: MOW Committee, II-A-417, NAACP Papers.

91. Randolph, "Keynote Address to the Policy Conference," pp. 9–10, September 26–27, 1942, Detroit, file: MOW Convention, 1942–43, II-A-417, NAACP Papers.

92. Ibid., 10.

93. For a discussion of the role played by the MOWM in introducing nonviolent direct action to African Americans during World War II, see Kapur, *Raising Up a Prophet*, 101–23.

94. "MOWM: What Do We Stand For!," box 26, APRP.

95. Randolph to Bennie Smith, October 15, 1942, box 25, APRP.

96. Randolph, "Keynote Address to the Policy Conference," p. 8.

97. "March on Washington Movement: What Do We Stand For!," box 26, APRP.

98. Report: March on Washington Policy Conference, p. 14. Minutes: Meeting of Board of Directors, September 14, 1942, pp. 2–3, II-A-134, NAACP Papers. For a fuller picture of the controversy over the MOWM and its relationship to the NAACP, see Wilkins to White, June 24, 1942; Memo: White from Wilkins, September 1, 1942; Randolph to White, September 9, 1942; White to Alfred Baker Lewis, September 21, 1942; Lewis to White, September 18, 1942; White to Randolph, September 21, 1942; White to Judge William H. Hastie, September 21, 1942; Memo: White from Morrow, September 11, 1942; all in II-A-417, NAACP Papers.

99. Walter White to William H. Hastie, May 20, 1941; Charles H. Houston to Randolph, May 20, 1941, both in MOWM, II-A-416, NAACP Papers.

100. Randolph, "Keynote Address to the Policy Conference," pp. 4–11.

101. For example, John Robert Badger, "World View," *Chicago Defender*, July 17, 1943, 15. Also *Chicago Defender* May 29, July 10, 1943; *Pittsburgh Courier*, June 6, 1942; August 14, 1943; and *New York Age*, September 4, 1943.

102. Pfeffer makes this same point in *A. Philip Randolph, Pioneer*, 298.

103. See the letter from C. B. Powell, publisher of the *Amsterdam News*, to Randolph in October 1942 stating that excluding white Americans from the MOWM was "undemocratic and denotes segregation and elimination of whites who would help the course of Negro advancement." [Although Powell later appreciated "the wisdom" of Randolph's position, his initial response was fairly typical. In Garfinkel, *When Negroes March*, 205, fn. 12 and 129.

104. Socialist Party principles quoted in James, *Holding Aloft the Banner of Ethiopia*, 127.

105. Quoted in ibid., 187.

106. For Garvey's Revenge, see ibid., 186–87.

107. Randolph, "Keynote Address to Policy Conference," p. 37.

108. Randolph to Bennie Smith, October 15, 1942, file: MOWM, box 25, APRP.

109. For keeping out the Communists, see Sitkoff, *A New Deal*, 315; John Sengstacke's column, *Chicago Defender*, January 18, 1941. For borrowing from Garvey, see Pfeffer, *A. Philip Randolph, Pioneer*, 58.

110. E. Pauline Myers, executive secretary, MOWM, "March on Washington Movement and Non-Violent Civil Disobedience," *Black Worker*, February 1943, 3.

111. Sitkoff, "Racial Militancy," 671.

112. Nancy Macdonald and Dwight Macdonald, "The War's Greatest Scandal! The Story of Jim Crow in Uniform," box 132, folder 8, BSCP Chicago.

113. Memo: White to Board of Directors, February 8, 1943; White to Randolph, February 3, 1943; White to Dr. Allan Knight Chalmers, February 11, 1943; White to Arthur B. Spingarn, February 11, 1943; II-A-416, NAACP Papers; Minutes: Board of Directors, April 12, 1943; Randolph to White, June 10, 1943; White to Randolph, June 11, 1943; box 30, BSCP-LC. Powell, *Marching Blacks*, 159.

114. Memo to White from Wilkins: March on Washington Convention in Chicago, July 7, 1943, p. 3, folder: MOW Committee: Conventions 1943, II-A-217, NAACP Papers.

115. Randolph, "Keynote Address to the Detroit Policy Conference," p. 6.

116. Garfinkel, *When Negroes March*, 144. See also, Sitkoff, "Racial Militancy," 673. *New York Times*, July 4, 1943, 12.

117. Payne, *I've Got the Light of Freedom*, 89. For the "piggybacking" strategy, see my chapter 7. Until we have the benefit of the many local community studies in process, we must continue to speculate about the relationship between the local and national NAACP during this period.

118. See boxes 25 and 26, APRP.

119. Meier and Rudwick, *CORE*, 15.

120. For Roosevelt's State of the Union Address, see *New York Times*, January 12, 1944, 12. For discussion of significance of the Economic Bill of Rights, see Eric Foner, *The Story of American Freedom*, 234; Weir, *Politics and Jobs*, 52; and Sullivan, *Days of Hope*, 167–68.

Chapter Eight

1. Weaver, *Negro Labor*, 28–40, 61–67; Lipsitz, *Rainbow at Midnight*, 69–95.

2. As Lipsitz summarized the situation, "they went on strike to get more blacks hired, and they went on strike to get blacks upgraded to higher-paying skilled jobs." *Rainbow at Midnight*, 74.

3. Randolph, "Keynote Address to the Policy Conference," p. 5, September 26–27, 1942, Detroit, file: MOW Convention, 1942–43, NAACP Papers.

4. See Chester Himes, "Now Is the Time! Here Is the Place!," *Opportunity* 10:9 (September 1942): 271.

5. My analysis on the economic situation of black workers during World War II would not be possible without the scholarship of Robert C. Weaver, whose *Negro Labor* provides the foundation for much of what follows. Weaver, *Negro Labor*, 18, 24, 65. See also Sullivan, *Days of Hope*, 134–35.

6. Weaver, *Negro Labor*, 18.

7. Ibid., 16–27.

8. Ibid., 60–65.

9. Ibid., 64.

10. Lipsitz, *Rainbow at Midnight*, 73.

11. Meier and Rudwick, *Black Detroit*, 120–24.

12. Ibid., 122–23; Lipsitz, *Rainbow at Midnight*, 74; Weaver, *Negro Labor*, 68.

13. Capeci, *Race Relations in Wartime Detroit*, 68.

14. Meier and Rudwick, *Black Detroit*, 183. Boyle, "There Are No Sorrows."

15. For Sojourner Truth controversy, see Meier and Rudwick, *Black Detroit*, 176–84; for composition of the Sojourner Truth Citizens Committee, see Capeci, *Race Relations in Wartime Detroit*, 83–84; for forces arrayed against black occupancy, see Korstad and Lichtenstein, "Opportunities Found and Lost," 797; Sugrue, *Origins of the Urban Crisis*, 72–75.

16. Capeci, *Race Relations in Wartime Detroit*, 75–99 (quotation from 88). Capeci documents a neighborhood improvement association, the Seven Mile–Fenelon Improvement Association, which was formed by whites who opposed black occupancy of Sojourner Truth.

17. For an excellent analysis of the housing situation in postwar Detroit, see Sugrue, *Origins of the Urban Crisis*, 218–29 (quotation from 218).

18. Capeci, *Race Relations in Wartime Detroit*, 142.

19. Quoted in Meier and Rudwick, *Black Detroit*, 164.

20. Ibid., 113–15, 163–64; James, Breitman, and Keemer, *Fighting Racism*, 235; "Forward with Action" (annual report, 1943, of Detroit branch of NAACP), especially 20–21, 37, Branch file: Detroit, II-C-87; "The Cadillac Charter," Branch file: Detroit, II-C-86, NAACP Papers.

21. Meier and Rudwick, *Black Detroit*, 164.

22. For Strong's threat to induct Alson in Army, see Marti Alston, interview by author, Detroit, December 11, 1999. Strong's threat to Alson was a dramatic contrast from his previous role as an interventionist who helped expand black economic opportunity; see Meier and Rudwick, *Black Detroit*, 158.

23. For details on the Packard strike of June 1943 and the firing of Christopher Alston, the chief steward of local 190 who walked off the job protesting the "union's indecisiveness" and propelled the situation into a crisis, see Meier and Rudwick, *Black Detroit*, 167–71. For pressure from draft boards to revoke deferments of insurgent workers, see Glaberman, *Wartime Strikes*, 50.

24. For "March behavior," see Leslie Perry to Walter White, May 4, 1943, "MOWC General," IIA-416, NAACP Papers.

25. Nelson Lichtenstein, "Defending the No-Strike Pledge," 272.

26. Ibid., 276.

27. For the "increasingly strained" relationship between Hardin and Thomas and dissolving of the interracial committee, see Meier and Rudwick, *Black Detroit*, 117–18, 212–13.

28. Capeci, *Race Relations in Wartime Detroit*, 68–69.

29. See Leslie Perry to Walter White, May 4, 1943, "MOWC General," II-A-416, NAACP Papers.

30. Ibid.

31. Ibid.

32. George McCray, "Labor Front," *Chicago Defender*, June 26, 1943, 8.

33. *Chicago Defender*, June 12, 1943, 1, 20; James, *Fighting Racism*, 252–54; Meier and Rudwick, *Black Detroit*, 164–65. On the working-class character of the Detroit branch of the NAACP, see Korstad and Lichtenstein, "Opportunities Found and Lost," 797–98.

34. Walter White, "An Open Letter to Negro Workers," *Chicago Defender*, May 1, 1943, 15.

35. "Forward with Action," Annual Report 1943, Detroit NAACP, p.15, II-C-87, NAACP.

36. Finally, there were many exceptions to the Packard pattern. For example, when Briggs Manufacturing Company, Kelsey-Hayes Wheel Company, and Consolidated Brass Company initiated programs of upgrading black workers to higher-paying defense jobs, no trouble erupted. Weaver attributes the difference to the firm stand that both management and labor took in expediting the transfers. Another incident, at the Chrysler Corporation, reinforces this reasoning. Chrysler ordered all loaders and boxers at Dodge transferred to defense work at the Chrysler Highland Park plant and manage-

ment declared that the transfers would take place despite rumors of a white workers' hate strike. Management was backed by both the local and international union. When a stoppage did occur, union representatives told "management to fire all workers who refused to return to their jobs." One day after the transfer, management said all was well. Weaver, *Negro Labor*, 71.

37. Lipsitz, *Rainbow at Midnight*, 92, 99; for the transfer of black workers out of Packard foundry, see Meier and Rudwick, *Black Detroit*, 173; Glaberman, *Wartime Strikes*, 51–60.

38. For influence of the tightening job market, see Sugrue, *Origins of the Urban Crisis*, 26; Korstad and Lichtenstein, "Opportunities Found and Lost," 799.

39. Meier and Rudwick, *Black Detroit*, 196; Wynn, *The Afro-American and the Second World War*, 70; Sitkoff, "The Detroit Race Riot of 1943"; Sugrue, *Origins of the Urban Crisis*, 29; Charles S. Johnson, "News Summary of National Events and Trends in Race Relations," August 1943, prepared for Julius Rosenwald Fund, pp. 4, 17–21, file: Rosenwald Fund, II-A-513, NAACP Papers.

40. These two incidents are related in Sitkoff, "Racial Militancy," 672.

41. "Negroes in the Armed Forces," *New Republic* 109 (October 18, 1943): 542–43.

42. Sitkoff, "Racial Militancy," 669–70.

43. Ibid., 673.

44. Sugrue, "Crabgrass-Roots Politics: Race, Rights, and the Reaction against Liberalism," 564. See also, discussion in Sugrue, *Origins of the Urban Crisis*, 72–75.

45. Sitkoff, "Racial Militancy," 680.

46. See ibid., 678–79; and Lawson, *Running for Freedom*, 11.

47. Edwin R. Embree to Walter White, May 10, 1943; telegram: White to Embree, May 20, 1943; "Minutes," Special Committee Called by the Rosenwald Fund, June 3, 1943, Chicago; Jeanetta Welch to Walter White, "The Chicago Charter Committee on Employment," June 30, 1943; Rosenwald Fund, II-A-513, NAACP Papers.

48. For the relationship between militant black workers and the NAACP in Detroit, see Korstad and Lichtenstein, "Opportunities Found and Lost," 797–98. For the collaboration between the UAW and NAACP in organizing a campaign to defeat reelection of Mayor Jefferies in Detroit after the race riot, see Meier and Rudwick, *Black Detroit*, 196–97.

49. Capeci, *Race Relations in Wartime Detroit*, 162; Korstad and Lichtenstin, "Opportunities Found and Lost," 797.

50. Quoted in Von Eschen, "African Americans and Anti-Colonialism," 75.

51. Ibid., 79, 9.

52. Merl Reed, *Seedtime*, 94–98 (quotations from 98).

53. Sullivan, *Days of Hope*, 157–58.

54. For arousing the southern bloc, see Merl Reed, *Seedtime*, 92, also 75; for publications critical of African American behavior, see 92–94.

55. Harris, "Federal Intervention in Union Discrimination: FEPC and West Coast Shipyards," 325–47 (quotation from 346).

56. Merl Reed, *Seedtime*, 106; for treating them like children, see Arnesen, "The Failure of Protest: Black Labor, the FEPC, and the Railroad Industry," 5; *Pittsburgh Courier*, January 23, 1943, 1; *Chicago Defender*, January 30, 1943, 6. For another interpretation of the FEPC hearings on the railroad industry, see Arnesen, *Brotherhoods of Color*, chap. 6.

57. Merl Reed, *Seedtime*, 116.

58. Weaver, *Negro Labor*, 78–79.

59. For politicizing the home front, see Lipsitz, *Rainbow at Midnight*, especially 71, 338.

60. Randolph, "March on Washington Movement," 137.

61. Weaver, *Negro Labor*, 306.

62. Dittmer, *Local People*, 9. Tyson observes this same phenomenon in North Carolina; see his "Wars for Democracy," 253–75.

63. Boggs, *American Revolution*, 79.

64. Hughes, "Let America Be America Again," 189–91.

65. Thelma K. Wheaton, interview by author, January 5, 1995.

66. Logan, *What the Negro Wants*, 136.

BIBLIOGRAPHY

Manuscript Collections

Barnett, Claude A. Papers. Chicago Historical Society, Chicago.

Bethune, Mary McLeod. Papers. Microfilm. Library of Congress, Washington, D.C.

Brotherhood of Sleeping Car Porters. Papers. Library of Congress, Washington, D.C.

Brotherhood of Sleeping Car Porters. Papers. Chicago division. Chicago Historical Society, Chicago.

Burgess, Ernest W. Papers. Joseph Regenstein Library, University of Chicago, Chicago.

Carnegie-Myrdal Study of the Negro in America Papers. Microfilm. Schomburg Center for Research in Black Culture, New York Public Library, New York, and Library of Congress, Washington, D.C.

Civil Rights Documentation Project. Moorland-Spingarn Research Center. Howard University. Washington, D.C.

Dellums, C. L. Papers. Bancroft Library, University of California at Berkeley.

Dieckmann, Annetta M. Papers. YWCA Papers. University of Illinois at Chicago.

Du Bois, W. E. B. Papers. Microfilm collection. Butler Memorial Library, Columbia University, New York.

Edwards, Thyra. Papers. Chicago Historical Society, Chicago.

Federal Bureau of Investigation. Archives. Preprocessed files obtained under the Freedom of Information/Privacy Acts. Subject files consulted: National Negro Congress and A. Philip Randolph. Federal Bureau of Investigation, Washington, D.C.

Fitzpatrick, John. Papers. Chicago Historical Society, Chicago.

Gaines, Irene McCoy. Papers. Chicago Historical Society, Chicago.

Ganley, Nat. Collection. Archives of Labor and Urban Affairs, Walter Reuther Library, Wayne State University, Detroit.

Harsh, Vivian. Collection. Carter Woodson Regional Library, Chicago Public Library, Chicago.

Herstein, Lillian. Papers. Chicago Historical Society, Chicago.

Ickes, Harold. Papers. Library of Congress, Washington, D.C.

McDowell, Mary. Papers. Chicago Historical Society, Chicago.

McLaurin, Benjamin F. Papers. Schomburg Center for Research in Black Culture, New York Public Library, New York.

National Association for the Advancement of Colored People. Library of Congress, Washington, D.C.

National Negro Congress. Papers. Microfilm. Schomburg Center for Research in Black Culture, New York Public Library, New York, and Library of Congress, Washington, D.C.

Olander, Victor A. Papers. Chicago Historical Society, Chicago.

Park, Robert E. Papers. Joseph Regenstein Library, University of Chicago.

Pullman Company. Papers. Newberry Library, Chicago.

Randolph, A. Philip. Papers. Library of Congress, Washington, D.C.

Taylor, Lea D. Papers. Chicago Historical Society, Chicago.

Wells, Ida B. Papers. Special Collections, Joseph Regenstein Library, University of Chicago, Chicago.

Wheaton, Thelma Kirtpatrick. Papers. Chicago Historical Society, Chicago.

Newspapers and Periodicals

American Mercury

Amsterdam News

Atlantic Monthly

Afro-American (Baltimore)

Black Worker.

BroadAx (Chicago)

Bulletin. City Club of Chicago.

Chicago City Directory.

Chicago Daily News

Chicago Defender

Chicago Evening Journal

Chicago Tribune

Chicago Whip

Crisis

Current History

Daily Worker

Detroit Free Press

Detroit News

Federated Press

Half-Century Magazine

Heebie Jeebies

Light and Heebie Jeebies

Messenger

Michigan Chronicle

Nation

New York Age

New York Times

New Republic

New Masses

Norfolk Journal and Guide

Opportunity

Pittsburgh Courier

Pullman News

Pullman Porter

Pullman Porters' Review

Record-Herald (Chicago)

St. Louis Argus

St. Louis Star-Times

Survey Graphic

Interviews

Alston, Marti. Interview by author. Detroit. December 11, 1999.

Black, Timuel. Interview by author. Chicago. May 3, 1995.

Blacks in the Labor Movement. Oral histories. Archives of Labor and Urban Affairs. Walter Reuther Library, Wayne State University, Detroit.

Burroughs, Margaret Taylor. Interview by author. Chicago, May 6, 1995.

Crowder, Ulus. Interview by Greg LeRoy. Chicago, October 27, November 16, December 8, 1977. Tapes in Chicago Historical Society.

Flory, Ishmael P. Interview by author. Chicago, August 31, 1994; January 7, April 11, May 4, July 13, 14, 1995.

Hayes, Charles. Interview by author. Chicago, March 15, 1995.

McLaurin, Benjamin. Interview by Greg LeRoy. Chicago, January 22, 1981. Tapes in Chicago Historical Society.

Nixon, Edgar Daniel. Interview by Stanley Smith. Montgomery, Ala., February 1968. Civil Rights Documentation Project, Moorland Spingarn Research Center, Howard University, Washington, D.C.

Randolph, A. Philip. Interview by Wendell Wray. 1972. In *The Reminiscences of A. Philip Randolph.* Oral History Collection of Columbia University.

Randolph, A. Philip. Interview by Robert Martin, New York City, January 14, 1969. Transcript in Howard University Civil Rights Documentation Project, Moorland Spingarn Research Center, Howard University, Washington, D.C.

Rustin, Bayard, Jr. Interview by Ed Edwin. In *The Reminiscences of Bayard Rustin.* New York City, January 1985. Transcript in A. Philip Randolph Institute, New York City (I read transcript in 1991; since that time, the Institute has relocated to Washington, D.C.).

Seeger, Pete. Interview by author (telephone). Fairfield, Vermont. January 12, 1989.

Webster, Milton P. AFL-CIO Speech. 1961. Tape in author's possession.

Wheaton, Thelma K. Interview by author. Chicago, September 1, 14, 1994; January 5, 1995.

Wilkins, Roy. Interview. April and May 1970. Civil Rights Documentation Project, Moorland-Spingarn Research Center, Howard University, Washington, D.C.

Books, Articles, and Theses

Abraham, Henry J. *Freedom and the Court: Civil Rights and Liberties in the United States.* 4th ed. New York: Oxford University Press, 1982.

Adelman, William. *Touring Pullman: A Study in Company Paternalism.* Chicago: Illinois Labor History Society, 1972.

Anderson, Charles Frederick. *Freemen Yet Slaves under "Abe" Lincoln's Son or Services and Wages of Pullman Porters.* Chicago: Enterprise Printing House, 1904.

Anderson, Jervis. *A. Philip Randolph: A Biographical Portrait.* New York: Harcourt Brace Jovanovich, 1973. Reprint, Berkeley: University of California Press, 1986.

——. *Bayard Rustin: Troubles I've Seen.* New York: Harper Collins, 1997.

——. *This Was Harlem: A Cultural Portrait, 1900–1950.* New York: Noonday Press, 1981.

Arnesen, Eric. *Brotherhoods of Color: Black Railroad Workers and the Struggle for Equality.* Cambridge, Mass.: Harvard University Press, 2000.

——. "Charting an Independent Course: African-American Railroad Workers in the

World War I Era." In *Labor Histories: Class, Politics, and the Working-Class Experience*, edited by Eric Arnesen, Julie Greene, and Bruce Laurie, 284–308. Urbana: University of Illinois Press, 1998.

——. "The Failure of Protest: Black Labor, the FEPC, and the Railroad Industry." Paper presented at Tenth Southern Labor Studies Conference, College of William and Mary, Williamsburg, Va., September 1997.

——. "Following the Color Line of Labor: Black Workers and the Labor Movement before 1930." *Radical History Review* 55 (Winter 1993): 53–87.

——. " 'Like Banquo's Ghost, It Will Not Down': The Race Question and the American Railroad Brotherhoods, 1880–1920." *American Historical Review* 99:5 (December 1994): 1601–33.

——. *Waterfront Workers of New Orleans: Race, Class, and Politics, 1863–1923*. New York: Oxford University Press, 1991.

Arthur, George R. *Life on the Negro Frontier*. New York: Association Press, 1934.

——. "The Young Men's Christian Association Movement among Negroes." *Opportunity* 1:3 (March 1923): 16–18.

Baker, Ray Stannard. *Following the Color Line: An Account of Negro Citizenship in the American Democracy*. New York: Doubleday, Page, 1908.

——. *The Industrial Unrest*. Garden City, N.Y.: Doubleday, Page, 1920.

Baldwin, James. *The Fire Next Time*. New York: Dell, 1962.

——. *Nobody Knows My Name*. New York: Dell, 1961.

Barrett, James R. *Work and Community in the Jungle: Chicago's Packinghouse Workers, 1894–1922*. Urbana: University of Illinois Press, 1987.

Bates, Beth Tompkins. "A New Crowd Challenges the Agenda of the Old Guard in the NAACP, 1933–1941." *American Historical Review* 102:2 (April 1997): 340–77.

——. "The Unfinished Task of Emancipation: Protest Politics Come of Age in Black Chicago, 1925–1943." Ph.D. diss., Columbia University, 1997.

Beale, Howard K. "On Rewriting Reconstruction History." *American Historical Review* 45 (July 1940): 807–27.

Bederman, Gail. " 'Civilization,' the Decline of Middle-Class Manliness, and the Ida B. Wells's Antilynching Campaign (1892–94)." In *"We Specialize in the Wholly Impossible": A Reader in Black Women's History*, edited by Darlene Clark Hine, Wilma King, and Linda Reed, 407–32. New York: Carlson Publishing, 1995.

Beifuss, Joan Turner. *At the River I Stand*. Memphis, Tenn.: St. Lukes Press, 1990.

Bell, Inge Powell. *CORE and the Strategy of Nonviolence*. New York: Random House, 1968.

Bennett, Leone, Jr. *Before the Mayflower: A History of Black America*. Chicago: Johnson, 1965.

——. *Confrontation: Black and White*. Chicago: Johnson, 1965.

Berlin, Ira, Barbara J. Fields, Steven F. Miller, Joseph P. Reidy, and Leslie S. Rowland. "The Wartime Genesis of Free Labor, 1861–1865." In *Slaves No More: Three Essays on Emancipation and the Civil War*, 77–186. New York: Cambridge University Press, 1992.

Bernstein, Irving. *The Lean Years: A History of the American Worker, 1920–1933*. Boston: Houghton Mifflin, 1960.

——. *Turbulent Years: A History of the American Worker, 1933–1941*. Boston: Houghton Mifflin, 1969.

Berry, Mary Frances, and John W. Blassingame. *Long Memory: The Black Experience in America*. New York: Oxford University Press, 1982.

Blackmar, Elizabeth. *Manhattan for Rent, 1785–1850*. Ithaca, N.Y.: Cornell University Press, 1989.

Bloom, Jack M. *Class, Race and the Civil Rights Movement*. Bloomington: Indiana University Press, 1987.

Boggs, Grace Lee. *Living for Change*. Minneapolis: University of Minnesota Press, 1998.

Boggs, James. *The American Revolution: Pages from a Worker's Notebook*. New York: Monthly Review Press, 1963.

Bontemps, Arna, and Jack Conroy. *Anyplace but Here*. New York: Hill and Wang, 1966.

Boris, Joseph J., ed. *Who's Who in Colored America, 1928–1929: Dictionary of Notable Living Persons of African Decent in America*. New York: Who's Who in Colored America, 1929.

Boyd, Melba Joyce. "Canon Configuration for Ida B. Wells-Barnett." *The Black Scholar* 24 (1991): 8–13.

——. *Discarded Legacy: Politics and Poetics in the Life of Frances E. W. Harper, 1825–1911*. Detroit: Wayne State University Press, 1994.

Boyle, Kevin. " 'There Are No Sorrows That the Union Can't Heal': The Struggle for Racial Equality in the United Automobile Workers, 1940–1960." *Labor History* 36:1 (Winter 1995): 5–23.

Bracey, John, Jr., and August Meier. "Allies or Adversaries?: The NAACP, A. Philip Randolph and the 1941 March on Washington." *Georgia Historical Quarterly* 75:1 (Spring 1991): 1–17.

Braden, Anne. *The Wall Between*. New York: Monthly Review Press, 1959.

Branham, Charles Russell. "The Transformation of Black Political Leadership in Chicago, 1864–1942." Ph.D. diss., University of Chicago, 1981.

Brazeal, Brailsford Reese. *The Brotherhood of Sleeping Car Porters: Its Origins and Development*. New York: Harper and Brothers, 1946.

Brier, Stephen. "Labor, Politics, and Race: A Black Worker's Life." *Labor History* 23:3 (Summer 1982): 416–21.

Bright, John. *Hizzoner Big Bill Thompson*. New York: J. Cape and H. Smith, 1930.

Brinkley, Douglas. *Rosa Parks*. New York: Viking Penguin Books, 2000.

Brody, David. *The Butcher Workmen: A Study of Unionization*. Cambridge, Mass.: Harvard University Press, 1964.

——. *Labor in Crisis: The Steel Strike of 1919*. Philadelphia: Lippincott, 1965.

——. "The Origins of Modern Steel Unionism in the SWOC Era." In *Forging a Union of Steel: Philip Murray, SWOC, and the United Steelworkers*, edited by Paul F. Clark, Peter Gottlieb, and Donald Kennedy, 13–29. Ithaca, N.Y.: ILR Press, 1987.

——. *Steelworkers in America: The Nonunion Era*. Cambridge, Mass.: Harvard University Press, 1960.

Brown, Elsa Barkley. "Negotiating and Transforming the Public Sphere: African American Political Life in the Transition from Slavery to Freedom." *Public Culture* 7 (Fall 1994): 107–46.

——. "Womanist Consciousness: Maggie Lena Walker and the Independent Order of Saint Luke." *Signs* 14 (Spring 1989): 610–33.

Brunn, Paul. "Black Workers and Social Movements of the 1930s in St. Louis." Ph.D., diss., Washington University, 1975.

Buckler, Helen. *Doctor Dan*. Boston: Little Brown, 1954.

Buder, Stanley. *Pullman: An Experiment in Industrial Order and Community Planning, 1880–1930.* New York: Oxford University Press, 1967.

Canaan, Gareth. " 'Part of the Loaf' Employment Opportunities, Working Conditions, and Living Conditions for African American Workers in Chicago, 1920–1929." University of Illinois, Chicago, 1996. Unpublished seminar paper.

Capeci, Dominic J., Jr. *Race Relations in Wartime Detroit: The Sojourner Truth Housing Controversy of 1942.* Philadelphia: Temple University Press, 1984.

Capeci, Dominic J., Jr., and Martha Wilkerson. *Layered Violence: The Detroit Rioters of 1943.* Jackson: University Press of Mississippi, 1991.

Carby, Hazel V. " 'On the Threshold of the Woman's Era': Lynching, Empire, and Sexuality in Black Feminist Theory." *Critical Inquiry* 12 (Autumn 1985): 262–77.

Carson, Clayborne. *In Struggle: SNCC and the Black Awakening of the 1960s* Cambirdge, Mass.: Harvard University Press, 1981.

Carter, Dan T. *Scottsboro: A Tragedy of the American South.* 2d ed. Baton Rouge: Louisiana State University Press, 1984.

Carwardine, William H. *The Pullman Strike: The Classic First-Hand Account of an Epoch-Making Struggle in U.S. Labor History.* Chicago: Charles H. Kerr, 1894. Reprint, 1994.

Cayton, Horace, and George S. Mitchell. *Black Workers and the New Unions.* Chapel Hill: University of North Carolina Press, 1939.

Chafe, William H. *Civilities and Civil Rights: Greensboro, North Carolina, and the Black Struggle for Freedom.* New York: Oxford University Press, 1980. Reprint, 1981.

——. "Epilogue from Greensboro, North Carolina: Race and the Possibilities of American Democracy." In *Democracy Betrayed: The Wilmington Race Riot of 1898 and Its Legacy,* edited by David S. Cecelski and Timothy B. Tyson, 277–86. Chapel Hill: University of North Carolina Press, 1998.

Chateauvert, Melinda. "Marching Together: Women of the Brotherhood of Sleeping Car Porters, 1925–1957." Ph.D. diss., University of Pennsylvania, 1992.

——. *Marching Together: Women of the Brotherhood of Sleeping Car Porters.* Urbana: University of Illinois Press, 1998.

Childs, Marquis W. "Samuel Insull I: The Rise to Power." *New Republic* 72 (September 21, 1932): 142–44; "Samuel Insull II: Chicago in His Vest Pocket," ibid. (September 28, 1932): 170–73; "Samuel Insull III: The Collapse," ibid. (October 5, 1932): 201–3.

Clarke, John Henrik. "A. Philip Randolph: Portrait of an Afro-American Radical." *Negro Digest* 16 (March 1967): 17–19.

Cohen, Lizabeth. *Making a New Deal: Industrial Workers in Chicago, 1919–1939.* New York: Cambridge University Press, 1990.

Chicago Commission on Race Relations. *The Negro in Chicago.* Chicago: University of Chicago Press, 1922.

Collomp, Catherine. "Unions, Civics, and National Identity: Organized Labor's Reaction to Immigration, 1881–1897." *Labor History* 29 (Fall 1988): 450–74.

Commission on Industrial Relations. *Final Report and Testimony Submitted to Congress.* 64th Cong., 1st sess., S. Doc. 415. Vols. 1, 10. Washington, D.C.: Government Printing Office, 1916.

Cronon, E. David. *Black Moses: The Story of Marcus Garvey and the Universal Negro Improvement Association.* Madison: University of Wisconsin Press, 1969.

Cruse, Harold. *The Crisis of the Negro Intellectual.* New York: William Morrow, 1967.

——. *Plural but Equal: A Critical Study of Blacks and Minorities and America's Plural Society*. New York: William Morrow, 1967.

——. *Rebellion or Revolution*. New York: William Morrow, 1968.

Dalfiume, Richard M. *Desegregation of the Armed Forces: Fighting on Two Fronts: 1939–1953*. Columbia: University of Missouri Press, 1969.

——. "The 'Forgotten Years' of the Negro Revolution." *Journal of American History* 60 (June 1968): 90–106.

Daly, Kathryn W. "The International Ladies' Garment Workers' Union in Chicago, 1930–1939." Master's thesis, University of Chicago, 1939.

Davis, Angela Y. *Women, Race, and Class*. New York: Vintage Books, 1983.

Davis, Colin. *Power at Odds: The 1922 National Railroad Shopmen's Strike*. Urbana: University of Illinois Press, 1997.

Davis, David Brion. *The Problem of Slavery in Western Culture*. Ithaca, N.Y.: Cornell University Press, 1966. Reprint, New York: Oxford University Press, 1988.

Davis, Ralph N. "The Negro Newspapers and the War." *Sociology and Social Research* 27 (May–June): 373–80.

Dawson, Mitchell. "Insull on Trial." *Nation* 139 (November 28, 1934): 611–13.

Dickerson, Dennis C. *Out of the Crucible: Black Steelworkers in Western Pennsylvania, 1875–1980*. Albany: State University of New York Press, 1986.

Dilliard, Irving. "Civil Liberties of Negroes in Illinois since 1865." *Journal of Illinois State Historical Society* 56:3 (Autumn 1963): 592–624.

Dittmer, John. *Local People: The Struggle for Civil Rights in Mississippi*. Urbana: University of Illinois Press, 1994.

Douglass, Frederick. "The Significance of Emancipation in the West Indies." Address delivered in Canandaigua, N.Y., August 3, 1857. In *Frederick Douglass Papers: Speeches, Debates, and Interviews*, vol. 3, edited by John W. Blassingame, 183–208. New Haven: Yale University Press, 1985.

Doyle, William. *Inside the Oval Office: The White House Tapes from FDR to Clinton*. New York: Kodansha International, 1999.

Drake, St. Clair, and Horace R. Cayton. *Black Metropolis: A Study of Negro Life in a Northern City*. Chicago: University of Chicago Press, 1945. Reprint, 1993.

Draper, Theodore. *American Communism and Soviet Russia*. New York: Octagon Books, 1960.

Du Bois, W. E. B. *Black Reconstruction in America*. New York: Harcourt, Brace, 1935. Reprint, New York: Atheneum, 1992.

——. *Darkwater: Voices from Within the Veil*. 1920. Reprint, New York: Schocken Books, 1969.

——. *The Philadelphia Negro: A Social Study*. Philadelphia: University of Pennsylvania Press, 1899.

——. *The Souls of Black Folk*. 1903. Reprint, New York: New American Library, 1969.

Du Bois, W. E. B., Kelley Miller, and Mary Church Terrell. *The Negro Church: A Social Study*. Atlanta: Atlanta University Press, 1904.

Duncan, Otis Dudley, and Beverly Duncan. *The Negro Population of Chicago: A Study of Residential Succession*. Chicago: University of Chicago Press, 1957.

Eagles, Charles W., ed. *The Civil Rights Movement in America*. Jackson: University Press of Mississippi, 1986.

Ellis, Mark. " 'Closing Ranks' and 'Seeking Honors': W. E. B. Du Bois in World War I." *Journal of American History* 79 (June 1992): 96–124.

Ellison, Ralph. *Shadow and Act*. New York: Random House, 1953.

Embree, Edwin R. *13 against the Odds*. New York: Viking Press, 1944.

Engelbrecht, Lester E. "Lillian Herstein: Teacher and Activist." *Labor's Heritage* 1:2 (April 1989): 66–75.

Escott, Paul D. *Slavery Remembered: A Record of Twentieth-Century Slave Narratives*. Chapel Hill: University of North Carolina Press, 1979.

Eskew, Glenn T. *But for Birmingham: The Local and National Movements in the Civil Rights Struggle*. Chapel Hill: University of North Carolina Press, 1997.

Evans, Linda. "Claude A. Barnett and the Associated Negro Press." *Chicago History* 12:1 (Spring 1983): 44–56.

Fairclough, Adam. *Race and Democracy: The Civil Rights Struggle in Louisiana, 1915–1972*. Athens: University of Georgia Press, 1995.

Faue, Elizabeth. *Community of Suffering and Struggle: Women, Men, and the Labor Movement in Minneapolis, 1915–1945*. Chapel Hill: University of North Carolina Press, 1991.

——. Review of *Marching Together: Women of the Brotherhood of Sleeping Car Porters*, by Melinda Chateauvert. *American Historical Review* 104:3 (October 1999): 1327–28.

Fields, Barbara Jeanne. "Ideology and Race in American History." In *Region, Race and Reconstruction: Essays in Honor of C. Vann Woodward*, edited by J. Morgan Kousser and James M. McPerson, 143–77. New York: Oxford University Press, 1992.

——. "The Nineteenth-Century American South: History and Theory." *Plantation Society* 2:1 (April 1983): 7–27.

——. "Slavery, Race and Ideology in the United States of America." *New Left Review* 181 (May–June 1990): 95–118.

Fink, Leon. *Workingmen's Democracy: The Knights of Labor and American Politics*. Urbana: University of Illinois, 1983.

Finkle, Lee. "The Conservative Aims of Militant Rhetoric: Black Protest during World War II." *Journal of American History* 60:3 (December 1973): 692–713.

Fishel, Leslie H., Jr. "The Negro in the New Deal Era." *Wisconsin Magazine of History* 48 (Winter 1964): 111–26.

Foner, Eric. *Freedom's Lawmakers: A Dictionary of Black Officeholders during Reconstruction*. New York: Oxford University Press, 1993.

——. "The Meaning of Freedom in the Age of Emancipation." *Journal of American History* 81:2 (September 1994): 435–60.

——. *Nothing But Freedom: Emancipation and Its Legacy*. Baton Rouge: Louisiana State University Press, 1983.

——. *Politics and Ideology in the Age of the Civil War*. New York: Oxford University Press, 1980.

——. *Reconstruction: America's Unfinished Revolution, 1863–1877*. New York: Harper and Row, 1988.

——. "Reconstruction Revisited." *Reviews in American History* 10 (December 1982): 82–100.

——. "Rights and the Constitution in Black Life during the Civil War and Reconstruction." *Journal of American History* 74:3 (December 1987): 863–83.

——. *The Story of American Freedom*. New York: W. W. Norton, 1998.

Foner, Philip S. *Organized Labor and the Black Worker, 1619–1973*. New York: Praeger, 1974.

——. *Women and the American Labor Movement: From Colonial Times to the Eve of World War I.* New York: the Free Press, 1979.

——, ed. *The Life and Writings of Frederick Douglass.* Vol. 4, *Reconstruction and After.* New York: International Publishers, 1955.

Franklin, John Hope. *The Color Line: Legacy for the Twenty-First Century.* Columbia: University of Missouri Press, 1993.

——. "Whither Reconstruction Historiography?" In *Race and History: Selected Essays, 1938–1988,* 24–40. Baton Rouge: Louisiana State University Press, 1989.

Franklin, John Hope, and August Meier, eds. *Black Leaders of the Twentieth Century.* Urbana: University of Illinois Press, 1982.

Franklin, John Hope, and Alfred A. Moss Jr., eds. *From Slavery to Freedom: A History of African Americans.* Vol. 2, *From Civil War to the Present.* 7th ed. New York: McGraw Hill, 1998.

Frazier, E. Franklin. "Chicago: A Cross-Section of Negro Life." *Opportunity* 7 (March 1929): 71–72.

——. *The Negro Family in Chicago.* Chicago: University of Chicago Press, 1932.

Friedman, Tami J. Review of *Marching Together: Women of the Brotherhood of Sleeping Car Porters,* by Melinda Chateauvert. *Business History Review* 73:2 (Summer 1999): 294–96.

Fusfeld, Daniel R., and Timothy Bates. *The Political Economy of the Urban Ghetto.* Carbondale: University of Southern Illinois Press, 1984.

Gaines, Kevin K. *Uplifting the Race: Black Leadership, Politics, and Culture in the Twentieth Century.* Chapel Hill: University of North Carolina Press, 1996.

Garfinkel, Herbert. *When Negroes March: The March on Washington Movement in the Organizational Politics for FEPC.* Glencoe, Ill.: Free Press, 1959.

Garland, Phyl. "A. Philip Randolph: Labor's Grand Old Man." *Ebony* 24 (May 1969).

Garvey, Amy Jacques. *Garvey and Garveyism.* New York: Macmillan, 1970.

Giddings, Paula. *When and Where I Enter: The Impact of Black Women on Race and Sex in America.* New York: Bantam Books, 1984.

Gilmore, Glenda Elizabeth. *Gender and Jim Crow: Women and the Politics of White Supremacy in North Carolina, 1896–1920.* Chapel Hill: University of North Carolina Press, 1996.

Glaberman, Martin. *Wartime Strikes: The Struggle against the No-Strike Pledge in the UAW during World War II.* Detroit: Bewick Editions, 1980.

Glen, John. *Highlander: No Ordinary School, 1932–1962.* Lexington: University Press of Kentucky, 1988.

Glickman, Lawrence. "Inventing the 'American Standard of Living': Gender, Race and Working-Class Identity, 1880–1925." *Labor History* 34 (Spring–Summer 1993): 226–27.

Goodwin, Doris Kearns. *No Ordinary Time: Franklin and Eleanor Roosevelt: The Home Front in World War II.* New York: Touchstone Book, 1995.

Gosnell, Harold. *Machine Politics: Chicago Model.* Chicago: University of Chicago Press, 1937.

——. *Negro Politicians: The Rise of Negro Politics in Chicago.* Chicago: University of Chicago Press, 1935. Reprint, 1967.

Gottlieb, Peter. "Making Their Own Way: Southern Blacks' Migration to Pittsburgh, 1916–1930." Ph.D. diss., University of Pittsburgh, 1977.

Graves, John Temple. "The Southern Negro and the War Crisis." *Virginia Quarterly Review* 28 (1942): 507–8.

Greenberg, Cheryl Lynn. *"Or Does It Explode?" Black Harlem in the Great Depression.* New York: Oxford University Press, 1991.

Greenberg, Jack. *Crusaders in the Courts: How a Dedicated Band of Lawyers Fought for the Civil Rights Revolution.* New York: Basic Books, 1994.

Greene, Lorenzo J., and Carter G. Woodson. *The Negro Wage Earner.* New York: Russell and Russell, 1930.

Griffler, Keith. "What Price Alliance? The Black Radical Intellectual, the Black Workers, and the Program for Labor, 1918–1938." Ph.D. diss., Ohio State University, 1993.

Grossman, James R. "Blowing the Trumpet: The *Chicago Defender* and Black Migration during World War I." *Illinois Historical Journal* 78:2 (Summer 1985): 82–96.

———. *Land of Hope: Chicago, Black Southerners, and the Great Migration.* Chicago: University of Chicago Press, 1989.

Hall, H. N. "The Art of the Pullman Porter." *American Mercury* 23 (July 1931): 329–35.

Hall, Jacquelyn Dowd. *Revolt against Chivalry: Jessie Daniel Ames and the Women's Campaign against Lynching.* 1979. Rev. ed. New York: Columbia University Press, 1993.

Halpern, Eric Brian. " 'Black and White Unite and Fight': Race and Labor in Meatpacking, 1904–1948." Ph.D. diss., University of Pennsylvania, 1989.

Halpern, Rick. *Down on the Killing Floor: Black and White Workers in Chicago's Packinghouses, 1904–54.* Urbana: University of Illinois Press, 1997.

———. "Race, Ethnicity, and Union in the Chicago Stockyards, 1917–1922." *International Review of Social History* 37 (1992): 25–58.

Hamilton, Charles V. *Adam Clayton Powell, Jr.: The Political Biography of an American Dilemma.* New York: Collier Books, 1992.

Harding, Vincent. *There Is a River: The Black Struggle for Freedom in America.* New York: Harcourt Brace Jovanovich, 1981.

Harlan, Louis R. "Booker T. Washington and the Politics of Accommodation." In *Black Leaders of the Twentieth Century*, edited by John Hope Franklin and August Meier, 1–18. Urbana: University of Illinois Press, 1982.

Harris, William H. "Federal Intervention in Union Discrimination: FEPC and West Coast Shipyards during World War II." *Labor History* 22 (Summer 1981): 325–47.

———. *The Harder We Run: Black Workers since the Civil War.* New York: Oxford University Press, 1982.

———. *Keeping the Faith: A. Philip Randolph, Milton P. Webster, and the Brotherhood of Sleeping Car Porters, 1925–1937.* Urbana: University of Illinois Press, 1977.

Haywood, Harry. *Black Bolshevik: Autobiography of an Afro-American Communist.* Chicago: Liberator Press, 1978.

Henderson, Elmer W. "Political Changes among Negroes in Chicago during the Depression." *Social Forces* 19 (October–May 1941): 538–46.

———. "A Study of the Basic Factors Involved in the Change in the Party Alignment of Negroes in Chicago, 1932–1938." Master's thesis, University of Chicago, 1939.

Hendricks, Wanda A. *Gender, Race, and Politics in the Midwest: Black Club Women in Illinois.* Bloomington: Indiana University Press, 1998.

———. "Ida B. Wells-Barnett and the Alpha Suffrage Club of Chicago." In *One Woman, One Vote: Rediscovering the Woman Suffrage Movement*, edited by Marjorie Spruill Wheeler, 263–75. Troutdale, Ore.: New Sage Press, 1995.

Henry, Alice. *The Trade Union Woman*. Minneapolis: University of Minnesota Library, 1915. Reprint, New York: Lenox Hill, 1973.

Higginbotham, Evelyn Brooks. "In Politics to Stay: Black Women Leaders and Party Politics in the 1920s." In *Women, Politics and Change*, edited by Louise A. Tilly and Patricia Gurin, 199–220. New York: Russell Sage Foundation, 1990.

———. *Righteous Discontent: The Women's Movement in the Black Baptist Church, 1880–1920*. Cambridge, Mass.: Harvard University Press, 1993.

Hill, Herbert. *Black Labor and the American Legal System*. Madison: University of Wisconsin Press, 1985.

Hill, Robert A., ed. *The FBI's RACON: Racial Conditions in the United States during World War II*. Boston: Northeastern University Press, 1995.

Himes, Chester B. "All God's Chillun Got Pride." *Crisis* 51:6 (June 1944): 188–89, 204.

———. "Zoot Riots Are Race Riots." *Crisis* 50:7 (July 1943): 200–201, 222.

Hine, Darlene Clark, and Kathleen Thompson. *A Shining Thread of Hope: The History of Black Women in America*. New York: Broadway Books, 1998.

Hirsch, Arnold R. *Making the Second Ghetto: Race and Housing in Chicago, 1940–1960*. New York: Cambridge University Press, 1983.

———. "Massive Resistance in the Urban North: Trumbull Park, Chicago, 1953–1966." *Journal of American History* 82:2 (September 1995): 522–50.

Hogan, Lawrence D. *A Black National News Service: The Associated Negro Press and Claude Barnett, 1919–1945*. Cranbury, N.J.: Associated University Presses, 1984.

Holbrook, Steward H. *The Story of American Railroads*. New York: Crown Publishers, 1947.

Holt, Thomas C. "The Lonely Warrior: Ida B. Wells-Barnett and the Struggle for Black Leadership." In *Black Leaders of the Twentieth Century*, edited by John Hope Franklin and August Meier, 39–61. Urbana: University of Illinois Press, 1982.

———. "Marking: Race, Race-Making, and the Writing of History." *American Historical Review* 100 (February 1995): 1–20.

———. "The Political Uses of Alienation: W. E. B. Du Bois on Politics, Race, and Culture, 1903–1940." *American Quarterly* 42 (June 1990): 301–23.

Honey, Michael K. *Southern Labor and Black Civil Rights: Organizing Memphis Workers*. Urbana: University of Illinois Press, 1993.

Horowitz, Roger. *"Negro and White, Unite and Fight!": A Social History of Industrial Unionism in Meatpacking, 1930–1990*. Urbana: University of Illinois Press, 1997.

———. "The Path Not Taken: A Social History of Industrial Unionism in Meatpacking, 1930–1960." Ph.D. diss., University of Wisconsin, 1990.

Huggins, Nathan Irvin, ed. *Voices from the Harlem Renaissance*. New York: Oxford University Press, 1975. Reprint, 1995.

Hughes, Alvin Cicero. "Toward a Black United Front: The NNC Movement." Ph.D. diss., Ohio University, 1982.

Hughes, Langston. "Let America Be America Again." In *The Collected Poems of Langston Hughes*, ed. Arnold Rampersad, 189–91. New York: Vintage Books, 1995.

Hunter, Tera W. *To "Joy My Freedom": South Black Women's Lives and Labors after the Civil War*. Cambridge, Mass.: Harvard University Press, 1997.

Husband, Joseph. *The Story of the Pullman Car*. Chicago: A. C. McClurg, 1917.

James, C. L. R., George Breitman, and Edgas Keemer, eds. *Fighting Racism in World War II*. New York: Monad Press, 1980.

James, Winston. *Holding Aloft the Banner of Ethiopia: Caribbean Radicalism in Early Twentieth-Century America*. London: Verso, 1998.

Jaynes, Gerald David. *Branches without Roots: Genesis of the Black Working Class in the American South, 1962–1882*. New York: Oxford University Press, 1986.

Jones, Jacqueline. *Labor of Love, Labor of Sorrow: Black Women, Work and the Family from Slavery to the Present*. New York: Basic Books, 1985. Reprint, New York: Vintage Books, 1986.

Jones, Lester M. "The Editorial Policy of Negro Newspapers of 1917–1918 as Compared with That of 1941–1942." *Journal of Negro History* 29 (January 1944): 24–31.

Jordan, William. " 'The Damnable Dilemma' African-American Accommodation and Protest during World War I." *Journal of American History* 81:4 (March 1995): 1562–83.

Joyner, Charles. *Down by the Riverside: A South Carolina Slave Community*. Urbana: University of Illinois Press, 1984.

Kaczorowski, Robert J. "To Begin the Nation Anew: Congress, Citizenship, and Civil Rights after the Civil War." *American Historical Review* 92:1 (February 1987): 45–68.

Kapur, Sudarshan. *Raising Up a Prophet: The African Amerian Encounter with Gandhi*. Boston: Beacon Press, 1992.

Katznelson, Ira. *Black Men, White Cities: Race Politics and Migration in the United States, 1900–1930 and Britain 1948–68*. London: Oxford University Press, 1973.

Kelley, Robin D. G. *Hammer and Hoe: Alabama Communists during the Great Depression*. Chapel Hill: University of North Carolina Press, 1990.

———. "Hammer n' Hoe: Black Radicalism and the Communist Party in Alabama, 1929–1941." Ph.D. diss., University of California, Los Angeles, 1987.

———. "Memory and Politics." *Nation* 259 (October 3, 1994): 352–55.

———. " 'We Are Not What We Seem': Rethinking Black Working-Class Opposition in the Jim Crow South." *Journal of American History* 80:1 (June 1993): 75–112.

Kempton, Murray. *Part of Our Time: Some Ruins and Monuments of the Thirties*. New York: Simon and Schuster, 1955.

Kennedy, Louise Venable. *The Negro Peasant Turns Cityward: Effects of Recent Migrations to Northern Centers*. College Park, Md.: McGrath, 1930.

Kerlin, Robert T., ed. *Voice of the Negro*. Lexington, Va., 1920. Reprint, New York: Arno Press and New York Times, 1968.

Kesselman, Louis Coleridge. *The Social Politics of FEPC: A Study in Reform Pressure Movements*. Chapel Hill: University of North Carolina Press, 1948.

Kessler-Harris, Alice. *Out to Work: A History of Wage-Earning Women in the United States*. New York: Oxford University Press, 1982.

Kilson, Martin. "Political Change in the Negro Ghetto, 1900–1940's." In *Key Issues in the Afro-American Experience*, edited by Nathan I. Huggins, Martin Kilson and David M. Fox, 167–92. New York: Harcourt Brace Jovanovich, 1971.

Kirby, John B. *Black Americans in the Roosevelt Era: Liberalism and Race*. Knoxville: University of Tennessee Press, 1980.

Kluger, Richard. *Simple Justice: The History of Brown v. Board of Education and Black America's Struggle for Equality*. New York: Alfred A. Knopf, 1976.

Kornweibel, Theodore, Jr. "An Economic Profile of Black Life in the Twentieth Century." *Journal of Black Studies* 6:4 (June 1976): 307–20.

———. *No Crystal Stair*. Westport, Conn.: Greenwood, 1975.

Korstad, Robert, and Nelson Lichtenstein. "Opportunities Found and Lost: Labor,

Radicals, and the Early Civil Rights Movement." *Journal of American History* 75 (December 1988): 786–811.

Krieg, Richard M., and Judith A. Cooksey. *Provident Hospital: A Living Legacy*. Chicago: Provident Foundation, 1998.

Kruman, Marc W. "Quotas for Blacks: The Public Works Administration and the Black Construction Worker." *Labor History* 16 (Winter 1975): 37–51.

Lahr, John. "Speaking across the Divide." *New Yorker*, January 27, 1997.

Laidler, Harry W. *The Role of the Races in Our Future Civilization*. New York: League for Industrial Democracy, 1942.

Larch-Quinn, Elisabeth. *Black Neighbors: Race and the Limits of Reform in the American Settlement House Movement, 1890–1945*. Chapel Hill: University of North Carolina Press, 1993.

Lasswell, Harold D., and Dorothy Blumenstock. *World Revolutionary Propaganda: A Chicago Study*. New York: Alfred A. Knopf, 1939.

Lawson, Steven F. "Freedom Then, Freedom Now: The Historiography of the Civil Rights Movement." *American Historical Review* 96:2 (April 1991): 456–71.

———. *Running for Freedom: Civil Rights and Black Politics in America since 1941*. Philadelphia: Temple University Press, 1991.

Leab, Daniel J. " 'United We Eat': The Creation and Organization of the Unemployed Councils in 1930." In *The Labor History Reader*, edited by Daniel J. Leab, 317–32. Urbana: University of Illinois Press, 1985.

Lemke-Santangelo, Gretchen. *Abiding Courage: African American Migrant Women and the East Bay Community*. Chapel Hill: University of North Carolina Press, 1996.

Lerner, Gerda. *Black Women in White America: A Documentary History*. New York: Pantheon, 1972.

———. *The Majority Finds Its Past: Placing Women in History*. New York: Oxford University Press, 1979.

LeRoy, Greg. "The Founding Heart of A. Philip Randolph's Union: Milton P. Webster and the Chicago's Pullman Porters Organize, 1925–1937." *Labor's Heritage* 3:3 (July 1991): 22–43.

———. "Scandalized, Analyzed, Paternalized, Fraternalized, Nationalized and Company Unionized, but Nowhere Near Recognized: Pullman Porters, 1913–1924." Paper presented at Illinois Labor History Society, Chicago, October 9, 1981.

Leuchtenburg, William E. *Franklin D. Roosevelt and the New Deal, 1932–1940*. New York: Harper and Row, 1963.

Levine, Lawrence W. *Black Culture and Black Consciousness: Afro-American Folk Thought from Slavery to Freedom*. New York: Oxford University Press, 1977.

Lewis, David Levering. *W. E. B. Du Bois: Biography of a Race, 1868–1919*. New York: Henry Holt, 1993.

———. *When Harlem Was in Vogue*. New York: Oxford University Press, 1979.

Lewis, Earl. "Connecting Memory, Self, and the Power of Place in African American Urban History." *Journal of Urban History* 21:3 (March 1995): 347–71.

———. *In Their Own Interests: Race, Class, and Power in Twentieth-Century Norfolk, Virginia*. Berkeley: University of California Press, 1991.

———. "Invoking Concepts, Problematizing Identities: The Life of Charles N. Hunter and the Implication for the Study of Gender and Labor." *Labor History* 34 (Spring–Summer 1993): 292–308.

———. "To Turn as on a Pivot: Writing African Americans into a History of Overlapping Diasporas." *American Historical Review* 100:3 (June 1995): 765–87.

Lichtenstein, Nelson. "Defending the No-Strike Pledge." In *Workers' Struggles Past and Present: A Radical America Reader*, edited by James Green, 269–87. Philadelphia: Temple University Press, 1983.

Lindsey, Almont. *The Pullman Strike: The Story of a Unique Experiment and of a Great Labor Upheaval.* Chicago: University of Chicago Press, 1942.

Lipsitz, George. *Rainbow at Midnight: Labor and Culture in the 1940s.* Urbana: University of Illinois Press, 1994.

Lockard, Metz T. P. "The Negro Press in Illinois." *Journal of Illinois State Historical Society* 56:3 (Autumn 1963): 570–91.

Locke, Alain. "The Unfinished Business of Democracy." *Survey Graphic* 31:11 (November 1942): 458–62.

———, ed. *The New Negro: Voices of the Harlem Renaissance.* 1925. Reprint, New York: Atheneum, 1992.

Logan, Rayford W. *The Betrayal of the Negro, from Rutherford B. Hayes to Woodrow Wilson.* New York: Da Capo, 1997. Orginally published in 1954 as *The Negro in American Life and Thought: The Nadir, 1887–1901* (New York: Collier Books, 1954).

———, ed. *What the Negro Wants.* Chapel Hill: University of North Carolina Press, 1944.

Logsdon, Joseph A. "The Rev. Archibald J. Carey and the Negro in Chicago Politics." Master's thesis, University of Chicago, 1961.

McLemore, Frances Williams. "The Role of the Negroes in Chicago in the Senatorial Election, 1930." Master's thesis, University of Chicago, 1931.

McMurry, Linda O. *To Keep the Waters Troubled: The Life of Ida B. Wells.* New York: Oxford University Press, 1998.

McNeil, Genna Rae. *Groundwork: Charles Hamilton Houston and the Struggle for Civil Rights.* Philadelphia: University of Pennsylvania Press, 1983.

Maiken, Peter T. *Night Trains: The Pullman System in the Golden Years of American Rail Travel.* Chicago: Lakine Press, 1989.

Marable, Manning. "A. Philip Randolph and the Foundations of Black American Socialism." *Radical America* 14 (March–April 1980): 7–29.

———. *Race, Reform, and Rebellion: The Second Reconstruction in Black America, 1945–1982.* 1984. Reprint, Jackson: University Press of Mississippi, 1989.

Marshall, Thurgood. "The Gestapo in Detroit." *Crisis* 50 (August 1943): 232–33, 246.

Martin, Charles H. "The International Labor Defense and Black America." *Labor History* 26 (1985): 165–94.

Martin, Tony. *Race First: The Ideological and Organizational Struggles of Marcus Garvey and the Universal Negro Improvement Association.* Westport, Conn.: Greenwood Press, 1976.

Martin, Waldo E., Jr. *The Mind of Frederick Douglass.* Chapel Hill: University of North Carolina Press, 1984.

Mays, Benjamin E. *Born to Rebel: An Autobiography.* 1971. Reprint, Athens: University of Georgia Press, 1987.

Meier, August. *Negro Thought in America, 1880–1915: Racial Ideologies in the Age of Booker T. Washington.* Ann Arbor: University of Michigan Press, 1963.

Meier, August, and John H. Bracey Jr. "NAACP as a Reform Movement, 1909–1965: 'To Reach the Conscience of America.'" *Journal of Southern History* 59 (February 1993): 3–30.

Meier, August, and Elliott Rudwick. *Black Detroit and the Rise of the UAW*. New York: Oxford University Press, 1979.

——. *CORE: A Study in the Civil Rights Movement: 1942–1968*. Urbana: University of Illinois Press, 1975.

——. "Origins of Non-Violent Direct Action in Afro-American Protest: A Note on Historical Discontinuities." In *Along the Color Line: Explorations in the Black Experience*, 307–404. Urbana: University of Illinois Press, 1976.

Meier, August, Elliott Rudwick, and Francis L. Broderick, eds. *Black Protest Thought in the Twentieth Century*. Indianapolis: Bobbs-Merrill Company, 1965.

Mergen, Bernard. "The Pullman Porter: From 'George' to Brotherhood." *South Atlantic Quarterly* 73:2 (Spring 1974): 224–35.

Mink, Gwendolyn. "The Lady and the Tramp: Gender, Race, and the Origins of the American Welfare State." In *Women, the State, and Welfare*, edited by Linda Gordon. Madison: University of Wisconsin, 1990.

Montgomery, David. *The Fall of the House of Labor: The Workplace, the State, and American Labor Activism, 1865–1925*. New York: Cambridge University Press, 1987.

Morris, Aldon D. *The Origins of the Civil Rights Movement: Black Communities Organizing for Change*. New York: Free Press, 1984.

Murray, Florence, ed. *The Negro Handbook*. New York: Current Reference Publication, 1944.

Murray, Hugh T., Jr. "The NAACP versus the Communist Party: The Scottsboro Rape Case, 1931–1932." *Phylon* 28 (1967): 267–87.

Myrdal, Gunnar. *An American Dilemma*. Vol. 1, *The Negro in a White Nation*. New York: Harper and Row, 1944. Reprint, New York: McGraw-Hill, 1964.

——. *An American Dilemma*. Vol. 2, *The Negro Social Structure*. New York: Harper and Row, 1944. Reprint, New York: McGraw-Hill, 1964.

Naison, Mark D. "Black Agrarian Radicalism in the Great Depression: The Threads of a Lost Tradition." *Journal of Ethnic Studies* 1:3 (Fall 1973): 47–65.

——. *Communists in Harlem during the Depression*. New York: Evergreen Edition, 1985.

Nelson, Bruce. "Organized Labor and the Struggle for Black Equality in Mobile during World War II." *Journal of American History* 80 (1993): 952–88.

Norrell, Robert J. "Caste in Steel: Jim Crow Careers in Birmingham, Alabama." *Journal of American History* 73:3 (December 1986): 669–94.

——. *Reaping the Whirlwind: The Civil Rights Movement in Tuskegee*. Chapel Hill: University of North Carolina Press, 1998.

Odum, Howard W. *Race and Rumors of Race: Challenge to American Crisis*. Chapel Hill: University of North Carolina Press, 1943.

O'Neill, Eugene. *The Emperor Jones*. New York: Horace Liveright, 1921. Reprint, New York: Vintage Books, 1972.

Osofsky, Gilbert. *Harlem: The Making of a Ghetto: Negro New York, 1880–1930*. New York: Harper and Row, 1963.

Ottley, Roi. *The Lonely Warrior: The Life and Times of Robert S. Abbott*. Chicago: Henry Regnery, 1955.

——. *"New World A-Coming" Inside Black America*. New York: World Publishing, 1943.

Payne, Charles M. *I've Got the Light of Freedom: The Organizing Tradition and the Mississippi Freedom Struggle*. Berkeley: University of California Press, 1995.

——. "Men Led, But Women Organized." In *Women in the Civil Rights Movement:*

Trailblazers and Torchbearers, 1941–1965, edited by Vicki L. Crawford, Jacqueline Anne Rouse, and Barbara Woods, 1–11. Brooklyn, N.Y.: Carlson, 1990.

Perata, David D. *Those Pullman Blues: An Oral History of the African American Railroad Attendant*. New York: Twayne, 1996.

Pfeffer, Paula F. *A. Philip Randolph, Pioneer of the Civil Rights Movement*. Baton Rouge: Louisiana State University Press, 1990.

———. "The Women behind the Union: Halena Wilson, Rosina Tucker, and the Ladies Auxiliary to the Brotherhood of Sleeping Car Porters." *Labor History* 36:4 (Fall 1995): 557–78.

Pinderhughes, Dianne M. *Race and Ethnicity in Chicago Politics: A Reexamination of Pluralist Theory*. Urbana: University of Illinois Press, 1987.

Pliven, Francis Fox, and Richard Cloward. *Poor People's Movements: Why They Succeed, How They Fail*. New York: Pantheon Books, 1979.

Plummer, Brenda Gayle. *Rising Wind: Black Americans and U.S. Foreign Affairs, 1935–1960*. Chapel Hill: University of North Carolina Press, 1996.

Posadas, Barbara M. "The Hierarchy of Color and Psychological Adjustment in an Industrial Environment: Filipinos, the Pullman Company, and the Brotherhood of Sleeping Car Porters." *Labor History* 23:3 (Summer 1982): 349–73.

Potter, David M. *The Impending Crisis: 1848–1861*. New York: Harper Torchbooks, 1976.

Powell, Adam Clayton. *Marching Blacks: An Interpretive History of the Rise of the Black Common Man*. New York: Dial Press, 1945.

Rachleff, Peter. *Black Labor in Richmond, 1865–1890*. Philadelphia: Temple University Press, 1984. Reprint, Urbana: University of Illinois Press, 1989.

Rae, William Fraser. *Westward by Rail: The New Route to the East*. 1871. Reprint, New York: Arno Press, 1973.

Randolph, A. Philip. "March on Washington Movement Presents Program for Negro." In *What the Negro Wants*, edited by Rayford W. Logan, 133–64. Chapel Hill: University of North Carolina Press, 1944.

———. "A New Crowd—a New Negro." *Messenger* 2 (May–June 1919): 26–27.

———. "New Leadership for the Negro." *Messenger* 2 (May–June 1919): 9–10.

———. "Why I Would Not Stand for Re-Election in the National Negro Congress." *American Federationist* (July 1940): 24–25.

Rawick, George P., ed. *The American Slave: A Composite Autobiography*. Vols. 9, 10. Westport, Conn.: Greenwood Press, 1972. Supplement ser. 1: vol. 6, 7, 1977; Supplement ser. 2: vol. 5, 10, 1979.

Reagon, Bernice Johnson. "Songs of the Civil Rights Movement, 1955–1965: A Study in Culture History." Ph.D. diss., Howard University, 1975.

Record, Wilson. *The Negro and the Communist Party*. Chapel Hill: University of North Carolina, 1951.

———. *Race and Radicalism: The NAACP and the Communist Party in Conflict*. Ithaca, N.Y.: Cornell University Press, 1964.

Reed, Christopher Robert. *The Chicago NAACP and the Rise of Black Professional Leadership, 1910–1966*. Bloomington: Indiana University Press, 1997.

———. "A Study of Black Politics and Protest in Depression-Decade Chicago: 1930–1939." Ph.D. diss., Kent State University, 1982.

Reed, Merl E. *Seedtime for the Modern Civil Rights Movement: The President's Committee on Fair Employment Practice, 1941–1946*. Baton Rouge: Louisiana State University Press, 1991.

Reich, Steven A. "Soldiers of Democracy: Black Texans and the Fight for Citizenship, 1917–1921." *Journal of American History* 82 (March 1996): 1478–1504.

Reiff, Janice L., and Susan E. Hirsch. "Pullman and Its Public: Image and Aim in Making and Interpreting History." *The Public Historian* 11 (Fall 1989): 99–112.

Robb, Frederic H. *The Negro in Chicago, 1779–1927*. Chicago: Atlas Printing, 1927.

Robertson, James Oliver. *American Myth, American Reality*. New York: Hill and Wang, 1980.

Robinson, George F., Jr. "The Negro in Politics in Chicago." *Journal of Negro History* 17 (Spring 1932): 180–229.

Roediger, David R. *The Wages of Whiteness: Race and the Making of the American Working Class*. London: Verso, 1991.

Rosenzweig, Roy. "Organizing the Unemployed: The Early Years of the Great Depression, 1929–1933." *Radical America* 10 (1975): 37–62.

Ross, B. Joyce. *J. E. Spingarn and the Rise of the NAACP, 1911–1939*. New York: Atheneum, 1972.

——. "Mary McLeod Bethune and the National Youth Administration: A Case of Power Relationships in the Black Cabinet of Franklin D. Roosevelt." In *Black Leaders of the Twentieth Century*, edited by John Hope Franklin and August Meier, 191–219. Urbana: University of Illinois Press, 1982.

Royster, Jacqueline Jones, ed. *Southern Horrors and Other Writings: The Antilynching Campaign of Ida B. Wells, 1892–1900*. Boston: Bedford Books, 1997.

Ruchames, Louis. *Race, Jobs, and Politics: The Story of FEPC*. New York: Columbia University Press, 1953.

Salem, Dorothy. *To Better Our World: Black Women in Organized Reform, 1890–1920*. Vol. 14 of *Black Women in United States History*. Edited by Darlene Clark Hine. Brooklyn, N.Y.: Carlson, 1990.

Salvatore, Nick. *Eugene V. Debs: Citizen and Socialist*. Urbana: University of Illinois Press, 1982.

Sancton, Thomas. "Something's Happened to the Negro." *New Republic* 108:6 (February 8, 1943): 175–79.

Sandberg, Carl. *Chicago Race Riots*. New York: Harcourt, Brace and Howe, 1919.

Santino, Jack. *Miles of Smiles, Years of Struggle: Stories of Black Pullman Porters*. Urbana: University of Illinois Press, 1989.

Savage, Barbara Diane. *Broadcasting Freedom: Radio, War, and the Politics of Race, 1938–1948*. Chapel Hill: University of North Carolina Press, 1999.

Schechter, Patricia A. " 'All the Intensity of My Nature': Ida B. Wells, Anger, and Politics." *Radical History* 70 (Winter 1998): 48–77.

——. "Unsettled Business: Ida B. Wells against Lynching, or, How Antilynching Got Its Gender." In *Under Sentence of Death: New Essays on Lynching in the South*, edited by Fitzhugh Brundage, 292–317. Chapel Hill: University of North Carolina Press, 1997.

Schultz, Rima L., ed. *Historical Encyclopedia of Chicago Women*. Bloomington: Indiana University Press, 2001.

Scott, Daryl Michael. *Contempt and Pity: Social Policy and the Image of the Damaged Black Psyche, 1880–1996*. Chapel Hill: University of North Carolina Press, 1997.

Scott, Estelle Hill. *Occupational Changes among Negroes in Chicago*. Project 665-54-3-336, Work Projects Administration. Washington, D.C.: Government Printing Office, 1939.

Shaw, Stephanie J. "Black Club Women and the Creation of the National Association of Colored Women." *Journal of Women's History* 3:2 (Fall 1991): 10–25.

Sitkoff, Harvard. "The Detroit Race Riot of 1943." *Michigan History* 53 (1969): 199–204.

——. *A New Deal for Blacks: The Emergence of Civil Rights as a National Issue: The Depression Decade*. New York: Oxford University Press, 1978.

——. "Racial Militancy and Interracial Violence in the Second World War." *Journal of American History* 58:3 (December 1971): 661–81.

Skinner, Robert E. "The Black Man in the Literature of Labor: The Early Novels of Chester Himes." *Labor's Heritage* 1:3 (July 1989): 51–65.

Skotnes, Andor D. "The Black Freedom Movement and the Workers' Movement in Baltimore, 1930–1939." Ph.D. diss., Rutgers University, 1988.

Solomon, Mark. *The Cry Was Unity: Communists and African Americans, 1917–1936.* Jackson: University Press of Mississippi, 1998.

Spear, Allan. *Black Chicago: The Making of a Negro Ghetto, 1890–1920*. Chicago: University of Chicago Press, 1967.

Spero, Sterling D., and Abram L. Harris. *The Black Worker: The Negro and the Labor Movement*. New York: Columbia University, 1931.

Stein, Judith. *The World of Marcus Garvey: Race and Class in Modern Society*. Baton Rouge: Louisiana State University Press, 1986.

Sternsher, Barnard, ed. *The Negro in Depression and War: Prelude to Revolution, 1930– 1945*. Chicago: Quadrangle Books, 1969.

Stovall, Mary E. "The *Chicago Defender* in the Progressive Era." *Illinois Historical Journal* 83 (1990): 159–72.

Streater, John Baxter, Jr. "The National Negro Congress, 1935–1947." Ph.D. diss., University of Cincinnati, 1980.

Strickland, Arvarh E. *History of the Chicago Urban League*. Urbana: University of Illinois Press, 1966.

Sugrue, Thomas J. "Crab-Grass-Roots Politics: Race, Rights, and the Reaction against Liberalism in the Urban North, 1940–1964." *Journal of American History* 82:2 (September 1995): 551–78.

——. *The Origins of the Urban Crisis: Race and Inequality in Postwar Detroit*. Princeton, N.J.: Princeton University Press, 1996.

Sullivan, Patricia. *Days of Hope: Race and Democracy in the New Deal Era*. Chapel Hill: University of North Carolina Press, 1996.

——. "Southern Reformers, the New Deal and the Movement's Foundation." In *New Directions in Civil Rights Studies*, edited by Armistead L. Robinson and Patricia Sullivan, 81–104. Charlottesville: University of Virginia Press, 1991.

Tannenbaum, Frank. *Slave and Citizen*. New York: Alfred A. Knopf, 1946. Reprint, Boston: Beacon Press, 1992.

Tarry, Ellen. *The Third Door: The Autobiography of an American Negro Woman*. New York: David McKay, 1955.

Taylor, A. A. "Historians of the Reconstruction." *Journal of Negro History* 23 (January 1938): 16–34.

Terborg-Penn, Rosalyn. "African American Women and the Woman Suffrage Movement." In *One Woman, One Vote: Rediscovering the Woman Suffrage Movement*, edited by Marjorie Spruill Wheeler, 146–54. Troutdale, Ore.: New Sage Press, 1995.

——. *African American Women in the Struggle for the Vote, 1850–1920*. Bloomington: Indiana University Press, 1998.

Thomas, Bettye. "Black Operated Shipyard, 1866–1884: Reflections upon Its Inception and Ownership." *Journal of Negro History* 59 (January 1974): 1–12.

Thomas, Richard W. *Life for Us Is What We Make It: Building the Black Community in Detroit, 1915–1945*. Bloomington: Indiana University Press, 1992.

Thompson, Mildred I. *Ida B. Wells-Barnett: An Exploratory Study of an American Black Woman, 1893–1930*. Vol. 15 of *Black Women in United States History*, edited by Darlene Clark Hine. Brooklyn, N.Y.: Carlson, 1990.

Tilly, Louise A., and Patricia Gurin, eds. *Women, Politics, and Change*. New York: Russell Sage Foundation, 1990.

Trotter, Joe W., Jr. *Black Milwaukee: The Making of an Industrial Proletariat, 1915–1945*. Urbana: University of Illinois Press, 1985.

——. "Black Migration in Historical Perspective." *The Great Migration in Historical Perspective: New Dimensions of Race, Class, and Gender*, edited by Joe W. Trotter Jr., 1–21. Bloomington: Indiana University Press, 1991.

——. *River Jordan: African American Urban Life in the Ohio Valley*. Lexington: University Press of Kentucky, 1998.

Trotter, Joe William, Jr., and Earl Lewis. *African Americans in the Industrial Age: A Documentary History*. Boston: Northeastern University Press, 1996.

Tucker, David M. "Miss Ida B. Wells and the Memphis Lynching." *Phylon* 32 (Summer 1971): 112–22.

Turner, Robert E. *Memories of a Retired Pullman Porter*. New York: Exposition Press, 1954.

Tushnet, Mark V. *The NAACP's Legal Strategy against Segregated Education, 1925–1950*. Chapel Hill: University of North Carolina Press, 1987.

Tuttle, William M., Jr. "Labor Conflict and Racial Violence: The Black Worker in Chicago, 1894–1919." *Labor History* 10 (Summer 1969): 408–32.

——. *Race Riot: Chicago in the Red Summer of 1919*. New York: Atheneum, 1970.

Tyson, Timothy B. "Wars for Democracy: African American Militancy and Interracial Violence in North Carolina during World War II." In *Democracy Betrayed: The Wilmington Race Riot of 1898 and Its Legacy*, edited by David S. Cecelski and Timothy B. Tyson, 253–75. Chapel Hill: University of North Carolina Press, 1998.

U.S. Bureau of the Census. *Historical Statistics of the United States, Colonial Times to 1957*. Washington, D.C.: Government Printing Office, 1960.

——. *Negroes in the United States, 1920–1932*. Washington, D.C.: Government Printing Office, 1935.

U.S. Bureau of Labor Statistics. *Monthly Labor Review*. November 1924. Washington, D.C.: Government Printing Office, 1925.

Vincent, Theodore. *Black Power and the Garvey Movement*. Berkeley: Ramparts Press, 1972.

Von Eschen, Penny Marie. "African Americans and Anti-Colonialism, 1937–1957: The Rise and Fall of the Politics of the African Diaspora." Ph.D. diss., Columbia University, 1994.

——. *Race against Empire: Black Americans and Anticolonialism, 1937–1957*. Ithaca, N.Y.: Cornell University Press, 1997.

Walker, Juliet E. K. "The Afro-American Woman: Who Was She?" In *Black Women's History: Theory and Practice*, Vol. 2, edited by Darlene Clark Hine, 659–69. Brooklyn, New York: Carlson, 1990.

Washburn, Patrick S. *A Question of Sedition: The Federal Government's Investigation of the Black Press during World War II*. New York: Oxford University Press, 1986.

Washington, Booker T. "The Negro and the Labor Unions." *Atlantic Monthly* 111 (June 1913): 756–67.

——. *Up from Slavery*. 1901. Reprint, Cutchogue, N.Y.:Buccaneer Books, 1996.

Waskow, Arthur I. *From Race Riot to Sit-In, 1919 and the 1960s: A Study in the Connections between Conflict and Violence*. Gloucester, Mass.: Doubleday, 1966.

Watson, Richard L. "The Defeat of Judge Parker: A Study in Pressure Group Politics." *Mississippi Valley Historical Review* 50 (September 1963): 213–34.

Weaver, Robert. *Negro Labor: A National Problem*. New York: Harcourt and Brace, 1946.

Webster, Milton P. "Labor Must Organize." In *The Negro in Chicago, 1779–1927*, edited by Frederick H. Robb. Chicago: Atlas, 1929.

Weir, Margaret. *Politics and Jobs: The Boundaries of Employment Policy in the United States*. Princeton, N.J.: Princeton University Press, 1992.

Weisberger, Bernard A. "The Dark and Bloody Ground of Reconstruction History." *Journal of Social History* 25 (November 1959): 427–47.

Weiss, Nancy J. *Farewell to the Party of Lincoln: Black Politics in the Age of FDR*. Princeton, N.J.: Princeton University Press, 1983.

Wells, Ida B. *Crusade for Justice: The Autobiography of Ida B. Wells*. As told to Alfreda M. Duster. Chicago: University of Chicago, 1970.

Wells-Barnett, Ida B. "A Red Record: Tabulated Statistics and Alleged Causes of Lynchings in the United States, 1892–1893–1894." 1895. In *Selected Works of Ida B. Wells-Barnett*, edited by Trudier Harris, 138–252. New York: Oxford University Press, 1991.

——. "Southern Horrors: Lynch Law in All Its Phases." 1892. In *Selected Works of Ida B. Wells-Barnett*, edited by Trudier Harris, 14–45. New York: Oxford University Press, 1991.

Wesley, Charles H. "The Historical Basis of Negro Citizenship." *Opportunity* 2 (December 1927): 356–59.

——. "The Negro Has Always Wanted the Four Freedoms." In *What the Negro Wants*, edited by Rayford W. Logan, 90–112. Chapel Hill: University of North Carolina Press, 1944.

Whatley, Warren C. "African-American Strikebreaking from the Civil War to the New Deal." *Social Science History* 17:4 (Winter 1993): 525–58.

White, Deborah Gray. "The Cost of Club Work, the Price of Black Feminism." In *Visible Women: New Essays on American Activism*, edited by Nancy A. Hewitt and Suzanne Lebsock, 247–69. Urbana: University of Illinois Press, 1993.

White, John H. *American Railroad Passenger Car*. Baltimore: Johns Hopkins University Press, 1978.

White, Walter. "The Negro Problem in America." In *The Role of the Races in Our Future Civilization*, edited by Harry W. Laidler, 36–40. New York: League for Industrial Democracy, 1942.

——. *A Man Called White: The Autobiography of Walter F. White*. Bloomington: Indiana University Press, 1970.

Williams, Katherine E. "The Alpha Suffrage Club." *Half-Century Magazine* 1:2 (September 1916): 12.

Wilson, James Q. *Negro Politics: The Search for Leadership*. New York: Free Press, 1960.

Wilson, Joseph E. *Tearing Down the Color Line: A Documentary History and Analysis of the Brotherhood of Sleeping Car Porters*. New York: Columbia University Press, 1989.

Wittner, Lawrence S. "The National Negro Congress: A Reassessment." *American Quarterly* 22 (Winter 1970): 883–901.

——. *Rebels against War: The American Peace Movement, 1941–1960*. New York: Columbia University Press, 1969.

Wolters, Raymond. *Negroes and the Great Depression: The Problem of Economic Recovery*. Westport, Conn.: Greenwood, 1970.

Wood, Junius B. *The Negro in Chicago*. Chicago: Chicago Daily News, 1916.

Woodard, Komozi. *A Nation within a Nation: Amiri Baraka (Leroi Jones) and Black Power Politics*. Chapel Hill: University of North Carolina Press, 1999.

Woodward, C. Vann. *The Strange Career of Jim Crow*. 3d ed. New York: Oxford University Press, 1974.

Wright, Richard. *Black Boy*. New York: Harper and Row, 1966.

——. *Black Boy (American Hunger): A Record of Childhood and Youth*. New York: Perennial, 1991.

——. *12 Million Black Voices*. 1941. Reprint, New York: Arno Press and New York Times, 1969.

Wright, Richard R. "The Industrial Condition of Negroes in Chicago." B.D. thesis, University of Chicago Divinity School, 1901.

Wynn, Neil A. *The Afro-American and the Second World War*. New York: 1976.

Young, Paul. "Race, Class, and Radical Protest: Chicago Unemployed Council, 1930–1934." Paper presented at Organization of American Historians, San Francisco, April 19, 1997.

Zangrando, Robert. "The NAACP and a Federal Antilynching Bill, 1934–1940." *Journal of Negro History* 50 (April 1965): 106–17.

——. *The NAACP Crusade against Lynching, 1909–1950*. Philadelphia: Temple University Press, 1980.

Zieger, Robert H. *The CIO: 1935–1955*. Chapel Hill: University of North Carolina Press, 1995.